THE OTHER SIDE OF RACISM

My niece and nephew haven't been around very long. They aren't 42 or 85 or 104 like the rest of us. They are post-civil-rights-revolution children who may one day fully understand the meaning of Selma, Ala., and Philadelphia, Miss., and the other bloody battlefields of the movement. But I think it is going to be harder than some people expect to explain to them precisely and profoundly what those battles were all about. And that is because they simply assume—how could they not?—that it is acceptable for the folks who run things to send one person here and another there strictly because of the color of his skin. They think the half-Indianness of their friend down the street is good and sufficient reason for the authorities to decree that he be treated differently.

Is all that so benign? Is it self-evidently something we should accept as the social price of righting old racial wrongs? Should we have wandered into a morass of new discriminations, which we are teaching the children of this country to view as the normal democratic landscape? I wish the big hitters of our racial politics would get off the platitudes and talk about that.—Meg Greenfield, *Newsweek*

THE OTHER SIDE OF RACISM

A PHILOSOPHICAL STUDY OF
BLACK RACE CONSCIOUSNESS

ANNE WORTHAM

OHIO STATE UNIVERSITY PRESS

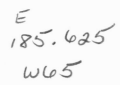
The quotation on page i is © 1977 by Newsweek, Inc. All Rights Reserved. Reprinted by permission.

The quotation on page 206 from "Men of Careful Turns, haters of fork in the road" is from *The World of Gwendolyn Brooks*, by Gwendolyn Brooks. Copyright 1949 by Gwendolyn Brooks Blakely. Reprinted by permission of Harper and Row, Publishers, Inc.

Quotations from "Black Student Revolt on the White Campus," by Frederick D. Harper, were published originally in the September, 1969, issue of the *Journal of College Student Personnel*. Copyright 1969 by the American Personnel and Guidance Association. Used with permission.

Extracts from *The Autobiography of Malcolm X*, by Malcolm X, with the assistance of Alex Haley. Copyright © 1964 by Alex Haley and Malcolm X. Copyright © 1965 by Alex Haley and Betty Shabass. Reprinted by permission of Random House, Inc.

Excerpts from *Blacker than Thou: The Struggle for Campus Unity*, by George Napper. Copyright © 1973 by William B. Eerdmans Publishing Company. Used by permission.

The quotation on pages 204–5 from "The Melting Pot," by Dudley Randall, is from *The Black Poets*, edited by Dudley Randall. Copyright © 1971 by Dudley Randall. Reprinted by permission of Dudley Randall.

The quotation on pages 257–58 from "Black People!", by LeRoi Jones, is from *Selected Poetry of Amiri Baraka/Le Roi Jones* (1979), by LeRoi Jones. Copyright © 1969 by LeRoi Jones. Reprinted by permission of William Morrow & Company.

Library of Congress Cataloguing in Publication Data

Wortham, Anne, 1941–
　The other side of racism.

　Bibliography: p.
　Includes index.
　1.　Afro-Americans—Race identity.　2.　United States—
Race relations.　I.　Title.
E185.625.W65　　　　　　　305.8′00973　　　　　　80-26346
ISBN 0-8142-0318-3

FOR BREWTON BERRY
AND HIS GENERATION

CONTENTS

PREFACE

After studying the principles of a free society and how those principles are best implemented to protect and preserve human liberty and human rights, I have concluded that even if that society's economic and political institutions are structurally constituted and maintained to achieve the maximum realization of its goals, it cannot hope to succeed except that its members make a vigorous effort to sustain the sovereignty of their individuality. The question every person is obliged to ask himself is not how free is my country, as compared with other nations, but: how free am *I*? Am I free of government coercion? Am I free of interference from my neighbor? But more importantly: Am I free of irrational ideas and unjust actions against my own human nature and best interest? For surely, a society or nation cannot be free unless it consists of individuals who are committed to matching external political and economic freedom with internal intellectual and spiritual freedom.

If the external freedom that enhances individuality is trampled to death by a society run amok politically or bogged in the swamp of philosophical inertia, it is because the internal freedom on which individuality rests was mutilated first in the minds of men. That is the basic premise of this study. Its specific purpose is to identify ethnic and race consciousness as an expression of mutilated internal freedom on the one hand and a revolt against external freedom on the other.

Ethno-race consciousness is itself "the other side of racism"—that state of awareness which entails the ideas, attitudes, and values of which racist dogma and behavior are expressions. But the title of this study represents a great deal more. The other side of racism is a personal psychointellectual dilemma of self-esteem: the conflict between an individual's values and the facts of reality, as opposed to the more publicized conflicts in race relations between groups. Politically, it is seen in the growing influence of "ethnic exclusivity" and "ethnic polity" on American public policy, as opposed to the American tradition of aiming toward a social system based on the rejection of racial, class, or national differences. It is the retributive "reverse discrimination" advocated *in favor* of ethno-racial minorities rather than the oppressive discrimination traditionally engaged in by the majority *against* such groups.

Finally, "the other side of racism" is descriptive of the particular approach of this study, which focuses on the microsociology of race relations between individuals as well as the macrosociology of race relations among groups. It is presented from an individualistic point of view different from the deterministic-collectivist context of most notable social scientists and social and political commentators. It is a view shaped by the definition of man as a reasoning being of volitional consciousness, requiring the freedom of self-regulation and self-responsibility for a productive and happy life.

I shall demonstrate first that race consciousness is not inherited but a set of attitudes, values, ideas, and behavior chosen by individuals; second, that it is a problem of self-esteem in general and an expression of social metaphysics in particular; and third, that when expressed in sociopolitical activities, it interferes with the human rights and liberty that are the prerequisites for harmonious and beneficial relations between individuals and groups in a multiethnic society.

There is an abundance of writing on the sociocultural problems of Negroes, but this is one of the few studies that name contemporary Negro individuals themselves as well as socioeconomic and political factors as the source of many of their problems. I have singled out Negroes, not because they are the only abusers of freedom and individual sovereignty, but because I am convinced that most Americans are so inundated by cries of freedom from Negro intellectuals and political leaders that they fail to recognize that, more often than not, these apostles of freedom are among its first violators. Yet, I hasten to add that the most eloquent and persistent opposition to the individuality and independence of man is found among white intellectuals and politicians. Practically every observation made here about Negroes can be made about individuals within any other race or group. In fact, the race-conscious attitudes of many Negroes would never come to fruition as racist dogma were it not for the intellectual, political, and financial backing they receive from whites who suffer from their own dilemma of race consciousness. It is not in the polarization of the races that I find the greatest threat to the stability of the American society, but in their combined efforts to undercut the stability of the single most important entity on which a rational social system and harmonious social relations depend: *the free and sovereign individual.*

A number of sociologists point out that race-conscious attitudes and behavior of Negroes are best interpreted as the victim's response to his oppression and his oppressor. This study does not deny that Negroes often act and think in response to white racism. But it asks whether certain forms of that response are always appropriate, realistic, and just. It takes the position that race consciousness held by any group is not just a response to external factors of social relations, but that it is also a response to internal pressures and is *goal*-directed. Though it is a response to others, it is not "others" who are the authors of that response, but the respondent himself. He may behave *in reference* to others; but the source of his attitudes and social conduct is himself, and he is to be held accountable for them whether they be right or wrong.

White racism is a reference point, but it is not the source of Negro social behavior. Many black power-seekers claim white racism as the cause of their desire to amass political privilege, and many people accept the idea that having political privilege will enable them to overcome racial oppression. This study questions the justification of political privilege as a means of achieving social and political advancement. And it suggests that although such means may eliminate overt racial oppression, it can only do so at the expense of individual rights and voluntary social relations.

Some people may conclude that my criticism of Negroes is a manifestation of hatred or contempt for these people of my own race. Or it may be interpreted by some as a confession of some shame I might feel in being a Negro. But any sensible person knows that criticism of Negroes cannot be automatically equated with antiblack sentiments. And only a moral coward would hold back valid criticism merely to escape the charge of being antiblack.

Some people have praised me for "having the courage to speak out against your own people," assuming that I am against members of my race and that it is with great trepidation that I make my views known. To those I say: first, I am not against Negroes and neither am I for Negroes; and this holds for any other group of people. I am for the individual, and what I have to say is always in defense of a particular kind of individual: the self-created person of authentic self-esteem, integrity, and honesty, whose individuality is endowed with a free spirit and an active commitment to reason as his only tool of knowledge.

No great battles are waged within me to achieve a courageous outpouring of polemics against race consciousness. I speak what I believe to be the truth, and I do so because I believe it is in my self-interest to share with my fellowman the truths I have found. To be sure, one pays a price for daring to suggest the priority of man's individuality during these times when ethno-racial collectivism is so prevalent in our society. And the price paid for such radicalism is even greater if one is a member of a group that is at once a victim of racism and in the forefront of the move toward statism. I pay it, in all its different forms, but always with the certainty that the price I pay is of lesser priority than the principles to which I adhere.

I harbor none of the trappings of race consciousness, neither in my own self-concept nor in my view of others. Thus, I have no reason to despise the fact that I am a Negro; the fact that I am simply is of no primary significance. The social significance of racial identity is not derived from the laws of nature, but from the conventional judgments of men. Racial identity is given to us by nature, but the natural laws of existence give it no significance in so far as human survival is concerned. Neither, then, do I. I perceive my racial identity according to the laws of nature, not the social conventions of men. I am who I am not because of my racial affiliation, but because of how I have chosen to be human, which includes how I deal with the reality of my racial affiliation and the response of others to it.

I have tried to present this study as carefully as my knowledge, context, and ability would allow, conveying only what I believe to be true and reasonable, and stating my opinions within the bounds of my present understanding. Its basic thrust is derived from the principles of individualism defined in Ayn Rand's philosophy of Objectivism and the principles of self-esteem and individuality defined in Nathaniel Branden's biocentric theories of human psychology. I sincerely hope that in presenting this view of ethno-race consciousness, I have not misrepresented the innovative ideas of these two thinkers. I have quoted often and liberally from the works of these and other scholars, employing their analyses of many of the issues covered here. However, the ultimate responsibility for what is said here is mine alone.

The philosophical seeds that eventually gave fruition to this work were sown many years ago by my father, Elder Johnny Wortham, of Jackson, Tennessee, whom I thank for his example and for having the foresight and courage to allow me to cultivate and assert my independence. Much of my thinking en route to this study has appeared in articles in *The Freeman*, the organ of The Foundation for Economic Education. I thank Paul Poirot, managing editor of *The Freeman*, and Leonard Read, president of the foundation, for giving me the opportunity to share my views with others. Sociologist and anthropologist Brewton Berry (Ohio State University), to whom this work is dedicated, was the first to read the manuscript and has since been steadfast in his conviction that it should be published. His textbook, *Race and Ethnic Relations*, has been indispensable as a guide to my understanding the sociology of race relations. I owe much to philosopher Tibor R. Machan, at State University of New York—Fredonia, whose expositions of the natural rights principle inform many of my judgments about the application of justice in the politics of race relations. I have also profited from the criticisms and suggestions offered by sociologist Peter Berger at Boston College.

I am particularly grateful to my friend, artist Frank Porpat, of Georgetown, California, whose creations and convictions have fueled my inspiration when it was needed most. Pillars of long-standing material and spiritual support are Mr. and Mrs. George Koether, Mr. and Mrs. William H. Barton, Dr. Ruth Dowling Bruun, Dwight Minkler, and Donald A. Feder. Finally, I wish to thank Weldon A. Kefauver and the Editorial Board at Ohio State University Press for accepting the work for publication and Robert S. Demorest and Kummi Ranjit for seeing it through the production stages.

Anne Wortham
Brighton, Massachusetts

INTRODUCTION

This study identifies ethno-race consciousness as a self-esteem problem among ethno-racial minorities in general and Negroes in particular. It is not an indictment of a whole race, however, and does not proceed without a consideration of race consciousness among the majority group as well. But in its defense of human individuality, it challenges that view of race relations which places the collective identification of ethno-racial groups above the individual identity of their members.

Part I, The Foundations of Ethno-Race Consciousness, begins with the observation that ethno-racial minorities are just as plagued by race consciousness as members of the majority. It defines the concepts of race relations and the ramifications they have for this particular examination of race consciousness among Negroes. In demonstrating how ethno-race consciousness is a negation of self-consciousness, Chapter 1 describes the components of the concept by beginning with a definition of racial and ethnic categories. The concept *ethno-race consciousness* is used to allow for an analysis of racist attitudes and behavior that often overlap those of ethnocentrism. It is also introduced to designate more than just the dynamics of group contact and conflict, but to focus on the awareness and thinking of individuals engaged in such relations.

Chapter 2 defines the difference between ethno-race consciousness and ethno-racism: *ethno-race consciousness* being a personal crisis of self-esteem—a state of awareness in which the individual seeks to escape his own consciousness and that of others by means of his own or someone else's ethnic and/or racial identification; ethno-racism being the politicization and institutionalization of ethno-race consciousness—the translation of it into a sociocultural dogma that is given political and economic expression in a society. Chapter 2 also takes a look at how ethno-race consciousness is being legitimated as a force in the political action of ethno-racial minorities. Reverse discrimination and neo-ethnicity are discussed as political expressions of ethno-race consciousness that are no more than an effort to seek political privilege at the expense of the rights of others. They represent "retributive" discrimination *in favor of* groups as opposed to the traditional "oppressive" racism that discriminates *against* groups.

Chapter 3 relies on Robert K. Merton's study of the variations of prejudice and discrimination as its base in presenting a view of ethno-race consciousness as it is expressed in prejudiced attitudes and discriminatory behavior. Not all the dimensions of prejudice and discrimination are presented in this study, but an effort is made to broaden the general characteristics supplied by Merton and others. The analysis goes beyond Merton's typologies of prejudice and discrimination among majority members and applies them to members of minorities.

Chapter 4 offers a new look at the process of assimilation that is central to understanding the response of minorities to their marginal situation. This chapter might well have been entitled "The Moral Meaning of Assimilation." It begins with a brief review of the altruistic "melting pot" theory and the statist "Americanization" theory and how their failure to achieve successful ethno-racial relations has contributed to the bad name given to assimilation. In resurrecting this most misunderstood and misrepresented concept from its negative reputation, chapter 4 demonstrates that assimilation is as much a function of individual self-determination as it is of group contact; that it can be beneficial (self-assertive) or inimical (self-immolating), depending on the perspective of the individual toward himself and the relationship he establishes with his social environment.

Part II, Ethno-Race Consciousness: A Dilemma of Self-Esteem, argues that a great deal of the social and political activity of race-conscious individuals represents the attempt to achieve public solutions (often at the expense of the rights of others) to very personal psychointellectual problems of self-esteem that sustain, if not motivate, the dilemma of ethno-race consciousness. Invaluable to the delineation of this dilemma is Nathaniel Branden's work on the concept of "social metaphysics"—a form of pseudo self-esteem characterized by an individual's reliance on the minds of others as his means of understanding and dealing with reality.

By developing a synthesis between the concepts of Branden's social metaphysics and those of Everett Stonequist's theory of marginal personality, chapter 5 defines the race-conscious individual as a *marginal social metaphysician: marginal* in the sense that he suffers from incomplete assimilation, fluctuating between his desire for membership in the dominant culture and his loyalty to his ethno-racial subculture; and a *social metaphysician* in that he views either or both groups as objects of cognitive and evaluative authority and relies on them for a perception of reality and a definition of his identity.

While Stonequist's conception of marginality as a crisis of maladjustment illuminates the dilemma of ethno-race consciousness, this study does not take the position that marginality is necessarily punishing or the result of psychological and cultural conflict. Marginality as conformist or anomic, as presented here, is not exclusive. The "other-directed" marginality of the social metaphysician is discussed as the antithesis of the "inner-directed" marginality of the individualist who, by definition, does not figure as a marginal social metaphysician. Other-directed marginality is focused on not because it is viewed as the only form of the phenomenon but because it is a significant factor of the other-orientation of ethno-race consciousness. The moral conflict that underlies the psychological conflict of other-oriented marginality is analyzed by bringing Branden's ethical meaning of social metaphysics to bear on Stonequist's characterization of the negative psychological correlates of marginality.

Chapter 6 discusses the civil rights/ "black identity" movements as manifestations of the ethno-race consciousness of their constituents. Its main point is that although many Negro civil rights activists direct their action toward the pursuit of genuine political and economic freedom, the activism of others represents an evasion of the responsibilities of personal freedom and a rationalization of their fear of increased social and political freedom. Their revolt against authentic self-identity and self-assertiveness is an effort to make some adjustment to their marginal situation—to move from the position of having a conflict of loyalties between their ethno-racial group and the dominant group to the position of loyalty to a single authority group. The various forms of rhetoric and activism they choose are summarized as a prelude to part III, which gives a comprehensive account of these solutions.

Tracing from Nathaniel Branden's very generalized conception of the motivational trends and rationalizations that are dominant among five types of social metaphysicians, Part III, Profiles of Race-Conscious Negroes, portrays five types of race-conscious Negroes. These typologies are constructed according to the solutions these individuals seek as they attempt to adjust to the alienation of self-immolating assimilation and their dependency on the groups from which they seek approval and acceptance on the one hand, and their fear and hatred of them on the other. The "significant other" orientation of ethnic marginality is presented as the antithesis of individualism. However, it is not the in-between position of the ethnic marginal that defines him as anti-individualistic. Rather, it is *his perception* of that position that defines him as such, evidenced most clearly by his reliance on significant others as cognitive and evaluative authorities and by the solutions he seeks.

Since integration, like assimilation, is often misunderstood, chapter 7 begins with a discussion of the distinction between desegregation and integration and the philosophical differences between the laissez-faire and coercive implementations of the integrationist expectation in the practical life of the community. Against this background the profile of the *Conventional Integrationist* is drawn as a person whose solution to his dilemma is voiced as: "*If you want to join them, be like them.*" Entailed in his advocacy of coercive integration is the desire for automatic acceptance and friendliness he hopes to achieve by creating an egalitarian system that would eliminate the differences of human capability and achievement altogether.

The *Power-seeking Nationalist* in chapter 8 is the individual who has failed to win approval of others as he had hoped and is fearful or contemptuous of competing in the open market of material acquisition and political participation. His alternative is to gain control over men's judgment of him by means of political and economic separatism. Two types of Power-seeking Nationalists are profiled: (1) the reactionary nationalists, more popularly known by their "Black Power" rhetoric and advocacy of territorial separatism; and (2) the pragmatic nationalists, who have achieved a synthesis between integration and separatism in order to make black ethnic polity a source of power in the formulation and implementation of public policy. The formula chosen by the reactionary nationalists is: "*If you can't join them, lick them.*" The pragmatic nationalists, who are presently the most vocal among black politicians and organization leaders, have as their formula: "*If you can't join them, protect and depend on yourself.*"

There is argument among pragmatic nationalists, however, as to whether Negroes should seek political and economic gains along racial lines or whether their programs and policies should be deracialized to promote class interests. By and large, the tactics of the pragmatic nationalists remain racially and ethnically oriented, as seen in their support of such programs as affirmative action quotas, busing, open admissions, and black capitalism. Achieving power or redressing grievances on the basis of race or ethnicity is clearly not in accord with the American tradition of giving no formal recognition to ethnic groups as political entities. Suggestions as to how the pragmatic nationalists have made their ethnicity a powerful force in the shaping of public policy are presented in a review of the Negro's history of forced separation from the mainstream of American life and a summary of sociologist Nathan Glazer's conceptualization of the moral sanction given to the creation of specially benefited group categories.

The *Spiritual Separatist* in chapter 9 is the intellectual counterpart of the Power-seeking Nationalist. In fact, most of the attitudes that move the Spiritualist are also significant in the Power-seeker's philosophy. They differ in the sphere of activity each chooses to express his solution, but their relationship is one of interdependence. The cultural nationalism of the Spiritualist is employed to legitimate the political nationalism of the Power-seeker. Fearful of individual authenticity and of competing in the open market of ideas and men's judgment, the Spiritual Separatist advocates psychointellectual and ethno-cultural chauvinism, proclaims himself above the understanding of those whose acceptance he craves but has not achieved, and withdraws into a world of "blackness" that promises automatic acceptance. His solution is stated thusly: "*If you can't join (or be like them), join (or be like) your own group.*"

The Independent Militant in chapter 10 resorts to destructive rebellion against those he is afraid to join and cannot control by political or economic means. Unlike the Power-seeking Nationalist or the Conventional Integrationist, who would use peaceful means to achieve their goals, the Independent Militant is committed to his "violent revolution." The others want only to change the attitudes of men and the social system to favor their interests, but the Militant wants to destroy the society. His solution is expressed as follows: "*If you can't lick them, destroy their world.*"

Of the five types, the Ambivalent Appeaser in chapter 11 is posited as the most tragic of the ethnic marginals because, possessing greater intellectual independence than the others, he has the greatest potential to reverse his crisis of duality and consequently his social behavior. His crux is that although he gives no cognitive authority to either of the cultures he stands between, he does render evaluative authority to them. He is further paralyzed by the conflict between his private convictions and his public denial of those convictions. Privately, he rejects aspects of both the dominant culture and his own ethno-racial subculture; but fearing disapproval from their members, he appeases both publicly, believing that to be the only "practical" solution to his problem. He states his solution as follows: "*If you can't join either group, don't let them know it.*"

While these are profiles of Negro individuals, in so far as their attitudes and behavior are expressions of social metaphysics, they are just as applicable to race-conscious individuals in other ethnic and racial groups. A repeated theme of this study is that the ethno-race consciousness of both the discriminator and the discriminated against is an anathema to rational human relations. With this in mind, part IV, Commentary on Race Relations and Public Policy, discusses the effects of antiracism legislation on the private affairs of individuals and on voluntary association.

In examining whether the use of force is justified in eliminating the irrationality of private ethno-race consciousness and the immorality of private discrimination, chapter 12 asks and answers the following questions: Does every act of prejudice and discrimination constitute the violation of the rights of others? Should an individual be punished by the state for his attitudes of prejudice? Does one's desire to create a community of harmonious association between groups justify his taking steps to force that goal into existence?

The answers to these questions lead to the assertions made in chapter 13. This concluding chapter does not propose specific legislative and institutional programs that would modify or eliminate existing programs. Rather, it challenges the ideology that legitimates such programs, and urges a counterpolicy of social interaction based on the achievement of self-identity, self-responsibility, and self-assertiveness.

PART I. THE FOUNDATIONS OF ETHNO-RACE CONSCIOUSNESS

1

Ethno-Race Consciousness versus Self-Consciousness

Science is at a loss to explain why Newton and Mozart were full of creative genius and why most people are not. But it is by all means an unsatisfactory answer to say that a genius owes his greatness to his ancestry or to his race.—Ludwig von Mises, *Human Action: A Treatise on Economics.*

In his introduction to the Bantam edition of the 1968 *Report of the National Advisory Commission on Civil Disorders*, journalist Tom Wicker writes that the task before the commission and the American society it represented was to define what could be done to deal with "the sheer humanness of racism." Racism *is* human, though not intrinsically so as Tom Wicker implies. Neither can racism be claimed human from the grotesque and faulty proposition that it is a function of an alleged evil in human nature. Racism is human because it is one of several choices men make in expressing their response to contact with other men. It is not a function of "the way man is," but an expression of the way some men *choose* to be. It is an immoral choice, to be sure, but not the manifestation of inherent, universal evil. It is a doctrine decided upon by individuals or a group of individuals in *contradiction* to what is human. It is immoral because it negates the nature of man and the requirements of his survival. It is an expression of the kind that only man is capable of: the capacity to consciously act *against* his survival.

3

And because racism is a matter of human choice, it is not exclusive to white Americans as the report implies in the following indictment: "What white Americans have never fully understood—but what the Negro can never forget—is that white society is deeply implicated in the ghetto. *White institutions created it, white institutions maintained it, and white society condones it.*"

Wicker echoes the sentiments of the commission when he states that "until the fact of white racism is admitted, it cannot conceivably be expunged." In so saying, Mr. Wicker joins the many who, even in the face of the ever-increasing politicization of "reverse discrimination," continue to deny that the sword of racism is two-edged and forged in the psychointellectual fires of race consciousness found in Negroes as well as whites; that America's racial dilemma is not just a matter of whites against Negroes, but of whites and Negroes against each other; and that it does not include merely the racist behavior of these two groups but encompasses also the ethnocentricity of a great many American subcultures. Until *these* facts are admitted, there is no hope that a rational view of American racism will ever be developed, not to mention the means of eliminating it from human relations and institutional functions.

When the National Advisory Commission on Civil Disorders concluded that the cause of the 1967 racial violence was "white racism," it told only half the story—and perhaps not even half. The commission's report did not altogether discount Negro race consciousness, but it was conspicuously lacking in any detailed examination of race consciousness among Negroes as a factor in the polarization of the races. Even in its accounts of violence, its participants, and its effects, the commission failed to identify the problems of many Negroes for what they are. In presenting a historical perspective of the Negro's experience in Negro-white relations in America, the commission saw Negroes as having been primarily respondents to a racist society. For instance, it did not identify Black Power activism as the reverse racism that it is, but chose to call it instead "an accommodation to white racism." In each discussion of the factors it names as contributors to racial violence, the commission failed to consider the Negro as being even remotely the cause of many of his problems. Having named white racism as the cause of Negro alienation, dissatisfaction, and violence, the commission did not feel obliged to investigate the nature of white racism and left the impression that whites in this country are either of working-class Archie Bunker extraction or KKK vigilantes disguised as policemen, both preoccupied with ideas as to how they can make life miserable for Negroes.

Racism is usually viewed as a collective illness, as a doctrine conditioned in one by his culture and shared by him with his contemporaries, but the *cause* of racism—a symptom of one's lack of self-esteem—is individual. That the self-esteem of a great many in a society is so ravaged by fears, doubts, and envy that it gives rise to and then is swallowed up by their race consciousness is what makes a social disease of racism. If racism were in fact caused by "society" or one's "culture," no one could escape it. But there is ample evidence that not all men are race conscious and that those who are have *chosen* to be so. There is as much evidence that no one racial or ethnic group has a monopoly on racism; that as the affliction of racism transcends geopolitical boundaries, so does it transcend the racial boundaries of man.

In his book, *Reluctant Reformers*, Robert L. Allen disagrees with the idea that Negroes and other ethno-racial minorities are as much contributors to historical racism in America as the white Anglo-Saxon majority. To contend that they are, writes Allen, "would be like arguing that the existence of crime is to be understood in terms of the behavior of the victim."[1] Indeed, Negroes and other minorities *are* victims of white racism, but so too are whites victims of Negro racism and ethnic prejudice. And as this study will show, before most individuals and groups are victims of contemporary racism from without they are victims first of their own race consciousness from within. Indeed, many of the "crimes"—acts infringing on human rights in the name of civil rights for minorities—could not have succeeded during the last two decades of liberalism and social reform without the complicity of the victims.

This study aims to lift the shroud of social sanctity from racial "victimization" to reveal the other side of the coin of American racism—the side which few are courageous enough to admit is there and has always been there.

But first I must define what I mean by race consciousness.

Defining Racial and Ethnic Groups

A racial group is defined as one whose members through biological descent share distinctive hereditary physical characteristics. An ethnic group is defined as one bound together by

5

ties of cultural homogeneity, often possessing distinctive folkways and mores, customs of dress, art and ornamentation, moral codes and value systems, and patterns of recreation, and often expressing allegiance to a monarch, a religion, a language, or a territory.[2]

What makes a group racial or ethnic is not as clear-cut as these definitions seem to indicate. While the universal distinction of racial groups is biogeographical[3] and the distinguishing characteristic of ethnic groups is cultural, some ethnic groups may be coincidentally populations of one of the major races. The American Indians, for instance, are not only a major racial group, but, within the United States, they constitute one of its major ethnic groups. Most Semitic-speaking peoples are of the local Mediterranean race. Jews were once a subtype of this race, but they have mixed with other peoples until the name Jew has lost all racial meaning. However, Hebrew, the traditional language of Jews, is a Semitic language and links them in this regard to other Semitic-speaking peoples in Arabia, Jordan, Israel, Syria, Iraq, Egypt, and other North African countries.

Yet even the factor of common language is not sufficient to link groups of people into an ethnic category. Among the Semites are Jews whose Judaic religion and Hebrew literature differ substantially from the Islamic religion and Arabic literature of the Arabs. Yet both these groups are classified as members of the European race, which includes populations throughout Europe, the United States, in the Middle East, and north of the Sahara in Africa.

Even the religious allegiance of an ethnic group is not sufficient to link a people whose subgroups are separated by national boundaries and historical development. Although language, nationality, and religion are elements of ethnic identification, an ethnic group is ultimately distinguished by the fact that its members "consist of those who conceive of themselves as being alike by virtue of their common ancestry, real or fictitious, and who are so regarded by others."[4] Ethnic categories remain significant bases for group identification because people *believe* them to be the natural divisions of mankind.[5]

As there is no monolithic "Negro culture" that embraces all the world's Negroes, neither is there an all-encompassing "Jewish culture" that distinguishes all the world's Jews. Jews, like Negroes, are scattered all over the world and there is as much difference between the ethnocultural heritage of Russian Jews and that of the Arabian Jews of Palestine as there is between the ethnocultural heritage of American Negroes and that of the Negroes of Madagascar. Such are the facts, but this is not what many Jews and Negroes *believe*—or would have others believe when it is to their advantage.

It must be stressed here that such elements as nationality, language, religion, accomplishments, or customs, which make up a people's culture, have no relation to race. There is, for example, no such race as the "English-speaking race," since people of many races speak English and language is a cultural trait and not determined biologically. As seen above, the Semitic-speaking Jews and Arabs are both members of the European race but one group category has nothing to do with the other. People often speak of the "German race," the "Italian race," or the "Welsh race." There are no such races, though there may be more or less distinct subpopulations in those countries. Similarly, there are no such races as French-Canadian, Chinese-American, Afro-American, or Greek-Cypriot. These terms refer to the national ancestry of subpopulations in Canada, America, and Cyprus.

Such overlapping of certain ethnic ties among racial subgroups is often misunderstood and some groups have been judged by their cultural traits as though those traits were racial attributes, with the result that people view other groups in terms of stereotypes. For instance, one often encounters a kind of chauvinism among English-speaking peoples toward those who speak the Romance languages—and vice versa. This is evident in the tension between the French and British Canadians in the predominantly French-speaking province of Quebec. The Catholic and Protestant Irish in Northern Ireland speak of each other as a "different breed," giving biological overtones to what is so obviously a matter of religious and political differences. When Negro entertainer Sammy Davis, Jr., converted to the Judaic religion and thereby became a Jew, many people protested that he had renounced his racial identity, as though that were possible and that his choice of religion had any relation to his *un*chosen, biologically determined racial identity. People often apply the characteristics of individuals to their judgments of groups as a whole, and they apply stereotyped group characteristics to individuals. For whatever combination of reasons, an individual may be dumb or intelligent, artistic or athletic, lazy or industrious, militant or pacifist; but there is no such race as a "backward race," an "artistic race," or a "militaristic race."

Many of the above judgments have nothing to do with race or culture either, but only the opinions or prejudices of those who make them. Yet people persist in judging cultural traits and individual characteristics as though they were natural extensions of a group's biogeographical heritage. Though there is a distinct difference in what makes a racial group and what determines an ethnic group, the confusion of race and culture in most people's minds and the overlapping of ethnic ties among racial groups make it almost impossible to speak of race consciousness and racism without also including attitudes of ethnic consciousness or ethnocentrism. (For instance, no study of "white racism" is complete without an analysis of how members of many Caucasian ethnic groups view themselves and others.)

Defining Ethno-Race Consciousness

Much of what is said about race consciousness can be said about ethnocentricity, and thus the term *ethno-race consciousness* will be used here to encompass the varying perspectives of both. Sociologists and political scientists use the term "ethnicity" to designate the complimentary and interchangeable characteristics of racial identity and ethnic awareness that are manifested in modern society and politics. It is basically a sociological concept which Glazer and Moynihan have defined as "the character or quality of an ethnic group"—the great pole around which group interests are mobilized for the pursuit of social, economic, and political goals.[6] And it is precisely the reference of ethnicity to collective identification that makes it an inadequate concept to describe the realm of individual identity and awareness focused on in this study.

As a concept of social psychology, ethno-race consciousness takes into account the interpersonal relations of individuals in society as well as their level of awareness and the nature of their thinking. Indeed, it is the very foundation of the dynamics of group expression and experience. Since all men belong to some ethnocultural group, they all possess a certain degree of ethnicity, or sense of peoplehood. But the nature and degree of each person's ethnic experience and expression is determined by the degree to which ethno-race consciousness is operative in his thinking and self-awareness. If ethnicity is defined as the character or quality of an ethnic group, ethno-race consciousness designates the character or quality of *individuals* within ethnic and racial groups. Because it constitutes a multitude of psychological responses toward others and cultural expressions of an individual's fundamental view of reality and his place in it, ethno-race consciousness is a very complex attitude to understand. An example of its complexity may be seen in the ethno-race consciousness among Jews. The ethnocentricity of Jews is so complex and difficult to understand precisely because, unlike other groups, there is little that ties them together existentially. Unlike the racial group, Jews are not bound together by common hereditary physical features (color, hair, eyes, etc.), and it is not on this basis that they are assigned a status in their community or excluded from full participation in the life of that community. Unlike a nation, they do not share the same political structure and territorial establishment (of course the state of Israel with its 90 percent Jewish population is an exception).[7] Neither do Jews make a religious group, as not all Jews adhere to the particular faith of Judaism—or any faith at all for that matter. Jews cannot even be strictly called an ethnic group, as they are not bound together by ties of cultural homogeneity.

What, then, is a Jew? According to rabbinical law, a Jew is a person who has a Jewish mother or who has converted to Judaism. Brewton Berry concludes that the only characteristic that is common to all who are included in the group is *the consciousness of being a Jew*—that is, "a Jew is a person who thinks of himself as a Jew and is treated by others as a Jew, regardless of the physical features which he bears, the nation of which he is a citizen, the language he speaks, and whatever religion, if any, he professes."[8] There are Negro Jews, Arabian Jews ("Arabian" meaning one who speaks the Arabic language), Brazilian Jews, Israeli Jews, Protestant Jews, as well as atheistic Jews.

As the world's Negroes are tied together only by their hereditary physical features, the obvious histocultural variations among the world's Jews leaves them very little in common except their consciousness of being Jews. Most Jews believe that the group is tied together by something other than Jewishness, but there is hardly any agreement as to what that factor is. Some believe that the Jewish people ought to be bound together by the common denominator of the faith of Judaism. But since Judaism is an inextricable mixture of religion and nationhood, there are considerable differences of opinion as to what the focus of Judaism ought to be.

The more liberal, or "secular Jews," among whom are Reform Jews and Conservatives, see their purpose as the search for a common denominator of faith within a broader idea of *Jewish peoplehood*. The Orthodox Jews, among whom are the anti-Zionist Satmar Hasidics and the Zionist Lubavitch Hasidics, are opposed to the secular Jews and demand that faith must come first and peoplehood second. At the other end of the spectrum is Reconstructionism, a kind of Jewish Unitarianism that grew out of the American naturalism and pragmatism of the 1920s and 1930s. A group formed out of he "Jesus Revolution" is Jews for Jesus, which believes in "Messianic Judaism."

In an attempt to find a concept to define what embraces the Jewish people as a whole, a group of Reform, Conservative, and Orthodox thinkers have come together under the umbrella of "Covenant theology," which is the belief that Jews are joined together by a special relationship to God; that in revealing himself to man, God established a special covenant with the Jews. Finally, however, with the creation of the state of Israel, the ethnic, religious, and political allegiances of most Jews have culminated to take either of two positions that express the degree of ethnic consciousness among them. And here the concept of peoplehood often outweighs religious considerations. There are Zionists of all Judaic backgrounds and persuasions and anti-Zionists of as many backgrounds and persuasions. Thus, for all of their differing political and religious allegiances, most Jews find that their pro and con position on Zionism is the one element in their culture that variously links them.

Since the Jewish group is not a race, we have to say that being Jewish is a matter of choice—the choice of Jewish parents that their children will be raised as Jews, which is usually the case; or the choice of children, when they are old enough, that they will share the Jewish affiliation of their parents or associates. While one may be born a Jew—i.e., of parents who are Jews—*being* "Jewish" is an *acquired* characteristic: a psychointellectual commitment to a Jewish identification as defined by the particular histocultural elements of the Jewish subpopulation in a given territory. Unlike one's racial identification over which he has no control, one either chooses to become a Jew or chooses to remain a Jew. Of course, one may also reject the Jewish affiliation into which he was born.

Unfortunately, however, many Jews and non-Jews put a moral price tag on Jewish affiliation and are quick to condemn Jews by birth who reject a commitment to "Jewishness." They are reacted to as though they were denying their physical racial identification which, of course, is not the case. There is nothing immoral about not wanting to be a Jew, providing one's reasons are not neurotically motivated. There is, however, *every*thing wrong with becoming or remaining a Jew as the substitute for one's lack of self-identity. (There is a mistaken idea held by some social scientists and most laymen that being a member of a racial group that is a minority in a given territory is to be race conscious by definition—that one's physiological attribute, such as skin color, and the reaction of others to it makes it virtually impossible to escape acquiring a sense of identity based on his race. This idea is presented as though it were the natural condition of racial groups. But, as we shall see, the issue of race consciousness and / or ethnic consciousness is psychointellectual, not metaphysical.)

As pointed out, much of what is said about race consciousness can be said about ethnocentricity. The difference between these attitudes is that while race consciousness is based on the perception of oneself and others as being *biologically determined* and on his judgment of himself and others according to their *biological attributes*, ethnocentricity is based on the perception of oneself and others as being *environmentally determined* and his judgment of himself and them according to their *ethnocultural heritage*. At the root of both, however, is the doctrine of psychological determinism, described by Nathaniel Branden as "an *epistemological* contradiction," which "denies the existence of any element of freedom or volition in man's consciousness."[9]

Crucial to constructing a definition of ethno-race consciousness is an understanding of what is meant by *consciousness*. " 'Consciousness,' in the primary meaning of the term," writes Branden, "designates a state: the state of being conscious or aware of some aspect of reality. In a derivative usage, 'consciousness' designates a faculty: that faculty in man by virtue of which he is able to be conscious or aware of reality."[10]

Branden defines consciousness as the regulator of an organism's behavior in the direction of life. From the single cell to man, there are three forms of self-regulatory activity: (1) the *vegetative* level, by which plant life is exclusively directed but which is operative in all higher life forms as well, is directed toward *maintaining* life; (2) the *conscious-behavioral* level (or sensory-perceptual level), which appears with the emergence of consciousness in animals, is required to survive—to *protect and sustain* life; (3) the *self-conscious* level (or conceptual level), which appears only in man, is required to activate thinking—to focus one's awareness, to initiate purposeful mental activity, *to maintain a proper cognitive contact with reality* by perceiving and identifying the facts of reality.[11]

"The basic function of consciousness—in animals and in man—is awareness, the maintenance of sensory and/or conceptual contact with reality," writes Branden. On the perceptual level awareness is automatic ("to look is to see"), but conceptual awareness must be activated and to activate one's awareness, one must focus his mind (to see is not necessarily to understand).

By combining the elements of ethnic and racial identification with the above view of consciousness, a definition of ethno-race consciousness may be constructed as follows: *a psychological, conscious, and volitional level of awareness at which an individual perceives himself and others according to characteristics of the racial categories to which they belong and the ethnic groups with which they are affiliated.*

Ethno-race consciousness is not just a network of attitudes and value judgments about oneself and others; it involves the suspension of purposeful awareness, the refusal to integrate one's knowledge so that whatever attitudes and judgments one has are a mass of floating abstractions unrelated to the facts as they are. This policy of evasion—i.e., "actively seeking unawareness as his goal"—is described by Branden as follows:

> As focusing involves expanding the range of one's awareness, so evasion consists of the reverse process: of *shrinking* the range of one's awareness. Evasion consists of refusing to *raise* the level of one's awareness, when one knows (clearly or dimly) that one should—or of *lowering* the level of one's awareness, when one knows (clearly or dimly) that one shouldn't. To evade a fact is to attempt to make it unreal to oneself, on the implicit subjectivist premise that if one does not perceive the fact, it does not exist (or its existence will not matter and not entail any consequences).

> Consciousness is man's tool for perceiving and identifying the facts of reality. It is an organ of integration. To focus is to set the integrative process in purposeful motion—by setting the appropriate goal: awareness. Nonfocus is non-integration. Evasion is willful *dis*integration, the act of subverting the proper function of consciousness, of

setting the cognitive function in reverse and reducing the contents of one's mind to disconnected, unintegrated fragments that are forbidden to confront one another.[12]

Ethno-race consciousness is not, as many believe, an automatic, nonvolitional level of awareness; it is not an innate feature of human nature and neither is it "conditioned" by society. It is a policy of sustained evasion that may become so primary to an individual's manner of thinking and so pervasive in the content of his thoughts as to appear automatic when in fact it is not. It involves willfully *arresting* one's awareness at the sensory-perceptual level in living and dealing with other men in a social context. Racial identification and ethnic affiliation, not man's rational faculty, become the loci of his thinking and conclusions about himself and others. Not reality, but other men, are the standard of his ideas and behavior. Not facts, but feelings, whims, and arbitrary desires are the standard of his evaluation and judgment.

What links race consciousness and ethnocentricity is the basic attitude that one's ethnic and/or racial group is the center of everything, and all others are scaled with reference to it.[13] He may view his group (and thus himself) as subordinate to the will of others; or he may perceive his group (and thus himself) as dominating the will of others. On the one hand, he may experience a sense of contemptuous inferiority—feeling inferior to others and contempt for their alleged superiority; on the other hand, he may experience a sense of condescending superiority—feeling superior to others and contempt for their alleged inferiority. It often involves not just a judgment of metaphysical condition, but of moral worth; that one is not only inferior or superior in fact, but that he is also found morally wanting or morally superior—that possessing a particular racial identification or belonging to a given ethnic group makes him more or less worthwhile than others of different ethno-racial groups.

It is important to note, however, that one may be conscious of his ethnic affiliation or racial identification without feeling either inferior or superior; he may experience either emotional evaluation for reasons that have nothing to do with his race or his culture. It is when he judges himself or accepts the judgment of others that he is inferior or superior *by virtue of* his ethno-racial ascription that he is defined as ethno-race conscious. It is when he views personal worth and efficacy as effects of ethno-racial attributes rather than as the

13

effects of an individual's state of awareness, his judgment of the facts of reality, and his ability to deal with them that he becomes ethno-race conscious.

Some individuals go out of their way to avoid referring to the racial attributes of others and refuse to acknowledge legitimate ethno-racial and cultural differences among men, all with the purpose of appearing unconcerned about such matters. But an interest in the history and culture of one's own and other racial or ethnic groups, or in the achievements of their members, does not constitute race consciousness. Rather, it is when one's own group and/or another group arise as *objects of cognitive authority* in his awareness that he may be called race conscious. He is race conscious if he believes that the interaction of men with one another and the relationships they form must be dictated by their ethno-racial differences or likenesses—if he believes that American Indians should live only with other American Indians, or that Jews should marry only Jews, or that only Negro professors should teach courses on the history of American Negroes.

While this study is critical of ethno-race consciousness and champions *self*-consciousness, it does not deny legitimate racial and ethnic differences among men. Rather it holds that such differences are insignificant when judging the characterological differences among individuals. Its position is that while a certain group of men may share the characteristics of a given racial and/or ethnic category, each man is distinctly independent of the other as an individual; that while all racial groups are equally members of the human species and all ethnic groups are equally members of the human social community, each racial group is distinguished by its hereditary physical characteristics (not by the physical attributes of the individuals of which it is composed) and each ethnic group by its cultural traits (not by the character of the individuals of which it is composed).

Thus, while no one can deny the cultural differences among the Protestant and Catholic Irish as groups, for example, we should reject the idea that these differences preclude interaction between individuals of these groups or that the character of a single Protestant Irish or a single Catholic Irish should be judged by the prevailing characteristics of the groups to which each belongs. To selectively focus on ethnic and racial differences does not, in itself, constitute ethno-race consciousness. Ethno-race consciousness

14

involves an *exclusive* focus on ethnic and racial categorical differences and the concomitant rejection of individual characterological differences.

Finally, a point that is central to the focus of this study should be reiterated. Ethno-race consciousness is not just a composite of feelings, attitudes, and evasions about one's own or another ethno-racial group. At its very core, ethno-race consciousness is flagrantly *anti-individual* and is motivated by a deep-seated fear of man's individuality. It is a flight from the reality of one's own consciousness.

1.   Robert L. Allen, *Reluctant Reformers: Racism and Social Reform Movements in the United States*, p. 3.

2.   Brewton Berry, *Race and Ethnic Relations*.

3.   The description of races as biogeographical is used here in consideration of the view held by most anthropologists today that the races of men are not only distinguished by their common genetic ancestry, but that their differing characteristics also result from thousands of years of living in the same area and exposure to common selective forces such as natural selection, mutation, genetic drift, and race mixture; that there are nine major *geographical* races extending throughout major continental areas and hundreds of smaller population units called *local* races; and that these larger and small groupings of mankind are the products of evolutionary change.

4.   Tamotsu Shibutani and Kian M. Kwam, *Ethnic Stratification: A Comparative Approach*, p. 47.

5.   Ibid., p. 46.

6.   See Nathan Glazer and Daniel P. Moynihan, eds., *Ethnicity*.

7.   There is some question in my mind as to whether Israel can remain politically "Jewish" without infringing on the rights of its citizens through its system of religious courts that have been in operation since the time of Turkish control. Under this system, courts operated by various religious groups have the only power to perform marriages or to hear divorce cases. But a religious court does not perform marriages between persons of different religions. As a result, such marriages cannot take place in Israel.

8.   Berry, op. cit. pp. 33–34.

9.   Nathaniel Branden, *The Psychology of Self-Esteem*, pp. 50–51. Branden's definition of the doctrine of determinism (of which ethno-race consciousness is a variety) is employed throughout this study. His full statement is as follows: "Psychological determinism denies the existence of any element of freedom or volition in man's consciousness. It holds that, in relation to his actions, decisions, values and conclusions, man is ultimately and essentially *passive*; that man is merely a *reactor* to internal and external pressures; that those pressures determine the course of his actions and the content of his convictions, just as physical forces determine the course of every particle of dust in the universe. It holds that, in any given situation or moment, only one 'choice' is psychologically possible to man, the inevitable result of all the antecedent determining forces impinging on him, just as only one action is possible to the speck of dust; that man has no *actual* power of choice, no

actual freedom or self-responsibility. Man, according to this view, has no more volition than a stone: he is merely confronted with more complex alternatives and is manipulated by more complex forces."

10. Ibid., p. 26.

11. Ibid., pp. 34 ff.

12. Ibid., p. 42.

13. This attitude applies not only to the race, tribe, or nation of which one is a member, but to one's other categorical and social affiliations as well—church, political party, fraternity, college, social class, community, sex, and age.

2

Race Consciousness, Racism, and Neo-Ethnicity

I have always been made sad when I have heard members of any race claiming rights and privileges, or certain badges of distinction, on the ground simply that they were members of this or that race, regardless of their own individual worth or attainments.—Booker T. Washington, *Up from Slavery*.

Though they spring from the same psychointellectual frame of reference and are exponents of the same morality, race consciousness and racism are not the same. The two concepts differ in circumstantial connotation: race consciousness being a psychointellectual doctrine and racism, a sociopolitical ideology.

Race consciousness is a state of awareness of individuals—a *personal* attitude rising out of ignorance, evasion, and/or the conflict between a person's values and the facts of reality.

Racism, however, is *the dilemma of race consciousness translated into a sociocultural dogma that is given political and economic expression in a society*. It is an institutionalized form of collectivism, such as the racism of Nazi Germany, the government-enforced discrimination in the United States, the militarized tribalism of many African countries, or the apparthied of South Africa.

Race consciousness is the motive of the fears expressed by a white woman who said: "I don't want them living next door to me for the simple reason that there might be a lot of nice ones but I got four kids and I don't want them growing up with colored next to them.

17

Because it's a proven fact they grow up, they think nothing of each other. They play together. Pretty soon they're in their teens, they start dating, and pretty soon they're marrying. I don't want my kids marrying a colored person."

However, the constitutional prohibitions against miscegenation that existed in sixteen states until the 1966 Supreme Court ruled to nullify bans on intermarriage were instances of racism, pure and simple.

When one believes, as author Cynthia Ozick does, that "the Jews are one people . . . you cannot separate parent from child, the Jews from Zion" and equates the survival of Israel as a state with the survival of the world's Jews as a people—that is race consciousness.[1]

When the White House feels the necessity of having a staff member who is "liason man" with the Jewish community—that is racism.

When one solicits the alliance or the financial and military aid of his country to aid a foreign country simply because that nation is his ancestral homeland—that is racism.

Race consciousness is expressed when Negroes ask country music star Charley Pride: "Why do you look like us and sound like them?"—meaning that Charley Pride's biological physical features indicate a limited appreciation for and ability to sing only certain kinds of music: jazz, rhythm and blues, or "soul."

When rhythm and blues singer Ray Charles says: "I don't know of any white person that could really sing the blues and know what he's talking about"—that is race consciousness.

When the Republic of South Africa bans the performances of black African singers before white audiences—that is racism.

White critic Richard Gilman expresses his own brand of race consciousness when he declares in his book *The Confusion of Realms* that whites have no right to judge books like Malcolm X's *Autobiography* or Eldridge Cleaver's *Soul On Ice* because "we whites . . . are, vis-á-vis the black, the imperialists. This is why our vocabularies of rational discourse are so different now from black Americans' (when a subject people finds its voice at last, it has to be different from its masters'). . . . We can no longer talk to black people, or they to us, in the traditional humanistic ways. The old Mediterranean values—the belief in the sanctity of the individual soul, the importance of logical clarity, brotherhood, reason as arbiter, political order, community—are dead as *useful* frames of reference or pertinent guides to procedure."

But it is a blatant act of racism when the Afro-American Society of a university presents the administration with the unconditional demand that no white teacher be permitted to teach Negro literature "because no person has the ability to stand outside his own conditioning—because to communicate with black men at all, the white man must recognize that he comes to black literature as an alien and ultimately as an enemy."

When a Negro businessman who has worked his way up the corporate ladder worries (regardless of contrary evidence) whether he will be denied further promotion because of his race—that is race consciousness.

When a young white male is seeking a producer-director job at a television station but is passed over in favor of a Negro trainee (who doesn't have as much experience and hasn't completed the station's training program) in order that the station may satisfy government-enforced "affirmative-action" racial quotas—that is racism.

When an individual thinks of his own achievements or failures in terms of what good or harm they do to the image of his ethno-racial group—that is race consciousness.

When a white student is twice denied admission to the University of Washington's law school while more than three dozen minority students with lower academic credentials are admitted—that is racism.

When the descendants of an oppressed or persecuted ethno-racial group feel bitter prejudice and antipathy toward their contemporaries because they are descendants of the oppressors and persecutors—that is race consciousness.

When the descendants of an oppressive racial group assume an unwarranted guilt for the sins of their ancestors—that is race consciousness.

It was an act of racism when, in order to disfranchise Negroes, state constitutions provided that persons could qualify as voters by showing that their fathers or grandfathers were eligible to vote before the adoption of the Fifteenth Amendment in 1870.

And it was an act of racism when, on December 4, 1971, the Department of Labor issued a rule requiring that affirmative-action programs specifically include "members of an 'affected class' [i.e.,

Negroes, Spanish-surnamed individuals, American Indians, and Orientals] who, by virtue of past discrimination, continue to suffer the present effects of that discrimination."

When it is assumed that the only way to achieve one's goals is through ethno-racial "solidarity"—that is race consciousness.

When the Congress of the United States allows the existence of a Congressional Black Caucus in its midst—that is racism.

It was racism when the 1972 National Black Political Convention called for a constitutional amendment to guarantee black congressional representation in proportion to population, with sixty-six representatives and fifteen senators.

He is expressing his race consciousness when a white homeowner says of blacks: "They're not responsible citizens. Until they live like we are, we don't want them [in our neighborhood]."

It is an act of racism when fair-housing regulations impose federally assisted housing upon communities in order to achieve residential integration.

Racism in Disguise

The distinction between race consciousness and racism is crucial to understanding the complexities of race relations and the differences between the *private* conflicts of individuals and the *public* policy that is often initiated to express or constrain these conflicts. Racism is often studied as a political and economic force in societies, but it is seldom presented within the context of the dilemma of race consciousness that is antecedent to it. And in judging the actions of men it is important to know when the individuals involved are responding to their own personal dilemma and when they are acting as agents of institutional racism.

For example, not every Arab wants to drive the Jews into the Mediterranean, but there are Jews who cannot encounter an Arab without simultaneously visualizing themselves being driven into the sea by him. The alleged threat the Jew perceives in the presence of an innocent Arab is of his own making, and he is the victim of his own race consciousness. At this point, his dilemma is purely his own private conflict. But when he begins to express that dilemma of race consciousness in ways that violate the individual rights of the Arab, it is that existential expression that is called racism. Likewise, the threat that an Arab may perceive in all Jews is race consciousness.

20

But the institutionalization by Arabs of an international boycott of businesses owned and operated by Jews *because* they are Jews is racism.

When most of us think of racism, the examples that come to mind are such acts of degradation as the holocaust of Nazi Germany, slavery and racial segregation in the United States, aparthied in South Africa, or the expulsion of Asian Indians from Uganda. In the United States we most readily think of racism as a policy of the Anglo-Saxon majority against ethno-racial minorities; we usually do not think of minorities as being as capable of espousing racist policies against majority groups. This commonsense view of racism is often confirmed by the theories and research of social scientists. One finds it implied in Louis Wirth's widely quoted definition of minorities: "We may define a minority as a group of people who, because of their physical or cultural characteristics, are singled out from the others in the society in which they live for differential and unequal treatment, and who therefore regard themselves as objects of collective discrimination."[2]

The "differential and unequal treatment" that makes for minority-group status does not necessarily result in lower-class status. As Milton Yinger points out, "A minority group is a group which, regardless of where it is on the class ladder, faces barriers to the pursuit of life's values that are greater than the barriers faced by persons otherwise equally qualified."[3] By this definition, what makes a minority is not whether the group is treated unequally, but whether that unequal treatment is also *unfair*—that is, whether the group is discriminated *against*. Because she views the treatment of businessmen as unfair compared to the treatment of workers, who make up the majority, Rand has designated them "America's persecuted minority."[4] But groups high in the social class hierarchy are not often thought of as objects of discrimination that impedes their life chances. Instead they are thought of as agents of discrimination, or inheritors of positions made possible by discrimination against minorities low on the socioeconomic scale.

It is easy to see why, on this view, the minority status of businessmen in relation to the majority status of workers is not accorded the same moral evaluation as the minority status of Negroes in relation to the majority status of whites. Indeed, many businessmen believe that they are rightly discriminated against on

21

the basis of their productivity in order to redress the discrimination against racial minorities within the majority work force. Since minorities are defined in terms of their economic and political powerlessness resulting from discrimination (not their numbers), businessmen are not usually included. It is especially difficult to consider contemporary businessmen as members of a minority when the power they lack is so often the economic power they give up in exchange for government protection and favors. (As discussed in chapter 8, the politicization of "victim status" makes the concept of minority status problematic.) In any case, the position here is that minorities are not always those with the fewest life chances, but they are always those who are discriminated *against*. (There are those, who in light of affirmative action policies, would name the White Anglo-Saxon Protestant male as America's newest minority.)

The idea that minority status results from unequal treatment that is unfair has enhanced the commonsense view that minorities are only the *victims* of discrimination of various forms, never the perpetrators. Thus, when racism emanates from minorities or is instituted on their behalf, observers and advocates give the concept a different name altogether.

The "third world mentality" is what social scientists call the race consciousness expressed by governments of developing nations toward the United States specifically and the Western world in general through international economic boycotts and cartels.

Some journalists have coined the term "ethnic diplomacy" as a polite description of congressional voting on foreign policy by legislators who are increasingly more concerned about the votes of their ethnic supporters at home than about the overall benefits of the United States; they are often more influenced by the sentiments of "ethnic lobbyists" than by the realities of international politics and economics. Thus, more than at any time since World War II, ethnicity is a major factor in U.S. foreign policy.

There are probably more advocates of racism today—granted, many unwittingly so—than at any other time in American history; there are certainly more victims of it. On the domestic front we are in the paroxysm of an abhorrent form of racism disguised as "affirmative action," which imposes racial and ethnic quotas on the employment practices of the industrial and business communities, colleges and universities.[5]

By another disguise racism becomes the forced busing of school children out of their community schools to allegedly achieve "quality education," but which a group of helpless and anguished parents in Brooklyn, New York, called "the destruction of our neighborhood schools under the guise of providing a more meaningful education through integration."

As the world's nations move ever closer to a state of international collectivism, there is a greater overt advocacy of ethno-racism among spokesmen of various subpopulations than at any other time in the twentieth century. As Glazer and Moynihan observe, in the past twenty years, "ethnic identity has become more salient, ethnic self-assertion stronger, ethnic conflict more marked." And as ethno-race consciousness and ethno-racism are becoming more a way of life, there is an increasing attempt by intellectuals, social scientists, and politicians to legitimize these attitudes and dogmas by attaching to them arbitrary definitions that defy logic and a moral superiority which in fact they do not have.[6]

When the 1968 Democratic National Convention directed the McGovern Commission to reform the rules for delegate selection, the commission created a set of "Guidelines," which amounted to a quota system. Later in a story about the commission, McGovern was quoted as saying: "The way we got the quota thing through was by not using the word 'quotas.' We couldn't have gotten quotas."

Like quotas, race today is a discredited idea. But it is, nonetheless, alive and well and the way to "get it through" the boundaries of rationality and moral values is by not using the word "racism" and substituting it with the more tolerated concept of "ethnocentrism" or the even greater dilution of ethno-race consciousness found in the term "ethnicity." Motivated by their lust for power, the intellectuals in the forefront of the movement to gain popular acceptance of the "new racism" go to great lengths to distinguish their own brand of racism from what most people think of as traditional forms of racism. Witness this attempt by author Robert L. Allen:

It certainly appears that ethnocentrism is generally distributed among human cultures, but ethnocentrism refers only to a socially shared feeling of in-group solidarity. It is not necessarily a racial phenomenon, and it certainly does not imply the development of institutional and ideological forms of oppression based on race. At worst, ethnocentrism is a form of inward-looking narrow-mindedness; whereas racism involves an inward-facing hierarchical ordering of human beings for purposes of racial oppression. The former may or may not be a universal facet of human nature, but the latter is definitely socially conditioned. The two should not be confused.[7]

Allen speaks from his premise that historically racism originates in white society and from his conclusion that blacks and other minorities are always the victims and never the cause of racism. According to Allen's view, racism is an inherent feature of the response of white society to minorities; ethnocentrism, on the other hand, is the response of minorities to the racist white majority; and of the two, ethnocentrism is the less harmful to human relations. But ethnocentrism, or ethnicity, is as much a feature of white response to minorities as it is of minority response. As Martin Kilson points out: "Neo-ethnicity among urban whites is in large part a response to the relative political success of an emergent black ethnicity. It is concentrated in marginal-income, working-class, lower middle-class, and even some middle-class city whites who retain some vestiges of ethnic lifestyles, values and perceptions."[8] In warning against the dangers of the deification of ethnicity in American political life, Professor Kilson observes that as white ethnicity includes an anti-Negro orientation, so does black ethnicity require "both anti-white activism and the denigration of white society and values . . . as effective tools in unifying blacks."[9]

Yet, Kilson does not seem to imply that he comprehends black ethnicity as being every bit a form of racism as white ethnicity is. Like Allen, he perceives a difference and does not want the two confused. He does not wonder if neo-ethnicity among whites could be a defensive posture in response to the political racism of blacks. In fact he does not admit to the existence of black racism but prefers to call it "black ethnocentric revitalization" or the "politicization of black ethnicity," which he characterizes as the translation of "the emergent power-mustering capacity of Negroes into public policies that will raise the standards of the Negro social system to levels comparable to those of white America." What he calls "the power-mustering dimension of ethnicity" when expressed by whites is called white racism (or political anti-Negro authoritarianism)—"an albatross, or worse, around the neck of American society." But when expressed by blacks and other non-WASP minorities, it is called ethnocentric revitalization (or ethnic legitimation)—"ethnic redress of differentials between subordinate and superordinate groups." Kilson does not deny Negro antagonism toward whites and he does not pretend that the only force of white neo-ethnicity is its anti-Negro sentiments. But he does manage to convey a justification for black ethnicity that is not granted to white ethnicity. "The new black ethnicity is reformist in thrust," he writes, "while the new white ethnicity is conservative."

Kilson's ethnocentric revitalization and Allen's definition of ethnocentrism as "a socially shared feeling of in-group solidarity" attach a kind of respectability to the doctrine of ethno-racial collectivism that it should not in fact have. Ethnocentrism is every bit as immoral as racism and, like racism, it has every potential for developing into ideological and institutional forms of oppression. Obviously aware of this, Kilson acknowledges the danger of both white and black ethnicity: "as an instrument of political mobilization ethnicity is curiously metapolitical—something more than politics. Herein lies the danger of neo-ethnicity in American political life—a danger still poorly appreciated by some liberal social scientists."[10]

The metapolitical nature of neo-ethnicity is seen in the ontological premises on which it is based. Its ethnocentric form views man as a socioculturally conditioned robot, while its racist form reduces man even further in degradation to a genetically determined hulk of protoplasm; both reject the evidence of man's rational capacity, his conceptual level of consciousness, and his self-determining action.

Traditionally, ethnocentrism and racism have acted as separate, if often overlapping, features of group relations and social change. But recently, the "inward-looking narrow mindedness" of ethnocentrism and racism's "inward-facing hierarchical ordering of human beings" (e.g., racial quotas, etc.) have coalesced to form the ritualistic and political expression of ethno-race consciousness that Kilson and others call ethnicity, but which I designate as *ethno-racism*.

Whether one calls it ethnic revitalization, ethnic awareness, the third-world mentality, ethnic diplomacy, affirmative action, ethnicity, or ethnic solidarity, ethno-racism remains what it is: *the transformation of ethno-race consciousness into political activism toward social advancement by instituting public policies and legislation in favor of an ethno-racial group at the expense of the rights of others.*

Ethno-racism in favor of minorities is most often referred to by its critics as "reverse racism". In his book, *The New Racism*, Lionel Lokos writes that reverse racism in American society has two prime targets: "the white teenager who wants to go to a good college, and the white wage earner trying to hold his own in a highly erratic economy."[11] But as Lokos goes on to show in his detailed accounts of reverse discrimination by Negroes, ethno-racism is not aimed at the white teenager and white wage earner per se. These are merely two of many groups of individuals (including Negroes) who are the victims that must be sacrificed as the New Racists move hellbent toward their altruistic goal of achieving a collectivist society. The white college applicant or any qualified high school graduate is but an obstacle in their effort to abolish academic competition and excellence in higher education. The wage earner is but a symbol of free-market productivity that the New Racists would replace with a welfare state greater than we have at present. The advocates of ethno-racism are concerned with actual human beings only in so far as they are the means to their altruist-collectivist ends. They want the unearned in status and the unearned in wealth, and their "in-group solidarity" is against the right of every individual to free ideas, free actions, and free association with his fellow man.

Glazer and Moynihan allude to these qualities of ethno-racism when they assert that ethnicity is a "new" social development:

We feel that to see only what is familiar in the ethnicity of our time is to miss the emergence of a new social category as significant for the understanding of the present-day world as that of social class itself. For in the welter of contemporary forms of group expression and group conflict there is both something new and something common: there has been a pronounced and sudden increase in tendencies by people in many countries and in many circumstances to insist on the significance of their group distinctiveness and identity and on new rights that derive from this group character.[12]

Elsewhere Glazer concludes that this "new" ethnicity—as expressed in "the creation of formal political entities with ethnic characteristics" and in social policies such as affirmative action ("positive public action on the basis of race and ethnicity to overcome a previous harmful public action on the basis of race and ethnicity")—threatens to overturn the American ideals of common humanity, equal justice, and the primacy of the individual.[13]

"We have a complex of education, culture, law, administration, and political institutions which has deflected us into a course in which we publicly establish ethnic and racial categories for differential treatment," writes Glazer, "and believe that by so doing we are establishing a just and good society. . . . But this has meant that we abandon the first principle of a liberal society, that the individual and the individual's interests and good and welfare are the test of a good society, for we now attach benefits and penalties to individuals simply on the basis of their race, color, and national origin. The implications of the new course are an increasing consciousness of the significance of group membership, an increasing divisiveness on the basis of race, color, and national origin, and a spreading resentment against the favored groups."[14]

Historian Daniel J. Boorstin also agonizes over the recent toleration and even admiration that is expressed for the power politics of "narrow self-seeking groups":

> When before has it been respectable for American politicians to declare themselves the candidates for their race, for Americans to accept uncritically a racial caucus in the Congress of the nation? Is a Black Caucus any more respectable than a White Caucus? In the past, with few exceptions, American politicians have been ashamed to call themselves the candidate of only one group of citizens. They have found it necessary at least to pretend to represent all their constituents equally.[15]

Civil rights leader Whitney Young wrote that to label "anti-white feelings" as reverse racism is "to equate the bitterness of the victim with the evil that oppresses him. Black 'reverse racism' is the response of angry people to their oppressors. It is based not on an existing caste system and the mythology that sustains it, but on very real grievances."[16]

Young did not condone the anti-white feelings of many Negroes but he asked that we understand its context and denied that such feelings can be labeled reverse racism. "Perhaps the most relevant analogy here is the position some Jews take toward Germany," he wrote. "They know that the people of Germany today cannot be held responsible for the atrocities committed by another generation captivated by Nazi ideology. But many Jews still refuse to include Germany on a vacation tour or to buy goods made in Germany. They recognize that their attitude is irrational, but the memory of the murder of 6 million Jews cannot leave them. No one calls this 'racism' or even 'reverse racism.' We realize that these are human feelings grounded in horrible experiences. So, too, anti-white feelings on the part of some black people should be seen not as a kind of racism but as a response to generations of overwhelming oppression. White racism is a cause; black racism is effect."[17]

While such actions by Jews is not racism in the sense that they are not political expressions against the people of Germany, such behavior does fall under the category of ethno-race consciousness as defined here. The irrationality of such behavior is found in the Jewish person's view of himself and his view of Germans as being trapped in the circumstances of a prior generation of Jews and Germans and the relationship of those in that generation to each other. The victimization of one generation of Jews by Germans ought not be the basis on which subsequent generations of Jews judge their German contemporaries. The same should be no less true of Negro and white race relations. The sins of previous generations of whites against Negroes should not be used as the justification for the violations by Negroes of the rights of the present generation of whites.

The whole point of this study is to demonstrate that black racism is not necessarily the effect of white racism as Young and others assert. Ethno-racism is not defined here by the racial or ethnic identification of its perpetrators, but by the attitudes, doctrines, and behavior that characterize it and the politicization and institutionalization needed to maintain and sustain it. Whether racism emanates from blacks or whites, it exists not necessarily as a cause or an effect but as a symptom of the lack of self-identity and self-esteem.

As stated at the outset of this study, racism is a two-edged sword that spares no one in its wake. The "old" oppressive racism of the white majority, which discriminates *against* individuals and groups of individuals on ethnic and racial grounds, has been outlawed. The "new" retributive racism, which discriminates *in favor* of individuals and groups of individuals on ethnic and racial grounds, is now Law of the Land. But neither could exist without having foundations in the ethno-race consciousness of a great many Americans in both the majority and minority groups.

Ethno-race consciousness is by definition a personal affliction, and it may harbor in the hearts of men who are otherwise the best intentioned. But however benign, ethno-race consciousness is still a cancer on the soul possessing every potential to perpetuate itself into the malignancy of public and institutional racism. We know how ravaging the disease is because the history of man is strewn with the wreckage of prostrate cultures and human devastation due to the institutionalization of ethno-race consciousness into the public policy of ethno-racism. When race consciousness eats into the very marrow of men's minds and becomes a seething hell that spills over into the socioeconomic and political policies of communities, states, and nations, then we can see its deadliness for what it is—only then it is too late to tame the maniacal passion of a collective that was once but a petty impulse of private prejudice.

Ethno-racism is so immoral and so reprehensible because its various forms require the denial of the basic conditions of human existence. It is not just the emotional abnegation of rationality but the *institutionalized* rejection of human rights and the prohibition or regulation and circumvention of their practical expression. *Slavery* is instituted on the premise that their biological and cultural heritage makes certain individuals unworthy of their own person. *Serfdom*, like slavery, is practiced on the basis that the bioethnic heritage of some men renders them undeserving of the product of their effort and the means to sustain their lives. *Expulsion, apartheid*, and *segregation* are instituted as denials of the right of individuals to freedom of mobility and association. *Discrimination* is practiced on the premise that conclusions reached about an ethno-racial group override the thoughts, actions, and character of the individuals belonging to that group. The ultimate among racist policies is the practice of *extermination* on the basis that their bio-ethnic heritage makes certain groups of individuals unworthy of life.

As a form of discrimination, *reverse racism* is instituted on the premise that their common bio-ethnic heritage makes one individual responsible for the ideas, actions, and character of another; that individuals of one generation must pay for the sins of their ancestors; that an entire country must bear the responsibility for the personal attitudes of private citizens; and that random individuals must pay for the injustices committed by the government.[18]

The underlying conclusion of all racist policies is that by virtue of their biological and/or cultural heritage certain men are *unworthy of living*—i.e., inherently *wrong* as persons—and that they are *unfit or incompetent to live*—i.e., inherently *wrong* in their conclusions and choices. Ethno-racism is the *explicit* negation of human life as the universal standard by which men choose their goals and actions; it is the invalidation of rationality as the universal condition of

29

man's survival. It is anti-life, anti-mind, anti-man—and profoundly resentful of a universe in which automatic knowledge and automatic evaluation of men's characters and actions are impossible. It is the systematic denial of the single most significant minority in any society and in any social circumstance: *the individual human being, a minority of one.*

1. Cynthia Ozick, "All the World Wants the Jews Dead," pp. 103–7.

2. Louis Wirth in Ralph Linton, ed., *The Science of Man in the World Crisis* (New York: Columbia University Press, 1945), p. 347.

3. J. Milton Yinger, *A Minority Group in American Society*, p. 22.

4. Ayn Rand, *America's Persecuted Minority: Big Business.*

5. For a critique of affirmative action and its denigrating impact on the quality of American higher education, see George Roche, *The Balancing Act.*
For an examination of how the administration of affirmative action programs has run counter to the intent of Congress in passing the 1964 Civil Rights Act, see Thomas Sowell, *Affirmative Action Reconsidered: Was It Necessary in Academia?*

6. See Ayn Rand, "Collectivized Ethics," in *The Virtue of Selfishness.*

7. Allen, *Reluctant Reformers,* p. 266.

8. Neo-ethnicity is defined by Kilson as "either the revitalization of weak ethnic collectivities (for example, Negro Americans) or the rehabilitation of dwindling ethnic cohesiveness (for example, Irish Catholics, Jews, Italians)." See Martin Kilson, "Blacks and Neo-Ethnicity in American Political Life," in Glazer and Moynihan, eds., *Ethnicity.*

9. Ibid., p. 244.

10. Ibid., p. 262. Kilson elaborates on this danger in "Political Change in the Negro Ghetto, 1900–1940s," in Nathan Huggins, Martin Kilson, and Daniel Fox, eds., *Key Issues in the Afro-American Experience* (New York: Harcourt Brace Jovanovich, 1971), p. 192. He objects to "attempts to deify ethnicity in American life," such as that by Michael Novak in *The Rise of the Unmeltable Ethnics* (New York: Macmillan, 1972).

11. Lionel Lokos, *The New Racism: Reverse Discrimination in America.*

12. Glazer and Moynihan, eds., *Ethnicity,* p. 3.

13. Nathan Glazer, *Affirmative Discrimination: Ethnic Inequality and Public Policy.*

14. Ibid., p. 220.

15. Daniel J. Boorstin, *Democracy and Its Discontents.* It should be noted that while Boorstin's point regarding a racial caucus in Congress is well taken, the Congressional Black Caucus is not alone in its narrow self-seeking. The ethnic exclusivity of the Black Caucus is matched by the special interests of other congressional organizations and clubs such as the Environmental Study Conference, the Congressional Rural Caucus, and the New England Congressional Caucus.

16. Whitney M. Young, Jr., *Beyond Racism: Building an Open Society,* p. 85.

17. Ibid., p. 86.

18. See Ayn Rand, "Moral Inflation—Part III."

Variations of Prejudice and Discrimination

Overcategorization is perhaps the commonest trick of the human mind. Given a thimbleful of facts we rush to make generalizations as large as a tub.—Gordon W. Allport, *The Nature of Prejudice.*

Entailed in the dilemma of ethno-race consciousness is the attitude of ethno-racial prejudice, which I define as *an emotional attitude of bias expressed by reaching conclusions about a person on the basis of his race or culture without considering the facts of his individual character and behavior.*

Emotional bias, writes Berry, runs the gamut of feelings from love to hate, from esteem to contempt, from devotion to indifference. But ethno-racial prejudice usually includes unfavorable, unfriendly attitudes toward others. It is a feeling of antipathy grounded in fear and resentment and fortified with stereotypes, compounded of fallacies and half-truths. As Allport points out in his definition of prejudice, it covers a wide range of attitudes, including hatred, aversion, dislike, enmity, and various other unfavorable feelings toward a group as a whole, or toward an individual because he is a member of that group.[1] The repulsiveness of ethno-racial prejudice lies not just in the *pre*judgment of men without facts but in the refusal to revise one's judgment *in face of evidence to the contrary.*

The prejudiced form of ethno-race consciousness is not something men can't help. It is not "just there," inherent in man's nature, but is an attitude toward others that is learned and consciously held. "You have to be taught," goes the song, "when you're seven or eight—to hate all the people your relatives hate." And as ethno-racial prejudice can be learned, so can it be rejected or unlearned.

When prejudice is given practical expression it is usually by means of discrimination, defined by Berry as "differential treatment accorded to individuals who are considered as belonging in a particular category or group,"[2] and more specifically defined by Hankins as the "unequal treatment of equals, either by the bestowal of favors or the imposition of burdens."[3]

Not everyone who is prejudiced practices discrimination. Many people, during these post–civil rights times, keep their racial prejudices to themselves or admit them to only a close network of associates who are sympathetic to their sentiments. Some individuals are without prejudice themselves but express no vocal opposition to the discriminatory practices of others. Some are unprejudiced and believe that they are justified in forcing their morality on others. There are those prejudiced persons who do not discriminate simply because it is illegal or impractical for their purposes. And then there are, of course, those individuals who are both prejudiced and active discriminators.

Robert K. Merton designated these four types of variations between the attitudes of prejudice and the overt behavior of discrimination as follows: (1) the unprejudiced nondiscriminator; (2) the unprejudiced discriminator; (3) the prejudiced non-discriminator; and (4) the prejudiced discriminator.[4]

The Unprejudiced Nondiscriminator

The unprejudiced nondiscriminators are neither prejudiced against members of other racial or ethnic groups nor do they practice discrimination. They believe implicitly in the American creed of justice, freedom, equality of opportunity, and dignity of the individual. While they are motivated to fight against forms of discrimination that mock these ideals and values, they succumb easily to the illusion that the consensus which prevails among themselves is taking hold in the larger community; they confuse discussion and the psychological support they give to each other with action; and since their own "spiritual house" is in order, they do not themselves feel any guilt for the plight of minorities, and accordingly shrink from any collective effort to set things right.

The above characterization is not altogether an accurate or up-to-date reading of the unprejudiced nondiscriminators Merton calls "all-weather liberals." Their self-righteousness and their belief that all will be well in the larger community as it is in their own "spiritual house" is typical of the liberal ethos of an earlier time, perhaps four or five decades ago. However, the lack of guilt and refusal to use collective means to set things right is characteristic not of modern liberalism but more the attitude of eighteenth-century liberals and many present-day conservatives. Modern Fair Deal and New Deal liberals are motivated by ancestral guilt such as that expressed in the lament of a liberal journalist on the occasion of the death of baseball great Jackie Robinson: "As a nation, we are deeply in his debt," wrote the journalist. "He helped us to fulfill our obligation to our ideals; he forced us to look in the mirror and be ashamed of what we saw."

Being ashamed of what they see and feeling that the society at large owes a great debt to American Negroes, the modern unprejudiced nondiscriminating liberals see collective effort as the only means of finding a solution to racial disharmony. The individual's self-interest must be sacrificed to the "public good," they say, and they will determine in their councils and academic workshops what constitutes the public and what is the good. They will do what they think is good for everybody. And when these reformers find that people do not want to be done good to, they inevitably invoke political coercion to put the nation's ethical house in order—solve the problems of racial discrimination by regulating and administering the individuality of man out of existence.

We are all brothers under the skin, these liberals declare, and in order to realize this false notion in practical reality, they would level all to the zero-sum of egalitarianism. For it is not just racial discrimination and prejudice they wish to eliminate from the ideas and actions of men; in the final analysis, they wish to control man's very *faculty* of discrimination—*his reason*—to declare it impotent and create a consensus against the legitimacy of its autonomy.

In the realm of ethno-racial relations, the unprejudiced nondiscriminators adhere to a "liberal expectancy" summarized by Glazer and Moynihan as "the expectation that the kinds of features that divide one group from one another would inevitably lose their weight and sharpness in modern and modernizing societies, that there would be increasing emphasis on achievement rather than ascription, that common systems of education and communication would level differences, that nationally uniform economic and political systems would have the same effect. Under these circumstances the 'primordial' (or in any case antecedent) differences between groups would be expected to become of lesser significance."[5]

This may appear to be a noble expectation until one realizes that it cannot be realized without the imposition of a way of life that some in these societies may not desire. Not even on the face of it does this notion reach toward a rational view of human relations, particularly when one considers that outweighing any differences between groups and antecedent to these differences are the differences between *individuals*. And the "liberal expectancy" is even more suspect when we consider the authors' conclusions that it "flows into the 'radical expectancy'—that class circumstances would become the main line of division between people, erasing the earlier lines of tribe, language, religion, national origin, and that thereafter these *class* divisions would themselves, after revolution, disappear."[6] Thus, the framework of the liberal expectancy is questionable because it views differentiation by achievement as only a necessary element of modernization that replaces differentiation by ascription, and which will itself be eliminated by the de-differentiation of egalitarianism. What modern liberalism desires, ultimately, is the triumph of collectivism over individuation.

As noted, not all unprejudiced nondiscriminators are liberals. There are those conservatives and libertarians who variously advocate an expectancy that I shall call the "individualist expectancy"—the expectation that individual character, ethical standards, and achievements *would not* necessarily eliminate cultural ascription and ethnic attachments or erase class circumstances as the lines of divisions between people; that such divisions between groups would be derived from the *self-interest* of the individuals of which they are composed; that common *interests* would make ethnic, racial, and cultural-based forms of social identification and class-based forms insignificant in social interaction; that individual character, personality, and ability would make these categories insignificant in one's judgment of others as beneficial or inimical to the achievement of his goals and the fulfillment of his interests; that the economic and political system in which such individual-based forms of identification and social interaction can best take place is capitalism, which would provide for the maximum voluntary human association, material and intellectual productivity, and laissez faire (uncoerced, unregulated, unadministered) exchange of ideas, services, and products.

Not all libertarians and conservatives endorse the "individualist expectancy" to the same extent or with the same degree of consistency. While they both advocate capitalism as the politico-economic system that can best eliminate racial disharmony, they are at irreconcilable odds over the moral foundations of capitalism. The traditionalist conservatives are committed to a defense of capitalism in terms of Judeo-Christian ethics, with emphasis on what M. Stanton Evans identifies as "the higher law above the sway of individual impulse, a stressed awareness of human reality, and the consequent need for authority, order and virtue."[7] One can see the contradiction of attempting to justify capitalism on the basis of faith, tradition, and order in a statement by Senator Barry Goldwater in announcing his plan to vote against the 1964 Civil Rights Bill: "I am unalterably opposed to discrimination of any sort, and I believe that though the problem is fundamentally one of the heart, some law can help—but not law . . . [with] provisions which fly in the face of the Constitution and which require for their effective execution the creation of a police state."

The difference between the traditionalist conservative and the libertarian is that while a conservative like Goldwater would concede to the state the power to enact *some* law to preserve order and decency, the libertarian position, which justifies capitalism on the basis of man's reason and his self-interest, would concede to the state *no* power in resolving problems of human relations that are fundamentally of the mind *and* heart—i.e., issues of ethical conduct that do not involve force, fraud, or harm to anyone.

The conservative moral defense of the capitalist system is determined from its view of man, and thus conservatives who see man as the Original Sinner are quite willing to legislate him back to the Judeo-Christian path of righteousness. Libertarians, on the other hand, view "human reality" in terms of man's free will and see him quite capable of discovering for himself what is the right path to take in human affairs. Believing that group differences arise out of individual differences, conservatives would disagree with the liberal expectancy that calls for the elimination of group differences in order to achieve unprejudiced nondiscriminating justice in modern societies. But they do agree with liberals that some law must be employed to stabilize group conflict; they differ only in *which* laws should be invoked.

Some libertarians suffer their own contradictions in applying the "individualist expectancy" to the realm of race relations. All libertarians—and there are as many different libertarian approaches as there are conservative—would agree with Barry Goldwater, who said in a 1964 campaign speech, "Our aim is neither to establish a segregated society nor to establish an integrated society as such. It is to preserve a free society. As far as the government is concerned, it must ensure freedom of association, but it cannot and should not ensure association itself." But not all would agree on what form that association should take. Libertarian anarchist Jerome Tuccille, in advocating voluntary association, believed that "whenever separatism is taken to mean absolute freedom of association (voluntary integration for those who want it, voluntary separatism for others like Roy Innis [National Director of the Congress of Racial Equality]), it should be supported by libertarians as a policy consistent with their own ideas."[8] And while Tuccille declared that "the right to separate voluntarily is equally as valid as the right to integrate voluntarily," he did not question whether the ethics of "racial separatism" as advocated by Roy Innis and others is in fact consistent with the principles of capitalism. Like conservatives, unprejudiced nondiscriminating libertarians are often guilty of evading the morality of the political action they support and defend. Tuccille urged libertarians to "actively support" black leaders such as Dr. Thomas W. Matthew, founder of the "black capitalist" National Economic Growth and Reconstruction Organization (NEGRO)— a self-help program which, though allegedly not financed by the federal government as is the Office of Minority Business Enterprise (OMBE), could not have fared as well as it did without the federal contracts awarded to the NEGRO factories for the manufacture of goods.[9]

The problem with many unprejudiced nondiscriminators—from the liberals who engage in what one journalist calls "masochistic fawning toward Negroes" to even the detached limited-government libertarians who are the most consistent advocates of the "individualist expectancy"—is that they are often tempted to "prove" their unprejudiced nondiscriminating position to skeptics who are convinced that no one, least of all a white person, is capable of resisting the pervasive race consciousness in our society. And it is in the "proving" of *themselves*—of their psychointellectual attitudes—rather than in providing the moral validation of their convictions that unprejudiced nondiscriminators undercut their position. When they are confronted with the choice of presenting arguments against prejudice and discrimination in the face of either moral condemnation or winning the approval of those who sit in judgment of them, too often they abandon the intellectual defense and opt for psychological approval.

The Unprejudiced Discriminator

The unprejudiced discriminators are free themselves of ethno-racial prejudice but keep their silence when bigots speak out. They will not condemn acts of discrimination lest they somehow lose status thereby; they will make concessions to the intolerant, and will acquiesce in discriminatory practices for fear that to do otherwise would "hurt business" or cause them to lose their jobs or harm their reputations. Their personal unprejudiced attitudes do not square with their public tolerance of discrimination, and herein lies their shame.

Robert K. Merton wrote about the variations between prejudice and discrimination in 1949 when white bigotry was more evident than black bigotry, and thus he saw the unprejudiced discriminators as persons who failed to condemn discrimination *against* Negroes and other minorities. To update Merton's description of the unprejudiced discriminators, I include those persons who fail to condemn discrimination *in favor of* Negroes and other minorities— i.e., reverse discriminators.

One's support of the American system of freedom, justice, private property, and individual rights necessarily places him in opposition to many programs and policies that allegedly favor the advancement of Negroes and other minorities. White liberals and minorities often denounce the politics of individual freedom as "racist" if advocated by whites (particularly if by southern whites), and "Uncle Tom" if advocated by Negroes. Senator J. William Fulbright was denounced by many Negroes for his consistent opposition to many civil rights issues that were indeed detrimental to the rights of all Americans. When Senator Goldwater voted against the 1964 Civil Rights Bill, in protest of the public accommodations title on the basis that it was an infringement of the property rights of all individuals, he was proclaimed a racist and represented in the press as insensitive to the aspirations of Negroes. Many Negroes and civil rights advocates condemned the appointment of historian Daniel J. Boorstin as Librarian of Congress on the grounds that as head of the Smithsonian Institution, he had opposed employment quotas.

Fearing similar indictments and repudiation, many Americans of all races are paralyzed by their moral cowardice as the orchestrated stripping away of individual liberty continues via housing programs, education programs, manpower efforts, and expansionary economic policies—all supposedly aimed toward the racial advancement of Negroes and the social progress of minorities. It is a sad commentary on the state of the American culture when, in the face of assaults on American ideals paraded as coerced reform in the name of justice and equality, politicians, intellectuals, and ordinary citizens who claim those ideals as their legacy stand mute and disarmed by their fear of being accused of bigotry.

There are many unprejudiced discriminators who are simply afraid to challenge discrimination against or in favor of ethno-racial groups. (How many Germans closed their eyes to the systematic extermination of their Jewish neighbors? How many Jews lend their voices to the denouncement of militant Zionism? How many unprejudiced Arabs are afraid to speak out against Arab terrorism? How many thousands of Negroes were silent when their fellows took to the streets looting and destroying property in the name of social justice? How long has the Catholic church acquiesced to southern intolerance by condoning segregated parishes and schools? How many black parents are afraid to join white parents in their opposition to forced busing of school children? How many university presidents have failed to challenge admissions quotas for fear of jeopardizing their institutions' chances of receiving federal financing?)

But many unprejudiced discriminators were former unprejudiced nondiscriminators of two categories: (1) those who believe that the best way to achieve their egalitarian ideal of equal conditions among men is by discriminating in favor of ethno-racial minorities; and (2) those who are driven to "prove" their unprejudiced attitudes by condoning discrimination in favor of their accusers. The former would sacrifice human rights and liberty to power and the tyranny of collectivism. The latter would sacrifice personal integrity to social approval. Both wish to fake reality—to force into existence conditions of human relations that are otherwise not forthcoming. One cannot establish equal conditions among men without violating each man's expression of the rights that are entailed in his nature as man. And one cannot sacrifice the lives of one group of individuals as proof of his sincerity toward another group without destroying his own self-esteem in the process.

Too many Americans have adopted the ways of the unprejudiced discriminators in order to save their faces or ease their consciences. The result is that we have become a nation caught in the vise of welfare statism, ruled by groups claiming their greater share of the "pie" they did not create, while envious and racist world leaders demand that the United States prove its unbiased intentions toward their countries by sacrificing the very productivity and defense of its citizens.

The Prejudiced Nondiscriminator

The prejudiced nondiscriminators are timid bigots who do not accept the American creed, but conform to it and give lip service when the slightest pressure is applied. Such a person is the employer who dislikes certain minorities but hires them rather than run afoul of some "Equal Employment" law. A great number of ordinary people fall into this category. They will sometimes admit, "Frankly, I don't like any of them," but will concede to the fact that "they should have a chance like everyone else." When such a person complies with antidiscrimination and other civil rights legislation, he does not take such action because he genuinely believes in the principles these laws allegedly uphold but merely because he believes one should obey the law. If left on his own, he would not give minorities "a chance like everyone else." But being forced to do so, he rationalizes his constrained position by giving lip service to the laws that hold him in check.

It should be pointed out that the prejudiced nondiscriminator is not necessarily *against* discrimination. He is nondiscriminating in practice because either (1) he does not have to deal with the individuals or groups toward whom he is prejudiced; (2) he is without the means to carry out discriminatory acts; or, (3) he is prohibited either by private ethics (religious or secular), professional standards, or public law from allowing his prejudice to be expressed in discriminatory behavior.

39

Of course the prejudiced nondiscriminator may not discriminate because he himself is the object of discrimination. But as we are witnessing in the case of reverse discrimination, even those who are traditionally discriminated against may resort to retributive discrimination if there is the opportunity and the kind of social tolerance, if not sanction, of such behavior as there is at present. And being the object of discrimination does not exempt him from having prejudiced attitudes toward members of the group discriminating against him.

Not all prejudiced nondiscriminators are entirely hostile to the so-called American creed as Robert K. Merton suggested. Many of these individuals actively deplore the discriminatory behavior of others and believe themselves to be quite free of prejudice until they are confronted with a personal issue such as giving consent to their son or daughter's marriage to someone of another racial or ethnic background. Since the days of the Abolitionist movement, it has not been unusual to find that the liberal approach of social and political movements advocating reforms that would benefit ethno-racial groups has been quite apart from the race consciousness of those who make up these movements.[10] Like many early abolitionists, some prejudiced nondiscriminating liberals believe that, as human beings, Negroes should be free but still believe them to be racially and culturally unequal to whites. Though quite committed to achieving social change that would benefit Negroes, they are nevertheless paternalistic in their attitudes and thereby betray their deep-seated notion that their racial inferiority renders Negroes incapable of achieving those ends on their own.

Eliminating racist policies in institutions does not in itself remove the curse of race consciousness from individuals. And race consciousness need not be characterized by the more virulent forms of racial bias. Some of the most ardent supporters of civil rights legislation are politicians who approach Negroes as though their political outlook were shaped primarily and overwhelmingly by race; as though the mere fact of their being black overrides differences in ideology, economic background, and the political tradition in which each individual was nurtured.

A most poignant example of the pervasiveness of race consciousness in our society is in the case of the white psychotherapist who feels incompetent to treat a Negro client because he believes the Negro's psychological conflict (particularly as it is a result of the client's response to social factors) is somehow of a different ontological nature than that of his white clients. He is a nondiscriminator who is committed to the idea that all men have a right to equal freedom and justice and actively supports civil rights for ethno-racial groups. Yet in his role as psychotherapist his ability to assist a Negro client is overwhelmed by the prejudicial belief (compounded by psychosocial determinism and psychocultural relativism) that being a Caucasian precludes him from understanding what it is like to be a Negro and that therefore he cannot deal with the inner state of a Negro.

Without any factual evidence or contrary to factual evidence, he concludes that the content of a Negro's consciousness is to be analyzed and understood not on the basis of his identity as man *qua human being*, but as man *qua racial being*; that the malfunctioning of his mental state is not a problem of human cognition and evaluation but one of "social adaptability."[11] His race consciousness is evidenced not by any sense of enmity toward his Negro client *because* he is a Negro, but by his approach to the individual's *peculiar* mental state as though it were but a reflection of the collective inner state of a race of people. He sees in the person before him not an individual with problems common to most men that can be scientifically identified and objectively treated, but a symbol of an entire race of people, their history, and their present sociocultural circumstances as he understands them. And of course, any attempt to treat the client on these premises is most likely to cause all kinds of complications.

A psychological disorder of otherwise healthy persons is a *thinking* disorder. It is not an issue of one's hereditary lineage or the dynamics of his ethno-racial subculture, but an issue of his psychoepistemology—i.e., how he thinks, how he apprehends reality, what emotional and cognitive responses he makes to the circumstances of his daily life.

There is no denying that psychological conflicts are contextual and that the treatment of them should take this into consideration. But that context is *individual*, not racial or ethnic. The resolution of a psychological disorder that is related to racial issues does not remove those issues from existence; it can only resolve the disorder in how the person apprehends and evaluates such issues. The psychotherapist who cannot see past an individual's racial or ethnic category to his self-identity could have a more debilitating effect on

41

the client's unstable self-esteem than any amount of prejudice and discrimination he may encounter elsewhere.

It should be noted that there are Negroes who would welcome the help of a white psychotherapist in their fight for civil rights, but would not seek his professional services because they, too, believe their racial differences preclude the achievement of successful therapy. This example of the prejudiced psychotherapist is not meant as an indictment against the profession. Rather, it is presented to demonstrate that one of the milder forms of prejudice in nondiscriminating individuals can be nevertheless as destructive in its subtlety as the more overt variations of prejudice and discrimination.

The Prejudiced Discriminator

The prejudiced discriminators are the bigots, pure and unashamed. For them there is no conflict between attitudes and behavior. They do not believe in the American creed, nor do they hesitate to give expression to their prejudice both in speech and in action. They practice discrimination believing that it is not only proper that they do so, but is, in fact, their duty. A statement by Theodore Roosevelt is a good example of the sentiments expressed by the prejudiced discriminator: "I don't go so far as to think that the only good Indians are dead Indians, but I believe nine out of every ten are, and I shouldn't like to inquire too closely into the case of the tenth. The most vicious cowboy has more moral principle than the average Indian."[12]

As this burst of hatred from Roosevelt indicates, the prejudiced discriminator believes that white supremacy entails a moral superiority as well as biological and cultural superiority. He believes that since ethno-racial minorities are less than whites in human attributes, they should therefore be less free and enjoy an inferior economic and sociopolitical status in society; that their political freedom should be circumscribed by the perception of those who believe they are incapable of fully actualizing human liberty.

The prejudiced discriminator is usually thought of as a member of the Ku Klux Klan, a vigilante in a lynch mob, or a Jim Crow politician. But prejudiced discriminators are not found only among whites. Negro advocates of militant separatism, Black Power, and political terrorism are every bit as racist and dangerous as the hooded Klansman and the political segregationist. The rule of law and an increasing public intolerance of their lawlessness have rendered them powerless and forced the diehards to the fringes of society, leaving the more pragmatic among them to take the position of the law-abiding prejudiced nondiscriminator.

Merton's description of the prejudiced discriminator is a narrow one, depicting a person who is hostile toward the American creed, psychologically committed to his bias, and actively engages in discrimination. The expanded view presented here, however, includes people like Theodore Roosevelt whose attitudes and behavior often contradict each other, especially with respect to their belief in the American creed. Unlike the prejudiced non-discriminators who are constrained from action by the law, these individuals, whom I shall call *passive* prejudiced discriminators (as opposed to the violent type mentioned above), are constrained by their moral convictions. Theodore Roosevelt believed all Indians were immoral and that the world would be a better place without them; and like most political leaders from the colonial years until the middle of the twentieth century, he did not actively oppose discrimination against minorities. But he believed in the American creed, and such is the contradiction of most passive prejudiced discriminators.

Most Americans do not express their prejudice in violent acts against the person and property of those they wrongly judge. And most people haven't the political or economic means nor do they encounter the circumstances in which to engage in active discrimination themselves. More often than not the average prejudiced discriminator quietly hoards his prejudice unless provoked and either passively allows for the discrimination of others or lends his nonviolent support, as in the case of voting for discriminatory legislation.

Prejudice taints the hearts of some of the most upright people among us; many of the most stalwart defenders of the American creed were slaveholders; and even today men and women who fancy themselves guardians of the democratic ideal lend their support to measures of government-enforced discrimination. Arguing from a general metaphysical principle, Aristotle, the father of Logic, maintained that "some men are by nature free, and others slaves, and that for these latter slavery is both expedient and right." But, as Jones notes, Aristotle could not reconcile this view of men as means and ends of each other with his moral principles and with his view that some natural slaves are actual masters and some natural masters are actual slaves.[13]

The complexity of prejudice and its expression via discrimination may be seen in the case of Thomas Jefferson, great apostle of human liberty,[14] author of the Declaration of Independence, and a Founding Father of the American nation. Being intellectually committed to the principles of human liberty and dignity, Jefferson's advocacy of the emancipation of slaves was lifelong. Yet he owned slaves, and though he manumitted some, allowed them to run away, and emancipated others in his will, these were only a fraction of the number he owned. Being a slaveholder necessarily makes Jefferson a discriminator, as slavery is one of the more severe forms of discrimination, regardless of whether the slaveholder is a "good master" as Jefferson reportedly was.

Jefferson knew slavery could not last in the American society and, as his writings indicate, he feared that if emancipation did not come "by the generous energy of our minds," it would surely come as the result of violence and bloodshed. But in the manner of the unprejudiced discriminator, his commitment to emancipation stopped short of the point at which open opposition to slavery might cost him his political prestige. Turning down an invitation to become a member of the Society for the Abolition of the Slave Trade, he wrote to one of the members: "You know that nobody wishes more ardently to see an abolition not only of the trade, but of the conditions of slavery and certainly nobody will be more willing to encounter every sacrifice for that object. But I am here as a public servant, and those whom I serve having never yet been able to give their voice against this practice, it is decent for me to avoid too public a demonstration of my wishes to see it abolished."[15]

Jefferson's prejudice was inconsistent, but present nevertheless. In his "Notes on Virginia," he writes of his suspicion that blacks are an inferior race:

> Comparing them by their faculties of memory, reason, and imagination, it appears to me that in memory they are equal to the whites; in reason much inferior; as I think one can scarcely be found capable of tracing and comprehending the investigations of Euclid. . . . The opinion, that they are inferior in the faculties of reason and imagination, must be hazarded with great diffidence. To justify a general conclusion, requires

many observations. . . . I advance it, therefore, as a suspicion only, that the blacks, whether originally a distinct race, or made distinct by time and circumstances, are inferior to whites in the endowments of both body and mind.[16]

Yet years later he wrote the following to Benjamin Banneker, the Negro mathematician, farmer, astronomer, and surveyor whom he recommended to assist with laying out the boundaries of the District of Columbia: "Nobody wished more than I do to see such proofs as you exhibit, that nature has given to our black brethren, talents equal to those of other colours of man, and that the appearance of a want of them is owing merely to the degraded condition of their existence both in Africa and America. I can add with truth that nobody wished more ardently to see a good system commenced for raising the condition both of their body and mind to what it ought to be."[17]

In an 1809 letter to Henri Grégoire, who had sent him a volume entitled "Literature of Negroes," Jefferson wrote:

> Be assured that no person living wishes more sincerely than I do, to see a complete refutation of the doubts I have myself entertained and expressed on the grade of understanding allotted to them [Negroes] by nature, and to find that in this respect they are on a par with ourselves. My doubts were the result of personal observation on the limited sphere of my own State, where the opportunities for the development of their genius were not favorable, and those of exercising it still less so. I expressed them therefore with great hesitation; but whatever be their degree of talent it is no measure of their rights. . . . Accept my thanks for the many instances you have enabled me to observe of respectable intelligence in that race of men, which cannot fail to have effect in hastening the day of their relief.[18]

The views of Aristotle and Jefferson are pointed to not to dilute the moral contradictions implicit in policies of racial prejudice and discrimination. There should be no tolerance in our thinking for the notion that if it was so for these two giants of human civilization it cannot be all bad. The point of these examples is that discrimination *is* all bad and that some of the most intelligent and benevolent men can be sabotaged by notions that are unjust and irrational.

This discussion has by no means exhausted the variety of attitudes and behavior expressed along the spectrum of prejudice and discrimination. However, enough has been mentioned to warrant a summary of the major points raised.

Among the *unprejudiced non-discriminators* we find four philosophical types:

1. There are the guilty liberal reformers and the self-righteous egalitarian liberals who would invoke political coercion to eliminate prejudice and discrimination and eliminate the differences between groups and individuals by expanding the power of the state to create a society of metaphysical equality.

2. The traditionalist conservatives believe that racial harmony can best be achieved in a capitalist society but would concede to the state limited power to enact laws to preserve order and moral conduct. Conservatives agree with liberals that some law is necessary to prescribe personal conduct and stabilize group conflict; they differ only in what laws should be invoked and which realms of personal conduct should be proscribed.

3. The individualists are truly unprejudiced and non-discriminating. While they respect the differences between groups, they view these differences as insignificant when judging the character and achievements of men. Unlike egalitarian liberals, they do not believe that the solution to group conflict is the elimination of group differences. Rather, they believe that the philosophical validation of individual differences must be the basis from which group differences are to be understood and that societal respect for individual differences will lessen the occurrence of group conflict. Thus, they do not see group differences as an inherent threat to social order and equal justice and, consequently, have no desire to see them eliminated by force. But neither would they support any move by groups to achieve political and economic gains on the basis of their ascriptive differences. They would oppose the proposed Equal Rights Amendment to the Constitution, for example, on the grounds that it cannot be enforced to protect the rights of women as a group without violating the rights of individuals. However, such opposition by individualists does not place them in league with conservatives who also oppose the ERA, but who do so not on principle but for pragmatic reasons, such as excluding women from the military draft.

46

4. Libertarians are similar to individualists in that they would leave men entirely free to choose their nonviolent solutions to group conflict. Being vigorous advocates of voluntarism in all spheres of human affairs, they stand with the individualists in opposition to governmental regulation of moral conduct. However, libertarians are not as consistent as individualists in applying the moral standards they share to political action. Some condone voluntary solutions such as economic and/or territorial separatism without specifying under what conditions such solutions are compatible with the capitalism they profess.

The *unprejudiced discriminator* traditionally refers to the individual in a segregated society who discriminates *against* ethnoracial minorities in order to conform to social pressures. But, with the recent intensification of reserve discrimination, the concept may also include the individual who discriminates *in favor of* minorities to prove to them his unprejudiced attitudes and sentiments of goodwill.

In most cases unprejudiced nondiscriminators of all political persuasions "enjoy talking to themselves," as Merton observed, and engage in "mutual exhortation" about group conflict in the larger community, but, when they do act, the liberal egalitarian becomes an unprejudiced discriminator who advocates preferential treatment to ethno-racial minorites in order to eliminate what they perceive as the effects of past injustices. Desiring to prove their unprejudiced sentiments, other liberals, conservatives, and libertarians as well are driven to the unprejudiced-discriminator position, condoning discriminatory policies and programs of favoritism toward ethno-racial groups. While they do not approve of the egalitarian ideal, these individuals are much more concerned with avoiding accusations of bigotry than in defending individual opportunity against imposed equality.

Being a nondiscriminator does not necessarily mean one is *against* discrimination. More correctly, it means also that one *does not practice* discrimination. The unprejudiced nondiscriminator does not engage in discrimination against others first because he lacks the prejudiced attitudes that feed the desire for a segregated society. The *prejudiced nondiscriminator*, on the other hand, *would* act out his prejudice in discriminatory behavior but is constrained by his compliance with ethical standards, the law, or social convention. While much of the civil rights legislation has been aimed at correcting institutional ethno-racial discrimination, a great deal of it has been aimed at changing the private attitudes of individuals. But while it has ended much discrimination, prejudice still persists. Like the traditional unprejudiced discriminator, then, the public behavior of the prejudiced nondiscriminator contradicts his private attitudes. He obeys laws that oppose his conscience. The unprejudiced discriminator discriminates against people he believes are entitled to equal freedom and justice. The prejudiced nondiscriminator, on the other hand, advocates equal freedom and justice for people he believes are inferior human beings.

At one end of the prejudice/discrimination spectrum stands the unprejudiced nondiscriminator who advocates equal freedom and justice for all men. At the opposite end of the spectrum stands the *prejudiced discriminator* who discriminates against men he believes are inferior human beings and therefore *not entitled* to equal freedom and justice. Not all prejudiced discriminators are hooded ogres brandishing flaming crosses and bent on cleansing white society of ethno-racial contamination; neither are they rock-tossing children of warring Irish neighbors, or black militant firebrands, or officers of the Arab Boycott Office. Most prejudiced discriminators are nonviolent discriminators and among these many rarely have the opportunity or means to transform their prejudice into action. Nevertheless, they condone the discrimination of others.

The picture of the prejudiced discriminator that we are most comfortable with is that of the irrational dogmatist or the white-supremacist slaveholder and his spiritual descendants. But we cannot possibly understand the complexities of prejudice and discrimination until we are prepared to examine how it was that a man like Aristotle, the father of Logic, could believe in slavery and that his intellectual heir, Thomas Jefferson, the apostle of Liberty, could be a slaveholder and suspect that Negroes were inferior.

It is commonly assumed that unprejudiced nondiscriminators consist primarily of the political left and prejudiced discriminators are on the political right. But, as we have indicated by the differing philosophies of the unprejudiced nondiscriminators and the contradictions of men like Thomas Jefferson, there are various reasons why an individual's political action with regard to race relations may not reflect his ethical convictions.

The Discriminator and the Discriminated Against

The previous discussion has shown that, as an expression of ethno-racial prejudice, discrimination may be directed *against* individuals in an ethno-racial group by denying them the fullest expression of their rights; or it may be directed *in their favor* by according them preferential treatment. However, this is not to say that the ethno-race-conscious individual is that way one hundred percent of the time or on every issue and circumstance confronting him. Other social identifications to which he is attached—e.g., national, religious, socioeconomic class, or sex—may act as the context from which he judges himself and others. As sociologist Daniel Bell points out, "There are few, if any, identifications of a broad social character that are exclusive as a mode of emotional attachment. There is such a multiplicity of interests and identities that inevitably they cross-cut each other in extraordinary fashions."[19]

Ethno-racial prejudice is but one of the many attitudes expressed along the ethno-race-conscious spectrum and, as we have seen, that prejudice is characterized by its own variety of emotions and rationalizations. And again, it must be emphasized that ethno-racial prejudice is a *learned* attitude, not inherent in man's nature; it may be generalized to the point of saturation in a person's outlook, or it may be situational in response to certain people and particular experiences of contact with others.

A person may act as an unprejudiced discriminator in one situation and quite differently as an unprejudiced nondiscriminator in another. Negroes and whites may experience no ill-feelings toward each other in a work situation but would most vigorously oppose the marriage of their children to each other. A white laborer might generally have no serious attitudes toward Puerto Ricans and respond to them in neither one way nor the other. He simply does not think about them. Then one day he learns that he is losing his seniority and will be laid off while a recently hired Puerto Rican is allowed to stay. This could set off feelings of antipathy toward the trainee that caroms into a sustained hatred for all Puerto Ricans, whom he now regards as "people who are after my job."

Ethno-racial prejudice may be short-lived or lasting. There are Negroes who will always hate or suspect whites. And there are whites who have modified their anti-Negro position to accommodate the prescriptions of political and economic liberalism. The former governor of Alabama, George Wallace, shifted from his prejudiced-discriminating position to assume at least a non-discriminating outlook in order to receive any support at all for his political ambitions.

Until the death of Elijah Muhammad, the Nation of Islam, commonly known as the Black Muslims, was so anti-white that it forbade members to have close relationships with whites, whom they called "blue-eyed devils." But in 1975, following the death of his father, Wallace Muhammad, the new leader, declared the Universities of Islam, which are private elementary and secondary schools, open to all children and invited whites to join the Nation of Islam. Thus, the public policy of the group has shifted from that of the radical prejudiced discriminator to the moderate prejudiced nondiscriminator.

The dimensions of ethno-racial prejudice are many. Berry refers to a study by B. M. Kramer, who pointed out that not only are there discrepancies between how people *feel* toward ethnic groups and how they *act*, but people differ also as to what they *think* about other groups, how they *talk* about them, the extent to which they are averse to *contact* with them, and the *intensity* of their hostility toward them.[20]

Berry goes on to make the following observation: "Nor does one hold a single attitude toward Negroes, Jews, and foreigners, but varies his opinion with respect to their social, political, and economic aspirations. The same individual, too, will hold different degrees of prejudice toward the various minority groups, being bitterly hostile, say, toward Negroes, moderately hostile toward Greeks, but having no animosity whatever toward French Canadians."[21]

Still another complex dimension of prejudice is that antipathy or "social distance" felt toward ethno-racial minorities often varies with the occupational or social status of individuals within those groups. Antipathy is felt not just toward, say, Negroes "in general," but toward Negro doctors, teachers, bookkeepers, ditchdiggers, etc. Berry reports on a study by Frank R. Westie who found that the prejudices of whites varied significantly depending upon the Negro's occupation. "The higher the occupational status of the Negro, the less distance expressed toward him." According to Berry, Westie also found whites most rigid in their antipathy toward Negroes when it came to personal relations and residential proximity, and least rigid with respect to the Negroes' achieving positions of prestige and power in the community. Westie found still another dimension: "The higher the socioeconomic status of the responding white, the greater the alteration of response with variations in the occupational status of the Negro."[22]

Ethno-racial prejudice and discrimination are by no means attitudes and acts of race consciousness held only by the majority for the minorities. The affliction of prejudice is often shared by the discriminated against as well as the discriminator. Those who hate are hated in return. (The Negro character George Jefferson in the television comedy series "The Jeffersons" is every bit as prejudiced and disgusting as the white Archie Bunker of "All In The Family.") Both Negroes and native-born whites share prejudices toward other ethnic minorities. Jews are prejudiced toward Gentiles and some Jews are even anti-Semitic. The antipathy of whites and Indians for each other is vividly portrayed in motion pictures and television. The prejudice of the Boston Brahmin toward the Boston Irish, and vice versa, is well known. Policies instituted to repress and/or annihilate are often responded to, in time, with policies of revenge designed to exact unjustified retribution, such as those found in some aspects of civil rights activism, international Zionism, and the "third world" movement, to name a few.

Why the antipathy? Why the discrimination? There are as many theories explaining prejudice as there are variations in its attitudes and expressions.[23] At this point in the presentation, however, I will mention only the conclusion made by many that they are either superior or inferior to others. The discriminator expresses antipathy toward others because he judges them to be bioculturally inferior (or superior). And the discriminated feels inferior (or superior) because he is discriminated against (or in favor of) because of biocultural heritage. For instance, some blacks hate whites precisely because they believe whites are culturally superior to them; and some whites hate blacks because they believe blacks are biologically superior to them.

However, it must be stressed that discrimination, *by its nature*, does not cause one to feel inferior, and the existence of discrimination is not the proof of inferiority in men. We cannot say that an individual must be inferior or he would not be discriminated against. Neither can we say that an individual would not feel inferior

51

if he were not discriminated against. His sense of inferiority existed *before* discrimination occurred, and it is his sense of inferiority that allows discrimination or antipathy to have such a debilitating effect on him. Others may act toward an individual *as though* he were inferior; discrimination may even be the direct cause of his inferior status in the social hierarchy; but his actual feelings of inferiority are always self-imposed. Those feelings are representative of his self-evaluation, albeit reinforced by the evaluations of others.

Antidiscrimination laws aimed at sparing one from a sense of inferiority are worthless, as they have no power to change his psychology. While ridding the society of racism sanctions the fact that men are worthy of justice by virtue of their human identity, such action, in and of itself, is powerless to confer a sense of worth to any individual or group of individuals.

Not all persons who are objects of ethno-racial antipathy and discrimination conclude from such treatment that they are bioculturally inferior. But those who do are as ethno-race conscious as those doing the discriminating; both are engaged in a form of self-immolation. In hiding behind a collective judgment of men the discriminator is continually trying to escape the reality of each individual's sovereign identity, and, in his attempt to escape, he undermines his own power of awareness. In his conclusion that he is made inferior by forces beyond his control (biological and cultural heritage, or political forces), the discriminated sentences himself to the impotence of a sense of lack of worth. Though pitted against each other, they are most often unaware that they are two variants of the same disease: *the lack of self-esteem.*

The flight from reality by both the discriminator and the discriminated dominates the present state of ethno-racial relations in America. It is all around us, as the sustained popularity of "The Jeffersons" and "All In The Family" indicates. But in order to "prove" our lack of bias, how many of us laugh approvingly at the sometimes offensive ethnic humor of comedians Don Rickles, Flip Wilson, or Richard Pryor? These comedians earn their living telling us that race consciousness is too ridiculous to take seriously, that the best we can do is mock the disease by laughing at the stereotypes they portray of ourselves. In the meantime, however, while we are all laughing, one group after another is claiming itself politically "revitalized" and in the name of freedom usurping the freedom of us all. Ethno-race prejudice *is* ridiculous, but there is nothing funny about it—least of all the performances of these comedians, who are themselves carriers of the disease.

1. Gordon W. Allport, *The Nature of Prejudice*, p. 10.

2. As racism (racial discrimination) involves differential treatment according to race, ethnocentrism involves differential treatment according to cultural elements; ethnonationalism [a concept coined by Walker Connor in "The Politics of Ethnonationalism," *Journal of International Affairs*, 27(1)(1973)]—according to national origin; tribalism—according to tribal affiliation; sexism (feminism as well as male chauvinism)—according to sexual attributes. And all of these doctrines are negations of the individuality of man.

3. Frank H. Hankins, *An Introduction to the Study of Society*, quoted in Brewton Berry, *Race and Ethnic Relations*.

4. Robert K. Merton, "Discrimination and the American Creed," in *Discrimination and National Welfare*, ed. Robert M. MacIver (New York: Harper and Brothers, 1949), quoted in Berry, *Race and Ethnic Relations*. In the discussion that follows I am relying heavily on Berry's summary of Merton's study. For the only reprint of MacIver in which Merton appears see Robert M. MacIver, ed., *Discrimination and National Welfare*.

5. Glazer and Moynihan, eds., *Ethnicity*, p. 7.

6. Ibid.

7. Evans, M. Stanton, "Varieties of the Conservative Experience," in *The Conservative Alternative*, ed. David Brudnoy.

8. Jerome Tuccille, *Radical Libertarianism: A Right Wing Alternative*.

9. See chapter 9 for a discussion of "black capitalism" as a contradictory concept and as a program designed to avoid competition in the free market.

10. For an analysis of the effects of racism on the social reform movements in America, see Allen, *Reluctant Reformers*.

11. See Nathaniel Branden's discussion of "The Concept of Mental Health" in *The Psychology of Self-Esteem*.

12. In Richard Hofstadter, *The American Political Tradition*, p. 274.

13. W. T. Jones, *A History of Western Philosophy*, pp. 243–44.

14. My characterization of Jefferson in this manner is not meant to be facetious. For all the contradictions in his ideas and actions, Jefferson stands out in my mind as a committed seeker after the truth. He came to know the truth regarding the humanity of Negroes but failed to act consistently on that knowledge. But this breach of his own principles of human liberty does not constitute an invalidation of those principles; neither does it discredit his enormous contribution to the establishment of a society in which all men would be free.

15. "The Western Report," *The Papers of Thomas Jefferson*, ed. Julian Boyd (Princeton: Princeton University Press, 1958), vol. 12, p. 578; quoted in M. Thomas Bailey, "The Attitude of Thomas Jefferson toward Slavery during the Revolutionary and Early National Period."

16. "Notes on the State of Virginia," in *The Portable Thomas Jefferson*, ed. Merrill D. Peterson, pp. 188–93.

17. "Letter to Benjamin Banneker, August 30, 1791," ibid., p. 454.

18. "Letter to Henri Grégoire, February 25, 1809," ibid.

19. Glazer and Moynihan, op. cit., p. 158.

20. B. M. Kramer, "Dimensions of Prejudice," quoted in Berry, op. cit., pp. 374–75.

21. Berry, op. cit., p. 375.

22. Frank R. Westie, "Negro-White Status Differentials and Social Distance," quoted in Berry, op. cit., p. 375.

23. See Allport, op. cit.

Ethno-Race Consciousness versus Assimilation

America had been called "the melting pot," with good reason. But few people realized that America did not melt men into the gray conformity of a collective: she united them by means of protecting their right to individuality.—Ayn Rand, *The Virtue of Selfishness.*

Prejudice, discrimination, or the more conspicuous forms of ethno-racial conflict such as riots, lynchings, annihilation, or expulsion are not the only consequences of contact between groups. These conflicts, writes Berry, "create the impression that racial and ethnic groups are naturally and continually at each other's throats. . . . More common by far is the fusion of the two (assimilation and amalgamation) or the reaching of some *modus vivendi* (accommodation)." The fact is that even as intergroup conflict occurs, there are always some individuals who manage to penetrate the ethno-racial boundaries that separate them and create harmonious relations in which the exchange of ideas and customs can occur. And no examination of the ethno-race consciousness that impedes intergroup harmony would be satisfactory without giving consideration to the process of assimilation—a concept that is greatly misunderstood because of the link it has often been given in sociological literature to the "melting pot" theory and the theory of Americanization.

55

The Other Side of Racism

The Process of Assimilation

Before attempting to revive assimilation back to a state of conceptual "grace," let me review the political developments in America that occasioned its fall. The melting pot theory prevailed prior to World War I, when it was supposed that the multitudes crossing the Atlantic were undergoing a process of "fusion" that would eventually produce a great civilization and a race of supermen. "Great has been the Greek, the Latin, the Slav, the Celt, the Teuton, and the Saxon," wrote William Jennings Bryan, "but greater than any of these is the American, who combines the virtues of them all."[1] (Note that Bryan did not include Negroes, Indians, and Orientals.)

Assimilation, via the melting pot, was considered easy, rapid, natural, and inevitable; it would take care of itself. But, as Berry notes:

> The First World War gave a rude shock to this comfortable theory. It became apparent that assimilation had not been working as automatically as had been supposed. When the nation began to take stock of itself, the startling fact emerged that there were millions in the country who could neither read, speak, nor write the English language; less than half the foreign-born white males of voting age were citizens; there were thousands of organizations flourishing among the foreign element, and hundreds of newspapers and periodicals published in foreign languages; immigrants were concentrated in "colonies" in the cities, and foreign governments were in the habit of encouraging their nationals to retain their old allegiance, not without some success.
>
> As a result of these disclosures a new philosophy of assimilation came into being, and a program, known as the "Americanization Movement," was inaugurated. No longer would the assimilation of alien peoples be left to the operation of natural forces. No longer would assimilation be regarded as an inevitable outcome of the meeting of cultures. Deliberate, organized efforts would be made to divest the immigrant of his foreign heritage, to suppress his native language, to teach him English, to make him a naturalized citizen, and to inject into him a loyalty to American institutions. Many agencies participated in the movement— public schools, patriotic societies, chambers of commerce, women's clubs, public libraries, social settlements, and even industrial plants where foreigners were employed.[2]

The movement was characterized by a spirit of coercion, condescension, and suppression; it implied that American culture was a finished product, in an Anglo-Saxon pattern, that it was

56

superior to all others, and that aliens should promptly acquire it. Needless to say, the idea of "Americanization" fell into disrepute, from which it has never recovered. Although the melting pot theory represented the doctrine of laissez-faire applied to the realm of race and culture contact, it identified the melting pot as America where God (or some other force) was making the American—a mythical entity fused from all the European races. This view met a fate similar to that of Americanization.[3]

Unfortunately, however, in rejecting the theories of the melting pot and Americanization, Americans have also rejected the idea of assimilation itself and thus have failed to identify its legitimacy. As one Negro writer put it, assimilation in regard to Negroes is "a proposition calculated to blow the black mind to bits."[4] This one-sided view of assimilation as a threat to ethno-racial identification and subcultural allegiances underlines the following excerpts from a full-page advertisement placed in *The New York Times* by the Board of Jewish Education of Greater New York entitled, "Survival through Education and The Decline of American Jewry":

> The problem of a declining American Jewish population is more of a reality than a threat. . . .
> Many factors have contributed to this decline. Chief among them are a lower birthrate. However, feelings of alienation, and an intermarriage rate which has been estimated at 31% are major causes. These have their roots in, and are exacerbated by a lack of a positive Jewish identity in our youth.
> . . . It is not uncommon to read of Jewish children intermarrying, joining Jews for Jesus and many other groups which serve as outlets for their identification needs. Or, they go through life without association with any group, alienated, disaffected, and with an unfulfilled need to "belong."
> Why is it that our Jewish teenagers must turn to other religions and other modes of expression for satisfactions that should be and indeed can be achieved within the context of their own religion and culture? The answer lies in their lack of the knowledge and early experiences essential for the development of a positive identification with Judaism. . . .
> A Jewish education is the best way of combatting the corrosive effects of assimilation.

The misconceptions surrounding assimilation persist, and they do so amid sociological discussions of ethno-race relations that view it as a phenomenon of group contact with little or no reference to the nature of the individuals who make up the groups under study.[5] For the most part, sociologists still view assimilation as Donald L.

Horowitz does: "the process of erasing the boundary between one group and another" in which there are generally two kinds of change: (1) *amalgamation*, in which "two or more groups may unite to form a new group, larger and different from any of the component parts"—i.e., biological mixing; or, (2) what Horowitz calls *incorporation* and others call *acculturation*, in which "one group may lose its identity by merging into another group, which retains its identity."[6] While amalgamation often occurs simultaneously with assimilation they are not one and the same and contrary to what is popularly believed, miscegenation is not the necessary end result of assimilation. But it is misconceptions such as this, aided by the theory that assimilation must be inevitable and complete, that leaves many people with the conception of assimilation as a *dis*-value—a one-way process of adaptation or adjustment that involves the discarding of the traditional cultural values and behavior of one group and the adoption of those of another group.

What is assimilation? By employing the theoretical models of several writers on the subject, I have arrived at the following definition consistent with the individualistic approach of this study: *Assimilation is the process by which individuals and groups from different cultures come to share a common culture. It is achieved by the process of selection and exchange in which individuals acquire (by conscious choice) the memories, sentiments, attitudes, and values of other individuals, and by which their shared experiences and history are incorporated into a common way of life.*

What distinguishes this view of assimilation from others is its acknowledgement of the individual as the acting agent of the dynamics of group relations and therefore of assimilation. Emphasis is placed on the conscious selectivity of cultural elements, rather than their passive internalization. Assimilation occurs in individuals before it becomes a group phenomenon. It is the process of bringing the attributes of one's subculture and those of the dominant culture into synchronization with one's values and goals.[7] However, cultural synchrony does not mean the forceful subordination of one culture over another, nor necessarily the sacrifice of one's cultural values to gain the acceptance of individuals of another cultural affiliation. The idea of synchrony holds that at any given time, in a given sociocultural context, the individual thinks and behaves in that manner appropriate to maximizing the achievement of goals he believes to be in his self-interest.[8] It involves the *identification, selection,* and *exchange* of cultural attributes to meet certain needs and desires. (Just what his needs and desires may be and whether the synchrony he achieves is in his self-interest qua man is an issue that will be taken up later in this chapter.)

Assimilation is often misunderstood to mean the same as adaptation or adjustment. The dictionary definition of adaptation is "the act of changing *to fit* (emphasis mine) different circumstances or conditions; the condition of being altered for a different use." Adaptation is usually employed to connote the biochemical responses of living organisms to their environment—an evolutionary and maturation process that occurs in man as well as plants and animals. It is an automatic and natural process, whereas assimilation is not. Assimilation involves rejection as well as acceptance of cultural elements within the social environment.

Unlike adaptation, adjustment refers only to human beings, meaning the process by which a person adapts himself to particular natural or social conditions around him. Adaptation is essentially a passive response to existential conditions but adjustment is an active dynamic response. If a person used to a warm climate moves to a colder climate, he adjusts to the climatic conditions by wearing more clothes. Wearing more clothes (the adjustment) increases his body temperature (the adaptation).

The fine but significant difference between adjustment and adaptation is that adjustment is an act of choice, and therefore engaged in only by human beings. An animal adapts *automatically* to the colder climate by growing a thicker coat of hair or fur, or by migrating from the area to a warmer region. But the person from a warm climate *chooses* to adjust to the colder climate by adapting his body temperature with more or heavier garments. If he does not dress to increase his body temperature, it will not do so on its own but will decrease to the point where his life is endangered.

Man is constantly adapting and adjusting things in his environment to suit his needs and desires. We adjust the volume of sound from the radio to the level that is pleasant to our hearing; we adapt the shape of a sheet of paper to a given use so that instead of remaining flat it may be rolled in the shape of a cone to be used as a funnel or scoop. But man himself is not the volume dial on a radio to be adjusted to suit someone's desires, and neither is he a sheet of paper to be molded to meet someone's purpose.

Adjustment is not just a matter of body, but of mind also. This is particularly evident in the individual's response to the social conditions around him. As man is not compelled to adjust to natural conditions, neither is he compelled to adjust to his social environment. In dealing with both natural and social circumstances and conditions, the issue for a human being is whether those conditions are beneficial or inimical to his survival and how he should deal with them. His degree of adjustment or lack of it is determined by his value judgment of the facts he observes.

While adaptation involves the change or alteration of body functions in order to meet survival requirements in the natural environment, adjustment properly involves fitting one's choices to the requirements of a beneficial existence in both the natural and social realms. However, adjustment does not necessarily mean the selection of choices consonant with the values of the larger society. Nor does it mean imposing the arbitrary standards held by one individual or group of individuals on the society—i.e., all those who choose to live together according to a distinct system of social organization, values, and behavior. The issue of adjustment is one element of the assimilation process, but always it is directed by the individual's choice from among many alternatives in his social environment. Unlike adaptation, it involves not only the acceptance of elements in the culture, but also the rejection of certain elements.

The issue is not between man and society, but between the individual's choices and the requirements of his existence qua man. It is not society, as such, to which he must adjust, but to the laws of reality. It is not to arbitrary cultural attributes he must adjust, but to the requirements of his nature as a rational being of volitional consciousness. His priority is to be a human being, not a cultural "entity." Thus an individual's proper adjustment to those facts of reality relevant to the achievement of a beneficial existence (as opposed to arbitrary cultural attributes) may well constitute resistance to whatever structure, values, and behavior may be prevalent in his sociocultural environment at a given time.

But men do not always make the proper adjustment to the laws of reality; they are just as capable of evading reality and tailoring their identity after those social values and systems that run counter to their self-interest qua man but which serve as the substitute for their lack of autonomous, authentic self identity. Adjustment to the facts of objective reality would require, for instance, that Jewish parents resist the appeal by the Board of Jewish Education of Greater New York for Jewish education to develop in their child "a positive identification with Judaism." Their resistance to Jewish education as "the most effective instrument for transmitting Jewish heritage to Jewish youth" and the best means of developing an "early sense of 'belonging' " would not constitute a denial of the Jewish heritage, as such, or the problems of Jews as a group in the society. It would represent, instead, their desire not to impose an ethnocultural context on their child before he has reached an age to make his own choice of cultural attributes. The issue for them would not be the survival of American Jewry over the "corrosive effects of assimilation," especially since they know assimilation is not necessarily corrosive, but the survival of their child's self-identity over the corrosive elements of ethnocultural identification. Their concern would be with the well-being of their child as a human being, not just as a person born of Jewish parents. They know that he must know *who* he is before *what* he is can be understood from the proper perspective, and that this is not achieved by blind loyalty to the Jewish context but by experiencing himself as the single, unattached being he is.

The overriding issue in assimilation is the selection of elements from one's social context that may be successfully integrated into one's psychointellectual context. But, as I shall demonstrate later, what one selects will depend on what one judges as beneficial or inimical to one's self-interest. Orlando Patterson, who opposes the view that ethnic identity is involuntary and cannot be changed, makes the following observation which, by contrast, may shed some light on the individualistic view of assimilation presented here: "From a structural and contextual viewpoint, there is an important sense in which the significance of a given ethnic attribute can change and, as such, one can be said to have some choice in the matter, since one can choose the sociological and psychological significance of the given trait. And the way in which this is done is simply by changing one's social context or seizing the opportunity offered by a change, over time, in one's social context."[9]

Among several examples of changing one's social context, Patterson cites the case of the "highly Americanized" black Puerto Ricans who, far from melting involuntarily into the context of the larger culture or their own subculture, "consciously choose and manipulate different ethnic identities to serve their own best

61

interests." Patterson continues: "In certain contexts (for example, running for local office or applying for a job in which Affirmative Action has created a black bias) he will emphasize his blackness. In other contexts (for example, personal relations with whites) he may choose to mute the impact of his dark skin by emphasizing his Latin background, especially his Spanish accent."[10]

What is most significant about Patterson's view, considering the deterministic approach of his fellow sociologists, is his recognition that the process of assimilation does entail individual choice. But while it is true enough that individuals often change or shift the emphasis they place on certain ethnic or subcultural attributes to fit a given social context (i.e., conformity to social structures and expectations), it is just as true that individuals will emphasize attributes that run counter to that social context. In some cases, such as intermarriage, the individual may abandon his ethnic allegiances altogether. In any case, the fact that most people change to fit the external context does not mean that the choices are made for them "out there." The social context may imply what significance a given ethnic or cultural attribute should have, but the final judgment must be derived from the individual's psychointellectual context and value preferences. He must have the last word on the significance of a cultural attribute—not the sociocultural environment he happens to be in at a given time. He is the one who must decide the significance or insignificance of his Jewish heritage, Spanish accent, skin color, Anglo-Saxon ancestry, ghetto argot, "soul" food, Polish weddings, hillbilly folk music, or Sicilian "family."

Assimilation is not a condition; it is not the end result of social contact, but a *process* of subcultural give and take. Neither is it by definition a dis-value, but a process of human interaction in which men deal with one another voluntarily for mutual benefit. The cliché "association brings about assimilation" is often used to describe the process of integration within a culture. Of course, this slogan is meant to reflect the view that assimilation is something *done* to a person—an attitude that pervades the written history of emigrants to the United States and in the recorded attitudes of native-born Americans and the United States government toward these emigrants.[11] But nothing could be further from the truth, as evidenced by the history of Negroes in America who have had a longer and closer "association" with the dominant culture than any other minority, albeit the greater period of that association was characterized by slavery and racial segregation. Nevertheless, if association alone were the determining factor of assimilation, no group of people should be more assimilated than Negro Americans.

The degree to which any group of people assimilate into the mainstream of American life is the degree to which the individuals within that group take vigorous responsibility for their own individual self-determination—a fact that sadly has not been accepted and acted upon yet by many members of the various ethno-racial minorities. There are many existential factors, including association, that influence the nature and rate of a person's assimilation, but the one factor on which all the others depend is his power of volitional choice—whether he chooses to view the *culture* as his maker—or *himself*, a creator of the culture.

Self-Immolating Assimilation versus Self-Assertive Assimilation

Sociologists see many variables at work in assimilation, but the models they construct are drawn primarily from the social dynamics of groups.[12] Since this is a study of ethno-race consciousness in individuals, I shall go behind the scenes, so to speak, of the sociology of (group) assimilation to focus on the process as it is experienced in the psychointellectual realm of individuals. At this level, assimilation may be characterized by either of two perspectives held by individuals toward themselves and their relationship to their social environment. There is negative *self-immolating* assimilation engaged in by individuals who see themselves as creations of the culture around them. There is the positive *self-assertive* version engaged in by individuals who function on the policy that they are the creators of their self-identity and as such are capable of contributing to the structure and dynamics of the culture. However, these two variations of assimilation in the psychointellectual dimension are not definitions of assimilation; rather, they characterize the *valuations* given assimilation by those undergoing the process. Neither does this distinction mean to imply that one's assimilation must be all of one kind or the other. Quite the contrary, at different stages in his psychointellectual growth, for different reasons and in different circumstances, an individual may engage in both positive and negative assimilation.

The definition of assimilation as the process by which individuals and groups from different cultures come to share a common one does not identify *what kind of* process it is, and it does not define *what kind of* common culture may result. It is a process of selection and exchange, but this definition leaves open the question of what kind of selection and exchange. As human beings are neither intrinsically good nor evil, neither is assimilation intrinsically beneficial nor inimical to human relations. Left open to question are the standards by which we judge the process as being either one or the other as it occurs in different individuals and groups.

Using man's nature as a rational being as the standard for judging the quality of assimilation, *beneficial* assimilation is defined as that which is appropriate to the requirements of man's self-esteem; the cultural give and take involved is that which serves the rational self-interest of individuals and requires objective self-assertiveness; the common way of life that results is one that encourages voluntary association and the expression of human dignity and justice. *Inimical* assimilation is that which violates the requirements of man's self-esteem. It is employed by men of pseudo self-esteem as a means of *escaping* self-responsibility—what Branden calls the social metaphysician's "mindless conformity to the values of others." There is cultural give and take, but rather than being honest, just, harmonious, and benevolent, this altruistic assimilation is characterized by cognitive parasitism, psychointellectual blackmail, deceit, manipulation, role playing, and appeasement. When such is the case, one's assimilation *is*, as Brown suggests, a proposition calculated to blow one's mind to bits—calculated, however, by oneself.

But assimilation need not be such an odious and self-immolating experience. The individual who perceives himself as self-created rather than culture-created employs assimilation as a means of *asserting* his self-responsibility. *His* assimilation involves what Branden calls the healthy man's judgment of his "sense-of-life affinity" to others and to their ideas, their values, their spiritual and intellectual achievements.[13]

Finding affinity—a likeness of oneself in others or in their achievements—is an important psychological need that Branden calls the need for *psychological visibility*: "the desire to see [one's] own values embodied in the person of others, to see human beings who face life as he faces it; [to see in others] a reaffirmation of his own view of existence."[14] Because psychological visibility is a need of man's self-esteem, it is a primary factor of assimilation; but like assimilation, the kind of visibility one seeks depends on the nature of his self-evaluation.

It is man's need for psychological visibility that gives rise to his satisfaction of that need through assimilation; and the kind of visibility he desires will determine the kind of assimilation he will engage in. The sense-of-life affinity entailed in the psychological visibility that individuals seek is translated in the sociological realm into the cultural sense-of-life entailed in *transcultural* visibility achieved among groups. Indeed, on the macrosociological level of intergroup relations, assimilation is no more than the seeking of transcultural visibility achieved by identifying with certain attributes of another culture or subculture.

While finding visibility in others is important, the individuality of man's nature precludes that visibility, whether negatively altruistic or positively self-interested, be limited to the boundaries of one's racial, ethnic, national, sexual, or age group. The principle of visibility transcends all categories of men and all historical periods. This is why, for instance, we say that certain works of art are "timeless" or "ageless." A man of the twentieth century need not be limited to finding a reflection of himself and his values in the art produced during this century; he may find affinity with the works of art produced by men during the Renaissance; or he may find that he is more comfortable with the one-dimensional drawings of cavemen. He may find a reflection of himself in twentieth-century skyscrapers; or he may "see" himself in the mud huts of a tropical village. He may find that of all the past and present intellectuals, he can identify only with the view of man and reality as expressed by Aristotle some seventeen centuries ago; or, he may find that he can identify only with those views expressed by B. F. Skinner.

The race-conscious individual is often torn between allegiances to his ethno-racial subculture and those he has to the dominant culture. And what he desires is not the visibility one experiences in healthy relationships with individuals, but ethno-racial *identity*. His conflict is between his natural need for self-identity and the unnatural desire to rely on others to create that identity. Visibility— psychointellectual or transcultural—is not the equivalent of self-identity; but the nature of one's visibility is determined by the nature of his identity—whether it rests on an authentic self-esteem or pseudo self-esteem. As a factor of self-assertive assimilation, transcultural visibility requires an authentic self-image, which is precisely what the race-conscious person lacks. His identity is created in the image of whatever ethno-racial group he was born into and he feels himself trapped there.

One such personality so eloquently expressed is novelist James Baldwin whose anguished lack of transcultural visibility is reflected in his description of himself as "a bastard of the West." His lineage ends in Africa, not Europe, he says; Shakespeare, Bach, Rembrandt, the Empire State Building are not his creations and not part of his history. "I might search in them in vain forever for any reflections of myself," he writes. "I was an interloper; this was not my heritage."[15]

The man who cannot relate to the works of other men of other races, in other cultures or during other ages has no self of his own to relate. Having no psychointellectual authority with which to assert independent judgment, he is locked into the sociology of his biological or ethnic group, thinking what it thinks, doing what it prescribes. It is not Baldwin's racial identity that prevents him from identifying with European artists, no more than it is their race that prevents many Negroes from identifying with Baldwin. The achievements of individual men are not the achievements of whole races or cultures, but the identification of a culture depends on achievements (or lack of them) by individuals within that culture. Being of European descent gives Caucasian Americans no more special affinity with artistic, literary, and scientific giants of that part of the world than being of African descent gives Negro Americans any special affinity with tribal kings and priests of that part of the world. And as many American, Eastern European, and Russian Jews are learning, being Jewish gives them no automatic affinity with Middle Eastern Jews. Neither does the English ancestry of the Pitcairn Islanders give them any necessary affinity with the people of Britain.

The bridge between an individual and his affinity with the cultural attributes of another is his volitional choice, the instrument of his conceptual separateness. But the cultural determinism expressed by James Baldwin forbids individual choice; it forbids the transcultural nature of self-assertive assimilation. It demands that a man of African descent find inspiration in the tribal dance of Sub-Saharan

66

natives; that an individual born of Chinese parents see himself reflected only in the attitudes and lifestyle of traditional Chinese. This position holds that if one is Jewish, he must have a burning compulsion to prostrate himself before the Wailing Wall of Solomon's Temple in Jerusalem, even if he has to walk over the bodies of Moslems and Christians to do so. It requires that he lock his life and his self-identity into the cultural mold of his ancestors as his physical characteristics are locked into the biological mold of his genes. It requires that he dispose of his mind and spirit, becoming no more than any instinct-bound animal, and of no more consequence than a grain of sand in a dust storm.

But man is a rational animal: *he thinks*. He is a being of volitional consciousness: *he chooses*. He is a being of free will: he determines his identity and life's course. His existence depends not on a biological, ethnic, cultural, or national heritage, but on his intellectual heritage: what he chooses as his store of knowledge and how he applies that knowledge toward the maintenance of his existence. There may not be any Greeks in his biological lineage, and yet he may have more understanding of Aristotle's *Metaphysics* than the average native of Greece. He need not have Italian "blood" to be inspired by the work of Michelangelo Buonarroti. His ancestry need not include Africans to be able to appreciate the reggae music of the West Indies or *The Invisible Man* by Ralph Ellison. He need not be "country" to identify with country music. And as any Japanese fan of Elvis Presley will testify, one need not be "American" to be "turned on" by Western rock 'n' roll. He need not have Saxon ancestry or be a native of Great Britain to know what is meant by these lines from Shakespeare's *Hamlet*: "What a piece of work is man! how noble in reason! how infinite in faculty! in form and moving how express and admirable! in action how like an angel! in apprehension how like a god!"

The human mind is individual. There can be no such thing as a collective mind—a cultural mind, or a racial mind. The black child born in the deepest rain forest of Africa has the *capacity* to understand the meaning of the Empire State Building. It is not his biology, nor even the geography of his birth, nor the sociology of his tribal group that restricts that capacity. Rather, he is restricted by his *lack of knowledge* that the Empire State Building exists or what its existence implies. What is to prohibit those who *do* know of its existence and are aware of its implicit statement from identifying with it? Nothing, except the extent of their knowledge, context, interests, and values.

The fact that a man does not "see" his spirit in the meaning behind the Empire State Building has nothing to do with who his ancestors were, or in what part of the world they dwelled. It has only to do with the content of his mind and how he experiences himself. If he chooses to lock himself outside human achievement, per se, there will be no room in his intellect to evaluate the work of another man, regardless of that man's race, where he dwells, or the historical period during which he produces.

In his confession that he despises Negroes, "possibly because they have failed to produce a Rembrandt," James Baldwin lays bare but another aspect of ethno-race consciousness that gives whole groups of men a function they cannot and do not have in reality. Man's individuality is not the product of other men, neither biologically nor sociologically. The productivity of Rembrandt, the Dutch Caucasian, tells us nothing about the ability of Negroes, nor even of Rembrandt's countrymen or his family. No people produced Rembrandt. The Florentines did not produce Michelangelo's artistic triumphs and neither did they produce Niccolo Machiavelli's political philosophy. White Americans did not produce Thomas Jefferson and neither did they produce James Earl Ray. Negro Americans did not produce colonial patriot Crispus Attucks and neither did they produce Black Power anarchist H. Rap Brown.

That brand of ethno-racial determinism which advocates the opposite is not unlike that of Hitler who believed civilization to be the privileged responsibility of the "Aryan race." Human civilization is the achievement of individuals. It is individuals who have kept man civilized and only individuals can continue to keep man civilized. To quote a character from one of Rand's novels: "Civilization is the process of setting man free from men"—the process of establishing the primacy of man's self-identity over collective affiliation. If we destroy the individual, we will ultimately destroy civilization. And the most civilized society is one in which men are self-created, conceptually separate from other men, unchained to stereotypes, and free from the interference of those who fix themselves between the gripping jaws of the intellectual vise of ethno-racial and psychocultural determinism.

The many varied ways in which individuals express their need for psychointellectual visibility and their capability of achieving transcultural visibility cast a huge shadow of doubt on the notion that assimilation is but a process whereby one group of men dangle at the end of the subcultural strings of another group. It is not an automatic process and neither can it be externally calculated. Coercive assimilation is a contradiction that defeats its own purpose, as evidenced by the resistance of slaves to "deculturalization" and by the failure of the government-sponsored "Americanization Movement" inaugurated to assimilate foreign immigrants. We are presently witnessing a similar failure of coercive integration, calculated to force men to associate or live next to one another.

Some social analysts have concluded that assimilation was so difficult for Negro slaves because the American culture was not suited to them. If, by this statement, they mean that the culture has taken shape largely to reflect the ideas and interests of free white *men*, one would have to agree. But it must be said immediately that the history of American culture is of an endless stream of individuals who have challenged this contradiction in a nation established on the principles of individual rights and equal freedom. As the slaves struggled to survive the bondage of the plantation subculture, they also embraced the ideals of freedom that permeated the larger culture. They may not have experienced the *fact* of that freedom, but they were nonetheless fervent in their belief that they were entitled to it. Most immigrants to America from 1619 to the present day shared the same belief. The issue was not whether an individual was *capable* of assimilating aspects of the larger culture, but whether, regardless of his cultural heritage or biological ancestry, he would be granted the legal protection necessary to make beneficial, self-interested assimilation *possible*—in this case, to meritoriously rise to the level that his intelligence and industry would allow. This is the issue that stirred the advocates of women's suffrage and moves those who protest racial discrimination. And it is this same issue that waits to be faced in deciding the still-unresolved fate of American Indians.

Neither can one bypass the self-responsibility that self-assertive assimilation requires by making the observation that Negroes have been consciously denied opportunities to assimilate. While this observation is true in some respects, it is inconclusive in that it excludes the fact that from the beginning of the country's history, so many Negroes have assimilated themselves despite the socioeconomic and political restrictions placed on them. Restrictions by the majority group may explain the *difficulty* of achieving positive assimilation, but it is not an adequate explanation for *why* an individual in a basically free society does not ultimately achieve that goal. I suggest that the rest of the explanation is found in the person's motives, his self-evaluation, and his response to his situation. For if we are to understand assimilation, either in its self-assertive or self-immolating form, we will have to begin with an understanding of the individuals involved in the process.

1. Quoted in Berry, *Race and Ethnic Relations*, p. 211.
2. Ibid., pp. 212–13.
3. Ibid.
4. Susan Love Brown, "The Rape of the Black Mind."
5. My insistence on an individualistic foundation for the study of group relations (see chapter 1) is shared in part with Orlando Patterson who writes: "All hypothetical statements regarding ethnicity must be microsociological, since the critical problem is to explain the individual's relation to the group, not the group itself. A concern with the ethnic group shifts the theoretical emphasis from ethnicity to the macrosociological level of intergroup relations." ("Context and Choice in Ethnic Allegiance," in Glazer and Moynihan, eds., *Ethnicity*, p. 311.)
6. Donald L. Horowitz, "Ethnic Identity," in Glazer and Moynihan, eds., *Ethnicity*, pp. 111–40.
7. Subculture is used here according to the definition in *The Random House Dictionary*: A group having social, economic, ethnic values, and behavior patterns or other traits distinctive enough to distinguish it from others within the same culture or society. For an analysis of subculture, see Milton M. Gordon, "The Concept of the Sub-Culture and Its Application," *Social Forces* 26 (October 1947): 40–42.
8. Though I disagree with his application of cultural synchrony ·to his behaviorist theories of early education, I must credit Dr. Myron Woolman with introducing me to the concept. See Myron Woolman, *Cultural Asynchrony and Contingency in Learning Disorders*.
9. Orlando Patterson, in Glazer and Moynihan, eds., op. cit., pp. 306–7.
10. Ibid., pp. 307–8.
11. See Milton M. Gordon, *Assimilation in American Life*. See also Nathan Glazer and Daniel Moynihan, *Beyond the Melting Pot* (Cambridge, Mass.: MIT Press, 1963).
12. Gordon has examined what he calls the politics of assimilation, an aspect that became highly visible during the Black Power movement of the sixties.
13. For a wider discussion of "sense-of-life affinity," see Branden's discussion of psychological visibility in *The Psychology of Self-Esteem* and Rand's essays on "Philosophy and Sense of Life" and "Art and Sense of Life" in Ayn Rand, *The Romantic Manifesto*.

14. Branden, *The Psychology of Self-Esteem,* p. 191.
15. James Baldwin, *Notes of a Native Son*, p. 4.

PART II. ETHNO-RACE CONSCIOUSNESS: A DILEMMA OF SELF-ESTEEM

The Social Metaphysics of
Ethno-Race Consciousness

When—in any age—a man attempts to evade the responsibility of intellectual independence, and to derive his sense of identity from "belonging," he pays a deadly price in terms of the sabotaging of his mental processes thereafter.—Nathaniel Branden, *The Disowned Self.*

There is no denying the fact that many of the problems an individual faces are brought on by the state of the society in which he lives. But the problem of ethno-race consciousness does not originate in the society at large. The prejudiced attitudes and discriminatory behavior of ethno-race-conscious individuals is certainly a response to actual or vicarious contact with individuals of different ethnic and racial groups. But these attitudes and behavior are symptoms, not of negative group contact, as such, and its resulting conflict, but of a *characterological* conflict—the conflict between a man's values and the facts of reality—between what he *wishes* to be and what is— between *his* definition of the situation and the situation as it is. There are, for example, people who like to think that certain or all of their racial or ethnic attributes are superior when in fact they are not. It is, at bottom, a problem of self-esteem: *the conflict between an individual's legitimate (natural) need for self-identity and his irrational attempt to acquire that identity by means of group affiliation.*

Precisely what is the social situation of race-conscious individuals, and what is their definition of their situation? The position of this study is that the race-conscious individual emerges from a marginal situation and that his particular attitudinal and behavioral response to that situation is motivated by the psychointellectual policy of social metaphysics. The marginal situation of the race-conscious minority is that *he is straddling two cultures—his own ethno-racial subculture and the dominant culture—having one foot in each.*[1] The conflict of self-esteem that he experiences is not the result of any conflict that may exist between these two cultures, but is due to the fact that, as a social metaphysician, *he views either or both groups as objects of cognitive and evaluative authority and relies on them for a perception of reality.*[2] He is, by these definitions, a *marginal social metaphysician.*

Even when the ethno-race-conscious person declares that his internal conflict would not exist were it not for the external conflict, he only confirms the extent to which he has internalized that conflict at the expense of his self-esteem. He cannot transcend it because his policy is to be defined by it.[3] *His* definition of the situation amounts to a definition he believes is *itself* defined by the situation.

Before delineating further the marginal social metaphysician, it is necessary to establish the context of the present application of the theory of marginality and to show its relation to the theory of social metaphysics.

Elements of the Marginal Situation

Marginality presupposes a marginal situation. Theoretical and empirical investigations show a distinction between *a position in the social structure* (marginal situation) and *a set of psychological traits* that may develop in an individual occupying such a position (marginal personality characteristics).[4] The marginal situation itself may be delineated as a cultural phenomenon resulting from the transition and cultural conflict between two cultural groups; or, it may be analyzed as a structural phenomenon resulting from the disparity between two incompatible social categories. The cultural and structural dimensions of marginality may at times exist independently, but they are often related and go together, as in the case of the intersection of social class and ethnic identification. Even so, a distinction must be made between marginality as a response to conflicting choices in the realm of cultural behavior and marginality as a response to conflicting choices in the area of social structure.

The marginal person may be a racial hybrid of mixed-blood groups such as the Eurasians or Anglo-Indians of India, the metis of Brazil, or the mulattoes of the United States. He may be a cultural hybrid, such as the Europeanized African, the Occidental Oriental, the denationalized European, the second generation in an immigrant group, the "Gentile-oriented" Jew, or the Negro in the United States. Marginal situations may result from the inconsistency of status criteria, which is the case for South African Coloureds and American Negroes who experience inconsistency between cultural equality and social inequality. A marginal situation also exists where status based on individual achievement clashes with status ascribed to groups in terms of traditional expected characteristics and roles. Examples of marginal types found in this situation are the Negro physician, the woman engineer, or the boy university president. Marginals are also found at the intersection of ethnic group and social class within the social structure of the national society, such as the lower-class white Protestant, the middle-class Negro, the upper-class Jew, or upper-class white ethnic. Marginals may also be positioned between substructures of their own particular subculture, as in the case of "new" upper-class Negro entertainers, athletes, and actors whose lack of prestige among "old" upper-class and established middle-class Negroes is not commensurate with their high incomes; or such persons may be lower-class mulattoes whose low class position clashes with high ranking on the color hierarchy in the Negro subculture. Finally, marginality may be a manifestation of attitudinal inconsistency, as in the case of secularized Catholics; or ideological inconsistency, as in the case of "neo-conservatives"; or inconsistency of occupational roles, such as the academic intellectual; or discrepancy between role expectations, such as the adolescent parent.

Whether cultural (positioned between cultural patterns) or structural (positioned between classes), a further distinction must be made between individual and group marginality. The difference between these subtypes of marginality, writes Gordon, is that "although in the case of group marginality individuals do face problems of choice, they face them more or less in concert, so to speak, with other individuals who are in the same situation and who, collectively, make up a subsociety that provides a sociological home and a source of comfort for the members of the group."[5] Different groups face different kinds of barriers, have different degrees of social organization, and thus define their marginal situations differently. This is no less true for individuals whose different definitions of their groups' marginal situations are expressed in different behavior patterns, values, and aspirations. Indeed, the individual's definition of his marginal situation does not always conform to the definition held by his group of its marginal situation. It is clear that in some respects the Negro and white American cultures clash, but the impact is felt by individuals according to how they define the situation. And it is quite possible, as Aaron Antonovsky suggests, that notwithstanding the clash between the two cultural patterns, "individuals work out a way of life which can be relatively non-marginal."[6]

Marginality is a consequence of modernization, and like modernization, it has positive as well as negative attributes and consequences. While this study focuses on the negative philosophical and psychological correlates of marginality, as characterized by Everett Stonequist, it does not share Stonequist's view of marginality as necessarily punishing and a situation of crisis that is antithetical to psychological and cultural integration. As Antonovsky points out, marginality is distinguishable from alienation and anomie. "One can be anomic without being marginal, and marginal without being anomic."[7]

This study emphasizes that variant of marginality which is a situation of crisis—a self-esteem dilemma resulting from a conflict in values. But this emphasis should not be taken to imply that one is either marginal or he is not. We are all marginal in one context or another—indeed, in several contexts: in terms of ethnicity, social status, occupational roles, or economic class. However, some individuals experience their marginality as a self-esteem dilemma while the marginality of others is an expression of psychointellectual independence.

Like many social scientists, the marginal social metaphysicians delineated here have a dislike for marginality. They define their situation in much the same way as David Riesman claims social scientists view marginality. "As some sort of disgrace which should be abolished in all well regulated social and psychic systems.

Evidence of this . . . can be taken from contemporary efforts, from both sides of the ethnic line, to erase Jewish marginality, wherever found, to 'normalize' the Jewish situation."[8] Such normalization is seen in such forms as Zionist nationalism, ethnic pride campaigns by Negroes, and the revitalization of ethnicity by white ethnics. It is precisely this normalization that engages the marginals profiled in this work. Theirs are attempts to abolish the discontinuities of life and career which, according to their value-judgments as social metaphysicians, they regard as liabilities that must not be tolerated. Riesman believes that underlying such attitudes is a fear of looseness, and a fear of a certain amount of disorderliness and nonconformity. Continuity, order, "integration," and the forcing of identity are so emphasized (even by revolutionary militants) as to be perceived as being ethically superior to marginality.

Marginality is a fact of life in an open and mobile urban society. But it is neither an atypical fact nor an inimical fact. Whether imposed or chosen, one's marginal situation is not punishing by definition. Whether it is punishing or liberating depends on the individual's "own interpretation of what he is doing"—his definition of his situation. Riesman writes that some individuals enjoy "the very risk of their marginality . . . [They] seem almost to have consciously sought out the most precarious margins one could find in the society. . . . Marginality can foster insight and choice [or it] can freeze people with anxieties or nostalgia."[9]

Self-Esteem and Social Metaphysics

Authentic Self-Esteem. Inherent in man's nature is his need for self-esteem: *the need of a positive view of himself.* According to Nathaniel Branden, that positive self-evaluation consists of the integrated sum of *self-confidence* (the need to be right in one's conclusions and choices) and *self-respect* (the need to be right as a person, to be good).[10]

Self-esteem requires and entails intellectual independence, which consists of the will to understand, cognitive self-assertiveness, and the will to efficacy.

The *will to understand* is "the desire for clarity, for intelligibility, for comprehension of that which falls within the range of one's awareness."[11] It requires the commitment to *cognitive efficacy*—the control of the activity and growth of one's mind by the goals he sets—and the commitment to *cognitive efficiency*—"the policy of conceptualizing—of looking for and thinking in terms of principles."[12]

Cognitive self-assertiveness is "the policy of [rational self-regulated] thinking, of judging, and of governing action accordingly."[13]

The *will to efficacy* involves *metaphysical* efficacy—"the mastery and control over one's life"—and *particularized* efficacy—productive achievement and the growth and exercise of one's mental abilities.[14]

Since self-esteem entails the confidence in one's capacity to achieve values, the consequence of having achieved some particular value(s) is *pride*—"the pleasure one takes in himself on the basis of and in response to specific achievements or actions."[15] Since self-esteem also entails the capacity for the enjoyment of life, the consequence of having met the conditions of self-esteem is *pleasure*—"a metaphysical concomitant of life, the reward and consequence of successful action, . . . the state of enjoyment [that] gives [man] a direct experience of his own efficacy, of his competence to deal with reality, to achieve his values, to live."[16]

All of these conditions and consequences of self-esteem presuppose that man is a rational being, that reason is his basic tool of survival, and that his rational faculty is volitional. Therefore, they cannot be met nor their consequences experienced except by men who are committed, consciously and subconsciously, to confirming their own human nature.

The man of self-esteem has a sense of goodwill toward himself. He *likes* who he is and *being* himself is a source of pleasure and pride. (It is worth noting here that *who* he is—i.e., the character and personality he has created—is the object of his pride and pleasure, not *what* he is—i.e., the biological or ethnocultural given. What is relevant to the issue of self-esteem is *self*-identity, not one's racial or sexual category or ethnocultural, national, religious, or professional affiliation.) Even during times when he is less pleased with himself, he does not feel unfit for existence. Even during times of temporary unhappiness, he does not retreat to the policy that he is undeserving of happiness and thereby short-circuit his ability to discover the cause of that unhappiness.

The man of self-esteem is an optimist—not a "cockeyed" optimist, but one whose sight on reality is on target and unwavering. He does not try to evade the ruination that results from man's irrationality, but neither does he see man as inherently stupid and doomed to destruction and extinction. His optimism for man is based on his conviction that to exclude the possibility of a rational existence for man is to exempt him from the responsibilities entailed in his possession of a rational faculty. If man is headed for destruction, it is not because that is his predetermined fate, but because he himself has determined destruction as his goal.

How can an individual be optimistic when all about him seems to be crumbling into disarray? The person of self-esteem is optimistic not about the society around him, as such, but about his ability to function in that society. He is optimistic about his ability to exist rationally in a society of men who are committed to irrationality.

Can such a rose exist in such a wasteland of thorns? Yes, so long as the thorns are not allowed to interfere with his life and livelihood. And even when such interference occurs, as it does in our statist society, he is not shaken in his resolve and refuses to sacrifice an objective view of reality and rational standards of existence to that view and those standards that are inimical to his survival. The commitment to rationality requires first that he acknowledge the fact that the briar patch in which he lives is not a rose garden and, second, that he act according to his judgment of that fact. He observes the *is* of his situation: *I am a rose living in a society of briars and brambles.* Then, in accordance with the facts of his own nature as a rose and that of the world around him, he determines the *ought* of the situation: *How ought I think and behave in light of these facts?*

The person of authentic self-esteem is the man who was not incapacitated by slavery; who was not impeded by segregation; and who is not impaired by prejudice. He is neither impressed nor incited by racist testimony in his behalf; he is not made indistinct by the assertions of others that his is a collective identity; and he is not irresolute in his conviction that *he* is the captain of his fate—not the genes of his ancestors nor the socioeconomic statistics of his social location. He is no all-seeing, all-knowing, error-free paragon of perfection, but an ordinary human being willing to think and discover the truth on which his life depends. He is an unbiased individualist—a person whose identity is based on self-interested self-consciousness, not ethnicity or race consciousness.

Pseudo Self-Esteem. There are thousands of Negroes who exemplify the character of the man of self-esteem. But we hear most about the Negro lacking self-esteem, who has a negative view of himself and of reality in general. (Of course, lacking self-esteem is not exclusive to Negroes. Self-esteem, or the lack of it, is an issue of crucial importance to all human beings—not just to racial or ethnic groups.) To him life is a burden, and the effort required to sustain it is an imposition. He views life as a token he does not deserve from some unnamed source, and its continuation is an act he engages in by permission of forces beyond his control. Its aim, he believes, is not the happiness of a creative existence, but the lingering death of inefficacy and safety. To him effective living is viewed as the exception, not the rule of man's existence.

He does not trust reality and he does not trust his ability to deal with it. He is suspicious of other men and quakes at the power he gives them over his life. He feels himself up against an unfathomable universe that he is doomed never to comprehend, and which he must somehow manage to outwit at every turn. The requirements of his existence are forced on him, he believes, for the sin of being man. He resents having to think; he fears having to make choices; and he is contemptuous of his need for values. Yet, he aches for some sign from someone that he is worthy of life and love.

But, as Nathaniel Branden points out, the base and motor of the man of pseudo self-esteem, and the principle that distinguishes his basic motivation from that of a man of self-esteem, is "the principle of *motivation by love* versus *motivation by fear*. Love of self and of existence—versus the fear that one's self is *unfit* for existence. Motivation by *confidence*—versus motivation by terror."[17]

The mind of the individual lacking in self-esteem is a winter of discontent, frozen by the howling winds of compulsion, whim, and faith. Reason, for him, is not a tool of cognition used to validate his thinking but a cheap Molotov cocktail hurled at reality to defend his reliance on his feelings and to rationalize his substitution of cognition with force as his sword in one hand and ethnic mysticism as his shield in the other. Believing his mind and body are two evils in a state of perpetual conflict, he has left his cognition at the mercy of the chilling tyranny of his emotions. And so, there are no tomorrows for him, only the blinding snows of the dismal Now.

He is a living dead man, crawling a burning-cold minefield with no pride to counter shame and guilt—no confidence to purge fear—no courage to challenge weakness—no honesty to correct error—no justice to rout the undeserved—no rationality to disperse doubt and confusion—no productiveness to slay destruction—and with no purpose to guide his way.

This state of spiritual devastation that is more often than not one of quiet despair may be a constant way of life or it may come and go, overwhelming his sense of identity like a flash flood that ravages everything in its path. But it is important to remember that the motives of this state of pseudo self-esteem are no more inherent than the motives of authentic self-esteem. It is not a person's genes or his "fate" that renders him so intellectually helpless and emotionally defensive. Neither is his devastation determined by the connivance of the Prince of Darkness or the wrath of the Lord God Jehovah. The moon and the stars have not conspired against him; neither has "capitalism" (or the lack of it) or the "Establishment" left him so prostrate before reality. His helplessness is *self*-caused, and in the end only *he* can extricate himself from that condition.

This man of pseudo self-esteem is no prehistoric savage running amok in the twentieth century; he is not the walking symbol of Evil incarnate. On the contrary, like the man of authentic self-esteem, he is an ordinary man; but unlike the man of self-esteem, he has chosen to turn his back on the one thing that distinguishes the savage from the human and renders evil impotent: an independent, self-regulating consciousness.

Social Metaphysics. Men lacking in self-esteem differ in the manner they choose to rationalize their fear and lack of self-confidence and self-respect. One solution an individual may seek in defending himself against anxiety, inadequacy, self-doubt, and guilt is to function and survive by means of the minds of others—to become what Branden calls the *social metaphysician*—to be "a parasite of consciousness."

In his analysis of the social metaphysician's self-alienation, Branden lists certain traits that are crucial to understanding how social metaphysics is related to the attitudes and behavior of ethno-race consciousness. The most fundamental of these traits, the one that makes all the others possible is what Branden identifies as "the absence of a firm, independent sense of *objective reality*. This is the vacuum that is filled by the consciousness of others—and this is the void that is responsible for that desolate feeling of *alienation* which is every social metaphysician's chronic torture."[18]

Men of pseudo self-esteem experience a breakdown in self-identity, self-assertiveness, and self-responsibility. But this state of personal incompleteness in the social metaphysician is compounded by a breakdown in his independent status among men. Instead of a harmonious and benevolent relationship with his fellow man, he experiences self-alienation and sociocultural discord. Instead of a relationship of mutual exchange in which he experiences himself and others as independent equals, he is plagued by psychointellectual dependency and fear of his aloneness in the universe. He faces reality, not as a self-created entity, but as an extension of others to whom he has sacrificed his mind and his judgment.

This view of personal disintegration is different from the Durkheimian conception of *anomie*—that state of social disruption caused by the breakdown in communality and the state of personal disintegration caused by sudden changes in social circumstances that disrupt the link between a person's aspirations and his available means of realizing them. The social metaphysician is not alienated from society, as such, but from his sense of self. His disharmony is not structural in origin, but psychointellectual. Although structural disruption may aggravate a person's sense of self, it does not do so *necessarily*; there is no one-to-one correlation between social integration and psychointellectual integration. The intervening factor that defines a person's response to social disruption is the cognitive and evaluative policy underlying his value judgment of the situation.

Branden offers the following explanation of existential and spiritual disharmony: "The experience of self-alienation and the feeling of being alienated from reality, from the world around one, proceed from the same cause: one's default on the responsibility of thinking. The suspension of proper contact with reality and the suspension of one's ego are a single act. A flight from reality is a flight from self."[19]

Shackled by the ball and chain of moral cowardice, the social metaphysician runs from the responsibility of his own self-interest and independent judgment as though they were jailers of his spirit and flees into the frigid wasteland of his dependence on others— either surrendering his mind to their judgment or manipulating their judgment to satisfy his whims. His soul is not his own, but in the words of John Steinbeck, "just a little part of a big soul"—the deified We—the great Public—the Significant Others—the Generalized Other.

Branden says of him: "He wishes to function within a context of others, to live by the guidance of rules for which he does not bear ultimate responsibility. He lives, not in a universe of facts, but in a *universe of people*; people, not facts, are *his* reality; people, not reason, are his tool of survival. It is on them that his consciousness must focus; reality is *reality-as-perceived-by-them*; it is *they* who he must understand or please or placate or deceive or maneuver or manipulate or obey. It is his success at this task that becomes the gauge of his efficacy—of his competence at living."[20]

Orientations of Marginality: Other-Directed and Inner-Directed

If marginal personality, as used here, meant the necessary manifestation of self-alienation resulting from one's interpretation of his situation of structural or cultural marginality, it would be correct to equate marginality with social metaphysics. But as Branden's theory of self-esteem and Riesman's idea of chosen marginality indicate, this is not necessarily the case. The social metaphysician's definition of his marginal situation is only one of several orientations of marginality. An elaboration of this point is necessary in order to fully conceptualize the marginal person who is also a social metaphysician.

In a modern urbanized society where there is extensive vertical and horizontal mobility there is no single common basis for marginality. As already noted, marginality may be a function of cultural discrepancies or structural discrepancies, or, as is most often the case, a combination of the two in multifaceted variations. Without denying that marginal personality characteristics reflect discrepancies between cultural patterns and/or social structures, Riesman points out that in some cases marginality may be more characterological than structural or cultural. His voluntaristic framework views marginality as a means by which individuals differentiate their personality from others.[21]

When groups occupy a place in the social system that is not clearly distinct from other places, individuals relate to one another on the basis of "marginal differentiation of personality." Differences in self-identity, character, and behavior become the basis of interpersonal relations. From this perspective marginality is not only a function of structural discrepancies, but also a function of "discrepancies between our internal states and those we sense in others." Individuals want to be "different from others without being too different."

Riesman's differentiated or characterological marginality is seen as a derivative of modern and highly mobile individuals' quest for personal identity, moral certainty, and social meaning. Quite apart from the marginality of the cultural and racial hybrids who arise out of contact and conflict of cultures, and within this context may be *born* into a marginal situation, characterological marginality is a psychological and behavioral stance adopted by individuals (whether in marginal or nonmarginal situations) to assert self-identification apart from traditional group identification.

According to this conception the marginal situation is not necessarily an imposed condition, but may be a situation that is sought after. Some individuals, like the ethnic intellectuals discussed by Gordon, respond to the marginal situation of their group by forming a subsociety composed of marginals who engage in "systematic primary group contacts across ethnic lines."[22] Or, as documented by Joseph Bensman and Arthur J. Vidich in their study of the "new" middle class of the 1950s and 1960s, individuals might adopt the lifestyles of nonmembership groups in order to differentiate themselves from the group they are in or the one they have left. To separate themselves in terms of lifestyle from the working class they left and the middle class they had moved to, many of the new arrivals to the upper middle class became "culture vultures," imitating the lifestyle of academics; others imitated the lifestyles of the country gentlemen, the serious-minded sportsmen, the jet-setters, and the old middle-class vulgarians.[23] And it is not unusual to find a member of the upper class differentiating himself from his group by "slumming" among the lower classes, or adopting certain lower-class lifestyle patterns.

Riesman's exposition of characterological marginality is presented from the context of his analysis of the "new" middle class of the 1950s in terms of *inner-directed* and *other-directed* social character.[24] His delineations of these character types suggest two major categories of value-orientation and worldview on which the choice of marginality and definitions of the marginal situation are based. I shall designate these orientations toward marginality as *inner-directed marginality* and *other-directed marginality.* Before discussing their precise meanings, it is useful to summarize Riesman's terminology and compare it with Branden's conceptualization of social metaphysics.

The "inner-directed" are those whose source of guidance in life is an internalized authority. There may be historical, cultural, and social variations in the development of these types, but they have one thing in common: "the source of direction for the individual is 'inner' in the sense that it is implanted early in life by the elders and directed toward generalized but nonetheless inescapably destined goals."[25]

The "other-directed" are those whose source of direction is externalized authorities. The development of these varies also. But "what is common to all the other-directed people is that their contemporaries are the source of direction for the individual— either those known to him or those with whom he is directly acquainted through friends and through the mass media. This source is of course 'internalized' in the sense that dependence on it for guidance in life is implanted early. The goals toward which the other-directed person strives shift with that guidance: it is only the process of striving itself and the process of paying close attention to the signals from others, that remain unaltered throughout life. This mode of keeping in touch with others permits a close behavioral conformity . . . through an exceptional sensitivity to the actions and wishes of others."[26]

Marginal differentiation of personality and behavior—characterological marginality—is described by Riesman as characteristic of "other-direction." It involves a "radar-like sensitivity to how one is navigating in the social world, and [the] tendency to make that navigation into an end of life as well as a means." It also involves "the awareness that one is different in secret and subtle ways." And often in order for the other-directed mobile person to appear sufficiently "different" from his fellows he must accentuate discrepancies between himself and others.[27]

It must be pointed out that, as a strategy of other-direction, being "different" is not contradictory to that particular stance toward oneself and the world. The characterological marginality of the other-directed person is not an expression of psychointellectual independence, but of social metaphysics. The ostensive self-assertiveness of the other-directed person is not what distinguishes him from the inner-directed person of authentic self-esteem; what distinguishes them are the forms and ends of their assertiveness. Nathaniel Branden's distinction between counterfeit individualism and authentic individualism is helpful in understanding why the "independence" of the other-directed person is not independence, but either subordination and manipulation or subjectivism and conformity. He writes:

> Individualism [in its ethical-political context] does not consist merely of rejecting the belief that man should live for the collective. A man who seeks escape from the responsibility of supporting his life by his own thought and effort, and wishes to survive by conquering, ruling and exploiting others, is not an individualist. An individualist is a man who lives for his own sake *and by his own mind*; he neither sacrifices himself to others nor sacrifices others to himself; he deals with men as a trader—not as a looter; as a Producer—not as an Attila. . . .
>
> Rebelliousness or unconventionality as such do not constitute proof of individualism. Just as individualism does not consist merely of rejecting collectivism, so [in its ethical-psychological context] it does not consist merely of the absence of conformity. A conformist is a man who declares, "It's true because *others* believe it"—but an individualist is *not* a man who declares, "It's true because *I* believe it." An individualist declares, "I believe it because I see in reason that it's true."[28]

As Riesman points out, the characterological marginality of the other-directed person is aimed toward being different *from oneself* in order to achieve the status and prestige that others have. His aim is to be different, but not too different. The characterological marginality of the inner-directed person of authentic self-esteem, on the other hand, is merely a consequence of his intellectual independence and self-reliance—of what Branden states as his refusal to sacrifice "his perception of *the facts of reality*, his *understanding*, his *judgment* . . . to the unproved assertions of others."[29]

Riesman provides an elaboration of the inner-directed and other-directed types that will move this discussion closer to a finer distinction between inner-directed marginality and other-directed marginality. There are among the inner-directed and the other-directed those who are striving for *adjustment* to their environment, those seeking to be *autonomous*, and those who become *anomic* in the face of failure to attain adjustment. The "adjusted" are people who "reflect their society, or their class within the society, with the least distortion. . . . Such people fit the culture as though they were made for it, as in fact they are." The "autonomous" are people "who on the whole are capable of conforming to the behavioral norms of their society . . . but are free to choose whether to conform or not. . . . [They] are capable of transcending their culture at any time or in any respect." The "anomics," who range from overt outlaws to catatonic types, "are those who lack the capacity to conform and who arise as by products . . . of the attempt to create inner-direction and other-direction."[30]

Riesman makes a point, similar to Branden's above, that is crucial to understanding the issue of adjustment as it concerns the individualist's inner-directed orientation to marginality and the social metaphysician's other-directed orientation:

> In determining adjustment, the test is not whether an individual's overt behavior obeys social norms but whether his character structure does. A person who has the appropriate character for his time and place is "adjusted" even when he makes mistakes and does things which deviate sharply from what is expected of him—to be sure, the consequences of such mistakes may eventually produce maladjustment in character. . . . Conversely, just as nonconformity in behavior does not necessarily mean nonconformity in character structure, so utter conformity in behavior may be purchased by the individual at so high a price as to lead to a character neurosis and anomie: the anomic person tends to sabotage either himself or his society, probably both. Thus, "adjustment" . . . means socio-psychological fit, not adequacy in any evaluative sense.[31]

As Riesman's analysis suggests, it is possible to find the adjusted other-directed type in a society of other-direction. It is also possible to find the adjusted inner-directed type in a society of inner-direction. Yet, both are variants of the social metaphysician, as the adjusted person (as defined by Riesman), whether found in a society of other-direction or one of inner-direction, merely accepts and adjusts to the society's goals as self-evident and obeys. Both may be marginal, either in terms of character differentiation or in terms of structural discrepancies; but in the former situation marginality is sought as a strategy of adjustment, and in the latter it is rejected as a threat to integration and normalization.

The situation of the autonomous person is quite different. It is not possible to find an autonomous other-directed type. However, it is possible to find the autonomous inner-directed type in a society that is other-directed as well as in a society of inner-direction. He differs from the adjusted person in that, whether in an inner-directed or other-directed society, he chooses his goals by "rational, non-authoritarian, noncompulsive means."[32] If he "fits" in a society of inner-direction, it is not due to blind obedience. In a society that is basically other-oriented, as the contemporary American society, the autonomous inner-directed person is necessarily marginal in that he is positioned between his own inner-directed character structure and the other direction of the social structure. Unlike the adjusted types, his characterological marginality is a *consequence* of the discrepancy between his intellectual independence and the other-direction of the society. And rather than viewing structural or cultural marginality as a threat, he defines it as a situation in which to enhance his independence and exercise freedom of choice.

It is against the recognition of choice as factor in marginality that a distinction can be made between *other-directed ethnic marginality* which involves the *concession* of cognitive and evaluative authority to the cultures one stands between and *inner-directed ethnic marginality* which involves the *retention* of such authority. In contrast to the other-directed marginal, on whom this study focuses, the inner-directed marginal does not mind his social position of "not belonging." He consciously seeks such a position as the most appropriate circumstance in which to assert his individuality. The "uprootedness" of the inner-directed marginal is quite the opposite from that of the *outcast* whose imposed marginality condemns him to wandering between normative expectations, cultural patterns, and social structures. On the contrary, the inner-directed marginal is an attitudinal and behavioral *emigrant* whose uprootedness is chosen as his means of transcending the entrapments of social conventions and social structure. The outcast has been rejected by his group or society; the emigrant, on the other hand, rejects society.

A point of clarification must be made regarding this theoretical distinction between the marginal who is an *other-directed outcast* and the marginal who is an *inner-directed emigrant*. There are *conformist* (or "adjusted") outcast marginals who rebel against their rejection by society. These are the cursed pariahs who wander between their subculture and the dominant culture or between structures. They are known by the ambivalence of their ethnic or social dualism and by their incessant search for social approval and integration. They do not want to be where fate or the social system has placed them. And all their social action is aimed toward adjusting to their situation—toward making it "normal" and comparable to other social situations in the larger society, toward becoming domesticated, as it were.

There are also *innovative* outcasts who, once rejected by society, assume the attitude of the inner-directed emigrant whose detachment was voluntary and innovative from the outset. That is, these outcasts, who in many cases are rejected because of their innovative deviance, join emigrants in the purposeful maintenance of a lifestyle of creative transcendence.[33] The difference between the *innovative outcast* and the *innovative emigrant* lies in their origins and in their methods of maintaining their marginality. Unlike the conformist outcast, who is rejected by society despite his efforts to conform, the innovative outcast, is rejected because he actively *defies* conventions that conflict with his values. His defiance is that of an adversary who, once rejected, seeks to maintain his exclusion. The conformist outcast, on the other hand, engages in *rebellion* against his imposed marginality and seeks inclusion. The innovative emigrant differs from both in that he *ignores* society's expectations and imperatives. He is certainly rejected because of his indifference, but he does not acknowledge any inherent conflict between himself and society. His marginality is a function of his cognitive and evaluative independence that is uncontested in a sense that is lacking in the independence of the innovative outcast.[34]

As it is possible that the innovative outcast may assume the attitudes and lifestyle of the innovative emigrant, so too is it possible that the conformist outcast may develop into an innovative outcast. These outcasts-turned-transcendents are known in common parlance as persons and groups who are adept at creating advantages out of disadvantages. This response is typical of European Jews, the Chinese in Southeast Asia, Asians in East Africa, Armenians in Turkey, Syrians in West Africa, Parsis in India, and Japanese in the United States. These groups who consciously seek to fortify a common marginal position in their host society of residence are called "middleman minorities."[35] Their marginality is both cultural and structural, but the form of their creative transcendence is most often only structural. Pushed out of desirable occupations and forced to make a living in marginal lines, middleman minorities manage to escape the lowest rungs of the economic order by maintaining internal solidarity and group pride and becoming entrenched in what Irwin Rinder calls the "status gap" between producer and consumer, employer and employee, owner and renter, elite and masses.[36]

Life in the gap is riddled with liabilities for the innovative outcast, which explains, in part, his defiant protectiveness of his marginal position against the forces of the larger society from which he is an outcast. No matter how successful these newcomers to the gap may be, writes Rinder, "the host society on either side of the gap, both high and low segments, regard the new arrivals as intruders and outsiders." In time, "as the vocational horizons of the higher and lower strata expand and as they experience difficulty in breaking into what are for them new fields, they are likely to feel hostile toward those already entrenched, especially when these are strangers in the land. When the hitherto despised monopoly of the outsider becomes a desirable object for the native, conflict results."[37]

Edna Bonacich, who elaborates on Rinder's concept of middleman minorities, writes of their situation: "The difficulty of breaking entrenched middleman minorities, the difficulty of controlling the growth and extension of their economic power, pushes most host countries to ever more extreme reactions. One finds increasingly harsh measures, piled on one another, until, when all else fails, 'final solutions' are enacted."[38] Such reactions have been directed toward the Jews in Europe, the Indians in East Africa (notably in Uganda), and the Chinese in Southeast Asia.

As the above observations imply, middleman minorities represent innovative outcasts who have originated as emigrants from other societies, but who function in their host society as outcasts. In this regard they differ from those secular and religious countercultures who are also innovative outcasts, but who originated within the native society.[39] Both differ from the nonadversary native innovative emigrant (the autonomous inner-directed marginal) who emigrates from selective structures and cultural patterns of both his subculture of origin as well as the dominant culture, while still functioning as a member of the national society. His emigration is attitudinal and behavioral in that he is not an abject conformist to prevailing values and expectations. It is structural in the sense that he designs his social mobility so as to live out his life and career between boundaries of stratification but not outside the total system. However, he is not beyond challenging the total system when it becomes a threat to his values or mobility between structures. In this regard he may find that his chief opponents are outcast marginals of other-direction who demand the elimination of boundaries as the means for achieving their sought after inclusion in the mainstream.

During these times of cultural pluralism, it is assumed that the person seeking a marginal position is motivated by self-hatred or hatred for the group he is leaving or his subculture of origin. This is particularly so when the individual is critical of his fellow ethnics. As Norman Friedman points out, regarding the organized Jewish community's "ethnic stress" (or marginality) explanation of the behavior of runaway Jewish intellectuals, "anyone who rejects or ignores [the affirmation of Judaism or Jewishness] must be suffering from some sort of irrational psychological stress."[40]

Those who choose marginality are often accused of "false consciousness." In choosing not to belong entirely to either of the cultures he stands between, the inner-directed ethnic marginal is not rationalizing a situation that is imposed on him by external forces (such as racial subordination), but is committed to maintaining that position so as to benefit from the best of both worlds. Unlike the other-directed marginal, his self-esteem is shaped not by the internalization of cultural conflict, but by transcultural needs and values. Being transcultural in orientation, the inner-directed marginal experiences the quality of "two-ness" not as a state of cultural schizophrenia but as representative of one's freedom and diversity. He is "at home" in no single cultural context, but is a "guest" in all cultures, including the subculture into which he was born. He is loyal to no single set of cultural elements, but is committed only to those ideas, values, and preferences (whatever their cultural origin) that affirm his self-concept and reflect his value system.

Although structurally the inner-directed marginal exists on the peripheries of his subculture of origin and the dominant culture, the space he occupies (his subculture of achievement) is itself a subsociety.[41] He is, as David Riesman puts it, an "inhabitant of a margin." If he is fixed anywhere it is in a transcultural subsociety where *not belonging* to any one ethnic subculture *is the norm*. He may be identified categorically as Negro, Jewish, or Chinese, but his self-concept, lifestyle, interests, and social attitudes would have to be characterized as nonethnic. This does not mean that he is "Americanized," or "deculturated"; it means, rather, that he is individualized.

Unlike the other-directed ethnic marginal who has not reconciled his dilemma of being "in-between," the transcultural marginal recognizes no dilemma of ethnic dualism that needs resolving. Being "in-between" is precisely where he wants to be, as it is there that he can assert himself best. It is there that he experiences not a crisis of marginality, but the creativity of marginality.

In reference to the structural marginality that results from social mobility, Riesman writes, "We should not be intimidated from seeking liberation by the fear of becoming marginal both to the groups we leave behind and the groups to which we aspire." As stated earlier, marginality is a fact of modern life; we are all marginal in some respect. There are many subtypes of marginality and dimensions of the marginal situation. It is how we define our marginal situations that will determine whether they will be experienced as zones of ecstacy or as zones of agony.

Although the inner-directed orientation of marginality is similar to the transcultural and self-interested orientation of assimilation discussed in chapter 4, inner-directed marginality, as such, is not the subject of this study. The purpose here is only to acknowledge its possibility and to point out its theoretical and existential relationship to other-directed marginality, which is similar to the orientation of the marginal social metaphysician. The remaining chapters are concerned not with the liberation that the marginal situation affords, but with the flight from liberation that the crisis of marginality represents—the crisis of self-esteem.

The Theoretical Utility of "Social Metaphysics"

The social metaphysician is certainly the other-directed type conceptualized by David Riesman. However, there are significant differences between Branden's conceptualization of the social metaphysician and Riesman's types of social character. As noted earlier, Riesman's other-directed type is the "product" of a society of other-direction, such as contemporary American society. He is of society and adjusted to it. His differentiation from others is only in terms of characterological marginality, an attitudinal and behavioral stance he assumes not in rebellion, rejection, or indifference but as a strategy for attaining status among his other-directed colleagues. He wants to be different, but not too different. Riesman draws a distinction between the other-directed type and the adjusted inner-directed type in that the former is adjusted to a society of other-direction while the latter is adjusted to a society of inner-direction. Branden's theory of social metaphysics would grant this distinction, but only as variants of social metaphysics. The fact that their character is derivative of their adjustment, albeit to different sociocultural orientations, defines the other-directed and the adjusted inner-directed types as social metaphysicians.

According to Riesman, those persons experiencing discrepancies between their character structure and the social structure are either autonomous inner-directed individuals who are capable of selective conformity and of transcending the other-direction of their society, or the anomic who are characterologically between inner-direction and other-direction, unable to adjust to either. Unlike the other-directed and the adjusted inner-directed, who are *of* society and *adjusted* to it, the autonomous inner-directed type is *in* society but not *of* it. The anomic type is *of* society but *maladjusted* to it.

Again, Branden's theory of social metaphysics would grant these distinctions, but based on premises that differ from Riesman's. Branden's social metaphysician of pseudo self-esteem and the individualist of authentic self-esteem are based on the premise that the character structure of all men is derivative of psychointellectual development. Riesman's types are based on the premise that character structure is derivative of social structure; his autonomous inner-directed type is an exception who comes close to being like Branden's man of authentic self-esteem but about whom Riesman confesses he knows little. In general, Riesman's types are differentiated along a spectrum of social adjustment and social integration; whereas Branden's are distinguished on a spectrum of psychointellectual independence and cognitive and evaluative integration.

In Riesman's conceptualization adjustment does not carry the evaluative connotation it does in Branden's theory. For Riesman, adjustment or conformity means "socio-psychological fit, not adequacy in any evaluative sense." And by adequacy, he means either "the culture's definitions of adequacy"—i.e., cultural norms—or, "those which (to a still culturally determined degree) slightly transcend the norm for the adjusted."[42]

Branden's view of adjustment is conceptualized not in terms of culturally defined adequacy, but within the context of man's nature as a rational being of volitional consciousness and in terms of the adequacy of rationality ("the acceptance of reason as one's only guide to knowledge, values and action").[43] His conceptualization proceeds on the premise that "man *needs* an integrated, objective code of moral values" that are "as indispensable to man's psychological survival [and therefore his character development] as it is to his existential survival [which includes his social interaction]"[44] and that "the psychological and existential results for his life [can be] devastating if he accepts a code of values that is inimical to his nature and needs."[45]

Branden's theory of self-esteem, in which social metaphysics is featured as a policy of thinking that is inimical to psychointellectual independence, recognizes man's need for social interaction. But it does not presuppose a human need to conform, even though conformity may be a cultural value and the psychointellectual policy of individuals and groups. It presupposes, instead, man's need of self-esteem.

As stated earlier, self-esteem is man's positive view of himself. He needs to know that life is worth living and that he is worthy of living it; that he is competent in using his mind to maintain his life; that he can live his life effectively; that he is capable of making the right choices and arriving at the right conclusions; that he can rely on his consciousness. Authentic self-esteem is the conviction that one is good—that he is right in his character—that he is good enough for a good life, the best life he is capable of creating and maintaining. It is the conviction that he is competent to rule his own mind and competent to deal with reality. It is the unshakeable conviction that he is worthy of happiness.[46]

The conditions and consequences of self-esteem are not dependent on norms defined by the culture, or even a person's own "particular successes and failures," as Branden points out, "since these are not necessarily in a man's direct, volitional control and/or not in his exclusive control."[47] To assign cultural norms—i.e., society's definition of adequacy—the primary role in the ongoing development of character, which is shaped by the state of his self-esteem, is to abnegate the very quality on which psychological and existential adequacy depends. In this sense, the theory of self-esteem does not consider the culture's normative definition of adjustment as an element of authentic self-esteem. However, culturally defined adequacy is a key element of the theory's conceptualization of pseudo self-esteem and the psychointellectual crisis to which it leads.

In Branden's theory of self-esteem, intellectual independence as a psychointellectual policy, is superior in ethical and psychological status to the policy of social metaphysics—superior, in that it meets the requirements of human nature. The theory defines other-direction as *irrational*—that is, contrary to man's nature qua man—and *unhealthy*—that is, inimical to man's self-esteem requiring self-sabotage by means of self-deception, evasion, repression, etc. It defines inner-direction as rational and consistent with the requirements of man's nature and the conditions of self-esteem. Thus, it would place the adjusted inner-directed type, along with the other-directed and the anomic, in the category of the social metaphysician. To be inner-directed simply because one's society is inner-directed is not the exercise of intellectual independence that is the basis of authentic self-esteem. To be inner-directed simply because others are is still a form of conformity.

Branden's theory is not anticonformity, as such, but it is an indictment against uncritical, dependent, parasitical, or manipulative conformity. Even if one lived in a society of inner-direction, he would have to reach the independent judgment that inner-direction is the proper and rational orientation toward himself and the world around him to be classed as autonomous. Falling short of that, whether as an adjusted inner-directed type, an adjusted other-directed type, or as an anomic, he would have to be classified as a social metaphysician. Only the autonomous inner-directed type would qualify as an individual of authentic self-esteem. The reason, however, according to Branden's theory of self-esteem, is not simply because he is capable of nonconformity and of transcending the norms of his society. The theory holds that *all* men are capable of such an orientation and behavior. The man of authentic self-esteem is one whose selective conformity and nonconformity are rationally self-regulated, based on his independent judgment, and carried out according to an integrated set of values and goals that serve his rational self-interest.

Discrepancy between a person's character structure and the social structure is not what defines a social metaphysician. Such discrepancy certainly exists for the inner-directed individual who lives in a society of other-direction. It is the assertion of his authentic self-esteem, not adjustment, that is the basis of his ability to function rationally in the face of the discrepancy. If, however, his self-esteem is tied to that discrepancy, he is to that extent a social metaphysician, and therefore other-directed. Social metaphysics is a cognitive and evaluative policy of other-direction that determines how one perceives, defines, and responds to reality. It is not external discrepancies that determine that policy, but the policy that defines the discrepancies.

This study is concerned not only with how men define their marginal situations and how they think and behave in light of their definitions. It is also concerned with whether their definitions are valid, whether their thinking is rational, and whether their action is good. It analyzes what race-conscious Negroes think, say, and do against a universal standard of values—that standard being man's nature as a being of volitional consciousness. It goes beyond the statement that they are other-directed to examine the psychointellectual policy that motivates their orientation and concludes that it is the policy of social metaphysics.

The Marginal Social Metaphysician

Keeping in mind the distinctions between authentic and pseudo self-esteem, the characteristics of the social metaphysician and the motivations underlying his pseudo self-esteem, a very general picture may be drawn of the type of social metaphysician focused on here: the marginal social metaphysician found among ethno-racial minorities.

By neglecting the content of their own consciousness and choosing the consciousness of others rather than objective reality as their frame of reference, most people are a mixture of the characteristics that describe the social metaphysician, albeit in varying degrees, for different reasons, and under varying circumstances. At any age or social level, in any occupation, from any nation or culture, an individual can suffer the lack of self-reliance and self-assertiveness that holds the social metaphysician in bondage.

The key concept that links social metaphysics and ethno-race consciousness is "others"—more precisely, *significant* others. This is strongly indicated in the review of prejudice and discrimination in chapter 3. While that review focused primarily on the response of the majority toward individuals or groups in ethnic or racial minorities, it indicated that prejudice and discrimination are not exclusive to the majority. Minorities are every bit as capable of responding with these attitudes and behavior toward the majority. In both cases antipathy toward each other is compounded by a view of their own group in terms of its ethnic and/or racial attributes. Both groups fear and resent the self-assertion of others and attempt to curve or influence that assertion by acts of prejudice and discrimination. The white segregationist may engage in racial discrimination in response to his fear that racial integration may bring about miscegenation; or he may fear the economic and political power minorities are able to achieve in an integrated community. The Negro separatist, on the other hand, may advocate programs of reverse racism in response to his fear that voluntary integration may lead to increased competition in which he feels inadequate to engage.

There is, however, a difference between the ethno-race consciousness of members in the majority and that of minorities. It lies in the *context* of their focus. Ethno-racial chauvinism (i.e., superiority) is expressed by the majority in its attempt to subvert the assertion of the minority, as in the doctrine of white supremacy. Minority ethno-racial chauvinism is operative in the case of black separatism or reverse racism where the minority attempts to subvert the assertion of the majority. On the other hand, the minority would like to dispel its sense of ethno-racial inadequacy (i.e., inferiority) either by gaining the approval of the majority or, if that fails, claiming itself superior in some area or declaring itself beyond the majority's comprehension. The majority may experience its inadequacy as a sense of ethno-racial guilt of which it would like to be absolved by gaining the approval of the minority or, if that fails, declaring that it is incapable of understanding the ways of minorities.

Any of the above attitudes may motivate the race-conscious social metaphysician of either group whose "others" consist of members of more or less favored ethno-racial groups and who desires authority over those in these groups and/or their approval. The social metaphysician of the dominant group generally does not want to join the minority subculture, however; whereas, the social metaphysician of the minority group fluctuates between his desire for membership in the dominant culture and his loyalty to his ethno-

99

racial subculture. This is the substantial difference between the two and which defines the minority social metaphysician as marginal. As stated earlier, he is marginal in that *he is straddling two cultures—his own ethno-racial subculture and the dominant culture—having one foot in each.* And he is a social metaphysician in that *he views either or both groups as objects of authority and relies on them for a perception of reality.*

The marginal social metaphysician is incompletely assimilated: either being *denied participation* as in the case of American Negroes and American Indians; or, *resisting participation* as do the Pennsylvania Amish and the Hutterites for religious reasons and some immigrant groups; or, at best, *selectively participating* the case of the French Cajuns of Louisiana.

Not all ethnic persons in a marginal situation are necessarily social metaphysicians; and not all social metaphysicians have marginal personalities. While he shares the personality conflicts of other social metaphysicians, the ethnic marginal who is also a social metaphysician perceives his dilemma as an *ethno-racial* conflict that transcends the "personality" conflicts experienced by the others. He differs from them in that his particular conflict is experienced within the context of his race consciousness: he is not just generally "other" conscious but, more specifically, *race* conscious. Compare him with, say, the social metaphysician whom Branden calls the "conformist." While the ethno-racial conformist may share the same motives as the committee-room conformist, the difference between them lies in the context of each individual's conformity. The motives of the former are rooted in his reliance on his own or another ethno-racial group for a perception of reality, and the motives of the latter are based on his reliance on a numerical majority opinion or consensus for a perception of reality.

The ethnic marginal social metaphysician experiences the external conflict between races and ethnic groups as a conflict within himself and is therefore a potential agent in perpetuating those social conflicts. His ethno-race consciousness alienates him not only from his sense of self, but from others as well. It constitutes a crisis situation in which he feels that he must choose among different ethno-racial allegiances; that he cannot fashion his own identity but must choose among sets of attitudes, values, and life-styles created by others.

The Social Metaphysics of Ethno-Race Consciousness

One journalist calls this crisis in American Jews the "crisis of freedom"—fear that by enjoying freedom and opportunity in the United States, the Jewish person will forget the traditions of his ethnic group and merge into the population; that the material benefits of living in a free society will undermine the spiritual traditions of his religious culture; that as he becomes an increasingly capable individual in a competitive society, he will become less capable of holding Judaism or "Jewishness" at the center of his identity. Jewish parents fear most the day when their offspring come to the realization that they cannot embrace every aspect of their Jewish heritage and be fully free individuals as well.

There would be no serious conflict if membership in both groups represented "pure appeal" without threat, or if membership in one group represented all threat and membership in the other only appeal. Indeed, there would be no conflict if group membership (of any kind) were not experienced as such a crucial psychointellectual vehicle by which the marginal social metaphysician views reality, to which he abdicates his judgment, and through which he seeks to express his tragic sense of life.

But like all social metaphysicians, group affiliation is the prerequisite to his identity. His conflict arises because he desires membership in two groups—his own ethno-racial group and the dominant culture—each group requiring (he believes) full membership or none at all. In this case, he cannot have both groups and he cannot give up either. But having participated in each he is able to look at himself from two standpoints: from that of the dominant culture as well as that of his own subculture. And, as Stonequist pointed out, "since these two standpoints are in conflict—the contempt and prejudice of the one conflicting with the self-respect and demand for loyalty of the other—the individual experiences this conflict." Consequently, he develops a dual personality, what Du Bois called a "double consciousness," based on an ambiguous self-identity and the ambivalence of divided loyalties. Du Bois pictured this conflict in the marginal Negro as follows:

> The Negro is a sort of seventh son, born with a veil, and gifted with second-sight in this American world—a world which yields him no true self-consciousness, but only lets him see himself through the revelation of the other world. It is a peculiar sensation, this double-consciousness,

this sense of always looking at one's self through the eyes of others, of measuring one's soul by the tape of a world which looks on in amused contempt and pity. One ever feels this two-ness—an American, a Negro; two souls, two thoughts, two unreconciled strivings; two warring ideals in one dark body, whose dogged strength alone keeps it from being torn asunder.[48]

Many Jews experience this "double consciousness," symbolized by their allegiance to the Stars and Stripes and devotion to the blue and white Star of David, Israel's flag; or, as with many Negroes—loyalty to the Negro subculture and respect for American institutions that are established and run by the white majority. Allen sees this in Bigger Thomas, the hero of Richard Wright's novel, *Native Son*, whom Allen calls "a neurotic personification of black oppression": "In him are seen the psychological results of lack of self-determination. He is caught between two worlds—denied the possibility of participating in the dominant culture, and unable to conceive of creating a viable and strong culture among his own people. His response takes the form of reactionary nationalism. He fears and hates whites, but he cannot reach out to blacks because of his own self-hatred."[49]

Because of his in-between situation, the marginal man may become an acute and able critic of the dominant culture, combining the knowledge and insight of an insider with the critical attitude of an outsider. Stonequist observed that if it is true that the origin of thinking is perplexity, confusion, or doubt, then the marginal man is likely to do more reflecting than the ordinary person. But what this position fails to include is that while the marginal man's "outside criticism" is often quite valid, it is not necessarily motivated by the perplexity that characterizes an assertive, consciousness-seeking understanding or the solution to a problem. In the case of the marginal social metaphysician his criticism is motivated by the perplexity of a frightened and desperate child. It is his way of rationalizing his fear of the independence and self-responsibility required to maneuver in the "outside world." What appears to be perceptive criticism is not a reflection of broader knowledge and sensitivity, which he surely may possess, but of intense self-alienation, profound loneliness, and suffocating uncertainty.

The other-directed marginal is at odds and disharmony with the members of the larger society because he and they are not sufficiently free of each other as "significant others." Each grants the other too large a role in his life. The very psychointellectual and physical independence of man requires that he face the facts of reality apart from the judgments, beliefs, opinions, and feelings of others. But it is not human independence other-directed people want to actualize; they want to be relieved of the responsibility of achieving an authentic identity. They do not want to be separate and independent; yet they cannot escape their need for self-esteem that is the result of this condition.

Assimilation becomes the other-directed marginal's escape route from his fear of independence and the means of sacrificing his identity to members of his own and other subcultures, or by the sacrifice of their identity to him. Of course, he fails and finds himself stalemated where others cannot grant him identity and refuse to give up their identity to him. He fails because his less demanding means of achieving self-esteem do not meet the requirements of self-esteem. He fails because what he desires is an impossibility. Self-esteem is not an end product of assimilation; but only men of authentic self-esteem are capable of achieving positive self-assertive assimilation. Thus, it is his lack of self-esteem that frustrates his desire for assimilation; and it is his lack of authenticity that freezes him into the marginal position of self-immolating assimilation. And there he remains—not an individual, but a "social product."[50]

The dilemma of the marginal social metaphysician is a phenomenon as old as the first time a caveman felt compelled to choose between his family and the family in the next cave as objects of psychointellectual authority. It is an oft-repeated story told in social histories and fiction varying in detail according to the particular experiences of individuals or a given group. Novelist James Baldwin has devoted most of his career to portraying various aspects of what is called "the black experience" in America. He views the Negro's dilemma of marginality as "the choice, either of 'acting just like a nigger,' or of *not* acting just like a nigger"—of being damned if he does and damned if he doesn't—knowing "how impossible it is to tell the difference."[51]

In a conversation with Margaret Mead, Baldwin spoke at length about his own personal experiences in America. Because one such experience so aptly typifies the self-esteem dilemma of the marginal social metaphysician, I will include it in its entirety as a capsule of how the social metaphysics of ethno-race consciousness is manifested in a member of an ethno-racial minority.

The Other Side of Racism

When I went south, I was a grown man. By this time—it's funny—I had a double reaction. . . . Essentially, I knew most white Americans were trapped in some stage of infantilism which wouldn't allow them to look at me as though I were a human being like themselves. I didn't expect them to. But I didn't expect what I found in the South, either. . . . I felt that I was walking on this rug, this wall-to-wall carpet. Beneath it is a complex system of wires, and one of those wires, if you step on it, will blow up the whole house.

And everybody in the South knows where that wire is except me. I've got to cross this rug, too. But I don't know how I'm going to get across it, because every step I take is loaded with danger. Every time I open my mouth I'm wrong. The way I look at people is wrong. The way I sound is wrong. I am obviously not only a stranger in town, I'm an enemy. I've arrived with a bomb, because I am a black from America *in* America.

I'm also endangering everybody else, which gives you another fear. Then you really get scared. When I worked with Medgar Evers for a little while, I would never dare open my mouth in front of other people around him. If he were working on a case or talking with white or black people, I wouldn't open my mouth because I had a Northern accent and I didn't know what that would trigger in the minds and hearts of the people he was talking to and what kind of danger it might place him in. He was already, God knows, in enough danger.

That's a grim, grim pathology. The situation forces you, the black cat in it, to become party to it, whether you like it or not. You cannot escape the pathology of a country in which you're born. You can resist it, you can react to it, you can do all kinds of things, but you're trapped in it. And your frame of reference is also the frame of reference of white people, no matter how you yourself try to deal with it. No matter what you tell your children, you're trapped: the despised darker brother in this great white man's house.[52]

Trapped—in the white man's frame of reference. *Feeling wrong*—as a person. *Afraid*—to be oneself for fear of rejection by others. *Contemptuous*—of having to be like them in order to survive. *Unloved*—by men he despises but whose approval he desperately desires. *Insecure*—in a malevolent universe where everyone knows the rules but him, where every step he takes "is loaded with danger."

Such is the dilemma of the race-conscious social metaphysician who is trapped between his and "their" definition of his self-identity as "the despised darker brother in this great white man's house."

1. Everett V. Stonequist, *The Marginal Man: A Study in Personality and Culture Conflict.* For a discussion of the analytical distinctions between cultural patterns of the national society and subcultural patterns of subsocieties, see Milton M. Gordon, *Human Nature, Class, and Ethnicity.*

2. Branden, *The Psychology of Self-Esteem*, pp. 161 ff.

104

3. In recent years scholars have become increasingly critical of that view of marginality put forth by Stonequist and his teacher, Robert E. Park (in *Race and Culture*), as a maladjustment phase of a one-way process of acculturation. In his work, *Black Culture and Black Consciousness*, Lawrence W. Levine establishes the pattern of simultaneous acculturation and revitalization of Negroes since slavery. He admits to the ambivalence that Negroes have experienced during acculturation, but is critical of the emphasis on that aspect of marginality presented here, which may be termed "pathological." There is a tendency, he writes, for "American scholarship to view almost any action of marginal groups—and particularly those of black people—as signs of pathological striving to conform to other people's standards, other people's images, other people's goals. In this area as in so many others, black Americans have been treated as passive subjects reacting in almost classic Pavlovian manner to external stimuli, rather than as people with a point of view and a cultural frame of reference who were able to respond with some degree of selectivity and intelligence to their environment." As will be shown presently, the position of this study is not in disagreement with Lawrence's criticism. It does not deny that marginality may be selective. The focus here is on the value-orientation of the spectrum of selectivity. It does not deny the distinctions between the national culture and the Negro subculture. It questions whether either culture should play the role of cognitive authority in the minds of its members.

4. Alan C. Kerckhoff and Thomas C. McCormick, "Marginal Status and Marginal Personality."

5. Gordon, *Human Nature, Class, and Ethnicity*, p. 280.

6. Aaron Antonovsky, "Toward a Refinement of the 'Marginal Man' Concept." See also David I. Golovensky, "The Marginal Man Concept: An Analysis and Critique."

7. Ibid.

8. David Riesman, *Individualism Reconsidered*, p. 159.

9. Ibid., 162–63.

10. Branden, *The Psychology of Self-Esteem*, pp. 105–8.

11. Ibid., p. 108.

12. Ibid., p. 110.

13. Ibid., p. 111.

14. Ibid., pp. 115, 120–21.

15. Ibid., p. 118.

16. Ibid., p. 120.

17. Ibid., p. 137.

18. Ibid., p. 172.

19. Ibid., p. 172.

20. Ibid., p. 167.

21. Riesman, *Individualism Reconsidered*, pp. 153–57.

22. Gordon, *Human Nature, Class, and Ethnicity*, pp. 279 ff. See also Charles H. Anderson, "The Intellectual Sub-Society Hypothesis: An Empirical Test," and "Marginality and the Academics."

23. Joseph Bensman and Arthur J. Vidich, *The New American Society: Revolution of the Middle Class.*

24. David Riesman, *The Lonely Crowd*. Riesman is careful to point out that by "character" he does not mean "personality," of which character is only a component. He distinguishes between personal character and social character as follows: "Character . . . is the more or less permanent socially and historically conditioned organization of an individual's drives and satisfactions—the kind of 'set' with which he approaches the world and people. 'Social character' is that part of 'character' which is shared among significant social groups and which, as most contemporary social scientists define it, is the product of the experiences of these groups."

This study disputes the sociological tenet that character is socially bestowed, and agrees with Nathaniel Branden that "A man's character is the sum of the principles and values that guide his actions in the face of moral choices." (*The Psychology of Self-Esteem*, p. 107). A person's character is a *self-creation*, even when it consists of values and attitudes shared by others. What Riesman calls social character, an attribute of classes, groups, regions, and nations, is more properly conceptualized as *Weltanschauung* or "sense of life," defined by Ayn Rand as "a generalized feeling about existence, an implicit *metaphysics*," which is expressed by a collectivity "in its 'life style'—in the kinds of actions and attitudes which people take for granted and believe to be self-evident, but which are produced by complex evaluations involving a fundamental view of man's nature." (Rand, *The Romantic Manifesto*, pp. 25–33, and "Don't Let It Go.")

25. Ibid., p. 15.

26. Ibid., p. 21.

27. Riesman, *Individualism Reconsidered*, p. 156.

28. Nathaniel Branden, "Counterfeit Individualism," in Rand, *The Virtue of Selfishness*, pp. 136–37.

29. Ibid., p. 136.

30. Riesman, *The Lonely Crowd*, pp. 241–42.

31. Ibid., p. 242. For expositions of the price paid for conformity, in terms of character and self-esteem, see Branden's *The Psychology of Self-Esteem*, *Breaking Free*, and *The Disowned Self*.

32. Riesman makes this observation and further notes in *Individualism Reconsidered*: "An autonomous person has no compulsive need to follow the other-direction of his culture and milieu—and no compulsive need to flout it, either." Yet, having grasped this much about the autonomous person, his basic premise of social determinism prevents him from going beyond the *fact* of autonomy amid other-direction to a full explanation of its existence. He writes: "We know almost nothing about the factors that make for such positive results; it is easier to understand the sick than to understand why some stay well." In *The Lonely Crowd* he states quite accurately that "Many will even deny that there are such people, people capable of transcending their culture at any time or in any respect."

An understanding of how the autonomous person is possible in a society of other-direction and how he functions requires a validation of the ethical, political, and psychological contexts of individualism—a validation which mainstream social science lacks. For consistent validations of autonomy and the individualism from which it is derived, see the works of Ayn Rand and Nathaniel Branden. For social psychological expositions of self-actualization, flawed by their subjective humanism but put forth on the premise that in order to understand psychological and social pathology we need to understand psychological and social health, see Abraham H. Maslow's *Motivation and Personality, Toward a Psychology of*

Being, The Psychology of Science, and *The Further Reaches of Human Nature*. Frank Goble presents a readable summary of Maslow's theories in *The Third Force: The Psychology of Abraham Maslow*.

33.   A helpful, but incomplete, discussion of innovative deviance is in Robert K. Merton, *Social Theory and Social Structure*, pp. 195 ff, 230 ff. Merton includes the *manipulator* as a type of innovative deviant, but that type does not figure in this exposition of inner-directed innovators. While the manipulator is classed as a deviant in sociological terms, in terms of the individualistic framework of this study, he is a conformist. More specifically he is an *other-directed innovator*, a variant of the social metaphysician under examination here.

34.   The distinction between the innovative outcast and the innovative emigrant is fine, but crucial, in that it reflects the different philosophical premises underlying each person's definition of his relation to society. For an excellent dramatization of defiant innovation and indifferent innovation, see Ayn Rand's characterizations of Henry Cameron and Howard Roark in *The Fountainhead*.

35.   Irwin D. Rinder, "Strangers in the Land: Social Relations in the Status Gap."

36.   Ibid.

37.   Ibid.

38.   Edna Bonacich, "A Theory of Middleman Minorities."

39.   A close scrutiny of the ideologies and tactics of the counterculture movement of the sixties in the United States shows that it was in fact more conformist than is generally recognized. See Ayn Rand, *The New Left: The Anti-Industrial Revolution*; Leonard Peikoff, "The 'Spirit of the Sixties' "; and Robert Nisbet, *The Quest for Community*.

40.   Norman L. Friedman, "Problems of the Runaway Jewish Intellectuals: Social Definition and Sociological Perspective."

41.   See Gordon, *Human Nature, Class, and Ethnicity*, for a discussion of the intellectual subsociety as a milieu of permanent marginality.

42.   Riesman, *The Lonely Crowd*, pp. 242–43.

43.   Branden, *The Psychology of Self-Esteem*, p. 219.

44.   Ibid., p. 212.

45.   Ibid., p. 151.

46.   Ibid., pp. 104 ff.

47.   Ibid., p. 118.

48.   W. E. B. Du Bois, *The Souls of Black Folk*, p. 3.

49.   Allen, *Reluctant Reformers*, p. 248.

50.   When I refer to the marginal social metaphysician as a "social product," I am not subscribing to the doctrine of social determinism, which holds that man is merely a passive reactor to pressures in his social environment. I mean quite the contrary—that the marginal social metaphysician chooses to be so determined; he is a *willed* social product, *self*-willed.

51.   Quoted in Charles E. Silberman, *Crisis in Black and White* (New York: Random House, 1964).

52.   James Baldwin and Margaret Mead, *A Rap On Race*, pp. 25–26.

Response to the Dilemma of Ethno-Race Consciousness

The double life every American Negro must live, as a Negro and as an American, with double thoughts, double duties, and double classes, must give rise to double words and double ideals, and tempt the mind to pretence or revolt, to hypocrisy or radicalism.—W. E. B. DuBois, *The Souls of Black Folk.*

As pointed out, the marginal social metaphysician's dilemma of ethno-race consciousness is of his own making; his failure to initiate self-assertive assimilation is due to his lack of an authentic self-esteem. The conflict between his ethno-racial group and the dominant group is a conflict he experiences personally and he believes that it is in his mind that a solution must be found. His aim is not to give up his reliance on the consciousness of others, but to relieve himself of the in-between situation of the "double consciousness" he is so overwhelmed by—i.e., to move from his position as a marginal personality whose "significant others" consist of two or more groups, to the position of the traditional social metaphysician whose "significant others" consist of a single authority group. But in the meantime, he must make some adjustment to his marginal situation; he must try to make his dilemma a little more bearable than it is; he must attempt to make his lack of self-esteem less devastating than it is and more attractive in the eyes of others.

In the United States the marginal social metaphysicians whose response to ethno-racial conflict we have heard the most about recently are American Negroes. Presenting their conflict as a transformation in politics and psychology, social analysts observe that as the political life of Negroes shifted from the civil rights-integration movement of the fifties and early sixties to the black nationalist movement of the late sixties and seventies, so was there a transformation in the self-identity of Negroes. It was a change in values, attitudes, and opinions of themselves and the society in which they live. This identity transformation is described as the movement from a negative view of themselves as "inadequate, inferior and incapable of self-determination, and unable to cope with the intricacies of life in a complex society" to a positive view of themselves as "adequate, self-reliant, assertive and self-determinative."[1] In other words, Negroes are being perceived as having moved from a position of pseudo self-esteem to one of authentic self-esteem.

Ostensibly such a transformation appears undeniably worthwhile and indicative of positive growth, but further examination reveals that it was not a transformation from collective lack of self-esteem to individual self-value, as the foregoing description indicates. Rather it was merely a shift from one form of collectivism to another—from one form of ethno-race consciousness to another. Some refer to this movement as a transition from being "Negro" to being "Black"—from being preoccupied with "whiteness" to accepting only those values and attitudes that can be called "black."[2] But as much of the rhetoric and analyses of the black-identity movement indicates, the transition from Negro ("whiteness") to Black ("blackness") was merely the substitution of one authority group for another. It was not self-reliance that was the goal, but *group* reliance; not self-assertiveness, but *group* assertiveness; not self-determination, but *group* determination; not personal adequacy, but *group* adequacy; not self-identity, but *group* identity; not self-value, but *group* value; not individual pride, but *group* pride; not self-awareness, but *group* consciousness.

Search for a Second-Hand Identity

For many people the question "Who am I?" is made problematic by a clash between the answers they arrive at, consciously or

110

subconsciously, to the questions "Who do I say I am?" and "Who do they say I am?" Race consciousness is but one of many adjustments to the conflict. The most salient of all the expressions of black social metaphysics has been the emphasis on black identity and black consciousness. It has interlaced all the various economic, political, professional, intellectual, and educational programs of the civil rights movement, and remains the one constant in all the shifts of ideology and tactics of the protest movement. This should not be surprising, however, since it underlies all the specific psychointellectual solutions to the self-esteem dilemma of race consciousness.

Led by the cultural nationalists, the aim of the black-identity movement is to provide a defense against counter definitions of the reality of the Negro subsociety and the identity of its members. The mere existence of a black-identity movement is indicative of the lack of homogeneity on the meaning of black identification—that is, there is not yet a taken-for-granted definition for the majority of Negroes. For one thing, it is an all-encompassing world view that only a few intellectuals are aware of and understand. Secondly, different segments of the Negro community place different emphasis on its elements. Thirdly, various expressions of these different perspectives are modified to varying degrees by concurrent responses to social locations in the larger American society. Thus, in order to understand what black identification means as a significant factor in the black social metaphysician's definition of his situation, it is necessary to distinguish between the *ideology* of black identity and the *commonsense* orientations toward black identity; and these realms of meaning should be compared against the broader frame of reference entailed in the sense of life of the Negro subsociety.

Cultural Nationalism: Ideology of Black Identification. In its broadest sense cultural nationalism is a philosophy of counteridentity whose basic premises are as follows:

1. That of all the factors determining one's life chances, the most critical is the person's *race*; that one's place in society is determined by his *color*; that he is not being responded to as a person but in terms of the respondent's perception of his racial identification.

2. That the social forces that have determined the self-concept of Negroes have been and are detrimental to the self-esteem and sociocultural progress of Negroes.

3. That it was not just enslavement and segregation that determined the racial identification of Negroes but the *interpretation* of those situations by contemporaries, and by those who have since transmitted the cultural elements of Negro life to succeeding generations—folklorists, historians, writers and poets, musicians, sociologists, intellectual critics, and race leaders.

4. That the self-identity of individual Negroes must be determined by their group identification, which must be shaped primarily by the Negro subsociety and the forces at work in its relation to the dominant culture.

5. That in order to reverse the pathological self-concept of Negroes, those forces which have shaped it must be redefined and those which continue to do so must be overturned and new meaning constructed to revitalize an impaired self-concept.

6. That the sociopolitical revitalization of Negro identification is necessary in order to achieve uniformity between internal values and beliefs and external culture and institutions.

7. That ethical significance is to be found in the identification with race, or class, or group; that of these, identification with race must supersede identification with class; that the morality of ascribed status must be given primacy over the morality of achieved status.

8. That racial identification enhances the assertion of a "black" value system and insures Negroes against further contamination by the "white" middle-class Protestant American value system.

9. That the assertion of black identification and the value system it signifies must be supported by sociopolitical and economic structures that guarantee their power to shape the Negro community and influence the national community.

10. That the liberal-democratic ideal that individual rights without reference to group (racial) identification cannot be applied in the area of race relations; that since neither the law nor white Americans have treated Negroes as individuals, the only proper means of attaining the right to be treated as an individual without reference to racial

identification is to raise the status of the group by extending preferential treatment to close the historical gap in status between Negroes and whites.[3]

The problem of identity, as black-identity proponents view it, is stated by James A. Banks as follows:

A person in our society validates his identity through the evaluations of "significant others." However, the average black American has never been able to establish social or self-identity that is comparable in terms of social valuation to that of the white majority. The ideal self in America has been made synonymous with Caucasians, and particularly middle-class whites. In his quest for identity, the black man has begun to ask "Who am I in relation to other races and ethnic groups?" . . .

Since whites are the dominant and "significant others" in American society, and black children derive their conceptions of themselves largely from white society and its institutions, we are not going to progress significantly in augmenting the black child's self-concept until we either change the racial attitudes and perceptions of white Americans or create new "significant others" for black children.[4]

In order to release black children and adults from the "psychological captivity" of self-doubt and self-rejection, cultural nationalists offer a redefinition of black identification from which, in their view, self-identity is derived and on which it depends for validation and affirmation. They aim to create a "new" Negro, who will not be Negro at all, but *black*.

To call oneself "Negro" is, according to the cultural nationalists, to see oneself in the image of white America, which is, to them, the self-concept of Negro integrationists. According to Lincoln, their choice of "black" to describe Negro Americans is "deliberately chosen as a symbol of racial polarization. It intends to imply the solidarity of the black masses, here and abroad, to disavow any necessary commitment to white values or deference to the white establishment; to distinguish the masses from the integrationists; and to exploit new feelings of black nationalism and negritude that have taken hold in the Negro community since World War II. It answers, at least for the time being, all the important questions of identity and color."[5]

But, Lincoln asserts, this symbolization of black identity and its legitimation through cultural nationalism does not answer the fundamental question of "whether color alone is a unifying force sufficient to weld together in a monolithic (or, better, monochromatic) sociopolitical movement a black minority exhibiting immense spectrum of needs, wants, desires, and intentions based on conflicting systems of values. The question of identity has not been resolved. Color alone does not answer satisfactorily the questions about the self one needs to have answered as the basis for intelligent decision-making about oneself and others. Negroes in America still do not know who they are."[6]

Lincoln's reaction to the symbolization of black identity was written in 1967. Since then the cultural nationalists have presented definitions of black identification that are somewhat more sophisticated than the proposition that identity equals color. For them identity also equals consciousness. Hence, the *quality* of black identification from which black identity is derived is usually referred to as "black consciousness." Drawing from the criteria for the class-conscious definition of the class situation, Hraba and Siegman identify the criteria for black consciousness as

—a belief in racial barriers
—a belief in external controls
—the belief in racial deprivation
—a belief in racial discontent
—a belief in black interest collectivity
—belief in racial antagonism[7]

These are criteria for the individual's definition of the racial situation that the Negro community in general faces. In addition to those is the definition of one's own racial situation which the authors call "self-placement into black consciousness." It includes "self-placement" in all of the criteria above.

The beliefs constituting black consciousness emerge "cumulatively through a sequence, beginning with beliefs about racial conditions and culminating in a commitment to collective action." Socialization into black consciousness may be empirically determined by social and symbolic participation in the black movement, with reference to its ideological interpretations of racial conditions, such as discrimination in employment, housing, and so on, or by vicarious experience.

The ideology of black identity rejects the assumption that all cultural value and meaning must flow from the dominant culture. Yet, it incorporates the assumptions that whites serve as significant others for blacks and that whites have the power to define and label

114

psychological reality for blacks. But it incorporates these assumptions only to challenge them with the counterassumption that black culture is unique, with unique patterns of symbolic meaning and value, and that therefore Negroes do not derive their self-conceptions solely from the dominant culture; and that the reference groups from which Negroes derive their significant others are found in their subcultural milieu rather than the dominant culture. Since this is the case, say cultural nationalists, black consciousness must be the manifestation of the internalization of these counter definitions of black life and personality. Not only must blacks undergo re-socialization regarding the source of their identification, but theories about their identification must be transformed as well. Carmichael and Hamilton write:

> Black people must redefine themselves, and only *they* can do that. Throughout this country, vast segments of black communities are beginning to recognize the need to assert their own definitions, to reclaim their history, their culture; to create their own sense of community and togetherness. . . . When we begin to define our own image, the stereotypes—that is, lies—that our oppressor has developed will begin in the white community and end there. The black community will have a positive image of itself that *it* has created.[8]

It is both the ideological assumption of cultural nationalism and the commonsense assumption that as Negroes move up the social ladder they also move away from the structural location of their racial identification and the traditional (lower status) carriers of that identification, and are prone to deny their racial identification. The ideological position of black consciousness is that blacks who do not identify themselves in racial terms have lower levels of self-esteem, and prestige should be withheld from them. Thus, the ideological and commonsense orientations toward black consciousness hold that "when a black person incorporates the words *Negro* or *Colored* into his self-image, he is also internalizing the negative connotations associated with them. [That is], when a black person says 'I am colored,' or 'I am Negro,' he is also saying 'I am as white people see me.'"[9]

Black consciousness is more than the collective definition of the racial situation, and assumptions and judgments about racial self-image, however. It is a style of mind and "Black is Beautiful" is its article of faith. It is a cognitive and psychological escape from what W. E. B. DuBois called a "double-consciousness . . . [a] sense of

115

always looking at one's self through the eyes of others, of measuring one's soul by the tape of a world that looks on in amused contempt and pity."[10]

The heightened awareness of racial self-image that "black consciousness" entails is to be achieved by rejecting the old identity, including the term "Negro"; teaching and practicing African customs (including adopting African names and dress, and studying an African language); celebrating the distinctiveness of Negroes as it is manifested in cultural forms such as soul food, soul music, a black value system, black literature, black theater, Afro-American studies, and various patterns in the Negro subsociety that distinguish Negroes from othes; the exclusion of white participation from organizations and (in some cases) refusal of white financial support; and discouraging the honoring of blacks who have achieved success in mainstream American society. "Black Power," the ideology of political and economic nationalism, provides the philosophy and programs for the legitimation of black identification and black consciousness.

Commonsense Orientations of Black Identity. Political nationalists and cultural nationalists have insisted that the ideology they profess is widespread among the nation's Negroes. Historian Lerone Bennett has written that "in 1966 and 1967 a tidal wave of black consciousness swept over the black community." To know the definitions of intellectuals is not necessarily to know what definitions inform the attitudes and behavior of the masses. With this in mind, Neil Friedman set out in 1967, 1968, and 1969 to find out "whether the emergence of black consciousness has affected the sense of cultural identification and personal identity of Americans of African descent, the so-called Negroes."[11] Friedman conducted interviews with two groups of high school seniors and their mothers or female guardians, one group of college students and one group of adult males.[12] He found that "for each group, 'Negro' is the most preferred name. . . . only between 2 to 5 percent of the people in the five samples object to being called 'Negro.' " (This excludes the male adults.)

Why the rejection of the term "Black" when black consciousness was supposedly sweeping the Negro community? Friedman suggests that there is a difference between *experienced* connotations and *taught* connotations of "Black" and "Negro." He writes: "People are being taught the slave connotations of the name *Negro*. Many have

116

experienced the ugly connotations that *Black* has had in their community. . . . our data indicate that the mass media . . . notwithstanding, the facts are that as of February 1969 there were a lot of Negroes in the South and precious few black people."[13]

Friedman's findings are substantiated by the 1969 *Newsweek* Poll which found that while many Negroes believed in "soul," an aspect of the orientation toward black consciousness, they did not want to give up the name they had called themselves since the Civil War. "The word black was a painfully acquired taste, and only a minority, by the end of the 1960s, had acquired it." writes Goldman. "The overall returns show, not surprisingly, that 'Negro' was still the most liked and the least disliked name of all, and that more people rejected 'black' than accepted it."[14]

If most Negroes preferred to think of themselves as "Negro" or "Colored," how was it that the term "Black" became the prevailing concept of identification in the 1970s? Even though the *Newsweek* Poll substantiated Friedman's conclusion that the *orientation* toward black identification ("Negro") was considerably different from the *ideology* of black identification ("Black"), Goldman writes that it also showed that " 'Negro' was no longer a majority choice." Two factors were at work. First, "there remained a substantial dissent among the most conservative elements—the oldest and poorest blacks, particularly in the South—to whom 'Negro' had always been too close to 'nigger' and who felt more comfortable thinking of themselves as colored." Second, " 'Negro' was under challenge by the most militant elements as well—the young and the middle class in the Northern ghettos. 'Black' topped their list, and their choice carried weight beyond their numbers because they were so well placed to influence the vocabulary of race. The young and the middle class together provide much of the leadership and most of the activism in the ghetto; their people are regularly on television and in print; and by the end of the 1960s practically all of them, from the Urban League to the Panthers, were using 'black.' "[15]

In February and March 1972 *Ebony* magazine commissioned a study of the extent of black identification among its readers as compared with that in the Negro community as a whole. The study, which revealed little difference between *Ebony* readers and the national Negro community, showed that Negroes did not consider themselves "just Americans." Instead, the emphasis was equally on the term "Black" and a pride in being black: 62 percent considered

themselves equally Black and American; 24 percent considered
themselves first a Black and then an American; 12 percent thought
of themselves as first an American and then a Black; 2 percent were
not sure of their identification. As these figures show singular
emphasis was placed on black identification.[16]

What of the correlation of racial identification with self-esteem
that cultural nationalism assumes? Are commonsense orientations
commensurate with the ideological assumption that people who
identify themselves as "Negro" or "Colored" have internalized white
conceptions and definitions of black people? Was the fact that the
lower-status old and poor people in the South preferred to call
themselves "Colored" an indication of lower levels of self-esteem?
Does the emphasis on black identification in the *Ebony* poll indicate
a heightened self-esteem?

Cummings and Carrere found that "a low level of self-esteem does
not seem to be associated with whether or not a black person
identifies himself in racial terms. . . . Analysis of the measures of
self-esteem between the two groups, across three occupational
categories [white collar, skilled blue collar, and semi-skilled and
unskilled blue collar] showed that levels of self-esteem did not
significantly differ between occupational groups. . . . Thus, the
relationship between level of social status, racial self-image and
general level of self-esteem does not seem to be as clear as the
traditional literature suggest."[17]

The authors are not satisfied with their findings, however, and
suggest that "we may have designed a weak test of the idea that low
self-esteem is brought about through the internalization of the white
definitions ["Negro" or "Colored"] of blacks." It is possible, they
admit, that by creating two dichotomous groups (of blacks who do
and do not identify themselves in racial terms), they may have
glossed over some of the finer distinctions of degrees of internalization. Further, they take a position similar to Friedman's that "defining oneself as *Colored* or *Negro* may be a long way from the reality
of the process in which black people observe and subsequently
internalize the wide array of negative gestural and behavioral cues
transmitted to them by whites." It is possible also that black people
do not have the same "subjective meaning structure" associated with
Colored and *Negro* that white people have. "There may be a world
of difference between a white person saying 'he is colored,' or 'he is a

118

Negro,' and a black person saying 'I am colored,' or 'I am a Negro.'"

It is possible, they write, that as a white person does not internalize the negative meaning that blacks give to the term *white*, and therefore does not suffer an impaired self-esteem (because "black people are simply not part of his range of significant others"), so too is it likely that blacks who identify themselves as *Negro* or *Colored* do not suffer a consequent loss of self-esteem because whites are not in their range of significant others and thus their negative definitions are not internalized. "White people may or may not be significant determinants of variations in self esteem of blacks." And even when it is allowed that there are persons whose pathological responses are so determined, what remains unexplained, say Cummings and Carrere, is "the apparent fact that most blacks have developed social and psychological techniques to cope with these forces. What is not at all accounted for are the apparent facts of widespread tough-mindedness and resilience among blacks in this hostile white world rather than a widespread pattern of psychological instability."[18]

The discrepancies between theoretical/ideological assumptions about Negro identification and commonsense orientations are evident in other respects. Friedman found that while the majority of the students in his sample preferred the name "Negro," they also approved of the Afro hair style. The fact that they did may be interpreted as the main symbolic expression of black pride. But Friedman thinks their response to questions ("Do you approve of Negro women wearing wigs?" "Why do you approve/disapprove of the Afro?") call for a different interpretation. "Almost as many Tuskegee students approve of wigs as approve of Afros. It may be that an 'everybody do his thing' attitude prevails rather than an ideological 'come back to black' attitude."[19]

When asked why they approved of the Afro, the Tuskegee students mentioned *style* 30 percent of the time and *race pride* 44 percent. In the Birmingham sample of high school seniors *style* was mentioned 46 percent and *race pride* 24 percent. Of these figures, Friedman writes: "Our results indicate that the discovery of a new hairdo that 'looks good' . . . may be the propelling force behind the newest fad without any necessarily conscious mental tie-up under some of those Afros between the style and the ideology."[20] *Newsweek* found that while half the nation's blacks and three-fourths of the ghetto young approved of Afros, over half did not like the Afro-style clothes, indicating that "looking black" was as much a choice of style and personal preference as it was a declaration that "Black is beautiful."

Friedman asked other questions of his subjects regarding the acknowledgement of African ancestry and skin color preference and found that many reasons besides that of black consciousness can enter into responses. "Not every Dashiki-clad, Afro-topped student of Swahili is a Mau-Mau, Black Panther or even radical," he writes. "That is, items concerning names, hair, Africa, and skin color preferences are not, in the traditional sense of the word, political items. They do not in and of themselves tell us how the black pride and sense of identity will manifest itself or even whether it will."[21]

Identification is, as Friedman points out, multifaceted and multisituated. Thus, it is possible for a Negro who considers himself first an American and then a Black to prefer the Afro hair style and his preference could be a response to peer pressure rather than a statement of ideological commitment.

Between "Soul" and American Kinship

The discrepancies between the ideology of cultural nationalism and the commonsense orientations toward black identification reflect the class, power, regional, and generational divisions of the Negro community and the differential status situations in which these groups have been socialized to respond to the overall low status of the race. They are a long way from amounting to a *Weltanschauung* that transcends these differences and unites the Negro community. Yet there is a shared sense of life that threads through the Negro community, not uniting it but acting as a surrogate for solidarity and making possible a common frame of reference to which all in the subculture can relate. It consists of what Philip Mason calls widely based strands of "expectant emotion"— *impatience* to change the Negro's status now; *resentment* at oppression, at indifference, at patronage; and "the search for identity, a cultural pedigree."[22] It is the very"two-ness," or "double-consciousness" and ambivalence from which cultural nationalism proposes to escape by means of black consciousness. Finally, it is the "tough, hardy, invincible belief that the American dream was meant to include them, too," that *Newsweek* found prevalent in 1969, accompanied by what Lerone Bennett calls the "metaphorical myth of *Soul*"—the belief that most Negroes have a special spirit that most white people have not experienced—and the anxiety that the price of the American dream is the very "soul" on which they base their claims.

The Myth of Soul. According to the 1969 *Newsweek* Poll, cultural nationalism was most of all a phenomenon of the young and the middle class, but the element of black identification called "Soul" reached Negroes everywhere. "They agreed by two and a half to one that black people in fact partake of some special grace called soul," writes Goldman.[23] It was a clear rejection of the assumption voiced by Kenneth Stampp that "Negroes are, afterall, only white men with black skins, nothing more, nothing less."

What is Soul? Lerone Bennett writes that it is

the American counterpart of the African *Negritude*, a distinct quality of Negro-ness growing out of the Negro's experience and not his genes. *Soul* is a metaphorical evocation of Negro being as expressed in the Negro tradition. It is the feeling with which an artist invests his creation, the style with which a man lives his life. It is, above all, of the spirit rather than the letter: a certain way of feeling, a certain way of expressing oneself, a certain way of being. To paraphrase Sartre, *Soul* is the Negro's antithesis (black) to America's thesis (white), a confrontation of spirits that could and should lead to a higher synthesis of the two.[24]

Soul is an "implicit metaphysics" based on an ensemble of contradictions: "a relaxed and noncompetitive approach to being, a complex acceptance of the contradictions of life, a buoyant sadness, a passionate spontaneity, and a gay sorrow."[25] There is little that is "new" about Soul; it has existed since slavery, being, as it is, an American phenomenon. What is new are its contemporary manifestations and its legitimating function. It is not counteridentity per se, but counter*style*, a style of greater permanence than Afros and Afro-style clothes, or even "black power" for that matter. As Bennett points out, Soul is not genetic; it is rather a traditional style of life and personality that is learned and internalized to such an extent that it is taken-for-granted, as self-evident, as axiomatic.

It is a cluster of symbolizations, typifications, stereotypes, and generalizations that, as Goldman writes, defy codification. Some Negroes have it; others don't. Yet all Negroes can identify it in themselves or the lack of it in others. Below are attempts by *Newsweek* respondents to explain what it is:

It's the bringing up of the two races—there was more warmth and love in our people because they had nothing else to give their children. . . .

121

The Other Side of Racism

It's something inside of you that keeps you going even though you know you're being mistreated and taken advantage of. . . . We are a more compassionate people. . . . The white people can do the Watusi but we are the Watusi. . . . It's the ability to laugh in the face of adversity that would drive the average white to suicide. . . . I think it's more a happy and contented feeling—I've always gotten joy from being black for a reason I can't explain. . . . They don't have the gift of religion that we have, try with all their might. . . . It's a feeling of black nationalism—a kind of common destiny for survival. . . . You meet other Negroes and speak to them, you don't have to know them—there's just a kind of understanding. . . . Whites have had no problems, therefore no soul— no sincere feeling for anything at all. . . . Our belief in God is different—I think they believe God is white. . . . We have heart, whites just don't have it. . . . They can't stand the cold, we can stand the heat. . . . Sure 'nough—swinging and being happy. . . . They try to copy the Negro people—they see us dance and they wish they could do it too. . . . We like spirituals and jazz, they like way-out things we can't understand. . . . We got more rhythm—they don't move like us. . . . We're happy with the least or less. . . . It's more experience in life—the average Negro lives more in five years than the whites do in ten. . . . I wonder how the white man would survive if he were to be told all his life that he isn't as good as the black man or made to feel he isn't human. . . . It's from being down so long. . . . It's like you get to feeling the spirit. . . . It's so sweet. . . .

I can't describe it, man. You just have to be black. . . .

Soul is the colored person. . . .

Soul is you. Yourself.[26]

It must be emphasized that Soul is not the same as "black consciousness"; it is neither ideological black consciousness nor the commonsense orientation toward black consciousness. Soul is a sense of life—a *style of life*—of the Negro subculture; black consciousness is a *style of mind*—an expression of Soul that is by no means unanimous. Soul, with its traditional dialectic between "We" and "They," between "Us" and "Them," has persisted across the generations; black consciousness must be revitalized.

Estranged American Kinship. Just as thoroughly engrained as Soul in the *Weltanschauung* of black identification is a belief in The System modified by the old suspicion that The Man cannot be trusted; the hope that *"We'll achieve brotherhood someday,"* and the realization that *"We need each other,"* tempered by the alienating fact that *"You're not really a part of America. You're not really hooked into the real world"*; the frustration and bitterness over the fact that *"We tried to live with the white man for four hundred years. We didn't reject him—he rejected us,"* and the feeling that *"If these people would just get away from me and leave me alone, I wouldn't have most of the problems I do now."*[27]

As already indicated, the 1972 *Ebony* study of black identification in the Negro community showed that 62 percent considered themselves equally black and American. But, as the above comments indicate, being an American is not easy when one's need of belonging is continually frustrated. Yet belief in the American system persists. The *Ebony* study showed that 53 percent of its readers had faith in the American system, believed in its ability to solve its problems, saw integration as desirable, and were opposed to violence. Another 47 percent were troubled and helpless, more tolerant of violence and separatism, but did not really know what steps could be taken to resolve the serious problems in the American system. In the latter group 7 percent classified themselves as radicals who were almost totally dissatisfied with the American system, and saw violence and/or separatism as the means for resolving the problems that exist.[28]

Ebony's findings are similar to those in the 1969 *Newsweek* Poll. It found a "disquietingly large minority" or "spiritual dropouts" who approved of the idea of a separate black nation. (From 4 percent in 1963 and 1966 to 12 percent in 1969 who thought there *would* be a separate black nation and 21 percent who thought there *should* be.)[29] Yet, the overwhelming majority still wanted integration, "across the board . . . more deeply and urgently than ever." Two-thirds were against establishing a separate state. Gary Marx found similar results in his 1964 study of Negro attitudes. "Most respondents regarded a Negro nation not only as politically unfeasible, but as undesirable. Those questioned thought of themselves as Americans whose relatives had worked and died fighting for and building this country. Some were angered by the question and attributed it to white racists, apparently being unaware that a Negro group favored it as well."[30]

Since, except in the case of philosophically grounded pacifism, a refusal to fight for one's country is one of the indications of rejection and alienation from society, the *Newsweek* and Marx surveys measured the depth of estrangement by asking respondents if they felt America was worth fighting for. *Newsweek* found that in 1963 81 percent said the nation was worth fighting for; in 1964, Marx found that 89 percent responded affirmatively; in 1966 *Newsweek* showed 87 percent willing to fight; in 1969 the percentage decreased to 79 percent. Marx found that "subjects differed markedly in the intensity of their response and many qualified their answers. But it seemed that, for the majority of these respondents, the question of refusing to fight, if called upon, had never entered their minds."[31] This was far from the case in 1969, when the percentage of Negroes fighting in Vietnam and of those dead were roughly equivalent to their proportion of the population. In 1966, when the war was young, Negroes supported it; but in 1969, even though a majority felt the nation was worth fighting for, a 56-to-31 majority opposed the war because they had less freedom in this country.[32] Such a qualification as "*Not under a second-class citizenship. Hell no!*" cannot be ignored, but neither can such invincible patriotism as "*Yes, I would fight. This is home.*"

This is home, and the will to transform it into an integrated society runs deep. Writes Goldman: "Black people have been held apart all their lives, and the reasons are quite brutally plain to them; still they cling tenaciously to the belief that it has been a case of mistaken identity, that the white man would like them if only he would let them come close enough for him to see them. So they want integration as a proof of their common humanity; they want it so their children will grow up free of its crippling weight; they want it because it is right."[33]

Cultural nationalism was in part a response to white resistance to integration. Negroes responded strongly to the antiwhite sentiments of black power, but by 72 to 16 they rejected the proposition against working with whites at all and going it alone. "Ordinary blacks are not yet persuaded that integration has failed or that Whitey is beyond reach of reason or compassion," writes Goldman. Even though Black Power contended that there was no real choice between community control and integration, Negroes chose integration by six to one.

"*We just want to rule our own destiny,*" said one respondent to the *Newsweek* Poll. And they want to do so within the context of the system and values of the national community, as blacks and as Americans, not as Afro-Americans which in fact they have not been since the nineteenth century.

Talcott Parsons writes that even though it is no longer the case that a societal community is by definition an ethnic entity, "it is extremely important that any societal community, so far as it has the central property of solidarity, . . . is of the same generic sociological character is as the ethnic group. This is to say that it is a diffusely defined collectivity which has the property of solidarity and is a major point of reference for defining the identity of its members. To be identified as an American is not to have one's ethnic status identified, but it is very definitely a primary aspect of the 'identity' of any given individual so designated."[34]

Parsons's insight is confirmed by the *Ebony* survey cited above. One-third of the respondents placed differential emphasis on being American and being black, but what is significant is that none of those who knew their identity rejected their "American kinship."[35] And that in itself is verification of the property of solidarity of the American societal community. The survey results show singular emphasis on black identification, but they do not show ethnic identification to the exclusion of American identification.

The enduring *Weltanschauung* of the Negro community is itself a component of the transgenerational tradition of the national culture. The elements of transgenerational tradition—common language, shared history, shared fate—are acknowledged when one identifies himself as American, whether first or second to ethnic identification. This is acknowledged by angry black intellectuals like Lerone Bennett who, while declaring that "white people and Negroes do not belong to the same community," is also darkly proud of the fact that "the Negro shares the same basic culture as all other Americans and he is moulded, more or less, by the same forces. . . . The Negro—and this is the key point—is a product, an elaboration of American society. His basic culture, his basic responses are American and Western."[36]

It works both ways: as the Negro is American, so too is America Negroid: "Every American bears on his body or, deeper, his soul, the mark of fire of the Negro."[37]

As the cited studies of commonsense attitudes in the Negro community indicate, ethnic revitalization among Negroes was not a movement of the masses, by the masses, or for the masses. It was a middle-class movement; its leaders, definers, and legitimators were organization leaders, professionals, intellectuals, and students. It was primarily urban and northern, but it was managed, not in the ghettos, but on television, on the stage, on university campuses, at caucus sessions of professional meetings, at cocktail parties, and at publishing houses. In other words, it involved the most acculturated of the Negro community. Why did they respond as they did? Why the retreat to racial solidarity, and why this particular form of such a retreat?

As many studies of ethnic revitalization point out, relative deprivation was a powerful factor in the radicalization of the middle-class. The desire by the middle-class to eliminate the tensions of class-status inconsistency explains the embrace of "blackness" as a channel of communication with the masses that would diminish class-linked disunity; it also explains the middle-class use of ethnic identity as the basis for claims against the welfare state. Another explanation, offered by Richard Hamilton, is simply that these persons had the time to engage in this particular movement while the rest of the community was striving to survive. Hamilton writes that as the bases for strategies of radical white politics, considerations of "guilt" and "identity," were "special 'luxury' concerns which, in a sense, can be 'afforded' only by the relatively affluent and by relative leisured populations." Even in the case of ethnic or religious minorities, who are more likely to be concerned with "identity," such concern "is likely to appear only among that tiny segment of the minorities who have much free time for contemplation. It is the 'double vision' of the minority intelligentsia that, in part, gives rise to their distance from the dominant tendencies in the society, to their ambivalence, and to their identity problems. Having the luxury of considerable leisure, or, at minimum, having no demanding full time occupational commitments (which, by forcing choices, would end the ambivalent relationship), these persons are 'free' to think about their 'identity problems,' to read books about them, to write about them, to develop a language to handle those questions, and so forth."[38]

"Guilt" and "identity" were not the only interests that the black-conscious middle class shared with New Left ideology. At its height cultural nationalism was as vehemently anti-America (which included being antiwhite) as New Left radicalism. The animus that Negro intellectuals and youth had for assimilation-oriented middle-class Negroes (in many cases, their parents) was as intense as that which white student radicals had for their "work ethic"–oriented elders. Both condemned the universal standards of mobility in the American system of open competition. Both wanted to pull the reins on modernization and retreat into medievalism.

126

Response to the Dilemma of Ethno-Race Consciousness

While there is ample evidence that Negroes have been experiencing a change in self-concept in response to the demands of increased freedom, the change for many has not been progressive in nature, but regressive. What we witnessed in the late sixties and seventies was not a shift in sociocultural and political values, as such, but a different expression of the same values that were just as prevalent before and during the civil rights-integration movement. Their problems were the same then as they had been twenty years before. Those problems, which remain today, have to do with the manner in which they perceive reality, how they come to the conclusions they reach, and what motivates them to seek the solutions they seek. In a sense their dilemma is like that of the slaves who chose to remain on the plantation upon being told they were free to go: while they had been granted physical freedom, they did not have the political freedom needed to take advantage of it. While contemporary Negroes have been granted political freedom, many do not have the psychointellectual freedom necessary to take advantage of it. In fact, a comparison of the protest literature and speeches of Negro abolitionists and leaders of the freedmen with that of Negro spokesmen and activists of the past twenty years shows that those who had less freedom understood it better than those who now have more freedom.

Much of the cultural, political, and economic activity among Negroes is not an expression of increased freedom, but an expression of the conflict between their lack of internal freedom and the increased external sociopolitical freedom. Theirs is not an embrace of freedom, but a desperate flight *from* freedom. Their solution is not to achieve authentic self-identity, but to rationalize their choice of the less demanding alternative of "racial identity" and pass it off as a "positive transformation."

During the height of the boycotts and sit-in demonstrations in the South in 1962, Martin Luther King presented to President Kennedy a document prepared by the Southern Christian Leadership Conference (SCLC) that appealed "for national rededication to the principles of the Emancipation Proclamation and for an executive order prohibiting segregation." The concluding paragraphs of the document emphasized the organization's commitment to non-violence and called for the fulfillment of "the hopes and dreams

127

arising from the abolition of slavery." Portions of those paragraphs follow:

> We are confident that our peaceful resistance to unlawfully imposed segregation and discrimination will awaken the conscience and morality of those who, in ignorance and without love and respect for the dignity of man, seek to impose second-class citizenship upon us.

> We believe we need not and should not struggle unaided. Our efforts to achieve human decency and human rights by eliminating the unlawful restrictions upon the exercise of our civil and constitutional rights seek to uplift and enrich our entire country.

> . . . We appeal to you because we yearn for the time when we can stand in the full sunlight of human decency and join hands with our white brethren, north and south, east and west, and sing in joyous hallelujah.[39]

This appeal, which links the achievement of human dignity with the achievement of civil rights, represents the spirit of the civil rights movement up to 1964. It is not in itself a statement that can be attributed to social metaphysics. There is certainly no evidence in it of race-conscious motives on the part of those who drafted and supported it. The ideas a person has are no certain indication of his psychological state. There are marginal men who hold every kind of political philosophy, and some of the most ardent advocates of genuine human rights are men who feel pulled this-way-and-that by the authority they give to the dominant culture and their own subculture over their self-esteem. The marginal social metaphysician's dilemma is not a political crux, but a psychointellectual dilemma that may or may not be given political expression. And the only way we can know for certain that a given political stand is motivated by social metaphysics is to examine it in its full context against the psychology of the individual, which is not the purpose here.

The SCLC statement is an example of the kind of sentiments a social metaphysician might endorse, not for their objective purpose—in this case, the achievement of human decency and human rights—but for his own subjective desire for social approval. Now there is nothing wrong with wanting social acceptance, but what distinguishes the marginal social metaphysician from others is the value he places on social acceptance, the means by which he seeks it, and his response to social rejection. It is not just civil liberty he desires; he longs for freedom from rejection by his fellows. It is not just the status of second-class citizenship from which he wishes to be unleashed; he desires recognition as a first-class person. While in actuality the political sanction of civil rights is only the confirmation of the (universal) human rights inherent in man's nature, the marginal man interprets the social system's recognition of his civil rights as its approval of him as a (particular) person.

Having one's rights protected should be a personal issue for each individual in the society. But to the marginal man civil rights are an extension of a subjective appraisal of his character, not a political expression of the objective worth entailed in the individuality of every human being. Having the right to vote, for instance, is less the ability to express his judgment in the political realm of society than it is a statement of society's judgment of him. Hence, if he is a "language minority" and does not wish to learn the language of the dominant culture in order to fully express his right of suffrage, he may make it a test of that society's "respect for human decency" whether it will modify its election process to accommodate his language "disability" by establishing bilingual polls. Or, he may insist that the society narrow its commitment to the idea that all citizens must have a representative voice in government and allow for the special representation of his group, as in the case of the Congressional Black Caucus and the various ethnic lobbies in Washington.

And the society that confuses civil rights with political privilege rushes headlong into giving form to his whims, always at the expense of the rights of everyone else, in the name of "the public good," which is, in reality, the "good" (whatever they happen to define as good at the time) for only a few.

Solutions to Dilemma

Human liberty is a fundamental requirement of human survival, but as Branden observes: "Political freedom is not a metaphysical given; it has to be achieved."[40] And the key to achieving a free society is held by every individual in "a single action, a single basic choice to think or not to think"—to be properly man or to be something man was never meant to be. Those who seek freedom must *know* what it is they are about and what it is they seek.

The solution many marginal individuals have chosen is *not* to think but to adjust to their self-alienation, remaining "alone and afraid in a world [they] never made"; to rationalize their fear of independence and self-responsibility; and in the words of Branden,

129

"to make their plight more tolerable by directing their fear at some external object," persuading themselves that their fear is a rational response to "this great white man's house."

In short, their solution is to flee from the option of authentic self-esteem and the individual sovereignty on which the maintenace of social and political liberty is dependent and take on a "second-hand" identity, in the manner of the race-conscious social metaphysician. (Again, this is not to imply that all civil rights activists are race-conscious social metaphysicians. Neither does it mean that all those who are social metaphysicians are less than committed to the pursuit of civil liberty. It is quite possible that a person may believe in political liberty and be ensnared also by the social metaphysics of cognitive and evaluative dependence in other areas of his life. The concern here is with those activists who confuse the purpose of civil liberty with that of self-liberation and see political liberty not as a function of intellectual freedom but as a means of escaping the imperatives of intellectual freedom.)

As already established, what makes the race-conscious individual *marginal* is his policy of altruistic assimilation and fluctuation between his desire for membership in the dominant culture and his loyalty to his ethno-racial subculture. What makes him a *social metaphysician* is his view of either or both groups as objects of authority and his reliance on them for a perception of reality, including his self-identity and personal purposes and goals.

Race-conscious social metaphysicians vary in how they seek to adjust to their self-alienation and their dependency on the groups from which they seek direction, approval, and acceptance. A detailed account of these various solutions is presented in part III, but for now I will summarize the categories of solutions as derived from Nathaniel Branden's five typologies of the motivational trends and rationalizations that are dominant among social metaphysicians.

The first is the *Conventional* social metaphysician, whom Branden describes as follows:

> This is the person for whom reality "*is*" the world as interpreted by the "significant others" of his social environment—the person whose sense of identity and personal worth is *explicitly* a function of his ability to satisfy the values, terms and expectations of those omniscient and omnipresent "others." I am "as you desire me"—such is the formula of his existence, such is the "genetic code" controlling his soul's development.[41]

130

Response to the Dilemma of Ethno-Race Consciousness

Among the Conventional social metaphysicians is the race-conscious integrationist, whom I shall call *Conventional Integrationist*. He is the egalitarian conformist who denies the virtue of excellence, subverts variability among men, is envious of independent achievement, and offers "cultural deprivation" as the rationalization for the social favoritism and political privilege he seeks. "If you want to join them (meaning the white majority)," says the Conventional Integrationist, "be like them."

The second of Branden's social metaphysicians is the *Power-seeker*. Of this type Branden writes:

> To this type, the Conventional social metaphysician's path to pseudo-self-esteem is too frighteningly precarious; the spectre of possible failure and defeat looms too large to be endurable. . . . He longs for an escape from the uncertainty of "free market" social metaphysical competition, where he must win men's *voluntary* esteem. He wants to deceive, to manipulate, to coerce the minds of others; to leave them no choice in the matter. He wants to reach a position where he can *command* respect, obedience, love.[42]

Using Branden's Power-seeker as the reference point, I have constructed the *Power-seeking Nationalist* as a prototype among race-conscious Negroes. Having failed to win the approval of others as he had hoped and afraid to compete in the open market of material acquisition and political representation, the Power-seeking Nationalist attempts to gain control over men's judgment of him by means of political and economic separatism. "If you can't join them," says the Power-seeking Nationalist, "lick them."

Branden calls the third type the *Spiritual* social metaphysician:

> [His] claim to esteem rests on his alleged possession of a superior kind of soul—a soul that is not his mind, not his thoughts, not his values, not anything specifiable, but an ineffable composite of undefinable longings, incommunicable insights and impenetrable mystery. . . . If and when he fails to receive the acceptance and esteem he craves, he explains to himself that people are not fine enough to appreciate the "real" him.[43]

I call the race-conscious Spiritual social metaphysician, the *Spiritual Separatist*. Fearful of competing in the open market of ideas and men's judgment, the Spiritual Separatist advocates the psychocultural chauvinism of cultural nationalism, proclaims himself above the understanding of those whose acceptance he craves but has not achieved, and withdraws into a world of "black-

131

ness" that promises automatic acceptance. He expresses his solution as follows: "If you can't be like them, be like your own group."

The fourth type is the "counterfeit individualist" or "defiant nonconformist," whom Branden calls the *Independent* social metaphysician.

> [This is] the man who rebels against the status quo for the sake of being rebellious. . . . Overwhelmed by feelings of inadequacy in relation to the conventional standards of his culture, this type of person retaliates with the formula "Whatever is, *is wrong*." Overwhelmed by the belief that no one can possibly like or accept him, he goes out of his way to insult people—lest they imagine that he desires their approval. . . . While he may profess devotion to some particular idea or goal, or even posture as a dedicated crusader, his primary motivation is negative rather than positive; he is *against* rather than *for*.[44]

Among race-conscious Negroes the Independent social metaphysician is the person I call the *Independent Militant*, who resorts to destructive rebellion against those he is afraid to join and cannot control by political or economic means. His formula is: "If you can't lick them, destroy their world."

Finally, there is Branden's *Ambivalent* social metaphysician, whom he describes as follows:

> This is the person who, notwithstanding a major psycho-epistemological surrender to the authority of others, . . . retains a far greater measure of authentic independence than any other species of social metaphysician. . . . His bondage to social metaphysics is revealed in his . . . lack of confidence and freedom with regard to passing value-judgments, . . . and in his humiliating desire for "approval" and "acceptance." His superiority to other social metaphysicians is evidenced by . . . his desire to earn, through objective achievements, the esteem he longs for, . . . and by his tortured disgust at his own fear of the disapproval of others.[45]

Among the Ambivalent social metaphysicians is the race-conscious type I call the *Ambivalent Appeaser*. His conflict is between his private convictions and his public denial of those convictions. Privately he rejects aspects of both the dominant culture and his own racial group, but fearing their disapproval, he appeases both publicly, believing that to be the only "practical" solution to his problem. He expresses his solution thusly: "If you can't join (or be like) either group, don't let them know it."

Social theorists agree that the Negro protest movement has been as much a progression of attitudinal changes among Negroes as it is

132

one of change in political action and tactics.[46] Few admit, however, that race consciousness has been a motivating factor, and even fewer recognize race-conscious attitudes and racist policies as expressions of social metaphysics as such. Nevertheless, some descriptions of stages in the movement are very similar to the prototypes I've construed.

In his observation that Affirmative Action has inadvertently legitimized white ethnic consciousness, Nathan Glazer points to an attitudinal progression of the civil rights movement that echoes solutions expressed by race-conscious social metaphysicians:

> The saliency of ethnic identities has increased markedly since the middle sixties: since specifically, *the Negroes became blacks* [á la the Spiritual Separatist], and the dominant tone of black political rhetoric shifted from emphasizing "*we are like everyone else and want only integration*" [á la the Conventional Integrationist], to "*we are, of course, different from anyone else and want our proper share of power and wealth*" [á la the Power-seeking Nationalist] (emphasis mine).[47]

William Robert Miller presents a similar analysis of the civil rights movement, which he chronicles in terms of "the escalation of its vocabulary of slogans and rubrics from timidity to militancy, from accommodation to fullness of demand." In Miller's analysis we can see how the movement's focus moved from that of the Power-seeking Nationalist to that of the Independent Militant. That part of Miller's description which may be applied to the Integrationist is as follows: "First, a request for bare amelioration within an unjust system; next, the removal of odious restrictions (discrimination); then, the attack on segregated public facilities. These demands are combined and extended to an insistence on acceptance as a human person and the right to inclusion as such in every aspect of life— *freedom*, coupled with its ethical corollary *now*.[48]

Of course, desiring and working to achieve a just social system is not in itself an expression of social metaphysics. To determine the social metaphysics of a person's actions we must identify the reason for his behavior and judge whether his reasoning is motivated by the reliance on others for a view of reality. The social metaphysics of the Integrationist is evident in the contextual nature of his insistence on acceptance as a human being, the means by which he sets out to be included in every aspect of life, his concept of a "right" to such inclusion and his definition of "life." Having his race accepted as human beings is interpreted by him as having won blanket acceptance of himself—*his* character and personality, *his* values and virtues, *his* purposes and goals.

We all want to be accepted as human, and the demand for the respect of our human dignity is a noble one—the first we must ask of our fellow men. Indeed, human dignity should be the foundation on which our interaction with one another rests; but human dignity is an achievement of individuals, not a quality bestowed on men by other men. Others may *affirm* one's dignity but they have no power to *create* it. For the individual of authentic self-esteem, human dignity—the achievement of moral worth—is a function of his free will that can only be expressed in a free society. Yet a free social order can only facilitate human dignity; it cannot guarantee it. But for the Integrationist social metaphysician, human dignity is not a function of his free choice, but of what others say his worth is.

Finding guaranteed acceptance an impossible goal to attain, some Integrationists withdraw into a world where a modicum of acceptance is guaranteed—the world of their ethno-racial sub-culture. As Miller observes: "Finally these steps [of the integration-ist] are consummated in the demand to be oneself and to determine one's own values and control one's own destiny—to have the *power* which freedom makes real."[49]

Again, such goals are, of themselves, rational, appropriate, and noble. But in the mind of the race-conscious social metaphysician the meaning given to these statements is a function of the same cognitive parasitism that motivated the demand for guaranteed acceptance. On the one hand, the solution is expressed in terms of the Spiritual Separatist whose demand to be himself cloaks the desire for an identity determined by the collective values of his subculture and expressed primarily in intellectual pursuits that seek to legitimize racial exclusiveness and ethnic chauvinism. Other integrationists, however, find their solution in becoming Power-seeking Nationalists whose demand for identity and reliance on collective values is expressed in the politicization of ethno-racial identity.

The Conventional Integrationists, the Spiritual Separatists, and the Power-seeking Nationalists are all nonviolent freedom fighters, with emphasis on the word "fighters." Any course of action that necessitates the violation of human rights is an assault on freedom, and those engaged in such activity are indeed freedom fighters— fighters *against* freedom. The many Great Society programs, which followed the 1964 Civil Rights Bill, that proliferated under the direction of the Integrationists were established and maintained by continual social and *legislative* assaults on individual freedom and achievement. When such assaults on political liberty by Integrationists did not succeed in attaining acceptance and personal dignity, many opted for the solution of the Nationalist.[50] The black-identity movement of the Spiritualists is especially prevalent in education, the arts, and the social sciences wherein an *intellectual* and *psychocultural* assault is waged on freedom of the mind and man's individuality.[51] When the psychointellectual fight against freedom by the Spiritualists does not produce self-identity, some of them become Power-seekers whose aim is to "revitalize" attributes of their ethno-racial subculture by economic and political means.[52] Economic gimmicks like government-financed "black capitalism" and political devices as the Congressional Black Caucus are employed by Power-seekers to wage further *political* assault on freedom in the marketplace and in the political process of our constitutional democracy.

When individuals in any of these groups find that nonviolent measures do not in fact produce freedom *now*, some of them choose destruction as their solution—the destruction of the Independent Militant. Miller charts the course from nonviolence to violence as follows: "What was widely called 'the civil rights movement,' before 1960, therefore, in 1963, came to be called 'the freedom movement,' and those who had once called themselves 'nonviolent resistors' came to see themselves increasingly as 'nonviolent freedom fighters,' with the word 'nonviolent' soon slipping into parentheses, then into the discard."[53]

Thus, we see that the protest movement was not only a freedom movement in response to civil injustices, but a movement of coercion and reverse racism—a movement of revolt against psychointellectual freedom, espousing various solutions to the social metaphysical dilemma of ethno-race consciousness.

Before turning to an examination of the concrete implementation of those solutions in part III, it must be reiterated that, in so far as their attitudes and behavior are expressions of social metaphysics, the above profiles of Negro individuals are just as easily applicable to race-conscious and prejudiced individuals of other racial and ethnic categories. There are many "breast-beating" liberals among white Americans who fit the description of the Conventional

Integrationist. There is the Spiritual Separatist whose "Jewishness" has suffocated his individuality and snuffed out the candle of his spirit, leaving a dark and musty prison hole locked by the chains of historical martyrdom and collective vengeance. There is the American Indian who is so degraded by tribalism and government dependency that he cannot exert the individual effort and creativeness necessary to take the risks that freedom requires. There is the Italian, or Pole, or Irishman who has allowed the acid of ethnocentrism to burn a hole in his self-esteem so that he is always accompanied by the death of collective suspicion and forever haunted by the ghosts of those "others" who are allegedly out to harm him. Indeed, there is the person whose individuality is so overwhelmed by his duty as an "American" that there is nothing left of him that properly reflects what an American *really* is.

There is the Ku Klux Klansman who is as intensely fearful of an open society as any black Power-seeking Nationalist. There is the white Independent Militant whose skin color is the only significant difference between him and his black counterpart—that, and the fact that the black Militant would probably hesitate to include his parents among the "Establishment" he terrorizes and "rips off" in behalf of "the people."

Like the others, Ambivalent Appeasers exist in every ethno-racial group and on every socioeconomic level; they are the "silent majority" who continually sacrifice their own self-interest to the "public good" defined by the other four types. Their fear, appeasement, and lack of countervalues make the fodder for gluttonous parasites who will continue to exact a toll on civilization as long as they can count on the Appeasers to act as accomplices in their own victimization.

One last general observation should be made about the marginal dilemma of the race-conscious social metaphysician. Primarily, this is a study of the self-immolating, altruistic solutions to the external and internal conflict he experiences. However, as the discussions of assimilation and inner-directed marginality indicate, there are definite alternative solutions arising from self-assertive and self-interested thought and action. These solutions are put forth by Branden in *The Psychology of Self-Esteem* and by Stonequist in *The Marginal Man*. Stonequist suggests psychological integration "prompted by a realistic interpretation of the social situation and by understanding its influence on the personality" as the key to making ethno-racial identity secondary to self-identity. "What seems generally essential, if the individual possesses insight and wishes to maintain his self-respect," wrote Stonequist, "is that he shall not evade the issues, deceive himself, or act a role which does not have the fullest possible support of his deeper thoughts and sentiments."

And he added: "To confront the issues with courage will not necessarily solve the whole conflict, for the action of one person cannot eliminate, although it may significantly modify, the objective social situation. . . . But those who maintain their personal integrity—the 'I am myself' attitude—do reaffirm the rights of personality in the face of external pressures, and so become pioneers and creative agents in that new social order which seems to evolve as narrower group loyalties gradually give way to larger human values."[54]

Unfortunately, and inexcusably, narrower group loyalties have yet to give way to larger human values. The founding principles of the American society that rejected ethnic exclusivity are being betrayed and the United States is in danger of being transformed from "a union of states and a nation of free individuals" into "a nation of politically defined ethnic groups."[55]

1. William S. Hall, Roy Freedle, and William E. Cross, Jr., *Stages In The Development of a Black Identity*.

2. See C. W. Thomas, *Boys No More*; M. Sherif and C. Sherif, "Black Unrest As a Social Movement toward an Emerging Self-Identity."

3. August Meier, Elliott Rudwick, and Francis L. Broderick, eds. *Black Protest Thought in the Twentieth Century*, p. 379.

4. James A. Banks and Jean D. Grambs, *Black Self-Concept: Implications for Education and Social Science*, pp. 7-8.

5. Eric C. Lincoln, "Color and Group Identity in the United States," pp. 527-41.

6. Ibid., p. 539.

7. Joseph Hraba and Jack Siegman, "Black Consciousness," pp. 63-90.

8. Stokely Carmichael and Charles V. Hamilton, *Black Power*, p. 37.

9. Scott Cummings and Robert Carrere, "Black Culture, Negroes, and Colored People: Racial Image and Self-Esteem among Black Adolescents," pp. 238-48.

10. DuBois, *The Souls of Black Folk*, p. 3.

11. Neil Friedman, "Has Black Come Back To Dixie?," pp. 48-53.

12. The samples were as follows: In January 1967, 271 high school seniors and 258 of their mothers and female guardians (Montgomery, Ala.). In January 1968, 242 high school seniors and 223 of their mothers and female guardians (Birmingham). In February 1968, 410 college students at Tuskegee Institute. In February 1969, 279 adult males in Montgomery.

13. Friedman, *op. cit.*

14. Peter Goldman, *Report From Black America*, p. 155. This is the third in the series of *Newsweek* Poll reports. The first appears in William Brink and Louis Harris, *The Negro Revolution in America* (New York: Simon and Schuster, 1964); the second, in Brink and Harris, *Black and White: A Study of U.S. Racial Attitudes Today* (New York: Simon and Schuster, 1967).

15. Ibid., pp. 155–56.

16. Daniel Yankelovich, Inc., *An Insight into the Black Community* (A study prepared for *Ebony* magazine), New York: Daniel Yankelovich, Inc., 1973.

17. Cummings and Carrere, *op. cit.*

18. *Ibid.*

19. Friedman, *op. cit.*

20. Ibid.

21. Ibid.

22. Philip Mason, "The Revolt Against Western Values," pp. 328–52.

23. Goldman, op. cit.

24. Lerone Bennett Jr., *The Negro Mood*, p. 53.

25. Ibid.

26. Goldman, op cit., pp. 152–53.

27. Ibid.

28. Yankelovich, op. cit.

29. Goldman, op. cit.

30. Gary T. Marx, *Protest and Prejudice: A Study of Belief in the Black Community*, p. 29.

31. Ibid., p. 30.

32. Goldman, op. cit., p. 45.

33. Ibid., p. 180.

34. Talcott Parsons, "Some Theoretical Considerations on the Nature and Trends of Change of Ethnicity," in Glazer and Moynihan, eds., *Ethnicity*.

35. See David M. Schneider, *American Kinship: A Cultural Account* (Englewood Cliffs, N.J.: Prentice-Hall, 1968).

36. Bennett, op. cit.

37. Ibid.

38. Richard F. Hamilton, *Class and Politics in the United States*, p. 552.

39. Quoted in Thomas R. Brooks, *Walls Come Tumbling Down: A History of the Civil Rights Movement, 1940–1970*.

40. Nathaniel Branden, *The Disowned Self*, p. 254.

41. For the complete analysis of the social metaphysician and the five types discussed here, see Branden, *The Psychology of Self-Esteem*.

42. Ibid.

43. Ibid.

44. Ibid.

45. Ibid.

46. Meier, et al., *Black Protest Thought in the Twentieth Century*, and *From Plantation to Ghetto*.

Response to the Dilemma of Ethno-Race Consciousness

47. Glazer, *Affirmative Discrimination*.

48. William Robert Miller, *Martin Luther King, Jr.: His Life, Martyrdom, and Meaning for the World*, p. 157.

49. Ibid.

50. See Stokely Carmichael and Charles V. Hamilton, *Black Power*.

51. See Joyce A. Ladner, ed., *The Death of White Sociology*; Imamu Ameer Baraka (LeRoi Jones), "A Black Value System"; James A. Banks and Jean D. Grambs, *Black Self-Concept: Implications for Education and Social Science*; Philip Mason, "The Revolt Against Western Values." For discussions of the antiempirical bias of cultural nationalism, see Richard F. Hamilton, *Class and Politics in the United States*, pp. 550–52; Robert K. Merton, "The Perspectives of Insiders and Outsiders," in *The Sociology of Science*.

52. See William Julius Wilson, *The Declining Significance of Race: Blacks and Changing American Institutions*.

53. Miller, op. cit.

54. Stonequist, *The Marginal Man*, pp. 206–9.

55. Glazer, *Affirmative Discrimination*. See chapter 1, "The Emergence of an American Ethnic Pattern."

PART III. PROFILES OF RACE-CONSCIOUS NEGROES

7

The Conventional Integrationist

"If you want to join them, be like them."

The philosophy of nonviolent resistance does not seek to defeat or humiliate the opponent, but to win his friendship and understanding. It seeks to defeat injustice and not white persons who may be unjust.—Martin Luther King, Jr., *Stride Toward Freedom.*

Though it has not always been a goal shared by the majority of Americans, the achievement of an integrated society, like the pursuit of equal justice, has long been an ideal embodied in the American democratic method. But Americans are not agreed on just what racial integration should involve. Many people have condoned integration, thinking that it means the same as desegregation—the process of ending group separation. Others have resisted integration, believing that it inevitably brings about miscegenation. "If you want to get right down to the real outcome of this so-called 'integration,' what you've got to arrive at is inter-marriage," wrote Malcolm X in his autobiography. "I'm *with* the Southern white man who believes that you don't have so-called 'integration,' at least not for long, without intermarriage increasing. And what good is this for anyone? . . . What we arrive at is that 'integration,' socially, is no good for either side. 'Integration,' ultimately, would destroy the white race . . . and destroy the black race."[1]

143

Others who resist integration are motivated by a mistaken belief that the inevitable outcome of integration is assimilation, which they view as a threat to the perpetuation of their culture. The object of their resistance is, more properly, assimilation, not integration. For example, many groups, as do certain Jews, advocate ethnocultural solidarity (in resistance to assimilation) but are strong supporters of integration as an option for those who desire it. To some Americans integration implies social acceptance, and they support it or reject it on that basis. Black militant H. Rap Brown explained his rejection of integration on the basis of this interpretation as follows: "A lot of people, Black and white, have the impression that those of us who got involved in the Movement . . . were fighting for integration. That's the way the white press interpreted the sit-ins and freedom rides and all that. But what they didn't understand was that none of us was concerned about sitting down next to a white man and eating a hamburger. . . . We would've been some kind of fools to get beaten up, spat on and jailed the way a lot of folks did just to sit down at a lunch counter beside a white person. . . . We weren't fighting for integration. We were letting white folks know that they could no longer legislate where we went or what we did."[2]

To others integration implies sociopolitical and economic participation, and their support or rejection of it is defined within that context. This is basically the interpretation Bayard Rustin gave to integration in his advocacy of "coalition politics" as the best civil rights tactic to follow that of protest demonstrations. In 1965 Rustin wrote in *Commentary*: "There is a widespread assumption that the removal of artificial racial barriers should result in the automatic integration of the Negro into all aspects of American life." But, he asks, "What is the value of winning access to public accommodations for those who lack money to use them? The minute the movement faced this question, it was compelled to expand its vision beyond race relations to economic relations, including the role of education in modern society. And what also became clear is these interrelated problems, by their very nature, are not soluble by private, voluntary efforts but require government action—or politics."[3]

Still others view integration as the means of organizing the community according to an egalitarian ideal, and that definition is the foundation of their support or rejection. While some Americans

144

agree with Rustin's concept of economic and political integration, they nevertheless take exception to his egalitarianism, which holds that in order for the Negro to be integrated into American life, the political coalition he envisions (Negroes, trade unionists, liberals, and religious groups) must be concerned "not merely with removing the barriers to full *opportunity* but with achieving the fact of *equality*."[4]

It seems correct to say that while most Americans are unclear about the meaning of integration and that while there is disagreement over what they expect of it, most have accepted it as a worthwhile goal. It is popularly believed that only an unbiased person is capable of advocating integration and that only racists would reject it. And since most Negroes support integration, it is assumed that these supporters are not motivated by race consciousness. Of course, the interpretation of race consciousness presented in this study takes exception to this belief. The following profile of the Conventional Integrationist will show the value of integration to race-conscious Negroes. But before their specific expectations of integration are examined, let me present the definition of integration, as used here.

Defining Integration

Perhaps a definition of integration can be arrived at by stating first what it is *not*. It is most assuredly not segregation—the separation of groups of people by custom (de facto) or by law (de jure)—or as Berry puts it, "a [coercive or voluntary] form of isolation which places limits or restrictions upon contact, communication, and social relations."[5] Neither is it desegregation—the process of ending group separation. Integration is often thought of as synonymous with desegregation; another commonly held view is that desegregation implies the elimination of segregation by law, while integration is a voluntary process. But there is a significant distinction as indicated in the following passage by Thomas Pettigrew:

> During the course of desegregation, two or more separated groups may begin to act toward each other in new, friendlier ways. The process of integration goes farther, and refers also to the quality of the new relationship. A desegregated situation becomes integrated when it involves acceptance and friendship between persons in different groups. For example, a desegregated school is no longer all-Negro nor all-white—but there may be little friendship between the Negro and white

145

students. After student friendships form across racial lines, the school is truly integrated.[6]

This is a fairly simple distinction between desegregation and integration but it says more than meets the eye. Desegregation, which may be seen as a concept of social organization, is largely the process of decreasing the spatial separation or physical distance between groups (as in the desegregation of public transportation, schools, employment, housing, etc.). Integration, a concept of social interaction, involves the breakdown of psychointellectual and sociocultural distance between individuals within a desegregated situation. Desegregation, legal or voluntary, is essentially a tactic for eliminating racial barriers to the possibility of creating integrated situations and circumstances. The phrase "acceptance and friendship between persons," in Pettigrew's statement, means that to be achieved integration must occur between individuals; and since acceptance and friendship are the effects of selection and choice, integration ought to be voluntary. The public and political dynamics of desegregation may provide the atmosphere and social circumstances wherein integration may take place, but the process itself cannot be ordered into existence. Even in his indictment of integration, H. Rap Brown recognized the "impracticality" of forced integration: "Integration was never our concern," Brown writes of his faction of the civil rights movement. "In fact, integration is impractical. You cannot legislate an attitude and integration is based upon an attitude of mutual acceptance and respect between two racial or cultural groups in the society. A law can govern behavior, but attitudes cannot be forced or enforced, and what the Civil Rights Movement was concerned with was controlling the animalistic *behavior* of white people."[7]

Sociologist James S. Coleman, whose 1966 Coleman Report was used by civil rights leaders and the courts as the rationale for school desgregation and for court-ordered busing, echoed some of the facts of Brown's sentiments, though not their spirit, in a 1976 preliminary report on a new study of the effects of integration. In interviews with *Time* and *The New York Times*, he said: "As long as the court dealt with [the basic constitutional protection that eliminated segregation] it was O.K. But then it got into the other realm beyond the protection of constitutional rights. It attempted to eliminate all facets of segregation, not only that arising from state action, but that which arose from individual action.

146

"That is where it went wrong, because it is not set up to counter every individual action."[8]

While he had not ruled out state action altogether, Dr. Coleman believed that to succeed integration in the United States must depend on "voluntary factors," including more racial intermarriage. "It is ludicrous to attempt to mandate an integrated society," he said. "Integration must come through other means." To make integration work, "we still need to find some mechanism to make it to people's interest to be integrated."[9]

The main point to be drawn from the Pettigrew statement and those from the militant Brown and integrationist Coleman is that although integration is a possible outcome of desegregation, it is not the same as desegregation. Integration is dependent on the elimination of group separation but must itself evolve from the voluntary cooperation of individuals within those groups. Yet, to quote another writer on the subject, "court decisions against segregation are likely to remain meaningless unless integration does, in fact, take place."[10] This does not mean, however, that integration must be imposed to bolster desegregation laws.

In the broadest sense integration may be characterized in terms of any one or a combination of the categories that distinguish one group of individuals from another—race, religion, wealth, culture, or sex. Since the concern here is with both race and ethnic relations, the definition of integration that follows is limited to ethno-racial integration: *the voluntary process of eliminating sociocultural distance between groups and individuals of different ethnic and racial categories whereby individuals form personal and social associations that cross ethno-racial lines.*

As with assimilation, the definition of ethno-racial integration does not designate the kind or the quality of integration beyond the fact that it is voluntary. It does not characterize the rate of the process and neither does it entail a judgment as to whether the process is intrinsically good or bad for personal and group relations. It merely designates one of several forms of accommodation people make to the contact of different groups. Strictly speaking, the concept of integration does not imply the automatic achievement of harmonious relations between individuals of different groups. It may be engaged in with this goal in mind, but there is nothing about it that guarantees interpersonal and intergroup harmony. The quality and rate of the process is determined by the value people place on it, on what benefits (to them) they seek from it, and the means by which they choose to achieve it.

Those people who either support or reject integration as the best accommodation to group contact do so not only on the basis of their understanding of what integration is but also according to what they expect to achieve in the community at large and in their personal lives. The integrationist expectation is based on the belief that antipathy arises from ignorance, that stereotypes are false, that hostility is unnatural and unrealistic, and that prejudice will disappear if people are only given the facts. It holds that interracial contact and acquaintance brings about friendliness, tolerance, and sympathy; that a good community is based on benevolent and harmonious relations among individuals regardless of what characteristics distinguish them.

The integrationist expectation is not a monolithic attitude, however, as there are considerable variations in how people of different philosophical persuasions would implement it in the practical life of the community. There are, for instance, differing opinions as to just where the integration process occurs in the spectrum of group contact and association. There are those who believe that eliminating race-conscious attitudes by persuasion and education results in desegregation; others take the position that eliminating segregation and discrimination results in attitudes of friendliness and tolerance. Both solutions are attempted in the U.S. but the latter seems to be more widely received.

The two major variants of the integrationist expectation are the positions of (1) the *statist* integrationist and (2) the *laissez-faire* integrationist. While they share the belief in the *possibility* of an integrated society, what distinguishes them is the political means by which they would achieve such a community and the moral standards that guide the choice of those means. The statist variety of the integrationist expectation is guided by altruism, which regards integration as a goal to be achieved by "society as a whole," that it should be sought for the good of "society," or "the public," rather than for the interest of individuals. Opposing the altruistic standard is the self-interested ethic which does not presume that integration is best for everyone but rather that it is a goal chosen by individuals to serve what they define as their best interest.

The irreconcilable difference between the statist integrationist and the laissez-faire integrationist is that the former employs the force of law to achieve his goal and the latter relies on the voluntary actions of men.[11] The voluntarism of the laissez-faire integrationist holds that as men ought to be free to exchange which material goods and services in the market they deem beneficial to their livelihood, so they ought to be free to choose the individuals with whom they wish to associate. The belief that integration is possible and in some respects beneficial does not carry with it a mandate that societal integration be achieved at all costs.

There are various rationalizations for the use of force to bring about integration. Most often we hear from the utilitarians whose implementation of the integrationist expectancy is based on the belief that a good society takes priority over a free society. It is good, they say, that we create a community of human fellowship—one in which men associate with one another without reference to race, color, or creed. But, according to their reasoning, men cannot be left to achieve this goal on their own because they are naturally predisposed to evil thoughts and harmful behavior against one another. Thus, they must be forced to do what is good for themselves and for the community.

Some statists would go even further and advocate integration via egalitarian reforms that aim toward the elimination of individual differences altogether. Indeed, to many integration has become synonymous with equality and defined in terms of the requirement given to it by civil rights leaders and social scientists to achieve what Nathan Glazer calls the "statistical representation of categories"— in this case, ethno-racial balance via quotas. The idea that integration cannot be achieved unless everyone is equal in all respects finds support in the works of John Rawls, John Kenneth Galbraith, Daniel Bell, and others. However, most egalitarian integrationists argue their position in language similar to a statement by President Lyndon B. Johnson in his commencement address at Howard University in 1965:

> You do not take a person who, for years, has been hobbled by chains and liberate him, bring him up to the starting line of a race and then say, "You are free to compete with all the others" and still justly believe that you have been completely fair.
>
> Thus it is not enough just to open the gates of opportunity. All our citizens must have the ability to walk through those gates.
>
> . . . We seek not just freedom but opportunity. We seek not just legal equality but human ability, not just equality as a right and a theory but equality as a fact and equality as a result.[12]

149

The Other Side of Racism

It bears repeating here that integration is a process engaged in by individuals. Its purpose is not to equalize the distinctions of men that make them human instead of automatons. Neither is it to create a good society, as such, but to create meaningful, harmonious, and beneficial relations between individuals. An integrated society cannot come about except that it exists as the consequence of personal interracial associations maintained by a great many people. And, of course, this cannot occur by means of force; coercive integration, like coercive assimilation, is a contradiction that defeats its own purpose.

The American society, as a whole, has not reached that stage of social relations that would identify it as an integrated society. To be sure, many people live in integrated subcultures or have integrated experiences. There are numerous integrated relationships and circumstances between individuals and small interracial group associations such as occur in certain areas of the arts, the entertainment industry, academia, sports, and (probably to a lesser degree) the armed services and private industry. But, by and large, the society is still at the stage of desegregation where friendliness and acceptance across ethno-racial lines is a premium achievement.

The Conventional Integrationist

Up to now I have discussed the definition of integration in terms of the ethics and political implementation of the integrationist expectation. Keeping in mind that integration is, by definition, the voluntary elimination of psychointellectual and sociocultural distance between individuals within a desegregated situation, I will now turn to the psychological importance integration has for some people—specifically those race-conscious individuals I call marginal social metaphysicians.

The integrationist expectation is not race conscious by definition but some people who subscribe to it (as well as some who reject it) do so with race-conscious motives. The same factors that distinguish altruistic, self-immolating assimilation from self-interested, self-assertive assimilation also form the distinctions between the race-conscious integrationist and the unbiased integrationist. Some of the most ardent integrationists are altruistic whites who hope that by promoting interracial harmony they will somehow ameliorate the guilt they feel for injustices committed by their ancestors against Negroes and other minorities. This unwarranted assumption of

150

collective guilt is their tie to race consciousness. There are likewise Negro integrationists who are motivated by race consciousness.

Integration is most often seen as a political solution to ethno-racial segregation and conflict, but even among vociferous activists there are individuals whose stake in the integrationist expectation is as much psychological as it is political, if not more. One such person is the race-conscious social metaphysician, the Conventional Integrationist.

The Conventional Integrationist is adapted from Branden's conventional social metaphysician, the conformist: "the person whose values and view of life are a direct reflection and product of his particular culture or sub-culture. . . . He is the man who 'swims with the current.' "[13]

What makes an integrationist a conventional social metaphysician? Not all integrationists are social metaphysicians, but the individual who is seeks interracial associations and experiences not because he has concluded from his own reasoning that integration can be fulfilling and beneficial to him but simply because integration is held as a value by those "significant others" on whom he relies for a view of reality and whose value judgments he accepts without question. What motivates him is not the value integration may hold for him, but his desire for the approval of those for whom integration is a value. Integration is but a means of effecting his conformity to the expectations of others and to what others believe to be right.

When a Conventional Integrationist is motivated by race con-sciousness he expresses it in terms of his desire to conform to the values of others and to gain their approval. Conformity—in this case, to the integrationist expectation and its political implemen-tation—is chosen as the solution to his distressing need for ethno-racial acceptance and approval, which he hopes will result in a sense of identity he lacks and relieve him of the in-between situation of his marginality. He may fluctuate from one ethno-racial "authority" to another—at one time reaching a satisfactory "adjustment," then being thrown back into a condition of conflict, only to reach out again repeatedly for the approval he so desperately desires. His solution is voiced as follows: "*If you want to join them, be like them.*"

What has been said so far about the Conventional Integrationist as a race-conscious social metaphysician may be said about such a person of any ethnic or racial identification. The remainder of the discussion will focus on the Negro who is a Conventional Integrationist. In the conclusion "If you want to join them, be like them," the Negro Conventionalist means by "them" the white majority—the dominant culture and its value of integration.

The character of the Negro Conventional Integrationist may be heightened by a view of him from the perspective of those in his race who oppose him. His opposition—those of the radical black-identity movement—disapprovingly refer to the Conventional Integrationist as the "Negro" who has not yet encountered or acknowledged his "blackness." Black-identity proponents accuse him of being still dependent on an interpretation of reality according to "white values"—a view that is nonblack and antiblack. From their vantage point, the Conventional Integrationist

> believes that the world is, and should be, guided by American-European concepts, i.e., the sum total of his experiences, perceptions, are dominated by a white racist orientation. He believes that black people came from a strange, uncivilized continent and that the black search for historical relevance began around 1865. He believes that the white esthetic is superior to the black one; e.g., he uses white modes of expression, etc. He believes that the white man is superior intellectually, technically mystical, and capable of understanding him. He believes that large numbers of blacks are untrustworthy. This person believes that incorporation, integration, or assimilation is the black man's most effective weapon for solving his problems.[14]

(I should point out immediately that even in their protest of the Conventional Integrationist's apparent sellout of his "blackness," the black-identity advocates confess their own form of race consciousness and social metaphysics. As demonstrated in chapter 9, the essential argument between the integrationist and the black-identity separatist is not *whether* one's frame of reference should be defined by "significant others," but *who* should represent the "significant others" for Negroes—the white majority culture or the black minority subculture.)

While the above attitudes are obviously not true of all Conventionalists, the one they all share is the belief that their dilemma of marginality and pseudo self-esteem can be ameliorated best by integration. Confident that he can be whatever it takes to be accepted, the Conventionalist still believes that it is possible to join the "significant others" in the larger culture. He sees himself as the key personality in the contact of cultures, believing that it is *in his mind* that the cultures come together, conflict, and eventually work out some kind of mutual adjustment and interpenetration. And he believes that through his practical efforts the conditions of his self-esteem dilemma will be changed. He rightly believes that if he is to be entirely free, the socioeconomic, political, and psychocultural distance between the dominant culture and him must be decreased. More than anything else, he desires cultural synchrony out of which he hopes will come acceptance.

His intense hope is that by changing the external social situation to the political and cultural unity of an integrated society, he will ensure the kind of interracial situations that will provide sanction and approval of his ethno-racial identity. Being able to hold the same jobs as whites, to live in the same neighborhood and attend the same schools is not only an expression of the constitutional protection and implementation of his freedom; it is, in his mind, "proof" that he is as good as whites and he sees these desegregated situations as the means of gaining their acceptance. Like Branden's Conventional social metaphysician, whose "sense of identity and personal worth is a function of his ability to satisfy the values, terms and expectations of others," the Conventional Integrationist is very impressed with the dominant culture and willing to go to whatever lengths necessary to "prove" himself to its members. If he cannot achieve his goals by means of voluntary integration, then he advocates forced integration.

The rationale for integrating himself into the larger culture by force is provided in the following observation from an analysis of the integrationist by political scientist Charles V. Hamilton:

> The integrationist insists that the earlier struggles to overcome *de jure* segregation must be continued beyond merely declaring segregation to be unconstitutional. There is a heavy reliance on an interpretation of the Constitution that argues that officials must take affirmative action to insure that there will be integration of the races. This means busing of school children if necessary; it means deliberately placing blacks in public housing projects in all-white neighborhoods if necessary. In other words, the integrationist position is that there cannot be exclusive reliance on *voluntary* action of private citizens if a meaningful amount of racial integration (in schools, in housing, on jobs) is to occur in this country.[15]

Until about 1964 the civil rights movement was largely an integration movement that aimed to bring about an integrated society by means of desegregation and nondiscrimination. But the

153

movement's moral base was undercut by two assumptions held by many of its leaders and constituency who were Conventionalists. Underlying the polemics and protest was the assumption that coercive reduction of racial discrimination and segregation would produce a society of good men. A second debilitating assumption was that people's respect for one's human rights would necessarily mean their sanction of his individual character. Martin Luther King, Jr. wrote of this expectation as a central premise of the idea of "nonviolent resistance":

> Court orders and federal enforcement agencies will be of inestimable value in achieving desegregation. But desegregation is only a partial, though necessary, step toward the ultimate goal which we seek to realize. Desegregation will break down the legal barriers, and bring men together physically. But something must happen so to touch the hearts and souls of men that they will come together, not because the law says it, but because it is natural and right.[16]

Bypassing the question of whether it is right to bring men together by force, King urged that the message of Negroes to whites should be: "In winning our freedom we will so appeal to your heart and conscience that we will win you in the process."

As these and statements by other Negro and white civil rights advocates indicate, the Conventional Integrationist's desire for acceptance by the dominant culture often becomes confused with his desire for civil rights. He makes one the condition of the other, evading the fact that men may respect his rights without approving (rightly or wrongly) of his character. He desires the achievable dignity of man that a free society sets as its goal when it makes man's life, liberty, and property the standard of human association and interaction. But his error lies in the belief that the society, either the dominant culture or his own subculture, can achieve that dignity for him. It is true that human dignity requires political liberty, but all the political freedom imaginable will not produce the sense of worth that each man must achieve for himself.

Implicit in the concept of human rights is the principle that life itself is an absolute good; that each man has the right to his own life; that it is right for him to act to sustain his life—his highest value; that life is the standard by which he must guide his thinking and action. But the concept of life as man's highest value does not entail a judgment of the good or evil of men's character. Refuting B. F. Skinner's advocacy of a world in which men are automatically good, Tibor R. Machan writes: "There is no such thing as automatic goodness. . . . Man cannot be made automatically good *because* each person's virtue must be of his own making."[17] (Similarly, there is no such thing as automatic evil, as each person's vice must be of his own making.) Human life is good, which means that it is right as an aspect of nature. All human beings possess life and this—*their possession of life*—is good. But not all men choose to *make* their lives good. Human character is good or bad only insofar as it reflects an individual's *way* of living—whether he does so according to what is right for human life as an aspect of nature, or whether he follows standards that violate his nature and are inimical to a successful existence. When we ask the nature of a person's character we are inquiring after how *he* is living *his* life—not how he is judged by society or what statistical judgments are made about the ethnic, racial, sexual, or professional groups he belongs to.

"A good human life *means* the good life of a given individual being," writes Machan. "Every individual must realize it for himself. The guidance for that is provided by an understanding of what *kind* of being every individual is, namely a human being. But the implementation of goodness must be on the individual's particular level."[18]

In the Conventional Integrationist's universe of "others," his goodness is an issue "they" must decide and give confirmation of. Human dignity is not his personal achievement but a kind of attachment to his collectivized identity that should be guaranteed sanction by his fellowman even if it means the sacrifice of human liberty. As A. Philip Randolph told the throng at the 1963 March on Washington, the goal of the "massive moral revolution" was a "free democratic society" in which the sanctity of human personality would take priority over private property rights. And what is this human personality that must take priority over man's rights? For the Conventionalist it is a personality fashioned by those ethno-racial "others."

The amelioration of injustice, the elimination of governmental discrimination, and the desegregation of public facilities are undoubtedly symbols of society's acceptance of individuals *as human beings*. Indeed, such actions are often direct expressions of that acceptance. But they are not in fact the acceptance of *individual* human beings. The national community's acknowledgement of the Negro race as human beings is not equivalent to the independent judgments made of Negro individuals by other individuals. This is not to say that some individuals do not rely on collective judgments in reaching a specific evaluation of individual persons. Unfortunately, they do; they even project their judgments of individuals onto their characterization of a group as a whole. But the fact that they do has no bearing on the fact that the most objective evaluations of an individual ought to result from examinations of his character, conduct, purposes, goals, etc. The political action taken by the community is responsive to one's humanity, but it does not (and cannot) say whether any one member of the community is a good human being or not. A community may direct its actions to protecting and preserving the political liberty necessary for the possible achievement of human dignity; but it cannot guarantee that any one individual or group will achieve the moral worthiness that is human dignity.

Social justice is just that—*social*. It is the implementation of human rights in our relations with others; or, to quote Machan, it signifies "righteousness in human associations, interpersonal, community affairs."[19] And as Rand puts it, justice is "the act of judging a man's character and/or actions exclusively on the basis of all the factual evidence available, and of evaluating it by means of an objective moral criterion."[20] Social justice—what Machan defines as "the standards of legal righteousness" (as opposed to personal, moral excellence)—aims for the recognition of each person's equal moral status before the law. But it does not entail taking responsibility for the moral character and actions of individuals. It requires only that such character and actions be judged objectively and that such judgment be implemented *rightly*—in accordance with the human rights that ought to constitute the foundations of a community's legal system.[21]

But the Conventional Integrationist wants more than justice; he wants *unilateral acceptance* of his moral character. And behind his demand for "racial equality" via social justice lies the desire for a social system in which men's acceptance of him can be made an issue of legality.

The Conventionalist believes that to the extent that he has become partly assimilated, he is justified in expecting to achieve what he considers as complete assimilation into a culture that he and his ancestors helped to create. He sees whites as his fellow citizens and he is frustrated to be without the same opportunities they are privy to simply by virtue of their racial identity. He believes this "great white man's house" is his too and he wants to be included. "They"—intellectual and political authorities—say this is best achieved by desegregation and integration.

Now that de jure desegregation is a reality, how does the Conventional Integrationist go about achieving the *fact* of integration?

Integration via Egalitarianism

Some integrationists see competition as the practical route to achieving the friendliness and acceptance of integrated association. Among these are Conventionalists who believe Negroes should compete with whites as a group and not because they themselves necessarily value competition, as such, but because they believe *whites* value competition and that by competing with them they will earn their respect. Other Conventionalists believe that the only way to achieve integration is by creating a political and economic system that would eliminate the differences of human capability and achievement altogether. These egalitarian Conventionalists not only want legal equity with whites; they also want to be ontologically and structurally equal to whites—to be like whites. They want to eliminate what Arthur Shenfield calls "the head-on conflict between substantive equality and equality before the law."[22] Moreover, they believe that by equaling "the white man," they can remove, once and for all, the shadow of the stereotype, refute the stigma of inferiority, and demonstrate their ability to maneuver in the larger culture.

The egalitarian Conventionalist wants to be equal to others—to belong—to be a constituent of a common denominator. He not only wants to be integrated into the larger community, but he also wants to experience himself as an integrated person. Living in an integrated society will necessarily make him an integrated person, he believes. Added to his desire for integration is the desire for the ascriptive equality found in belonging to a group and meritorious equality found in economic performance. "Equality" is the watchword of his political action, and it carries more moral authority for him than freedom. In his mind, being "free and equal" extends far beyond the protection and preservation of the liberty of individuals seen as equal under the law. No, for him "free and equal" means free of his individual identity and self-responsibility and equal in fact and in condition to all others. When he calls for "equal opportunity" as a sociopolitical goal, he means it in the sense articulated by sociologist Daniel Bell, "the 'just precedence' of society . . . requires the reduction of all inequality, or the creation of *equality of result*—in income, status, and power—for all men in society."[23]

When some Conventionalists advocate egalitarian reforms they mean that men of excellence should be reduced to the lowest common denominator of the least among them.[24] Others advocate it meaning that the least among men should be raised by efforts other than their own to the level of men of excellence.[25] Today we witness an alliance between the two: on the one hand, there is the demand that the opportunities and rewards of excellence be conferred on all men whether or not they value excellence and/or have the ability to attain it. On the other hand, it is proclaimed that the best life for man is that he rise no higher than the lowest among him—that to do otherwise is necessarily to exploit his neighbor's weakness and misfortune.

The result of this alliance exists in the person who would bypass the cause and identity of excellence and declare that the worst human qualities and performance be deemed the excellent. Like the New Generation of Charles Reich's "Consciousness III," he "rejects the whole concept of excellence and comparative merit," substituting it with the zero-sum of invariability among men. "III refuses to evaluate people by general standards, it refuses to classify people, or analyze them," writes Reich. "Because there are no governing standards, no one is rejected."[26]

Not to be rejected—that is the Conventional Integrationist's prime motive; and the surest way to ensure against rejection, he believes, is to make everybody equal—to make everybody equally mediocre. Walter A. Weisskopf explains it this way:

> When people talk about equality and human dignity, they really want acceptance—I shy away from the word love, but that is what it is—in spite of all differences. They want to be accepted and loved as they are, even in spite of what they are. This love and acceptance—Christian theology calls it agape—is not primarily a creation of any social system; it is needed to soften the nonegalitarian harshness of society. This is the real meaning of the longing for a classless society and for a plurality of values.[27]

The concept *agape* that Weisskopf speaks of was a key element of Martin Luther King Jr.'s philosophy of nonviolent resistance, and its altruism is the motive power of the egalitarian approach to achieving integration. "*Agape* is disinterested love," wrote King. "*Agape* does not begin by discriminating between worthy and unworthy people, or any qualities people possess. It begins by loving others *for their sakes*." It is not a weak, passive love , but love in action and aimed toward seeking to preserve and create community. It is "a willingness to sacrifice in the interest of mutuality"—"a willingness to go to any length to restore community."[28]

Agape is plainly other-directed, springing from what King called "the *need* of the other person—his need for belonging to the best in the human family." It presumes to judge all white men as guilty of the sin of racial and economic oppression and claims them therefore in need of redemption. Wrote King: "Since the white man's personality is greatly distorted by segregation, and his soul is greatly scarred, he needs the love of the Negro. The Negro must love the white man, because the white man needs his love to remove his tensions, insecurities, and fears."[29] But this redemptive love carries a price with it: the sacrifice of self-interest and ultimately individual liberty.

Seeking the friendliness and acceptance of integration is in itself a rational and worthwhile goal. But the doctrine of *agape* provides the rationalization for the use of force ("We are doing this to save the souls of our misguided white brethren") if that friendliness and acceptance does not come forth voluntarily. As James Baldwin put it: "If the word *integration* means anything, this is what it means: that we, with love, shall force our brothers to see themselves as they are, to cease fleeing from reality and begin to change. . . . The price of this transformation is the unconditional freedom of the Negro; it is not too much to say that he, who has been so long rejected, must now be embraced, and at no matter what psychic or social risk."[30] Thus, we see the Conventional Integrationist concerned not only with seeking the acceptance of whites, but busily engaged in expounding ways by which whites may be released from the racist pathology that prevents them from granting friendliness and acceptance.

The Other Side of Racism

Even without its chief advocate, Martin Luther King, Jr., the psychotheological politics of redemptive love has continued to influence American public policy in the area of race relations. Conventionalists argue that their situation is not only caused by bad attitudes, but by bad social conditions brought on by the inequity of the economic system. Equality of opportunity simply does no good, they say, without a great deal of equality of condition. Having rejected the economic market as a mechanism for translating individual decisions into collective ones, they would replace it by a political market, supplemented by bureaucratic implementation. If the American society is to be cured of its disease of racist capitalism, say the Conventionalists, it must take "affirmative action" to extend special protection and benefits on the basis of group affiliation to overcome its heritage of discrimination. Thus, while they have not succeeded in obtaining unilateral acceptance and friendliness from members of the majority, they have succeeded in obtaining the institutional favor of government. They are now among the "official" minorities and reign supreme from their exalted position as glorified "victims." It should not come as a surprise, however. For, as shall be demonstrated later, the politics of victimization is but the logical consequence of the politics of redemption.

1. Malcolm X, *The Autobiography of Malcolm X*, pp. 272–81.
2. H. Rap Brown, *Die Nigger Die!*, pp. 55–56.
3. Bayard Rustin, "From Protest to Coalition Politics," in Marvin E. Gettleman and David Mermelstein, eds., *The Great Society Reader: The Failure of American Liberalism*, pp. 261–77.
4. Ibid.
5. Berry, *Race and Ethnic Relations*, p. 273.
6. Thomas F. Pettigrew, "Segregation." *World Book Encyclopedia.*
7. Brown, op. cit.
8. *New York Times*, June 7, 1975.
9. *Time*, June 23, 1975.
10. Thomas Brooks, *Walls Come Tumbling Down*, p. 63.
11. See the discussion of laissez-faire association in chapter 12.
12. Lyndon B. Johnson, "To Fulfill These Rights" (June 4, 1965), in Gettleman and Mermelstein, eds., op. cit. Also, for my critique of the doctrine of equality as a result, see Wortham, Anne, "Equal Opportunity Versus Individual Opportunity," p. 416.
13. Branden, *The Psychology of Self-Esteem*.
14. Hall, Freedle, and Cross, *Stages in the Development of a Black Identity*.
15. Charles V. Hamilton, "The Nationalist Versus the Integrationist."

16. Martin Luther King, Jr., *Stride toward Freedom*, p. 176.
17. Tibor R. Machan, *The Pseudo-Science of B. F. Skinner*, p. 193.
18. Ibid., p. 195.
19. Tibor R. Machan, "Law, Justice, and Natural Rights," p. 119.
20. Ayn Rand, *Introduction to Objectivist Epistemology*.
21. Machan, "Law, Justice, and Natural Rights."
22. Arthur A. Shenfield, "Equality before the Law," p. 114.
23. Daniel Bell, "On Meritocracy and Equality."
24. See John Rawls, *A Theory of Justice*.
25. See Arthur M. Okun, *Equality and Efficiency: The Big Tradeoff*.
26. Charles Reich, *The Greening of America*, p. 76.
27. Walter A. Weisskopf, "The Dialectics of Equality," in Donald M. Levine and Mary Jo Bane, eds., *The "Inequality" Controversy*, pp. 214 ff.
28. King, *Stride toward Freedom*, pp. 84–85.
29. Ibid.
30. James Baldwin, *The Fire Next Time*, quoted in Miller, *Martin Luther King, Jr.*, pp. 285, 287.

8

The Power-seeking Nationalist

"If you can't join them, lick them." "If you can't join them, depend on yourself."

Today blacks snicker at the refrain, "black and white together," from the theme song of the movement, "We Shall Overcome." If anybody still sings the theme, it is possibly a nostalgic white liberal.
—Paul Delaney, *New York Times.*

During the 1920s when separatist Marcus Garvey took to the streets of Harlem calling for the repatriation of Negroes to Africa, A. Phillip Randolph, an eminent figure among integrationists, attacked Garvey in his magazine *The Messenger* with what remains the basic premise of integration activism. "The United States is our home," Randolph said. "Our children are here. We have no other country. We have no other home. If there are wrongs in America, Negroes as Americans must help work and fight to correct them. If the problems of race and color are hard in the United States, so be it. Let us not lose heart and run away from them, but gird to solve them."[1]

And still today, over half a century later, Negro integrationists approach the problems of race relations from the position that this white man's house is theirs too and that the best way to gain acceptance as an equal resident is by the interracial drive against discrimination and segregation. Added to this purpose is the hope that the attitudes of whites will change. For, as pointed out, their

163

effort to ban discrimination and segregation is not done solely to right wrongs and reform injustices, but because they believe these changes entail the acceptance of Negroes on an individual basis. Further, they seek not only a place in the dominant culture, but the redemption of their white oppressors. As recently as 1976, a Memphis businessman told the *New York Times* that he saw "a new framework of blacks and whites working together to build Dr. King's dream of one nation." He continued: "If this country is to hold together—and it will—and if it is to prosper—and it will—it must finally include blacks in all its institutions. Black people, because of who we are, what we are and what we have gone through here, are in a position to lead white folks to freedom."

This was the view that dominated the civil rights-integration movement of the early sixties. But forced desegregation and antidiscrimination policies did not result in the universal acceptance of Negroes; they did not lead white folks to freedom; and they have not built on the dream of one nation. Instead, the nation has become increasingly group oriented, and the demands made by ethnic and racial minorities are being echoed by white ethnic groups who are now "revitalized" as political entities seeking their "fair share" of governmental benefits. (It is widely evident that while Negroes have not succeeded in winning the love of their fellowmen, they have been most successful in demonstrating to them the effectiveness of politicized ethnicity in obtaining political privileges and benefits.)[2] Private citizens and businesses are now prohibited from discrimination, and even natural, de facto segregation is arbitrarily interpreted by the courts as de jure segregation and summarily ruled unconstitutional. But there is suspicion and antipathy between the races. Taxpayers of both races resent the millions of dollars poured into Great Society programs and welfare claims that contributed to the further shrinking of the dollar's value and to the bankruptcy of many American cities. That Negroes and whites are not working together to build one nation is as true today as it was in 1968 when the Commission on Civil Disorders first issued that indictment of American society.

From Protest to Power

In 1968 the fact that this was a nation of two intolerant societies— one black and one white—stood out in bold relief. And as violence raged from city to city, it seemed that the two would never meet. The

164

thrust of the civil rights movement had changed from creating integration by changing the attitudes of whites according to the *agape* theory to building up political and economic power; from the integrationist desire to be like whites and the social system they represent to increased contempt for them and hostility toward the system; from the hope of entering the mainstream of American life to the effort to convert the system for the benefit of their ethno-racial interests. "We must start to turn our back on this country," said SNCC chairman Stokely Carmichael. "This country has never cared about black people. They didn't give two damns about us. And all of us always turn around worrying about what's good for America. Later for America. What's good for black people? That's what we want to know."

Carmichael's words expressed the doctrine of Black Power—an about-face from the A. Phillip Randolph position that had dominated the civil rights movement for half a century. Elements of the Black Power doctrine had always existed in the Negro community, but its nationalism was considered a deviant position by the majority of Negroes, who held to the tradition of seeking equal opportunity, justice, and racial harmony through the democratic process. But in the summer of 1965, during a voter registration drive in Lowndes County, Alabama, where none of its 80 percent black population were registered as voters, Carmichael first used the term *Black Power* to describe the desire of black people to control the black community. "That's why the word black power is meaningful to black people and frightening to white people," said one community leader. "Black Power means the power to control your own destiny. That's what black people want. They want to control the community, the economics of the community, the politics of the community. We're tired of having white representation downtown in city government. We're tired of having white merchants take care of our business. We're tired of having white teachers in our schools, white principals, white administrators We want all this to be black."

And in order for black politicians to be effective for the black community, said former Cleveland mayor Carl B. Stokes, "blacks have got to go outside the party [structure] and become a floating, self-interest group like the Jewish electorate, which remains energetic and sensitive to Jewish concerns and whose self-interest is not going to be determined by stock party answers but by individuals—from its support of Richard Nixon in 1972 to its support of Senator Henry Jackson today on Israeli issues."[3]

But Black Power demanded more than political power and separate economic and social institutions in the black communities. It abandoned the nonviolent resistance of the early sixties and called for Negroes to meet violence with violence. In the words of Mao Tse-tung, it held that "power comes from the barrel of a gun," and that this is what Americans respected, not the kind of "boot-licking" engaged in by Integrationists. Black Power also called for a change in the attitude of Negroes toward themselves. It glorified all things black, stressing that "black is beautiful," and insisting that Negroes adopt their own standards rather than "white" values. African clothing and hairstyles became fashionable, and "soul" was used to distinguish the black ethnic quality in everything from food to music. As a further expression of Black Power's rejection of all things "white," its leaders denounced the term *Negro* as a word applied to blacks by white society. They urged Negroes to refer to themselves as *blacks* or *Afro-Americans*.

Black Power was especially appealing to young people, intellectuals, and the middle class, who were impatient with the gradualism of the integration movement. *The Autobiography of Malcolm X* was their bible; "revolution" and "black pride" were their watchwords; and the raised clinched fist was their rallying posture of defiance. They transported the violence of the ghetto streets to university campuses, demanding separate black studies programs, open admission for disadvantaged minorities, separate dormitories for blacks, and more black professors and administrators.

The most feared and extreme among Black Power groups were the Black Muslims and the Black Panther Party. The Black Muslims urged the creation of a separate all-Negro state and prepared its followers for a final battle between the black and white races, called the "Battle of Armageddon." The Black Panther Party was founded in 1966 by Huey P. Newton and Bobby Seale to protect Negro communities from police brutality. But in time it became Marxist-Communist, advocating violent revolution to bring about social change. One of its major goals was to have the United Nations supervise an election among Negroes to determine whether they wished to remain a part of the United States. Another organization advocating the separatism of neo-Garveyism was the Congress of Racial Equality (CORE), which began in 1943 as an integrationist organization but was transformed into an all-black one between 1965 and 1970.

Black Power, writes Brooks, illustrated the transformation of the civil rights movement, not from "moderate" to "extremist," but from what history professor James Hitchcock called "a leadership which, however angry, is essentially pragmatic and concerned with specific problems and demands to a leadership of selfhood, inchoate anger, and fathomless frustration." The final stage was "the ritual assertion of a truism—that the oppressed group experiences a sense of selfhood not ultimately accessible to any outsider no matter how sympathetic, and that the group's liberation involves the bursting of bands which the oppressor does not even dream exist but which are in some sense more real than the obvious chains."[4]

Hitchcock's three stages of the movement are very accurate descriptions of the social metaphysics and political implementations of Black Power discussed in this and the two succeeding chapters. This chapter examines the social metaphysics and marginality of the Black Power pragmatist, whom I call the *Power-seeking Nationalist*.

The Power-seeking Nationalist

This is the individual for whom the Conventionalist's formula "I am as you desire me" has failed to win the approval of others as he had hoped. Like Branden's Power-seeker, he is not only afraid of failing to achieve the societal approval he seeks, but he is consumed by resentment and hostility toward those whose approval he desires and on whom he depends for a perception of reality. Branden gives the following description of the Power-seeker:

> [He] feels too unsure of his ability to gain the love and approval he desires; his sense of inferiority is overwhelming. And the humiliation of his dependence—of his *unrequited* dependence, so to speak—infuriates him. He longs for an escape from the uncertainty of "free market" social metaphysical competition, where he must win men's *voluntary* esteem. He wants to deceive, to manipulate, to coerce the minds of others: to leave them no choice in the matter. He wants to reach a position where he can *command* respect, obedience, love.[5]

Comparing the Power-seeker with the Conventionalist (from whom the Conventional Integrationist is derived), Branden writes:

167

Faced with the question, "What ᴄᴀn I to do with my life?" or "What will make me happy?"—the Conventional social metaphysician seeks the answer among the standard values of his culture: respectability, financial success, marriage, family, professional competence, prestige, etc.

Faced with the question, "How am I to make my existence endurable?"—the Power-seeking social metaphysician seeks the answer in aggressive and destructive action aimed at the external object of his fear: other people.[6]

It is interesting that while Branden names Adolf Hitler as the epitome of the Power-seeking social metaphysician, some twenty-five years earlier in 1937, Stonequist wrote of Hitler as an example of the category of marginal men he called the "denationalized nationalists" from the minority nationalities of Central and Eastern Europe. "Denationalization" is the process of coerced assimilation whereby ruling nationalities maintain their cultural dominance and political power over minority nationalities; it may also be a voluntary process whereby individuals from the minority nationality take on the attributes of the dominant group to escape nationalistic intolerance and oppression. Such was the case with Hitler, whose career Stonequist describes as follows: "Born in Austria (Bohemia) of an Austrian (German) father and a Czech mother, Hitler grew up in a Czech frontier village where the Germans were in the minority. This meant that he was 'teased and bullied by Czech boys and humiliated by Czech teachers. It ate into Hitler's soul; it gave him a fanatical devotion to Germanism and pride in being German.' "[7] In his own words he states, "I soon became a fanatical German Nationalist."[8]

German nationalism provided an escape from his personality conflicts. He was ashamed of his mother who spoke German with a Czechish accent, and resentful of his authoritarian father, an Austrian official. Shame of his mother facilitated hatred of the Slavs; resentment of his father found release in repudiation of the Austrian state. His half-peasant, half-bourgeois family was looked down on by Germans as well as by Austrians: "These subtle distinctions between in-group and out-group, and his own anomalous position in which he seemed to "belong" nowhere, deeply affected the boy."[9]

At the age of seventeen he went to the Austrian capital, Vienna. Here also he was angered by the presence of numerous Slavs; and when he heard a Czech deputy speaking in Czech in the Reichsrath his disgust was transferred to parliaments generally. His attachment to Germany caused him to develop intense hostility to the Austrian state. "Did not we boys already know that this Austrian State had and could have no love for us Germans?" In Vienna he intended to study painting, but failed in the entrance examinations. He was forced to earn his living by doing odd jobs. As a *declasse* he had to rub shoulders with socialistic workmen, and so became hostile to social democracy. Experiences with the large and important population of Jews in Vienna then turned him into an anti-Semite, especially when he learned that they were the leaders of social democracy: "for to my inward satisfaction I knew finally that the Jew was no German." At last he became convinced that Vienna was no place for him: "I hated the motley collection of Czechs, Poles, Hungarians, Ruthenians, Serbs, Croats, and above all that ever-fungoid growth—Jews and again Jews." He fled to Munich, Germany. He himself declares that it was his experiences in Vienna which determined his attitudes toward Judaism and social democracy, and so formed the basis for the post-war Nazi movement.[10]

In Stonequist's account of Hitler's denationalization, we can see both the process of self-immolating assimilation at work and, of course, the social metaphysical solutions Hitler chose therein. Stonequist's narrative provides a view of the ethnonationalism that plagues the peoples of Central Europe to this day, and it affirms a point made earlier: while it can be said that the German people helped create Hitler's Germany, they did not (and could not) produce Hitler. *Adolf Hitler* produced Hitler. So, too, did Malcolm X produce Malcolm X.

The case of Hitler is an extreme example of the Power-seeking Nationalist, and its citation here should by no means be taken as comparable to the dynamics of ethno-racial nationalism in American society. Though certain aspects of Hitler's early psychological conflict may parallel those of ethno-racial nationalists in this society, the politics of his ethnonationalism differed substantially from the solutions sought by nationalists among American ethnic and racial minorities. As Nathan Glazer points out, the level of nationalism and separatism permitted in American society exists within the context of the consensus to create a single national identity out of a mixed population. The subtle and complex adjustments to accommodate a wide variety of different ethnic and racial groups have been made for the most part according to one basic principle, says Glazer; "no formal recognition of the ethnic and racial groups, but every informal recognition of their right and desire to self-development, assimilation or integration at their own chosen rate, to an independent economic base,

169

independent social, religious, and political institutions, and political recognition as part of a united country."[11]

The system of ethnic and national politicization in which Hitler's dilemma of ethnonationalism occurred (the Austrian parliament recognized eight languages as official), differed in principle from the American pattern of reconciling national polity with group distinctiveness by self-regulated integration into the larger society. But his definition of his situation and that which the Negro separatist has of his own situation are quite similar. Hitler believed no country could last that gave equal political recognition to different nationalities; the Negro nationalist believes the lack of politically defined ethnic groups in America has made it all the more difficult for Negroes to compete with white ethnics and nonethnic groups who nevertheless act as special interest groups to influence American politics.

Hitler's story dramatizes the transition that marginal social metaphysicians make from wanting to belong and be accepted by the dominant culture to opposing that culture and retreating to the hoped-for automatic acceptance given him by his subculture. In his native Austria, Hitler was a German minority and his German-Czech parentage put him in the humiliating position of belonging nowhere—of being "in between." Like the nationalist who flees the multiracial culture of his birth to be embraced by the culture of his ethno-racial ancestors, Hitler escaped his "nowhere" position in Austria and fled to Germany, the "somewhere" of his ancestral origin. No one, most of all Jews, would be able to question his significance again; for, in his mind, Germany was his and he was Germany's.

Persistent in his desire to gain control over men's judgment of him, one way or the other, Hitler's formula for solving his dilemma became: *If you can't join them, lick them*, a solution chosen by Power-seekers throughout history.

The Power-seeking nationalist has been unsuccessful in his attempts to gain the kind of acceptance he wants from members of the dominant culture and is made even more insecure by his frustrated need for visibility from them. Having failed to gain unconditional love and acceptance, he seeks protection against the world that threatens and rejects him. To him that world is a hostile, humiliating place populated by those he can dominate or those who can dominate him. Since he lacks the power to dominate them, and since he refuses to accommodate the differences between them and him, his solution is to withdraw from their world in a frantic, determined, obsessive search for the "new selfhood" he hopes to find in his racial identification. But he has merely substituted the comfort of one group identification for the identity he failed to achieve in the other, without bothering to consider whether any group identity at all is necessary for his well-being.

The Negro nationalist wants to be "American," but the process of self-regulated integration that makes one a participant in the mainstream of American society is a slow process, especially in his case where the obstacles of prejudice and discrimination continue to plague him and undermine his efforts toward progress. "My people have been in this country for 300 years and look what we have to show for it," he says. "The Constitution was not written with me in mind. When the Declaration of Independence proclaimed all men to be equal, my people were not even thought of as men." The history of his people's suffering weighs heavily on him, and he wants relief— now! Impatient to overcome the irrational attitudes of prejudice and racial antipathy, he rejects the notion of a single national identification, calling it an Anglo-Saxon contrivance to dominate racial and ethnic minorities; instead, he opts for the ethnocentrism of "black awareness" and black nationalism.

Sociologist Robert K. Merton has criticized this solution as what he calls the doctrine of "insiders." When a once largely powerless group acquires a sense of growing power, as has been the case with many integrationists-turned-nationalists, "its members experience an intensified need for self-affirmation," Merton said. "Under such circumstances, collective self-glorification, found in some measure among all groups, becomes a frequent and intensified counter-response to longstanding belittlement from without."[12]

From his position of ethnic exclusivity, the Nationalist looks with disgust at what he perceives as the Integrationist's conformity to the ways and means of "white America." To him the Integrationist's desire to assimilate characteristics of the larger society is a form of self-hatred—a rejection of his ethno-racial identity. While the Integrationist views integration as a means by which whites may accept Negroes on an equal level, the Nationalist believes integration is merely used by whites to keep Negroes powerless and frustrate their aspiration. As black nationalist Roy Innis, director of Congress of Racial Equality (CORE), has said: "Integration, in fact, is not possible in the United States with the legacy of racism that exists. Even if possible, integration could in no way satisfy our need of self-determination."

One has only to consider integration as a process of personal association between members of different races and to think in terms of the self-assertiveness required in harmonious integration to understand why Innis would find integration incompatible with the need for the group identification he calls "self-determination." And he is partly right: the individual who defines the human need for self-determination in terms of *his* ethno-racial identification and attempts to fulfill that need by negating the requirements of authentic self-identity is not likely to achieve integration on a personal level or find satisfaction in an integrated society. His involvement in self-immolating assimilation only puts him farther from individual self-determination and self-regulated integration.

Nationalists say that the integration movement failed to achieve its goals. But the truth of the matter is that what was expected of integration, more correctly, desegregation, could not be realistically achieved. Integration requires the mutual consent of individuals and when consent is substituted with coercion, integration is near impossible. The promise of social harmony and political equality could not be fulfilled when their very requisites were so systematically negated. Power-seeking Nationalists did not make an objective inquiry as to why the integration movement failed and what little thought they did give to the matter always ended with the conclusion that white racism was the one and only cause. Since they could not achieve integration as they perceived it—Now!—they would simply declare it as irrelevant. Their salvation lay in a destiny separate from the rest of American society.

The most articulate of the anti-integrationists was Malcolm X during his days as a principle spokesman for the Black Muslims. His social theology was called "The Hate That Hate Produced," the title of the first-time documentary on the Black Muslims on CBS's *60 Minutes* in 1959. Malcolm X preached the hard-line separatism advocated by Elijah Muhammad, the leader of the Nation of Islam. "Our enemy is the white man," he told audiences in Muslim storefront temples across the country. "The white man is the devil!"[13]

As the civil rights movement gained momentum during the late fifties and early sixties, he called leaders of the Negro civil rights organizations "integration-mad puppets," "Uncle Toms," and "black bodies with white heads."

Why wasn't integration the answer to American Negroes' problems? "No *sane* black man really wants integration," he answered.

> No *sane* white man really wants integration! No sane black man really believes that the white man will ever give the black man anything more than token integration. No! . . . for the black man in America the only solution is complete *separation* from the white man! . . . Since Western society is deteriorating, it has become overrun with immorality, and God is going to judge it and destroy it. And the only way the black people caught up in this society can be saved is not to *integrate* into this corrupt society, but to separate from it, to a land of our *own*, where we can reform ourselves, lift up our moral standards, and try to be godly.

When integrationists equated his separatism with racism and segregation, Malcolm X explained, "We reject *segregation* even more militantly than you say you do. We want *separation*, which is not the same! . . . Segregation is when your life and liberty are controlled, regulated, *by someone else*."

The Integrationists appealed to whites in the words of Martin Luther King, Jr.: "In winning our freedom we will so appeal to your heart and conscience that we will win you in the process." But nationalists like Malcolm X directed their message to Negroes, summoning them to racial solidarity:

> The American black man should be focusing his every effort toward building his own businesses, and decent homes for himself. As other ethnic groups have done, let the black people wherever possible, however possible, patronize their own kind, hire their own kind, and start in those ways to build up the black race's ability to do for itself. That's the only way the American black man is ever going to get respect. One thing the white man never can give the black man is self-respect! The black man never can become independent and recognized as a human being who is truly equal with other human beings until he has what they have, and until he is doing for himself what others are doing for themselves.

> The black man in the ghettoes, for instance, has to start self-correcting his own material, moral, and spiritual defects and evils. The black man needs to start his own program to get rid of drunkenness, drug addiction, prostitution. The black man in America has to lift up his own sense of values.

This, in essence, was the philosophy of Black Power, preached and practiced by the Muslims long before Stokely Carmichael uttered those volatile words in Lowndes County. The Muslims advocated territorial separatism long before Roy Innis began his separatist campaign. They practiced economic separatism long before "black capitalism" schemes became fashionable.

Negro leaders had long scoffed at the Muslim approach and denounced Malcolm X's "militancy." And in the late sixties they and their white supporters were stunned by the growing number of young firebrands who, in the words of Carmichael, declared: "We want power, pure unadulterated political power. . . . We are out to take power legally, but if we're stopped by the government from doing it legally, we're going to take it the way everyone else took it, including the way Americans took it in the American Revolution."[14] Such calls for separation from the American community and its social institutions and the implied threat of war on whites were rejected out of hand by most leaders of the integration movement. But as they sought remedies to the racial violence of the ghetto that had spilled over onto college campuses, they began to take second notice of the philosophy that so many young Negroes adhered to.

They saw that, indeed, some of Malcolm X's angry words made sense, particularly his admonishment to blacks to overcome the shortcomings in their lives and in their communities. He had hit the nerve of self-sufficiency that had always been a driving force among Negroes determined to enter the mainstream of American life. Many weary Integrationists even began to see some validity in Carmichael's call to power. They could not see themselves becoming anarchists, but they began to see the practicality of relinquishing the hope of converting the attitudes of whites and directing their energy instead to employing racial solidarity to gain the political power necessary to achieve their dream of egalitarian integration. By the early seventies, they were moving increasingly in the direction of the assassinated Malcolm X, as he had begun to move toward their position after his ouster from the Muslims and subsequent pilgrimage to Mecca in 1964.

In a publicized letter from Mecca, Malcolm X put forth ideas that were decidedly the opposite of his previously held notions. Upon his return to the United States, he said, "My pilgrimage broadened my scope. It blessed me with a new insight. . . . In the past, yes, I have made sweeping indictments of *all* white people. I never will be guilty of that again—as I know now that some white people *are* truly sincere, that some truly are capable of being brotherly toward a black man. The true Islam [as opposed to Elijah Muhammad's religion] has shown me that a blanket indictment of all white people is as wrong as when whites make blanket indictments against blacks.

"Yes, I have been convinced that *some* American whites do want to help cure the rampant racism which is on the path to destroying this country!" But, he added, "the *problem* here in America is that we meet such a small minority of individual so-called 'good' or 'brotherly' white people. Here in the United States, notwithstanding those few 'good' white people, it is the *collective* 150 million white people whom the *collective* 22 million black people have to deal with!"

He no longer advocated complete separation from whites. He wanted to "deal" with whites, but never forgetting that "the seeds of racism are so deeply rooted in the white people collectively, their belief that they are 'superior' in some way is so deeply rooted, that these things are in the national white subconsciousness."

Upon his return from Mecca he tried to reshape his earlier public image and began to develop a black nationalist organization that would "instill within black men the racial dignity, the incentive, and the confidence that the black race needs today to get up off its knees, and to get on its feet, and get rid of its scars, and to take a stand for itself." All he wanted to do, he said, was to "help create a society in which there could exist honest white-black brotherhood." Apparently just a month before his death, he had even changed his views on integration and intermarriage. He told a television interviewer: "I believe in recognizing every human being as a human being—neither white, black, brown, or red; and when you are dealing with humanity as a family there's no question of integration or intermarriage. It's just one human being marrying another human being."

But while he seemed to have condoned private association between blacks and whites, he was still skeptical about whites joining black organizations to solve racial problems. White membership in black organizations could only make those organizations less effective, he said, because he believed "white people who want to join black organizations are really just taking the escapist way to salve their consciences." To white civil rights activists he said, "Work in conjunction with us—each of us working among our own kind. . . . Let sincere whites go and preach nonviolence to white people!" And he added:

We will completely respect our white co-workers. They will deserve every credit. We will give them every credit. We will meanwhile be working among our own kind, in our own black communities—showing and teaching black men in ways that only other black men can—that the black man has got to help himself. Working separately, the sincere white people and sincere black people actually will be working together. In our mutual sincerity we might be able to show a road to the salvation of America's very soul.

The transition of Malcolm X from hard-core opposition to all whites to the willingness to deal with some of them represents just two aspects of the Black Power ideology. Varying in emphasis, purpose, and implementation, its advocates have called for every kind of solution to their dilemma of marginality—from coalition politics to militant anarchy. Harold Cruse has described the Black Power movement as having several elements: "It has what I call a bourgeois economic reform element, and a separatist land element, and an identity rhetoric, and group culture values, and it also contains what we see in the streets, a revolutionary anarchist element. There is no one element that covers the whole range of Black Power ideas. However, fundamental to understanding it is seeing Negroes as a group seeking democratic parity within the American group and class structure. It is a group demand."[15] Between the two Black Power factions believing in permanent territorial separatism on the one hand and the use of temporary separatism as a tactic on the other, Cruse saw a middle ground with an implied objective of cultural pluralism as the most democratic method of accommodating the differences of racial and ethnic groups.

With the exception of its territorial separatism and militant retaliation, the Black Power philosophy continues to influence both Integrationists and Nationalists alike. However, "Black Power" as a concept is used less often to describe civil rights activism; terms like "black nationalism," "ethnic revitalization," and "politicized ethnicity" are used instead. These concepts represent a change in tactics but the goal of gaining "pure, unadulterated power" remains the solution to the dilemma of marginal social metaphysics that burdens the Power-seeker.

From Reactionary to Pragmatic Nationalism

Tactically the Black Power/Nationalist movement has shifted from the "lick them" solution of *reactionary nationalism* to the "protect and depend on ourselves" policy of *pragmatic nationalism.* The pragmatic nationalists occupy that middle ground which Cruse described as lying between permanent territorial separatism and temporary separatism. These are the individuals who no longer hope for black-white togetherness in pursuit of integration but are resigned to employing forms of community control as the instrument of political power to force an integrated society into being. "Our solution is not in the prospect of whites changing their attitudes, but in the building of our own black political and economic strengths," said a Tennessee legislator. He urged the "organization of blacks, not so much to oppose whites but to protect ourselves. We can only depend on ourselves."

As marginal men the pragmatic nationalists are caught between two appealing cultures; but as political social metaphysicians, they stand between the appeal of integration and the political advantages of black nationalism. Unlike the reactionary nationalists who rejected the integrationist approach altogether, the pragmatists still relate to the integrationist expectation, but are now addressing their grievances and expectations to the black communities in which they live or represent rather than to "white America." They may be educators, politicians, clergymen, intellectuals, students, and journalists who individually enjoy the benefits of social integration but often lack a sense of acceptance by their white colleagues. And even if they themselves are accepted by whites, they do not see that acceptance being extended by whites as a group to Negroes as a group. Having failed to achieve that, they concede it as a "limitation" of desegregation and attempt to solve the alienation it causes them by promoting the "self-determination" of their group. This is the position of many black legislators who occupy seats in an integrated Congress but nevertheless feel the necessity of a Congressional Black Caucus, which works for the passage of legislation that will benefit Negroes as a group.

Integrationists worked to solve the problem of white racism. But the pragmatic nationalists say: let whites who believe in brotherly love solve the problem of white racism; let blacks solve the problem of black powerlessness. Integration will become psychologically possible, they say, only after sufficient power has been generated to overcome not only the attitudes of prejudice and discrimination among whites but also the deep sense of inferiority that is one of the great problems of the Negro community. Their aim is to overcome the effects of the Negro's past separation from the American mainstream by turning the symbols of that separation into a source of power to be reckoned with by the larger society, particularly its economic and political institutions.

Many pragmatic nationalists have come to believe that the laws banning discrimination and the changing attitudes toward minorities are sufficient to relax the fight against racism per se and place greater emphasis on nonracial economic and political inequities. But others still believe racism is embedded so deep in the white psyche that even the most "liberal" nondiscriminators find themselves jolted occasionally by a wave of prejudice they thought they had exorcised for good. They would agree with Malcolm X that even the many "good" white people who sincerely want black-white brotherhood cannot escape the pull of the collective white racism that permeates American society. Indeed, it is true that while antidiscrimination laws and social pressure may have eliminated the threat of discrimination and segregation in some instances and deinstitutionalized it in most, they have not succeeded in correcting the attitudes and emotions of the prejudiced. As pointed out, the American society is largely desegregated, but not integrated. And that, says this group of nationalists, is because of white racism. Like the integrationists, they want a society of unprejudiced non-discriminators in which automatic acceptance of Negroes would prevail. And until that is achieved they continue to focus on racism as the primary cause of their problems. As Ronald Brown of the Washington bureau of the National Urban League put it: "One lesson that has emerged is that despite the good rationale for deracializing the campaign for better opportunity, it probably is not wise. Racism is at the root of most of our problems."[16]

Bayard Rustin, longtime advocate of coalition politics, disagrees. In a 1970 article critical of the separatist movement, Rustin wrote that it is time for the Negro to redefine his problem as one of economics rather than race. If he can appreciate the "economic dimension of racial injustice," wrote Rustin, he will see that the only solution to racial injustice is an alliance between him and the white worker against the white capitalist. "If the Negro chooses to follow the path of interracial alliances on the basis of class, he can achieve a certain degree of economic dignity, which in turn offers a genuine, if not the only, opportunity for self-determination."[17]

178

The real cause of racial injustice is not bad attitudes, said Rustin, but bad social conditions brought on by the concentration of wealth in the hands of a few. Neither the escapism of anti-integrationism and localism nor the guilt and misplaced sympathy of the breast-beating white liberal will solve the problem. "What is needed," he wrote, "is a political strategy that offers the real possibility of economically uplifting millions of impoverished individuals, black and white." That strategy must "rest upon an identification of those central institutions which, if altered sufficiently, would transform the social and economic relations in our society; and it must provide a politically viable means of achieving such an alteration." With such a strategy of coalition, he asserted, "the wealth of the nation can be redistributed and some of its most grievous social problems solved."

Charles V. Hamilton, a pragmatic nationalist and coauthor with Stokely Carmichael of *Black Power: The Politics of Liberation in America*, concurs with Rustin, the egalitarian integrationist, on the importance of deracializing certain issues that affect Negroes. In a paper he wrote at the request of the Democratic Advisory Council, Hamilton urged the Democratic party to couple the legislative implementation of President Johnson's "equality of results" doctrine with the search for deracialized solutions to civil rights issues. Hamilton said that some issues, such as affirmative action, busing, and redlining, "do not lend themselves to deracialized solutions"; however, proposals such as the improvement of "essential public services," the full employment program, and national health service "do not require special or particular reference to blacks."

He added: "Seeking such deracialized solutions to as many issues as possible need not be understood as a political device to avoid dealing with delicate matters. Rather, the argument could and ought to be made that this kind of approach makes substantive policy sense and the Democratic Party recognizes that fact, not in order to hold a political coalition together across racial lines, but to achieve a more civilized, humane society."[18]

Hamilton's position represents the synthesis between reactionary anti-white activism and the coalition politics of the moderate integrationists that began to take shape in the 1970s. It is the thinking prevalent among the new black politician class, which

179

Kilson characterizes as "based upon established or newly fashioned political machines rather than upon civil rights organizations and the clientage ties with liberal whites of the older Negro leadership."[19] While this pragmatic approach deemphasizes militancy and anti-white orientation, it functions within a political atmosphere of what Kilson calls "marked black-white polarization related to the ideological movement of black ethnocentric revitalization." Thus, it remains for the new black politician class to keep the "identity-sustaining benefits" of black ethnicity energized and to "translate the emergent power-mustering capacity of Negroes into public policies that will raise the standards of the Negro social system to levels comparable to those of white America."[20]

What all this means, in the simplest language, is that out of the Negro's protest against his forced separation from the American mainstream developed an appreciation by black and white politicians for the political power blacks hold as a pressure lobby. The marginal Power-Seeker may not be active in every aspect of the larger society, but his presence as a political force is felt by that society. Indeed, as the country becomes more and more of what one foreign visitor called "a federation of ethnic communities," it behooves the Power-Seeker to capitalize on his ethnic exclusivity (at least temporarily, say some) rather than mute it or reject it for the inclusiveness of being simply "an American." While in the 1960s he perceived his racial identification as being tied to victimization and oppression, in the 1970s he came to view his racial identification as the source of power and the rationalization for retribution. He is no longer just a seeker of power but in many instances a legitimate, duly elected holder of power. From the powerless "victim" of racist America whose salvation lay in separatism and anarchy has emerged the vigorous competitor who uses his ethnic exclusivity against the neo-ethnicity of Italians, Poles, the Irish, Jews, Greeks, Puerto Ricans, and others—all after the same power and benefits from the government he is after. The black-white polarization over civil rights has been transformed into a battle for political muscle that often cuts across racial boundaries to pit the ethnics (including Negroes) against the special-interest groups.[21]

The Tradition of Black Separation

While the politicization of black ethnicity is a recent development, ethnic exclusiveness is not new in Negro history; it only lacked the legitimation that certain groups like the Jews have capitalized on for years. The choice of nationalists to ameliorate their marginal position between cultures by focusing their attention and purpose on their black subculture has its roots in the folk traditions and social institutions of Negroes.[22]

From Reconstruction until the pre-welfare era of this century, self-determination among Negroes truly meant *self-determination*.[23] The Emancipation Proclamation freed Negroes of slavery, but it did not free them to participate fully in American life. There was no Office of Minority Affairs, no Office of Equal Opportunity, no Equal Employment Opportunity Commission to implement the freedom given slaves by the proclamation. The Freedman's Bureau, which sought the rehabilitation of whites and blacks after the Civil War, was restricted both by law and white resistance in how far it could go in its mission to rehabilitate Negroes as a group. The 1866 Civil Rights Act and the Fourteenth Amendment provided for the protection of Negro freedom, but little was done to implement it. That was something each Negro would have to do on his own—against the incredible odds of segregation, the doctrine of "white supremacy," poverty, ignorance, and disfranchisement. But these overwhelming obstacles to the actualization of freedom were no reason to abandon the hope that it was possible. Theirs was incomplete freedom, but they made the most of it by energizing the circumstances of their separation with ingenuity, skill, and knowledge. As historian John Hope Franklin points out, the experiences the Negro had in the social and economic world of whites convinced him more and more that the brunt of the burden of his development would have to be borne by himself.

The effort to achieve self-determination while being excluded from the mainstream of American society was a positive goal (like that of so many immigrants to this land), the purpose of which was to enable Negroes to improve their status and extend the parameters of freedom to the fullest. From their excluded position they developed their own social institutions and their own cultural life but with the idea that these would one day give way to the greater priority of the integration imperative. The questions before them were quite clear-cut: would they remain enslaved and separated, or free and separated? At the time neither the society nor its laws allowed for seriously entertaining the third alternative: free and integrated. But while they had no choice but to accept the free and

181

separate social life, it was the hope for a free and integrated social life that motivated the activities within their world.

The problem of achieving a desegregated social system was not one Negroes could solve alone, however; for it involved the society's acceptance of them as equally capable of participating in the affairs of a civilized community. As Franklin writes: "Negroes persistently sought opportunities to enter more fully into the affairs of American life, but the overtures were more frequently spurned than not. They were forced back into their own world, and as they erected more institutions and ways of life of their own the prospect of Americanization became more remote."[24] The prospect was indeed remote, but at no time did Negroes ever concede it to be impossible. For even as assimilation was denied to them as a group, the limited participation of individuals in the affairs of the larger community helped to shape Negro institutions and also promoted the integration of these individuals into the pattern of life of the community.

The fact is that nothing short of expulsion or annihilation could restrain the individual determined to assimilate attributes of the larger culture, and even to penetrate many of its barriers. Segregated America was nonetheless America.[25] The very nature of its social system was such that the only way the door of opportunity could be completely closed to Negroes was to close it to all Americans. And that could not be achieved without altering the very political and economic structure of the nation. Separated though they were, Negroes were nevertheless Americans and the taste of freedom continued to goad them on to achieve the fullness of their citizenship. Writes Franklin: "The growth and persistence of the Negro world did not result in the resignation of the Negro to life in this relatively small orbit. There were numerous manifestations of the effort to rise above the proscriptions that were thrown around the Negro community. These manifestations were reminiscent of the efforts that many Negro slaves made to escape their bondage and were also similar to them."[26]

Universal among Negroes after the Civil War and since was the idea that the key to complete freedom is knowledge. "The pursuit of education, therefore, came to be one of the great preoccupations of Negroes," writes Franklin, "and enlightenment was viewed by many as the greatest single opportunity to escape the increasing proscriptions and indignities that a renascent South was heaping upon Negroes."[27] Untold sacrifices were made and great inconveniences suffered so that Negro children could secure the learning that had been denied their fathers and mothers. It is perhaps accurate to say that greater than the imperative of integration was the imperative of education.

Both whites and Negroes knew that if knowledge did not lead to integration, it would certainly lead to self-sufficiency and power, however limited the actual exercise of that power might be. Separate schools and inferior education surely made the prophesy of white supremacy self-fulfilling, but to the intellectually impoverished Negro any education, even separate and unequal, was superior to none at all. If whites could do nothing to prevent Negroes from learning, they could at least make it difficult for them to learn well and amass the knowledge required to perform competitively in an open society. And failing that, they could restrict their opportunities to compete. But school segregation, inadequate facilities, poorly trained teachers, and lack of finances did not stop the progress of Negro education. Chroniclers of race relations in segregated America often ignore the fact that while thousands of Negroes fled to the industrial north for better opportunities, many thousands more remained in the agrarian south and educated their children, who became leaders of the Negro community; that the very foundation of Negro progress was being shaped in the segregated south, not the north.

While Negroes moved forward in education with the help of Northern philanthropists and educators, "the vast majority of Negroes were facing the difficult task of making a living and were becoming more and more convinced that they would have to work out their own salvation in terms of the means at their immediate disposal. . . . Frustrated in their efforts to participate in the development of businesses of the whites, they embarked on a program of 'Negro business enterprise' in which they undertook to be their own producers and employers."[28] And in doing so they adopted the business ideals and social values of the rest of America in order to assimilate themselves more completely.

The lack of opportunities for Negroes to participate fully in the affairs of other institutions caused many to concentrate their energy and attention on the church. "Perhaps the most powerful institution in the Negro's world is the church," writes Franklin. "Nothing in his world was so completely his own as his church. It provided self-expression, recognition, and leadership."[29]

The Negro press also performed an important function in the increasingly separate world of the Negro community. "Negro newspapers of the twentieth century became the medium through which the yearnings of the race were expressed, the platform from which the Negro leaders could speak, the coordinator of mass action which Negroes felt compelled to take, and the instrument by which many Negroes were educated with respect to public affairs.[30]

And all the while, as Negroes developed the institutions of their separate world, being nurtured in it were poets, novelists, composers, artists, athletes, entertainers in all fields, scientists, and educators who would one day burst the seams of their confinement like shooting stars to penetrate the larger culture with their talent and original ability.

The experience of participating in the ownership and control of their own institutions were exhilarating, writes Franklin. "It stimulated their pride and preserved the self-respect of many who had been humiliated in their efforts to adjust themselves to American life." But this was only a taste of freedom; it was not the full measure. Pride and self-respect would always hang in the balance until they were free and equal and integrated.

Between Separation and Integration

The achievements of Negroes as a group have occurred primarily during the last half of the century when greater national emphasis was put on the integration movement, and the trend toward conferring benefits on blacks and minorities reached its height during the Great Society era. But the history of American Negroes has been one of compulsory segregation, not integration. Most of the advances made by individual Negroes and by the group as a whole, from the early days of the republic and beyond, occurred within the context of their separation, imposed or otherwise. Thus, even as the integrationist movement gained increased momentum in its protest against the imposed segregation of Negroes, their separate way of life had become a tradition not easily relinquished by many.

When segregationists complained that integration threatened to destroy a way of life that both whites and Negroes valued, they were partly correct. Theoretically, the imposition of integration in every realm of society requires the dissolution of the Negro community and its social institutions as much as it does that of the white community. In a very real sense, one element of the Black Power/Nationalist movement was its pluralistic backlash to imposed integration. Laced throughout the rhetoric and writings of Black Power advocates was their condemnation of integrationists for selling out the black community to the man downtown. "Integration is irrelevant," said Stokely Carmichael. The pluralists among them wanted the legal ban on discrimination and de jure segregation as much as any egalitarian integrationist, but they did not expect that the implementation of antidiscrimination policies would have the effect of outlawing their separate way of life. For them, free and equal opportunity must also include the right to live and interact with people like oneself. They wanted to live in Negro neighborhoods, attend black churches, buy goods and services produced by black entrepreneurs, and send their children to neighborhood schools and to black colleges and universities. They wanted to work in black communities and affiliate with black social and professional organizations.

Early reactionary nationalists blamed the failure of integration on white racism alone, but pragmatic nationalists admitted rather guardedly that integration also failed because its price was more than blacks were willing to pay. Integrationist Harold Howe II of the Ford Foundation took a second look at the movement and wrote: "Early moves toward integration went too far in the direction of asking blacks and other minorities to join American society solely on white terms, to forget any pride of interest in their own heritage, or, if you will, to become white men." (It should be noted, however, that this was precisely what many Conventional Integrationists wanted in order to solve the dilemma of their marginal position.)

Howe continues: "Now we know that integration is a two-way street, that it is not just a simple matter of mixing people in some judicially or administratively determined proportion, that non-whites as well as whites must set the terms, and that these terms must include as a matter of dignity and right the opportunity for nonwhites to lead and control some of the institutions in our pluralistic society."[31]

But the integrationist movement was always one-sided in its interpretation that the absence of blacks in white communities and white-owned institutions as evidence of exclusion and that the absence of whites in Negro institutions as evidence of imposed separation. As Thomas Sowell points out, the element of choice is completely left out of the logic that goes from underrepresentation or no representation to exclusion.[32] To be sure, most Negro educational and social institutions were founded to provide education and social services for blacks who were segregated out of white institutions. But these institutions exist now because blacks either *prefer* them to integrated institutions or find that they are best suited to meet their limited financial resources and that as agents of remediation, they serve as invaluable points of transition from the debilitating effects of black-white separation to the demands of nonracial competition.

Indeed, even in housing, not all unintegrated residential areas are the result of racial discrimination, but the inability of blacks to afford such homes or their preference to live elsewhere. And many leaders complain as much about black flight from traditional black neighborhoods as they complain about white flight from center cities. Contrary to what many social theorists hold, job opportunities and quality education are not necessarily prerequisites for racial integration. As pointed out in chapter 7, integration is a matter of personal choice. Some of the most highly educated Negroes and those earning above-average salaries prefer to work and live among their own kind. That they do is not necessarily an indictment of integration; neither is it necessarily a response to exclusion. But it is most certainly an expression of their right to voluntary association, which ought to be protected.

Nowhere is the threat of de jure integration to the existence of traditional institutions in the Negro community as great as it is in Negro higher education.[33] "The Negro public colleges are in imminent danger of losing their identity through integration, merger with larger predominantly white public institutions, reduced status or outright abolition," reported the Race Relations Information Center in 1971. Even so, the majority of black students still attend predominantly black colleges—thirty-five public and sixty private. And even though philosophically their reason for being no longer exists, black educators and community leaders insist that a strong case can be made, on practical grounds, for preserving and strengthening them. As the *New York Times* reported, "The fear of administrators and faculties is more than a loss of black identity, but also possible loss of jobs, as has happened to Negro principals and teachers in public school integration."

To pragmatic nationalists and pluralists, the black college is not only a source of employment but is uniquely equipped to provide the intellectual and political leadership that is crucial to the politization of black ethnicity. But movement integrationists like social psychologist Kenneth Clark have argued that black colleges are relics of the past and should no longer be maintained as separatist institutions. "I'm not in favor of black colleges, whites colleges, or colleges for those who are five feet, eight inches tall. You can only have black colleges if you accept the absurdity of racism," he said. "I happen to take education seriously, and I think its purpose is to broaden people away from the institutionalization of racism. The question is—is Howard a good university? Does it stimulate creativity? Not, is it black?"[34]

The rapid advance of the integration movement has plainly caught the educational and other institutions in the Negro community unprepared for competition in a desegregated society. The contradiction of a free and separated Negro community is now threatened by the free and integrated society that blacks have fought for, for so long. And like their Jewish counterparts, the response of pragmatists is to put the reins on integration in favor of preserving the black institutions that symbolize their racial identification. As one N.A.A.C.P. official said, "We want integration, but not annihilation."

Implementing Nationalism

An important difference between the attitudes of present-day black nationalism and traditional Negro self-determination is the lack of ethnic exclusivity (chauvinism) in the latter. Negroes developed their own institutions during the late nineteenth and early twentieth centuries in order to *survive*, not to escape the risks and responsibilities of a pluralistic society. They were for the most part integrationists forced to live a separate way of life. Even as they developed their world, they fought against its existence—against the structural and cultural confinements to which their color condemned them. These free and separate Negroes of the era preceding the welfare state were compelled to fight for the sanction and protection of their human rights, not for the preferential treatment of political privilege sought by today's pragmatists. As their most well-known spokesman, Booker T. Washington, said: "the wisest among my race understand . . . that progress in the enjoyment of all privileges that will come to us must be the result of severe and constant struggle rather than of artificial forcing."[35]

By "privileges" Washington meant those social and economic conditions of opportunity that are the achievement of individuals and not the province of governmental policy and administration. He did not believe that members of his race should be granted unearned privileges in American society, but that they should create opportunities for themselves, voluntarily and within the confines of law and equal justice. He was critical of many applications of the law, especially those used to violate the rights of Negroes and to confer undue political advantages on whites, but he did not believe that such violations could be corrected by still further violations on the part of Negroes. He believed that ultimately it was not the law alone that would improve the lot of Negroes but their active participation in the free markets of ideas and economic industry. And the "severe and constant struggle" he spoke of was not just the struggle against white antagonism, but the Negro's struggle to assert his initiative in creating authentic self-earned privileges, albeit in a segregated society. The key to social and economic privilege, he believed, was human ability, not legislative manipulation. Unfortunately, Washington's approach had little influence on the integration movement, which became more and more egalitarian as the nation itself grew increasingly statist.

Today integrationists and nationalists alike believe that the only solution to Negro advancement is by conferring on them specially created privileges and benefits. Wishing to avoid the effort, competition, and risks of electoral politics, separatist nationalists at the 1972 black political convention said: "We want the establishment of Black Congressional representatives in proportion to our presence in the national population. We are at least 15 percent of the population. Through Constitutional amendment—or any other means necessary—we ought to have a minimum of 66 Representatives and 15 Senators; that until such time as the House and Senate represent black people fairly, our due seats are filled by persons elected at-large by the national black community. The same principle should obtain for state and local governments." In 1976, Mayor Richard Hatcher of Gary, Indiana, proposed a black representation of 25 percent among the delegates to the National

Democratic Convention. Both proposals are preposterously racist, and the only way they could be implemented is by a fundamental change in the American political system that would recognize ethnic groups as political entities.

Black students and their white supporters had a field day imposing their brand of reverse racism on educational institutions across the country. Afraid and contemptuous of open academic competition, they demanded that institutions of higher education accommodate their fear and inefficacy by establishing black-studies-for-blacks-only: their "territory, a private domain with frontiers that must be jealously guarded [at university expense] against the enemy." Said one student: "Competition is nothing more than an Anglo creation, created to keep certain people excluded from full participation." They pressured administrators into recruiting black faculty for black courses who would not have met the standards of the rest of the university programs. "If you're black and you're pushing a broom out there on the sidewalk, you are 'qualified' to teach black studies," said the publisher of *Liberator* magazine. Intimidated by the traditional "cold objectivity" of the academic environment, they complained of "institutional in-difference" to their culture, which, according to them, was driving black students away from courses. The solution, they said, was to recruit black instructors to the predominantly white campuses to give "a kind of black informedness accompanying the academic expertise that will have the over-all effect of humanizing the white university experience for the black student."

Afraid to win the voluntary esteem of their white college peers, nationalist students manipulated the uncertainty and fear of college administrators of universities like the University of Michigan, where a student-faculty policy board unanimously recommended that up to 400 black students be allowed to move into Afro-American and African culture living units in two university dormitories. Why did the black students demand this racial segregation? One of the leading advocates of the plan said it was a chance for black students "to get themselves together—to establish a power base."

The demand of reactionary nationalists for a "black perspective" in academia began in 1967 with student rebellions on the Negro campuses of Fisk, Central State, and Howard universities and spread, even more viciously, to predominantly white campuses from coast to coast. Among the most terrorizing disruptions to the education process and the very organizational structure and purpose of the universities were those on the campuses of San Francisco State College, Cornell University, and the City College of New York (CCNY). At City College the turmoil and state of siege caused by black and Puerto Rican dissidents ended only after administrators agreed to set up a dual system of admissions known as "open admissions," which would admit half of the freshmen class on the basis of grades and test scores and the other half, from poverty areas, without regard to conventional college admissions credentials.[36] The sacrifice of quality education and meritorious admission to mediocrity and ethnic balance took its toll on the City University system, and by 1975 this most prestigious of the nation's public college systems found itself bankrupt and on the verge of closing for good.

While open admissions and other for-minorities-only programs became the order of the day in educating America's college and university students, 1971 saw the beginning of the imposition of affirmative action programs on the academic world that required the establishment of numerical "goals and timetables" for increasing the "utilization" of minority groups and women. The affirmative action quota system in business and academic hiring became the most apparent implementation of the pragmatic synthesis between integration and separatism, which employs the priority of race as the means of achieving social integration. A letter to the president of the University of Arizona on March 31, 1971, from an HEW official ordered: "Department Heads should be advised that, in addition to the active recruitment of females, affirmative action requires that Government contractors consider *other factors than mere technical qualifications*"[37] (emphasis added).

In order to comply with HEW guidelines, San Francisco State College announced an affirmative action plan that called for "an employee balance which in ethnic and male/female groups, approximates that of the general population of the Bay Area from which we recruit. What this means is that we have shifted from the ideal of equal opportunity in employment to a deliberate effort to seek out qualified and *qualifiable* people among ethnic minority groups and women to fill all jobs in our area"[38] (emphasis added).

In a letter to deans and department chairmen, the president of Cornell University described the university's affirmative action policy as "the hiring of additional minority persons and females even if in many instances, it may be necessary *to hire unqualified or marginally qualified* persons"[39] (emphasis added).

One of the more publicized of the affirmative action horror stories is that of American Telephone & Telegraph (AT & T) being forced to pay $15 million to 15,000 employees as compensation for past discriminatory hiring and promotion practices. For this and other programs, the Equal Employment Opportunity Commission agreed to drop its opposition to rate increases for AT&T. Throughout the 1970s similar stories were reported almost daily in the newspapers. Most of them did not make the headlines or the television network news, but they made for many "small" tragedies that add up to one great tragedy whose episodes continue to unfold. Small businesses are destroyed, employees are laid off, promotions denied, careers damaged or ruined altogether, education disrupted, debts incurred, lives lost, hearts broken. In one court order and bureaucratic ruling after another, the priority of race continually usurps the priority of rights and reaches into every facet of American life.

Sometimes the power of politicized ethnicity is wielded in the most peculiar ways over the most trivial issues. In June, 1976, the school board of Winnetka, Illinois, voted to remove Mark Twain's *The Adventures of Huckleberry Finn* from the required reading list at New Trier High School because black parents said that their children were offended by the word "nigger" and by race relations depicted in the book.

Here was an instance in which the moral clout of black ethnicity was used to remove an American classic from a school's reading list.[40] Yet, when conservative parents and fundamentalist ministers in Kanawha County, West Virginia, objected (often with violence) to the textbooks that discussed sex, race, and patriotism in ways that they found "un-American, irreligious and obscene," a panel sponsored by the National Educaion Association issued a report that all but discounted their protest as racist. A summary of the report said that "despite the denial of the protesters, 'an occurrence of racism,' can be detected in [their] objections to the 'multicultural, multiethnic' language arts textbooks, which contain writings by black and other minority authors considered pornographic and profane by the demonstrators."[41] The national media all but ignored the action of the Negro parents in Winnetka, Illinois, but a great deal of attention was given to the white parents in Kanawha County, who were portrayed as racists. The complaints of the parents were virtually of the same kind, but the Winnetka school board's decision to remove *Huckleberry Finn* went unchallenged whereas a district judge ruled against a suit challenging the authority of the Kanawha board of education to introduce the disputed books.

These two cases are cited not to imply that one group of parents was any more right in its protest than the other (both are deplorable), but to demonstrate how public policy is often implemented in favor of Negroes not because their grievance is necessarily valid and deserving of redress but merely because they are black. The black parents of Winnetka, Illinois, were offended by Twain's depiction of race relations in his time and place, apparently with no consideration for the fact that the use of racist language by Twain's characters is no indication that Twain was himself a racist. Neither was any consideration given to the rights of those Negroes who are *not* offended by the word "nigger." Should they be denied the opportunity to study the works of a giant in American literature just because the speech used by his fictional characters offends the extra-sensitive?

Are we now to see Negro and white parents demanding that textbook selection committees and curriculum boards go through every book to find what may be offensive to some group? Will black parents next forbid the reading of *Gone with the Wind* because of its depiction of race relations during the Civil War? Could such sentiments spread to require that *Mein Kampf* be banned from reading lists because of Hitler's incessant denigration of Jews? Will black parents apply their distorted sense of justice to black comedian Richard Pryor and force the removal from the market of his comedy album *That Nigger's Crazy?* Will Don Rickles be banned from the nightclubs of America just to protect the sensitive from his offensive ethnic humor? Will the writers of the television series "The Jeffersons" be prohibited from using the term "honkey," a denigrating term used by the character George Jefferson to refer to whites?

These are just a few examples of how politicized ethnicity can get out of hand and threaten the rights of others in even the most innocuous circumstances. It is not likely that the particular cases of censorship cited above will come to pass, but some very similar to them have. One grotesque form of censorship, presumably in deference to ethnic sensitivities, occurs in the footnotes of at least two editions of *Familiar Quotations* by John Bartlett. In the 1938 edition, page 379, there is a note on Thomas Carlyle's use of the term "dismal science," indicating that he spoke of it in his 1849 essay *Occasional Discourse on The Nigger Question.* Obviously, only Carlyle can be held responsible for his use of the term "nigger" in the essay title; but one finds in the 1968 edition an editorial change of the title which reads ". . . The *Negro* Question." One wonders if the editors will change Carlyle's essay title yet again to read "The *Black* Question" since the term *Negro* is no longer favored by a majority of blacks.[42] Or why not call it "The *Afro-American* Question," since, in point of fact, Negroes were nearer to being Afro-American during the era of slavery than at any time since.

The tampering with Carlyle's essay title presumably to assuage potential indignation of blacks was done at the expense of an accurate record of Carlyle's work. Truth was distorted in favor of appeasement. Changing Carlyle's title is no earthshaking matter of public policy, but if this kind of censorship can be done voluntarily in response to social pressure, real or imagined, it can also be made a feature of government policy.

The Power Of Moral Clout

If the Power-seeking nationalist and other social metaphysicians kept their race consciousness to themselves, they would probably pass unnoticed by others; but since they perceive their personal problem as a societal problem—a problem caused and sustained by "others"—they are not content until they have succeeded in making it a public issue. The pragmatic nationalists have found that by racializing issues, they can project upon them an importance they do not inherently possess and exact from their resolution remedies that far exceed their actual parameters. And so, they "go public." Of such Power-seekers, Branden writes:

> To defeat the reality they have never chosen to grasp, to defy reason and logic, to *succeed* at the irrational, *to get away with it*—which means: to make their will omnipotent—becomes a burning lust, a lust to experience the only sort of efficacy they can project. And since, for social metaphysicians, reality means other people, the goal of their existence becomes to impose their will on others, to compel others to provide them with a universe in which the irrational will work.[43]

But if what they desire is so unprincipled and impractical, how have they been able to succeed? How have they been able to translate the desire to defeat reality in the realm of race relations into public

193

policy? Why are American colleges and universities burdened by the constraints of affirmative action if it has achieved nothing discernible in regard to the pay, employment, or promotion of women and minority academics?[44] Why is it that children, because of their race or ethnic group *alone*, are not allowed to attend the neighborhood schools of their choice, but forcefully transported to distant schools—this, despite the fact that in 1975, 74 percent of Americans opposed court-ordered busing? How is it that our public policy has moved from antidiscrimination in housing to the policy of integration by mandatory residential distribution by imposing federally assisted low-income housing and zoning measures upon communities? Surely this strangulation of freedom and individual rights is not due to any great political power held by the small percentage of the population who compose what Glazer calls the "protected minority constituencies," who are the supposed beneficiaries of statistical remedies for discrimination. How, then, has this sabotage of reality, liberty, and rights been accomplished? How have they been able to get away with it?

Glazer offers several explanations of why measures creating specially benefited group categories have established themselves so powerfully in such a short time. One simple answer, he says, is that the people do not determine what is constitutional; the courts do. The executive branch as well as Congress also play a great role in the creation of these policies. And added to the power of these branches is the administrative power they grant to the bureaucracy of specialized agencies. And that power of implementation is wielded, to a large extent, by government employees who are themselves members of the groups being benefited. Another factor is that of executive and congressional inaction due to political con- siderations, the cumbersome legislative process, and, as in the case of busing, the effort of each is often overmatched by the power of the courts.[45]

Glazer believes the preeminent factor that explains the action, or inaction, by government and its bureaucracy, as well as the sweeping remedies decreed by courts to implement the reverse discrimination of pragmatic nationalists, is what he calls "the distribution of morality, or rightness, as it is felt by the best educated and most enlightened parts of the community, and by a considerable part, too, of the affected electorate." It is the *moral authority* projected upon such policies as affirmative action that gives them their political

194

clout and causes the courts to impose upon them measures that most people oppose.[46] And how is this moral authority achieved? By placing morality outside the context of human rights and individual self-interest and redefining it to mean "the public interest." Or, as Walter Lippmann termed it, "the public philosophy"—those political ideas that have acquired legitimacy as an operative force in human affairs, having "the title of being right which binds men's consciences," and possessing "the mandate from heaven."[47]

Who is "the public?" What is its "interest"—its "philosophy?" As Rand puts it, "the public" is everybody and nobody; its "interest" is everything and nothing. "Since there is no such entity as 'the public,' since the public is merely a number of individuals, any claimed or implied conflict of 'the public interest' with private interests means that the interests of some men are to be sacrificed to the interests and wishes of others. Since the concept is so conveniently undefinable, its use rests only on any given gang's ability to proclaim that 'The public, *c'est moi'*—and to maintain the claim at the point of a gun."[48]

The Power-seeker—or "power-luster," as Rand calls him—"needs the irrational, undefinable slogans of altruism and collectivism to give a semiplausible form to his nameless urge and anchor it to reality—to support his own self-deception more than to deceive his victims."[49] But his victims—those whom the reactionary nationalist wants to "lick" and those against whom the pragmatic nationalist must "protect" himself—must be deceived, at all costs, into accepting the moral authority of "the public good" if he is to advance to the status of Power-holder whereby he becomes the collector of the good that is sacrificed. His demands must be seen not only as legitimate rights, but as ensconced in the armor of superior righteousness. As that archetypical Power-seeker, Hitler, wrote in *Mein Kampf*, the ruler cannot dominate except with a doctrine that tolerates no rival.

Witness how the public philosophy/heavenly mandate of "the public good" was utilized in the following invocation for enactment of the 1964 Civil Rights Bill by President Johnson to over 6,000 of the clergy and laity who met in Washington that spring for a convocation on civil rights. Johnson told them: "It is your job—as men of God—to reawaken the conscience of America . . . to direct the immense power of religion in shaping the conduct and thoughts of men toward their brothers in a manner consistent with

compassion and love." The pressure of the public
philosophy/heavenly mandate was applied as a doctrine with no
rival, and one senator from the West was overheard to grumble,
"Oh, I will have to vote for it in the end because you've got those
damned pastors on my neck!"

Accompanying the campaign for the moral righteousness of
politicized ethnicity are the assumptions manufactured by professors and journalists, presented in textbooks and mass media, believed by lawyers, religious leaders, and citizens—assumptions that
could not stand without the moral ramifications they are perceived
to have for deciding what is good for society in the area of race relations. They are untrue and ludicrous assumptions but nonetheless
powerful. Glazer cites them as follows:

> That minorities cannot make progress even if discrimination in
> employment is effectively outlawed, and that they can only make
> progress if quotas are set for them; . . . that any concentration of
> black students and teachers in schools must be due to segregation; that
> blacks cannot learn unless they are in schools in which they approximate
> their proportion in some larger population; that no blacks would live
> near other blacks if they could, but would distribute themselves evenly
> through a larger population; that resistance to quotas and school busing
> comes from racism, from resistance to the implementation of
> constitutional rights.

Finally, that "all those who believe these things believe they are
moral and the others who oppose them are immoral, that they
defend the best traditions of the United States, whereas those who
disagree with them would perpetuate discrimination, segregation,
and inequality."[50]

The potency of these assumptions is seen in the fact that almost
any claim for blacks and other minorities carries with it an
immediate moral force and justification. As one scholar has put it:
"The public probably has a rather benign view of affirmative action;
they think it just means being fair and letting blacks know that you
don't discriminate." Who would dare oppose such policies allegedly
designed to correct wrongs of past enslavement and legal
subordination? Any Negro opposing such measures would be
considered the worst kind of traitorous "Uncle Tom." Whites
opposing them would be ridiculed as racist bigots. Opposition is not
perceived as being in favor of human rights for all, but as being
against blacks.

196

Not only is the altruist-collectivist philosophy of policies such as affirmative action given more moral authority than human liberty, but the belief that these policies are necessary for the implementation of the ideal of equality is given support by the belief that measures ordered by the courts are necessarily moral. "By now there is an automatic assumption that morality demands that the decisions of the Federal courts be defended," writes Glazer. Even as parents send their children off to distant schools and employers wade through oceans of paper bearing specific goals and guidelines for affirmative action, these people are heard to say: "I don't like it, but the court has ordered it and we must obey and I suppose it will be for the best in the end."[51]

Few Americans are willing to engage in sustained defiance of the courts that order them to forfeit their rights, and nobody wants to be branded as a perpetrator of discrimination, segregation, and inequality. Everybody wants to be on the side of right. And at present the "right" public policy in race relations is whatever the pragmatic nationalists say it is.

Many Americans were genuinely surprised to find the nation's public policy shifting from the primacy of individual rights to that of ethnic polity. Indeed, many movement integrationists found it difficult to accept at first. They might have been less incredulous had they fully understood those entreaties from Martin Luther King, Jr. that men should go to *any* length to "restore community." They would have understood even better had they made the logical connection between the humility of King's "distinterested love" of the early sixties and, to use Rand's term, the "dictatorial presumptiveness" of the affirmative action statism that ensued. But they had neither understanding nor the courage of their convictions. Thus, with no effective moral or political opposition, the Power-seeking nationalists achieved the extraordinary feat of cashing in on the presumption of redemption by sacrifice and establishing themselves among the Power-holders of semifree America.

1. A. Phillip Randolph, quoted in Brooks, *Walls Come Tumbling Down*, p. 25.
2. See Mark R. Levy and Michael S. Kramer, *The Ethnic Factor: How America's Minorities Decide Elections*.
3. Paul Delaney, "Blacks Gaining Politically But Still Feel Frustrated."
4. Hitchcock's analysis, which appears in the March 1973 issue of *Commentary*, is quoted here from Brooks, op. cit., p. 272.

5. Branden, *The Psychology of Self-Esteem*, p. 175.

6. Ibid., p. 176.

7. Alice Hamilton, "Hitler Speaks, His Book Reveals the Man," *Atlantic Monthly*, October, 1933, p. 399. (*Note*: This footnote and those immediately following accompany Stonequist's narrative on Hitler.)

8. Adolf Hitler, *My Battle* (Boston, 1933), p. 4.

9. Frederick L. Schuman, *The Nazi Dictatorship*, (New York, 1935), p. 7.

10. Stonequist, *The Marginal Man*, p. 74 ff.

11. Glazer, "America's Race Paradox."

12. Robert K. Merton, "Outsiders and Insiders: A Chapter in the Sociology of Knowledge."

13. This and all the quotations following are from Malcolm X, *The Autobiography of Malcolm X*.

14. Stokely Carmichael quoted in, "Black Power" (editorial), *The New Republic*, 154:25, June 18, 1966, p. 5.

15. Cruse, participating in a discussion entitled "Black Power: Pluralism," at the 1970 International Committee for Cultural Freedom seminar held at Princeton, New Jersey; quoted in seminar proceedings by François Duchêne, ed., *The Endless Crisis: America in the Seventies (A Confrontation of the World's Leading Social Scientists on the Problems, Impact, And Global Role of the United States in the Next Decade)*, p. 115.

16. There is no doubt that most of the problems of Negroes, as a group, are caused by racism. But many of the charges of racism are made by black leaders not because racism is actually the cause but to use racism as blackmail against whites who still accept the notion of their collective guilt.

17. Bayard Rustin, "The Failure of Black Separatism."

18. Quoted in Charlayne Hunter, "A Black Professor Urges Softening of Racial Issues."

19. Glazer and Moynihan, eds., *Ethnicity*.

20. Ibid.

21. Glazer, "America's Race Paradox."

22. Allen, *Reluctant Reformers*, p. 247. See also, August Meier and Elliott Rudwick, *From Plantation to Ghetto*.

23. I do not mean that Negroes collectively gave its true meaning to self-determination, but that their circumstances and their relationship to the government were such that self-determination was very much a matter of personal survival. Most often their collective progress occurred as a result of individual action.

24. John Hope Franklin, *From Slavery to Freedom: A History of American Negroes*, p. 555.

25. Ironically, while there is no one-to-one correlation between segregation and capitalism, segregated America, being a more capitalistic nation than today, was a freer America than it is today. At least those Negroes who penetrated the barriers of segregation could do so without violating the rights of others. Today they can hardly compete effectively without taking advantage of privileges that entail the violation of individual rights.

26. Franklin, op. cit., p. 552.

27. Ibid., p. 377.
28. Ibid., pp. 390–91.
29. Ibid., p. 549.
30. Ibid., pp. 550–51.
31. Harold Howe, "Integration: The Lost Momentum."
32. Sowell, *Affirmative Action Reconsidered: Was It Necessary in Academia?*
33. My notice of the threat of de jure integration to black colleges is not with regret that this is so in the case of the public and government-subsidized private institutions. I do concede the value of black institutions, however, to those Negro students who still grow up in a relatively separate world and must be prepared to compete in desegregated society.
34. Holsendolph, Ernest, "Black Colleges Are Worth Saving."
35. Booker T. Washington, *Up From Slavery*, p. 157.
36. For a detailed account of the campus uprisings by black students, see Lionel Lokos, *The New Racism.*
37. Quoted in Glazer, *Affirmative Discrimination*, p. 60.
38. Ibid.
39. Ibid.
40. It should be noted that Negroes are not the only ones who object to "racist" language in textbooks and other forms of communication. Jewish organizations devote a great deal of finances and effort to ferret out and bring suit against expressions and behavior they consider to be anti-Semitic. In November 1974, community pressure in Pierceton, Indiana, forced the local school board to outlaw an English textbook series that contained profanity and selections from the writings of Eldridge Cleaver, the black militant, and Woody Guthrie, the folk singer.
41. *New York Times*, February 7, 1975.
42. See chapter 6.
43. Branden, *The Psychology of Self-Esteem*, p. 175.
44. See Sowell, op. cit., for his evidence supporting the contention that affirmative action programs have not advanced women and minority academics.
45. Glazer, *Affirmative Discrimination.*
46. Ibid.
47. Walter Lippmann, *The Public Philosophy*, p. 138.
48. Rand, *The Virtue of Selfishness*, p. 88.
49. Ibid.
50. Glazer, *Affirmative Discrimination.*
51. Ibid.

The Spiritual Separatist

"If you can't be like them, be like your own group."

Several of my black colleagues who are over fifty say "black, Negro, Afro-American" *in every sentence, because they don't know what they are going to get attacked for. What I try to do is if I am saying "In 1941 we said* _____ *" I say* Negro, *I do not say* black. *But I try to get* black *into the next sentence so that it is perfectly clear that I know what I should say now.*—Margaret Mead in James Baldwin and Margaret Mead, *A Rap on Race.*

As shown in chapter 7, besides redressing injustice and racism, Conventional Integrationists wanted the acceptance and friendliness of integrated association, but with a difference. They wanted, in the words of James Baldwin, "to be embraced, and at no matter what the psychic or social risk." And according to the altruistic ethic of *agape*, as advocated by Martin Luther King, Jr., they set out to redeem the souls of white men (by legislative coercion if necessary), with what King called "a willingness to sacrifice in the interest of mutuality." The psychic risk they took was paid for by the sacrifice of the self-interest of Negroes, of whites, and of the nation; the social risk, by the sacrifice of individual liberty. The quest for human dignity ended in constraining the expression of man's individuality; and the quest for civil rights became an assault on natural rights. Might became right, and all in the society are now enslaved by the system of legislated equality and distributive justice.

That is one view of the integration movement. Another view, held by the nationalists and black-identity advocates, explains the integration movement in quite different terms. Though risks were taken by both blacks and whites, the price paid was by blacks alone and what they sacrificed was their group identification. The acceptance they sought from the dominant culture through integration was paid for by their rejection of their own subculture. Integrationists, writes George Napper, assumed that the only way Negroes would gain justice, freedom, and equality in America was by sacrificing their blackness. Many blacks paid the price, he says, by "an unconditional acceptance, consciously or unconsciously, of the notion of white superiority and the white-oriented values of this society. Thus, the goal of that [integration] movement was to be 'let in,' to be assimilated. This being the case, the tendency in self-identification was to stress, psychologically, the whiteness of one's total make up and to degrade or dismiss one's blackness."[1]

But, he writes, the integration movement failed to keep its promise. "Both the price and the failure of integration ushered in the Black Power period." It called for a rapid shift from integration as a goal but it also demanded with equal swiftness "the replacement of a preoccupation with 'whiteness' by a priority concern with 'blackness.' The need to come to terms with 'blackness' by way of self- and group-identification became a crucial concern."

Thus, the Black Power movement involved not only the political separatism of the reactionary nationalists but was accompanied by a campaign to legitimize racial chauvinism. In fact, the reactionary and pragmatic nationalists have aimed to give political significance to what is otherwise a matter of psychological awareness. It was felt that Negroes needed revitalization not only to exorcise the bad habits of their conformity to "white" standards, but to regain their dignity and relieve their sense of inferiority. To be meaningful, a change in social status had to be accompanied by a change in self-concept.

The Spiritual Separatist

That new self-concept is seen in the race-conscious type I call the Spiritual Separatist. Unlike the Conventional Integrationist, this person, who is adapted from Branden's Spiritual social metaphysician, does not overtly seek the approval of others; neither does he necessarily seek to gain power over them like the Power-seeker; and he claims to abhor the violence and destruction of the Independent. His solution to his dilemma of self-esteem is to proclaim himself above the understanding of those whose acceptance he craves but has not gained. Branden writes of the Spiritualist:

> His chief virtue, he proclaims or implies, is that he is too good for this world. He must not be expected to conform to conventional standards. He must not be expected to achieve anything *tangible*. His friends and acquaintances must love and respect him, not for anything he does— *doing* is so vulgar—but for what he is. What *is* he? Not everything that can be communicated, after all. Some things—the important things— can only be *felt*. . . .
> [His] claim to esteem rests on his alleged possession of a superior kind of *soul*—a soul that is not his mind, not his thoughts, not his values, not anything specifiable, but an ineffable composite of undefinable long- ings, incommunicable insights and impenetrable mystery. . . . This sort of "solution" to the problem of self-esteem . . . spares [him] the necessity of effort or struggle (except, of course, the dreadful struggle to preserve this fraud *in* [*his*] *own eyes*).
> . . . If and when he fails to receive the acceptance and esteem he craves, he explains to himself that people are not fine enough to appre- ciate the "real" him . . . (It should be added that there are moments when the thought of people knowing what he is *really* like fills him with terror).[2]

The traditional Spiritualist may be anyone from a frustrated housewife to a religious fanatic. The race-conscious Spiritualist seeks to free himself of his dilemma by adopting the identity of the group with the most appeal (in most cases, his own racial or ethnic group) and claiming that group to be superior and beyond the perceptual understanding of the less-favored group (which may be either another minority or the dominant group). His solution is stated thusly: "*If you can't be like them, be like your own group.*"

While the Conventional Integrationist advocates *cultural accom- modation* and the Power-seeking Nationalist is an exponent of *political nationalism*, the Spiritual Separatist believes in *cultural nationalism*. The Negro Spiritualist responds to his marginal con- flict by rejecting everything that, by his standards, is considered nonblack and involves himself in a world of "blackness." Psycholo- gist William E. Cross describes what he calls this person's "immer- sion in blackness" as follows: "He behaves as if he feels that every- thing black is good. This person hungrily consumes black literature and devotes much contemplation to the forms of being black: e.g., he wears dashikies, cultivates an Afro [hairstyle], takes on an

African name, etc. . . . . He feels an overwhelming attachment to all black people. He feels excitement and joy in black surroundings. He begins to see whites as just people with the strengths and limitations that this perception implies. He engages in a cultural analysis of black life style. He comes to accept certain factors about the black experience and drops others. He behaves as if he has accepted certain factors that help explain the experience of being black in America and incorporates them into a style of life which forms the basis of a new life style."[3]

Many contemporary Spiritual Separatists originally gave expression to their marginal dilemma as activisits in the civil rights-integration movement, wanting to step into the "melting pot" of the dominant culture. Even though they openly acknowledge their error in believing in the melting pot theory of assimilation, and assimilation itself, they continue to view assimilation as analogous to the collective melting of different ethnic and racial subcultures, failing to grasp that it is properly a voluntary process initiated and sustained by individuals. (As Rand points out, "America did not melt men into the gray conformity of a collective: she united them by means of protecting their right to individuality.")[4]

The Spiritualist's view of collectivized assimilation—i.e., "Americanization"—and his transition from desiring that situation to resorting to psychocultural separatism is seen in Dudley Randall's poem, "The Melting Pot":

> There is a magic melting pot
> Where any girl or man
> Can step in Czech or Greek or Scot,
> step out American.
> *Johann* and *Jan* and *Jean* and *Juan*
> *Giovanni* and *Ivan*
> step in and then step out again
> all freshly christened *John*.
> Sam, watching, said, "Why I was here
> even before they came,"
> and stepped in too, but was tossed out
> before he passed the brim.
> And every time Sam tried that pot
> they threw him out again.
> "Keep out. This is our private pot.
> We don't want your black stain."

The Spiritual Separatist

> At last, thrown out a thousand times,
> Sam said, "I don't give a damn.
> Shove your old pot. You can like it or not.
> but I'll be just what I am."[5]

Having failed to "melt" into the larger society by means of coercive integration and being faced with the political "white ethnic backlash" to the equal opportunity movement, many black Spiritualists are disillusioned Integrationists who seek to fill the void of an unfulfilled dream with a new dispensation: "plot your own course to self-realization; seek it in your own heritage, portray it triumphantly in your own literature, art, and popular culture."

Although he rejects the context of integration, the Spiritualist is a peculiar mixture of the Integrationist's psychology and that of the political nationalist. While he desires the socioeconomic advantages and equal access of a desegregated society—i.e., "white things and white institutions"—he rejects what he calls the "white definition" of how people ought to live. He sees his progression from the protest demonstrations of the sixties to the ethnic assertiveness of the seventies as natural and healthy. As one civil rights worker put it, "Blacks are going to pull together to reach their goals. [We] now have to go beyond the acquisition of money and comforts. That's only the second part of the agenda and the first is blacks lifting their psychological heads and walking proud."

"When you start mixing with white people and you are looking for yourself you won't find yourself," said one young worker. "Black people have never been left alone to themselves to find out what they ought to be doing. We have been trying to mix and imitate and that hasn't brought any results for most black people. We haven't been accepted for it and we're still niggers to whites. That won't change, so we will just have to make sure that it is no longer an issue. We'll never control our own lives through integration and so it is defeatist."

While the Power-seeking Nationalist advocates politicized ethnicity as the rationalization for his fear of competing in the open market of material acquisition and political representation, the Spiritual Separatist advocates psychocultural exclusiveness as the rationalization for his fear of the demands of individual authenticity and of competing in the open market of ideas and men's judgment. The conviction that "only people who are like myself are good" is the defense he chooses against the threats he perceives in the outer "white" world. To make that world and the invisibility he feels in it "no longer an issue," he immerses himself in the "black world," which promises the visibility he so desperately needs.[6]

This search for visibility and the movement from "whiteness" to "blackness" is seen in reflections on her life and career by black poet Gwendolyn Brooks in a 1971 interview with *Essence*. She recalled that like many integrationists of the forties and fifties, her work was written on the premise that "the oppressor simply needed information about grievances to awaken the dormant conscience. . . . But then, I wasn't reading the books I should have read when I was young. If I'd been reading W. E. B. DuBois, I would have known. . . . I thought I was happy, and I saw myself going on like that for the rest of my days. I thought it was the way to live. I wrote. . . . But it was white writing, the different trends among whites. Today I am conscious of the fact that my people are black people: it is to them that I appeal for understanding."[7]

Discussing the black literature of the early sixties, she said: "All of those books . . . and my poetry too, show that those writers, whom I respect, felt that there was a future in integration and they had a high and mighty respect for whiteness. They stressed the genius of whites without stressing the genius and accomplishments of blacks."

In the pleading tone of the Conventional Integrationist seeking societal sanction, Miss Brooks wrote in 1949:

> Grant that I am human, that I hurt
> That I can cry
> Not that I now ask alms, in shame gone hollow
> Nor cringe outside the loud and sumptuous gate
> Admit me to our mutual estate.[8]

By 1968, with the self-righteousness of the Spiritualist, she merged her creativity with Black Power and went to the street life of South Side Chicago in search of a new consciousness: "I—who have 'gone to gamut' from an almost angry rejection of my dark skin by some of my brainwashed brothers and sisters to a surprised queenhood in the new black sun—am qualified to enter at last the kindergarten of new consciousness now. New consciousness and trudge-toward-progress. I have hopes for myself."[9]

With hopes for herself, Miss Brooks, who had been a leader in interracial literary circles since she won the Pulitzer Prize in 1949, asserted her "new consciousness" and culminated her immersion into blackness by severing her twenty-six-year relationship with Harper & Row Publishers for Broadside Press, a Negro publishing company based in Detroit.

As pointed out in chapter 7, true integration is neither coercive nor interracial, but voluntary and interpersonal, involving individuals who have common interests and attitudes that transcend their biological differences to which they give no significance. Unlike many Black Power and black-identity advocates, Gwendolyn Brooks had experienced the friendliness and acceptance of certain whites who had judged her on her own merits, not those of her race. No doubt many whites accepted her, not for her personal qualities and professional achievements, but as a receptacle for their magnanimity, to be boasted of as proof of their unbiasedness. Similarly, others must have seen in her the opportunity to assuage the guilt they assumed for the collective sins of their race against her race. And she might have wondered whether such honors as the Pulitzer Prize were accolades for *her* achievements or tokens of *their* atonement. Yet one would think that she would have been able to distinguish hypocritical tokenism from genuine esteem for her. In any case, what mattered was whether she herself had earned acceptance and acclaim, regardless of whether it was given to her.

Her integrated relations were undercut in one sense by her own perception of integration. She wanted for her race what she had achieved as an individual. "I thought integration was the solution," she told *Essence*. "All we had to do was keep on appealing to the whites to help us and they would." Like so many Conventional Integrationists, she didn't see that what she asked for her race could not be achieved—that even the force of law cannot make groups of people relate to one another as only individuals can. Thus, when the law failed she abandoned integration, not understanding that the solution to interracial conflict lay in the interpersonal cooperation she had experienced with whites who truly had been her friends. "They thought I was lovely. I was a real pet for them. They thought I was nice, and I was nice. I believed in integration, and so did they. But now, I rarely see these people, though a couple of them still call themselves my friends."

Besides being undercut by her misperception of integration, her support of the solution of interracial cooperation was further aggravated by her perception of herself. She did not see herself as

The Other Side of Racism

Gwendolyn Brooks—poet, but as Gwendolyn Brooks—black poet, representative of the Negro race to the white race. And therein lay the source of her dilemma: lacking autonomous self-identity and being trapped in a purgatory between black and white. Had she been Gwendolyn Brooks—the poet, the necessity to choose between the Negro race and the white race as her "significant others" would not have become an issue of self-esteem. But it was, and since she had come to view integration as requiring that she identify with a white frame of reference, she abandoned integration and "white writing" and chose instead to seek the understanding of her people. "The glorious thing about today [is] we aren't concerned about what whites think of our work," she said in the *Essence* interview. "Whites are not going to understand what is happening in black literature today. Even those who want to sympathize with it still are not equipped to be proper critics."

A newspaper article reporting Miss Brooks's change of mind was headlined: "Black Poet Now More Militant." Miss Brooks is hardly militant, least of all *more* militant. But she does credit young militant para-intellectuals for their role in her awakening. Militancy is not by definition the characteristic of the Spiritualist, but militants can find in the rhetoric of Spiritualists plenty of rationalizations for their behavior. If one scratches a Spiritualist, one will not necessarily find a Militant or Power-seeker, but beneath the surface of every Power-seeker and every Militant, one will find the psychology and epistemology of the Spiritualist.

Blackness and Black Awareness

While Gwendolyn Brooks was transforming her poetry from white to black, workshops were being held in Negro communities and on college campuses all over the country on the meaning of black awareness and how black identity and black pride are manifested. George Napper wrote of his idea of "whiteness" and "blackness." Of the term *whiteness*, he said: "In the most general sense, I am referring to the whole cultural value system on which Western society is based. More specifically, I am referring to the white middle-class model (or 'materialist-success syndrome')—which uses indices such as occupation, size of home, style of life, and size of income to assess the worth of an individual—along with the standards of good, evil, and beauty that emanate from this model."

208

His use of *blackness* is "to denote the culture of the black lower class, because this class embraces the overwhelming majority of black people in this country and because it is within this milieu that styles of life and characteristics distinctively 'black' find their greatest expression. Further, 'blackness' represents the emphasis that is placed on being a 'street Nigger' (an updating of the 'field Nigger' concept in the field Nigger–house Nigger distinction [that took place during slavery])."[10]

As pointed out in chapter 6, the marginal man's race consciousness exists as a kind of double consciousness; thus, as in the case of the Spiritualist, his "blackness" is explained within the context of how he perceives his position in a predominantly "white" society. Since reality for the race-conscious individual consists of "reality-as-perceived-by-others," his sense of identity is expressed in terms of that reality which others are so privileged to comprehend and master. Hence, many race-conscious Negroes express even their "blackness" from the perspective of that incomprehensible reality of the white world that awes and horrifies some, and which others envy and resent.

"White world" or "white America" does not only designate the world of Anglo-Saxons and other white ethnics; it is also used to designate the socioeconomic middle- and upper-classes that transcend racial boundaries. Thus "white America" includes those blacks who are referred to as "white Negroes"—middle-class blacks who are described as having been "socialized into accepting white standards," whose values are defined as "nonblack." It is a world which E. Franklin Frazier has described as the "make-believe" world that middle-class Negroes escape to, "rejecting both identification with the Negro and his traditional culture."[11]

So, too, does the symbol "black" refer to more than just the cultural attributes described by Napper. As Talcott Parsons puts it, the black community has chosen the term to symbolically " 'deny' the relevance of the white component of its ancestry. One might speak of this as 'getting back' for the obverse denial of the relevance of parenthood when a white person, notably a father, was a biological parent of a 'black' child."[12] There are also political reasons for using the term, which will be discussed later in this chapter.

In *The Souls of Black Folk*, DuBois very movingly described what it meant to be black in terms of the "two-ness" of being a Negro and an American—"two souls, two thoughts, two unreconciled strivings; two warring ideals in one dark body."[13] Today, the intensity of the blackness syndrome is varied according to whether the person perceives himself as being black in *white* America or whether he desires to be black in America without reference to its "white" attributes. Being black against a white frame of reference is described in the following passage by a young Negro student attending a predominantly white university:

> *Being black* means to open my textbooks and see pictures of white folks and to read white-washed theory, philosophy and history which are irrelevant to me.
>
> *Being black* means to go to a white counselor whom I don't trust, and who doesn't know how to handle my presence or my problem. . . .
>
> *Being black* is to watch whites look upon my natural hair, my moustache, my African garments, my black music and literature, my black community language, and my other symbols of black pride as being deviant. . . .
>
> *Being black* is to go into a class disadvantaged and find that I have a teacher who believes it is impossible for a black student to make an "A" or "B" grade.
>
> *Being black* is not having a penny in my pocket and seeing white students visit Europe and Mexico and driving fancy sport cars, and at the same time knowing that their parents and ancestors got rich off the sweat and pain of my parents and ancestors. . . .
>
> *Being black* means to be in an ocean of white stimuli, to be angry consciously or unconsciously, to continuously struggle with oneself to deny hostile feeling, angry feeling. . . .
>
> *Finally, being black* means to be lonely, hyperalienated, depressed, displayed, ignored, and harassed. Just the fact of being black is to be at the brink of revolt.[14]

A character in a comedy by Charles Gordone tries to ignore the "ocean of white stimuli" and describes his idea of blackness in the following manner:

> They's mo' to bein' black than meets the Eye!
> Bein' black, is like the way ya walk an' Talk!
> It's a way' a lookin' at life!
> Bein' black is like sayin', "Wha's happenin', Babeee!"
> An' bein' understood!
> Bein' black has a way' a makin' ya call some-
> Body a mu-tha-fuc-kah, an' really meanin' it!
> An' namin' eva'body broh-thah, even if you don't!

210

Bein' black, is eatin' chit'lins an' wah-tah-
Melon, an' to hell with anybody, if they don't
Like it!

.   .   .   .

Bein' black is havin' yo' palm read! Hittin' the
Numbers! Workin' long an' hard an' gittin' the
Short end'a the stick an' no glory! It's
Knowin they ain't no dif'rence between
White trash an' white quality! Uh-huh!

.   .   .   .

Yes! They's mo' to bein' black than meets
The eye!
Bein' black has a way'a makin' ya mad mos'
Of the time, hurt all the time an' havin'
So many hangups, the problem'a soo-side
Don't even enter yo' min'! It's buyin'
What you don't want, beggin' what you don't
Need! An' stealin' what is yo's by rights!
Yes! They's mo' to bein' black than meets the
Eye!
It's all the stuff that nobody wants but
Cain't live without!
It's the body that keeps us standin'! The
Soul that keeps us goin'! An' the spirit
That'll take us thooo!
Yes! They's mo' to bein' black than meets
The eye![15]

Blackness, as described by DuBois and the other two speakers, is a concept of attitudes, values, and a method of awareness peculiar to certain Negroes. It is not a concept of human biology and thus does not apply to everyone of African descent. It is rather a concept of psychointellectual orientation that designates how certain individuals perceive themselves and their existential circumstances. As Gwendolyn Brooks does, these Spiritual Separatists claim not to care what whites think about them, but their whole scheme of thought and behavior is predicated precisely on the fact that they feel rejected—if not by white individuals, then by the white society and its culture.

Since the self-identity of the Spiritualist is frustrated by what he perceives as the misconception of him by whites, he turns to his race for a black identity, which he claims is beyond the power of whites to grasp and understand. Having whiteness no longer entices him but is a threat he must escape by assuming a collective state of black awareness. As one black professor has said, it is necessary for the black community to see black people as the new saints and white people as devils. He no longer embraces the Integrationist's egalitarian dream of brotherhood and equality but sees himself as fundamentally different from whites in psychology—not as an individual whose difference from all other individuals is determined by the exercise of his free will, but dictated by his biological heritage and his subcultural environment.

Having failed in his attempts to achieve the blind approval of whites, his present claim to esteem rests on what Branden calls his "alleged possession of a superior kind of soul"—a soul superior in its illusiveness, that cannot be communicated, which whites can never know simply *because they are white*, and which all Negroes ought to know simply *because they are black*. He further rationalizes that the only means by which others can understand him is by the acceptance of "soul": soul-food, soul-music, soul-literature, soul-art, soul-language—even what Andrew Young once called "soul politics." As noted in chapter 6, "Soul" is the stereotype, the least common denominator, of personal and cultural attributes used by Spiritualists for the same reason stereotypes are created by prejudiced whites. Prejudiced whites have stereotyped Negroes as being variously biologically and culturally inferior to whites. Now prejudiced Negroes have stereotyped *themselves* as imperceptible to whites. This estimate of themselves and their subculture is imparted to others as an irreducible primary—not to be questioned and not subject to explanation by conventional means. "Soul" is something you have to be black to understand. And if you are black and do not understand soul, you are considered a neurotic.

By idealizing his "blackness" as unknowable to others, the Spiritualist exempts himself from their judgment. When he says "I'll be what I am," what he means is that he desires to be unaccountable as an individual and unidentifiable except as a member of the racial collective into which he was born. His race consciousness is certainly no different in its fundamental nature than that of any white bigot. The race-conscious white person resents any positive attempt by minority groups to remove the stigma of inferiority. As he feels the Negro should "remain a Negro," so does the Spiritualist think the Negro should "think black." And in a frantic attempt to evade the emotional sum of inadequacy, he professes to be privy to a special kind of consciousness—"black consciousness." As the white racist seeks to protect his pseudo self-esteem (expressed in the doctrine of white supremacy) by keeping the Negro segregated and "in his place," so does the Negro Spiritualist seek protection in the "black experience" as the Negro Power-seeker seeks protection in the separatism of "black politics" and "black capitalism." As the white racist placed "white" and "colored" signs over water fountains and waiting rooms, so does the Spiritualist insist on placing racial labels on such fields as journalism, advertising, history, sociology, literature, music, and art.

Whatever reasons are given for these solutions to racial conflict, they result in maintaining social distance and obstructing the opportunity for individuals of different groups to voluntarily develop a harmonious existence with one another. When the position of insecure individuals in the majority group is threatened, they respond with the fear and antipathy of racial prejudice and seek release from their dilemma through either de facto or de jure segregation. When the Negro Spiritualists and Power-seekers in the minority group feel their positions threatened by the majority, they respond with a reverse racial prejudice and set up their own form of de facto or de jure segregation. Both are wrong: neither act justifies the other.

Some commentators have argued that surely most people are sophisticated enough to know that a concept like black awareness is merely abbreviated use of the language. Social analysts, who know there is no such thing as a collective awareness, nevertheless use the term as literary convention without challenging that convention. Verbal economy in communication is certainly valid, but conceptual communication ends and anti-intellectual manipulation begins when concepts are inflated to the point where ambiguous metaphors, empty euphemisms, and the mumbo-jumbo of rhetoric are given the conceptual power that belongs to the original concepts they are meant to substitute for. (Black consciousness and black awareness are substitutes for *self*-consciousness and *self*-awareness.) The concern here is not just a matter of semantics or style, but with the political and social use to which semantics are put. Verbal economy at the expense of objective definitions contributes to the faulty reasoning that institutionalizes concepts like black consciousness and black awareness into such consequences as "black capitalism" and black political and professional caucuses. One might say that since the symbol black is, in fact, an irrelevant concept, its use should be of no pressing concern. In truth, it does not matter whether Negroes are called black, colored, Afro-American, Negro, or Bilalian as the Black Muslims now call themselves. However, it is the intention of Spiritualists and Power-seekers to *assign* relevance to the symbol black in order to give it a political legitimacy it does not otherwise possess and to employ this distortion of the language in their grab for political power and influence on the development of an American consensus on ethnic and race relations. This is why the concept takes on the importance of an issue worth discussing.

Very broadly, the symbol black came about as a response to white racism, but it is more fundamentally a symbol of disdain for individual identity and achievement. The disdain for individuality is evidenced by the explanation of the symbol black that Talcott Parsons reports was given to him by a student: "[the symbol black] concerned, she said, the internal stratification of the black community and the correlation between lightness of color and high status. She then said that one of the reasons for identification of all as blacks was to counteract this tendency to stratification and be sure that the least advantaged members of the group were fully included. In a sense this is a case of making a virtue of necessity."[16]

Without going into the finer points of the color-status hierarchy that is a source of disunity among Negroes, one interpretation of that explanation is that the symbol black is used to invalidate or lessen the economic, social, and educational differences between individuals of high status and those of least advantage. It is used to wipe out the relevance of individual character, personality, and performance (and hence, to negate the validity of self-identity) by making all Negroes equally "black," though they may differ in actual skin color, and attributing to them all a black awareness whether they have it or not.

Ironically, while the Spiritualist enjoys increased political and socioeconomic freedom, he rejects the individuality that is required to achieve the maximum benefits of that freedom. Individuality is seen by him as a threat to his blackness; individualism is redefined as the white man's concept used to weaken black solidarity, and capitalism is rejected as a trick employed by whites to keep blacks oppressed.

The Sin of Pride

While the symbol black is used to eliminate the differences in achievement among Negro individuals, it is also used to distort the meaning of the pride one knows from those achievements. The man is thought to be proud, wrote Aristotle, who thinks himself worthy of great things because he is worthy of them. The proud man claims what is in accordance with his merits. What, then, do we call the man who claims what is in accordance with the cumulative merits of his ancestors? He is properly to be called a chauvinist, but, according to the Negro Spiritualist, he is a man of racial pride—of *black* pride.

The Spiritualist believes that trying to be white and accepting white as superior to black has cost him a sense of worthiness. Thus he claims black pride as a counter to the denigration of his culture by white racists. But this affectation of virtues based on the traditions of one's ancestors is not the pride of self-esteem achieved but an attempt to disguise the lack of self-esteem. As Steven M. Lord points out: "Note that this kind of 'pride' is entirely unearned—the individual in question had nothing to do with who his ancestors were. The man who desires a sense of 'race pride' is a man looking for an automatic identity and a guaranteed self-esteem, a pseudo self-esteem that he will not have to work for and cannot lose, usually because he needs a substitute for the authentic pride that stems from personal achievements and virtues of character."[17]

Self-esteem is primarily a psychological need of man, but it is not a function of an individual's racial, national, sexual, occupational, or socioeconomic category. It is a function of man's cognition—of his volitional consciousness. It is personal—not an attribute of groups, but a quality that must be achieved singularly by each individual. To lessen the imperative of self-esteem by abstractly removing it from the personal sphere to a racial collective does not decrease by one iota the weight of its psychological significance as a basic need of which each man must meet the requirements. In the act of claiming that one's pride is based on the achievements of his ethnic or racial group it is pride itself that he must relinquish. To define one's self-esteem and pride by whether or not one asserts certain attributes of one's subculture is to short-circuit one's capacity to value oneself. Yet there are many Negroes who innocently accept the idea that it is "beautiful" to limit the experience of themselves and of existential reality to the ethno-racial aspect of their identity.

In reaction to what they called the "white is beautiful" syndrome, a group of Negroes opened a storefront school in Philadelphia that was intended to give young children from seventeen months to five years of age an education in black pride before they entered the public school system. The following is a portion of a drill session between the founder of the school and his pupils, as broadcast on CBS News in a 1968 special report "Blacks in America":

TEACHER: You, young lady—your nationality is American Negro. Yes?
PUPIL: No.
TEACHER: Don't play with me. You're a Negro.
PUPIL: No.
TEACHER: I am your teacher. *You are a Negro.*
PUPIL: No.
TEACHER: Suppose I threaten to beat you. What would you say? Aren't you a Negro now?
PUPIL: No.
TEACHER: What are you?
PUPIL: I'm black and beautiful!
TEACHER: What is your nationality?
PUPIL: My nationality is Afro-American!
TEACHER: . . . Suppose I gave you a dollar to say you're American Negro. This is money now. Money talks. . . . And if you don't say it, you don't get it. You're an American Negro, aren't you?
PUPIL: No.
TEACHER: You won't have any money. You know you need money, don't you?
PUPIL: Yes.
TEACHER: You need money to live, don't you?
PUPIL: Yes.
TEACHER: All right. All you have to say is that you're an American Negro. Aren't you an American Negro?
PUPIL: No.
TEACHER: What are you?
PUPIL: I'm black and beautiful.
TEACHER: What is your nationality?
PUPIL: My nationality is Afro-American.
TEACHER: Very good, man. Keep it up. Go sit down—You had to think about that for a minute, didn't you?
PUPIL: Yes.
TEACHER: All right. Everybody: What is your nationality?

ALL: My nationality is Afro-American!

TEACHER: Good. All right, what I did is what people are going to do to you in different ways when you get out of school. They're not just going to come up to you and offer you a dollar if you say you're an American Negro. But they're going to be very nice to you—some of them—and they're going to try to get you not to love black people—get you to be something other than what you are. They're going to try to make it seem as though you're different from the masses of black people. . . . But you must reject that.

At the end of the film, actor Bill Cosby, the narrator of the program, asked of the drill session: "Is it really brainwashing? Can you blame us for overcompensating when you take the way the black history got lost, stolen or strayed? When you think about the kids drawing themselves without faces and when you remember the fine actors who had to play baboons to make a buck, I guess you got to give us the sin of pride.

"Pride: *hubris*, in the original Greek. It's three hundred years we've been in this American melting pot and we haven't been able to melt in yet—and that's a long wait. Listen, we've been trying all kinds of parts to make the American scene. We've been trying to play it straight—and white; but it's been bit parts. Now, from now on, we're doing it black—*and* American, because we're proud of both. *Hubris*."

Cosby said that blacks should be allowed the sin of pride that they have been without so long. The notion that pride is a sin comes from mystics and the apostles of self-sacrifice who deride any attempt by a man to value himself and take pleasure in his achievements and character. What the teacher was drilling into innocent children was not pride, but what amounts to the sin *against* pride. As Lord puts it, the fact that one is a member of some particular race is simply nothing to be proud of. The doctrine of racial pride is the same as Brewton Berry has characterized most popular ideas about race itself, "no better than superstitions . . . born, not of cool, scientific thinking, but . . . smuggled into our heritage to justify exploitation, to protect privilege, to arouse nationalism, or to cover ignorance."[18]

The Spoils of Victimization

If authentic pride were actually a quality that Spiritualists wish to achieve, one of their first expressions of that pride would be to deracialize their attitudes and political activism. Deracialization, as used here, does not mean the deculturalization that many claim has robbed Negroes of their self-esteem. It means the de-emphasis of race as the measure of a person's self-identity, his ideas, and his behavior. A man of authentic pride has no need of this measure—not because he is ashamed of it, as black-identity advocates would claim, but because it is irrelevant, inappropriate, and insignificant to the maintenance of a free-functioning life. The truly proud man requires maximum freedom of spirit and would find the racial approach (or, indeed any form of collectivism) too confining and its cost in self denial too great. But the nonracial quality of an autonomous self-esteem and the pride derived from it is not what the Spiritualist seeks.

As indicated, the Spiritualist wants to exempt himself from self-responsibility, men's judgment, and the risks and uncertainties that that must be met in a free society. One way of doing this is to claim a sense of worthiness and self-identity based on the achievements of men who happen to fall in the same racial or cultural category as his. Their greatness is assumed as *his* greatness and offered as unquestionable evidence of his value and worth. He evades self-responsibility further by claiming that he is only a reactor to social and political pressures in a world he never made, that his membership in a historically oppressed group makes him a victim of past wrongdoing against his ancestors; and that he cannot be held responsible for how he responds to such unfair treatment. He may feel at once proud of his racial heritage and victimized because of it.

Thus, while the Spiritualist is engaged in changing his self-concept by exorcising the white frame of reference via racial pride, he nevertheless clings to his sociological identity as "a disadvantaged minority suffering from the cumulative effects of more than three and one-half centuries of racism, segregation and exploitation by white society." During the past decade Negro scholars in the social sciences have vigorously challenged the social pathological approaches to the Negro experience taken by mainstream "white" social scientists. Yet, in challenging such mainstream assumptions as "cultural deprivation," "tangle of pathology," and "social disadvantagement," (which, admittedly, should be challenged), these scholars assert victimization as the rationale for their own demands for "insider" scholarship as the only appropriate solution to generations of inaccurate "outsider" research.[19]

This paradox of racial pride and victimization in the Negro Spiritualist is very much like that of his Jewish counterpart in America. As Negroes have become increasingly interested in establishing an accurate account of their history and heritage, so too have Jews devoted a great deal of time and money to the study of their most recent past. The intent of both groups is not only to ascertain the truth and set the record straight but to counter the "corrosive effects of assimilation" on their collective ethnicity. Negroes say they cannot know who they are nor where they are going if they do not know where they came from. The Jews say they cannot survive if the world does not remember.

"The need to remember is the need to know the truth," says *Newsweek*, reporting on the efforts of Jews around the world to come to terms with the Nazi Holocaust during which six million Jews were starved, tortured, and murdered.[20] But what is the nature of this quest for the truth? They want to retrieve the Holocaust from the edge of historical awareness and have men relive it, but not in some vacant conceptual lot of their minds. For then the experience would be limited to only a minority of the world's people: the death-camp survivors, those German and Eastern European survivors of the war who were among the persecutors or were aware of their existence, and the children of both these groups. As in the case of slavery and lynching, when most people hear of the Holocaust they shudder in indignation, but they cannot live it, no more than the youngest generation of Negroes can live the very recent humiliation of Jim Crow.

But Spiritualist-minded Jews want to transform the memory of the Holocaust into a metamorphosis of actual experience and freeze its horror, pain, and death into a perpetual, everlasting Now. To conceptualize it as one of the many horrible things men are capable of doing to one another is to remove it from immediacy and place it in the past where it properly belongs. And this, say Spiritualist Jews, is to blaspheme their identity as Jews. For a great deal of being a Jew is to have the capacity to experience the omnipresent shadow of impending doom at the hand of one's non-Jewish neighbors. It is to be ever aware of a metaphysical threat. As Hyman Bookbinder of the American Jewish Committee has said, "As Jews, we've learned never not to worry."[21]

They worry that American Jewry may be disappearing because of its successful assimilation in America; they worry about the

219

declining guilt over the Holocaust, in face of the decreasing number of people alive who can be legitimately blamed for the event. They worry that support for Israel is not sufficiently fervent. They worry that the nations of Western Europe will bargain away Israel's security in return for access to Arabian oil; and they worry about the increased sympathy with which Americans have begun to examine the Arab cause. They worry about what they describe as the anti-Semitic remarks made by public officials. And all of this is culminated into the alarmist notion held by Gerald S. Strober (*American Jews: Community in Crisis*), that current trends will make "life rather unpleasant for the individual Jew" in America. Author and playwright Elie Weisel, survivor of Nazi concentration camps, has ventured a more sinister prospect for Jews: "the possibility of Jews being massacred in the cities of America or in the forests of Europe" because of "a certain mood in the making."[22] This, despite all the evidence to the contrary.

"From the moment the Germans set up crematoria," said Alain de Rothschild, a leader of the Jewish community in Paris, "a breach opened up in the human conscience."[23] A breach was indeed opened, but it was not the first and as present-day events signify, it most certainly will not be the last. Especially, as long as such breaches are frozen into position and the wound never allowed to heal. The greatest breach in the conscience of the American society was its constitutional and ethical toleration of slavery. And for the men, women, and children who suffered under that system, being treated as the property of another man was no less an injustice than the barbaric racism of the Holocaust. Yet the freed survivors of that Holocaust wanted more than anything to close the breach. But the Spiritualists among the Nazi Holocaust survivors do not want their experience of that event to stand the test of time and human progress. They are relentless in their resistance to history's persistent move onward. And when some attempt to close the breach by broadening the significance of the Holocaust to compare with other horrors, as done here with slavery, they protest, in the words of Elie Wiesel: "This tends to cheapen the experience and its meaning, and to deprive the victims of their own tragedy by broadening it."[24] And here, in Wiesel's words, is the essence of the spiritual separatism among many race-conscious Jews and Negroes. To transcend their Jewishness and blackness is to be deprived of their own tragedy and that of their ancestors.

220

For these Spiritualists the present and future are forbidden and locked out of their awareness by the past. And perhaps greater than their fear that the Holocaust will happen again is that their children and non-Jewish children, who do not know the experience firsthand, will not be able to act as sentinels over memories they do not have—or even over a collective sense of retribution they cannot sustain. "I think of Auschwitz once a week and have done so for 30 years," said historian Golo Mann, son of novelist Thomas Mann. "But you can't expect millions of Germans to don sackcloth and ashes and repent all the time. One likes to forget because what can you do with it?"[25]

What Spiritualist Holocaust survivors and their descendants are doing with their collective victimization is using it to sustain widespread immunity from criticism and to protect all things Jewish. Similarly, Negro Spiritualists use their victimization to rationalize economic and political revenge on those who had no hand in the sins of their fathers and grandfathers. It can be seen from this that what may appear at first to be a paradox between racial pride and victimization really is not, as the one flows out of the other. The doctrine of racial pride aims to secure an automatic self-esteem; the doctrine of victimization aims to make the lack of self-esteem (blamed on outside forces) the rationalization for imposing restraints on the actions of others. To retreat from racial pride such as Jewishness or blackness would mean giving up one's monopoly on tragedy and martyrdom, and it would rob one of the investment one has in seeking vindication and retribution. Most importantly, the maintenance of racial identification in terms of collective victimization can be translated into political power.

Elsewhere I have defined political privileges as special advantages peculiar to individuals and groups that exempt them from the usual course of law: "When men attempt to bypass reality by invoking the force of government to create opportunities for themselves at the expense of the rights of other men, the conditions (and circumstances) they create are not opportunities as such, but political privileges. . . . They wish to be excluded from the conditional nature of opportunities—to secure a guarantee against effort—to render effects immune to their causes—to secure protection against the facts of reality."[26] One set of circumstances used increasingly to justify a person's exemption from the usual course of law is his victimization.

221

The Other Side of Racism

Who is a victim? According to the dictionary a victim is a person who suffers from a destructive or injurious action or agency; he may be deceived or cheated, sacrificed or regarded as sacrificed. Some definitions note that one may be a victim of one's own emotions or ignorance, but we usually think of people as victims of another person's action or some impersonal, external agency or force beyond one's control such as natural catastrophes, accidents, physical handicaps or illness, psychological or physical abuse, or political and social injustice. However, even in these instances, a distinction is made between the suffering caused by people and their institutions and that caused by unforeseen mishaps, disease, or acts of nature. One may be victimized by a rapist, the Ku Klux Klan, or the Internal Revenue Service. But an earthquake victim is not "victimized" by nature, nor is the victim of an automobile accident "victimized" by his own or someone else's careless driving or a faulty engine, as the case may be. Neither is a victim of polio "victimized" by the poliomyelitis virus. Victimization, properly used, means that state of suffering caused by the destructive or injurious action of another person or institution.

Most Negroes have been victims of racial discrimination, either directly or indirectly, and most can cite aspects of their life circumstances that are influenced by it. The purpose here, however, is neither to enumerate specific instances of victimization suffered by Negroes, nor to challenge whether what they perceive and experience really is victimization. The focus is centered instead on a particular *response* of the Spiritualist to victimization. And as I've noted, that response is to transform his victimization into a political advantage—to institutionalize it as a symbol of status.

Victim status is a condition of political privilege that entails absolving individuals or groups from the responsibility for their behavior on the grounds of their psychocultural and/or socio-economic problems, real or imagined. One need not be an actual victim of the kind cited above to claim victim status. In the present sociopolitical climate of benevolent welfarism all he needs to do is claim that something or someone else is responsible for his unfortunate situation and that he is powerless (through no fault of his own) to reverse his misfortune. Since he cannot or will not deal with the risks and responsibilities of his life in the human community, the Spiritualist declares himself above those re-

222

quirements. It is quite easy to move from that position to the demand that others take those risks and responsibilities for him. It is especially easy if he can cite "evidence" that his inability to perform is caused by those collective "others" or their institutions. Then, in the name of justice and with the force of law, sympathizers rush to relieve him and punish his victimizers.

Once conferred, writes columnist Jeffrey Hart, "victim status is a very durable possession. The black who shoots the liquor store owner in the course of a holdup, or the teenager who slugs his teacher, retains in some larger sense 'victim status.' Victim status is also a highly valuable property to those who possess it. Because of their victim status, for example, Indians can seize property or destroy it with negligible chances of punishment. Paradoxically enough, victim status confers power."[27]

From its inception the American nation has been a refuge for the disadvantaged and victimized of the world. The Statue of Liberty, which personifies the country, is called "Mother of Exiles," and the words of welcome given to her by Emma Lazarus speak the national sentiment toward the world's less fortunate:

> Give me your tired, your poor,
> Your huddled masses yearning to breathe free,
> The wretched refuse of your teeming shore.
> Send these, the homeless, tempest-tost to me,
> I lift my lamp beside the golden door.

Through that door have come men, women, and children who believed their only hope was to flee the lands of their birth. They came to escape further victimization. Negroes, on the other hand, were forced from their homelands and brought to these shores already as victims. There was nowhere to escape to, and for almost two centuries the welcome to freedom was tarnished by the fact that behind the golden door were America's own huddled masses yearning to breathe free. Even when granted their physical freedom, they remained exiles from the protection and preservation of their rights.

But this was all changed by legislation brought on by the civil rights activism of the last forty years. By the 1960s the full weight of the law was put to the protection of the rights of Negroes. But having their legitimate (civil) rights guaranteed has not been enough for many Negroes. They want more. As the National Advisory

Commission on Civil Disorders reported in 1968, "Protest groups now demand special efforts to overcome the Negro's poverty and cultural deprivation—conditions that cannot be erased simply by ensuring constitutional rights." Having equated personal happiness, security, and economic well-being with political freedom, they expect the legal system to render them happiness and well-being *as a right*, even at the price of their own liberty and that of others if necessary. They no longer seek equal opportunity but equal results. They no longer want to be guaranteed of their natural right to *pursue* happiness; they want happiness itself provided as a political goal. Having the right to secure the blessings of liberty is not sufficient; they want those blessings produced and handed to them as a political right.[28] One way of justifying their claim to these conditions is to hold up their own material and spiritual impoverishment as evidence of the nation's breach of its commitment to human liberty.

With this as the general mood among minorities still euphoric over the impact of the 1963 March on Washington and mesmerized by Martin Luther King, Jr.'s "I Have a Dream" speech, the Johnson administration deliberately made an issue of the elimination of poverty. The Equal Opportunity Act of 1964 declared that it is "the policy of the United States to eliminate the paradox in the midst of plenty in this Nation by opening to everyone the opportunity to live in decency and dignity." This was no empty promise, as during 1965–70, some $2.3 billion was committed to a variety of anti-poverty programs. Overall federal expenditures for all welfare services rose from $24.9 billion in 1960 to $76.7 billion at the end of the decade. "It was the largest rise in such expenditures over a decade since the beginnings of the welfare state in the New Deal of President Franklin D. Roosevelt," writes Thomas R. Brooks.[29]

Much has been written about the fact that the War on Poverty did not originate as a demand of the poor. But the poor did not reject Johnson's declaration of war either. They wanted it as much as any of the professional reformers and politicians who planned and administered it.[30] In 1963 Whitney Young proposed a $145 billion "domestic Marshall Plan." In 1966 A. Philip Randolph proposed a $185 billion "Freedom Budget" to finance a ten year "*total* war" against poverty. In 1968 during the Poor People's Campaign, involving some eight thousand people encamped in the plywood-

224

and-canvas Resurrection City in Potomac Park, the Reverend Ralph Abernathy declared: "Unlike previous marches which have been held in Washington, this march will not last a day or 2 days, or even a week. We will be here until the Congress of the United States decides that they are going to do something about the plight of the poor people by doing away with poverty, unemployment, and underemployment in this country."

As her contribution to the Poor People's Campaign, Mrs. Martin Luther King, Jr. led a Mother's Day march of "welfare mothers" and, accompanied by several white women, told the five thousand participants at the concluding rally: "I must remind you that starving a child is violence. Suppressing a culture is violence. Punishing a mother and her family is violence. Neglecting school children is violence. . . . Ignoring medical needs is violence. Contempt for poverty is violence. Even the lack of will power to help humanity is a sick and sinister form of violence."

Standing on the shoulders of such "representatives" of the poor, Poverty incarnate reared its ugly head—its existence blamed in part on a "highly individuated, capitalistic society" and its victims proclaimed as the economically disadvantaged, the culturally deprived, the exploited, the powerless, the people left behind, the permanent poor, whom Michael Harrington called "the rejects of the affluent society"—the "other Americans." ("In Los Angeles they might be Mexican-Americans, in the runaway shops of West Virginia or Pennsylvania, white Anglo-Saxon Protestants," wrote Harrington. "All of them are poor; regardless of race, creed, or color, all of them are victims.")[31]

Negro and white Integrationists saw in the antipoverty movement the opportunity to redefine race and civil rights as a manifestation of conditions of poverty. And this, writes Elinor Graham, "opens a path for action. Where race and nationalism are vivid, emotion-based issues, not easily resolved through reason and logic, conflict between the 'haves' and 'have-nots' is well understood." Placing civil rights activism "in the context of a battle between the wealthy and the poor, between the 'power-lords' and the 'exploited underdog' " also enabled liberal whites to regain their place in the policymaking positions from which they had been excluded by separatists and nationalists. "Such a recasting of the Negro struggle cuts across racial boundaries to transform it into a fight for 'all humanity,' "

The Other Side of Racism

writes Graham. "A new struggle is created which has a great potential for rallying sustained activities within accepted political channels."[32]

While the Integrationists redefined the racial conflict as a conflict between the "haves" and "have-nots," the Power-seekers (backed by the Spiritualists) saw the War on Poverty as the opportunity to use poverty as evidence of their racial victimization. "The fact is that poverty is no accident," said Senator Eugene McCarthy during the 1968 presidential campaign. "Black people are poor because they are powerless and powerless because they are black." This view was also held by leaders of the Poor People's Campaign, which was dominated by Negroes, and it became clear that Negroes intended to use the poverty issue as a stepping-stone to power. Poverty and powerlessness had come to mean the same thing and the Negro was the symbol for both. This, despite Reverend Abernathy's claim that "the poor are no longer divided. We are not going to let the white man put us down any more. It's not white power, and I'll give you some news, it's not black power, either. It's poor power and we're going to use it."

It would be some time before blacks could actually use the power of victimization with any substantial consequence. First, they would have to gain that power and this was done through new jobs created by the antipoverty bureaucracy. Writes Graham:

The activity- and job-creating nature of its programs is presently opening and shaping new fields in the social services, a process that is certain to increase its range in the future. New professional positions in community organization and social planning, as well as the clerical and blue-collar jobs created to staff the research intitutions and service organizations of the "antipoverty" projects, are particularly accessible to the Negro. This is true, above all, for the now small but increasing ranks of the college-educated and professionally trained Negro.[33]

Besides the creation of jobs and status, programs that stressed "community action" and "community self-determination" provided a means to create new bases of political power. Writing of the power potential of the Community Action Programs, David Stoloff said, "From the beginning . . . it was clear to any alert politician that 'community action' and 'community participation' imply direct confrontation with established systems of political power and social control."[34] Successful confrontation enabled men like Kenneth Gibson, now mayor of Newark, New Jersey, who controlled money and jobs as vice-president of United Community Corporation, to move from power in the streets to power in City Hall.

The transfer of political and economic power into the hands of the poor through "community action" had another effect, pointed out by Daniel Patrick Moynihan: "re-creating the ethnic political-social organizations of the big city slums—the dismantling of which was so long the object of political and social reformers in the United States!"[35] The Integrationists had failed to achieve integration, but as "victims" of poverty the Power-seeking and Spiritualist leaders were able to achieve the power to demand special efforts to overcome the poverty and cultural deprivation of minorities. And the last thing they wanted was the dismantling of their organizational power base. Misfortune and victimization had become their badge of privilege, and they needed a rationale for maintaining their victim status and for expanding their power.

One way was to exempt their victimization from comparison with that of other groups that have made their way into the American mainstream—to make it exclusive of other kinds of misfortune—to claim continuous and permanent martyrdom that warrants greater restitution than that claimed by other minorities. Another method was to blame their victimization on past injustice that must be corrected, with the question of *how much* and *what kind* of correction to be decided by an ever-increasing army of caretakers and reformers.

Both of these rationalizations were enunciated by President Johnson in his speech at Howard University on June 4, 1965. First he defined the nature of the Negro's victimization: "Negroes are trapped—as many whites are trapped—in inherited, gateless poverty. They lack training and skills. They are shut in, in slums, without decent medical care. Private and public poverty combine to cripple their capacities." He acknowledged the "enormous accomplishments of distinguished individual Negroes" but pointed out that "they tell only the story of a growing middle class minority, steadily narrowing the gap between them and their white counterparts. But the great majority of Negro Americans—the poor, the unemployed, the uprooted, and the dispossessed—there is a much grimmer story. . . . Despite the court orders and the laws, despite the legislative victories and the speeches, for them the walls are rising and the gulf is widening."

Then, after reciting a litany of facts and statistics to substantiate "this American failure," Johnson explained why "Negro poverty is not white poverty." The "deep, corrosive, obstinate differences" were not racial differences, but "solely and simply the consequences of ancient brutality, past injustice, and present prejudice."

Neither did he view the experience of Negroes (the "black experience" claimed by the Spiritualists) as comparable, in its entirety, with that of other minorities. "They made a valiant and a largely successful effort to emerge from poverty and prejudice." But unlike the Negro, "they did not have the heritage of centuries to overcome, and they did not have a cultural tradition which had been twisted and battered by endless years of hatred and hopelessness, nor were they excluded—these others—because of race or color—a feeling whose dark intensity is matched by no other prejudice in our society."

Although two days earlier at a White House Conference on Civil Rights, the proposals Johnson offered "To Fulfill These Rights" had been repudiated by nationalists and militants as "pie-in-the-sky" goals, few could disagree that he had sounded a note of national sanction of the idea that Negro victimization was special and warranted special relief. By the end of the decade and $76.7 billion later the power of victimization was a durable possession of blacks and other minorities—but especially blacks. It was clear to all that in the welfare state one could get more attention—and power— by being a victim than he could being a nonvictim. "Anything and everything may serve as the rallying point for a new pressure group today, provided it is someone's *weakness*," writes Rand. "Weakness of any sort—intellectual, moral, financial or numerical—is today's standard of value, criterion of rights and claim to privileges. The demand for an institutionalized inequality is voiced openly and belligerently, and the right to a double standard is proclaimed self-righteously." And by this double standard virtue is defined not in terms of one's ability but in terms of his handicaps; not in terms of his achievements but in terms of his suffering; not in terms of his individual capacity to surmount racial discrimination but in terms of the collective oppression suffered by his ancestors. By this standard the "meek" claim inheritance to the "earth" they have not created while the creators are expected to be "tolerant" and "understanding." Says Rand:

"Tolerance" and "understanding" are regarded as unilateral virtues. In relation to any given minority, we are told, it is the duty of all others, i.e., of the majority, to tolerate and understand the minority's values and customs—while the minority proclaims that its soul is beyond the outsider's comprehension, that no common ties or bridges exist, that it does not propose to grasp one syllable of the majority's values, customs or culture, and will continue hurling racist epithets (or worse) at the majority's faces.

Nobody can pretend any longer that the goal of such policies is the elimination of racism—particularly when one observes that the real victims are the better members of these privileged minorities.[36]

No, the elimination of racism is not what the Negro Spiritualist intends. His goal is to make his racial identity—his blackness—a symbol of martyrdom and cash in on that martyrdom by demanding retribution from the majority that has rejected him. His aim is not to create harmonious relations between the races but to get even—to make "them" pay.

From Redemption to Retribution

To a large extent, the Integrationists who dominated the civil rights movement before 1965 were like their predecessors of the first half of the century in that their protest against racial injustice was directed primarily toward establishing the wrongs committed against Negroes and seeking the repeal of laws that permitted such offenses. Laws like the 1964 Civil Rights Bill and the Voting Rights Act were passed to *reform* the system of discrimination and segregation. Under the influence of Martin Luther King, Jr.'s *agape*, protestors sought to *redeem* the prejudiced souls of white men, women, and children. The enforcement of these laws might be called *redemptive* punishment, or what John Hospers calls a *utilitarian* form of punishment, which aims to produce "good" consequences— i.e., to bring about an integrated society and eliminate prejudice. It was thought to be capable of improving the offenders, preventing others from offending, and protecting the society.[37]

However, with the advent of the Black Power–black-identity movement, and in light of the white backlash of the mid-sixties, Militants and Separatists concluded that blaming the society and pointing out its evils in hopes that whites would change was not enough to ensure the success of civil rights goals. It became necessary that the society be punished—either violently, as the

229

reactionary militants advocated, or by coercive legislation, as the pragmatic nationalists advocated. The Integrationists had sought redress for themselves and redemption for whites. They had wanted love—*agape*—from the majority. But having failed to achieve the respect and friendliness of integration, the Power-seekers then sought revenge and the Spiritualists sought the majority's shame. As Stokely Carmichael put it: "Camus and Satre have asked, can a man condemn himself? Can whites, particularly liberal whites, condemn themselves? Are they capable of the shame which might become a revolutionary emotion? We have found that they usually cannot condemn themselves, and so we have done it."[38]

The Integrationists were victims who did not want to be victims. But the Power-seekers and Spiritualists wanted to enshrine their victimization—to make it the standard by which they deal with others. They would rather remain victims (or at least operate on the morality of victimization) than take the risks that their increased freedom demanded of them. ("The rebuilding of this society, if at all possible," said Carmichael, "is basically the responsibility of whites—not blacks.") They did not want justice, but power. They wanted to "get even" and to force others to provide conditions of success for them—while convincing them that such restitution was justified. Thus, in contrast to the Integrationist's future-oriented approach to achieve "good" through *redemptive* punishment, the Power-seekers and Spiritualists advocated *retributive* forms of punishment to "correct" past abuse and "compensate" the injured through such programs as affirmative action, racial quotas, residential distribution, etc. As Eugene D. Genovese put it, "The use to which [the advocates of Black Power] put that power depends not on our good wishes or on their good intentions, but on what they are offered as a *quid pro quo*."[39]

The quid pro quo was to provide the black-identity movement with political muscle so that, in the words of Malcolm X, "America's black man, voting as a bloc, could wield an even more powerful force [than the immigrants]"—so that "a ten-million black vote could be the deciding balance of power in American politics." Malcolm X called for politicized ethnicity in 1964 and by 1976 it was paying off to such an extent that no attempts were made to disguise the fact that it was not rights that many Negro leaders wanted but power. The 94 percent of black votes that helped gain Jimmy Carter the presidency in 1976 represented a "black claim to influence and power," said Vernon E. Jordan, executive director of the National Urban League.

In a *Newsweek* essay, Jordan wrote: "The black claim on Carter is not the traditional political claim for government jobs, although there is every indication that a Carter administration will feature blacks in high office. Rather, it is a moral claim for policies that would reverse the tragic decline of black living standards. . . . Other ethnic minorities have made their votes pay off in policies that helped them advance to middle-class status, and if our democracy is to work, then black votes will now have to pay off the same way."

Jordan was partially correct: Negroes are but the most recent of the ethnic groups to engage in pressure-group politics. And their electoral behavior is not unprecedented, since there has never been a time when Americans voted purely for their own individual self-interest. The history of American politics, particularly electoral politics, is the history of the competition for influence and power within and among various special-interest groups. And now, Negroes find that their behavior as a voting ethnic bloc can no longer be overlooked by other Americans. Levy and Kramer put it very plainly in their discussion of the impact the Negro vote could have on the 1972 Presidential race:

> Black voters are in an enviable position for 1972. The Democratic nominee cannot expect to win without the black vote. . . . The black voter is clearly in a position to make life miserable for the 1972 Democratic nominee. And the black voters may be so inclined. On the other hand the black leadership's opportunity to extract promises and commitments from the Democrats has never been better. The Democrats smell victory, and the blacks, if they wish, can stand in the way.[40]

The day of reckoning has come and the black Spiritualists and Power-seekers can now have their cake and eat it too. Having yet to join the American mainstream, their respective solutions to "join your own group" and "protect and depend on yourself," puts them in the position to remain "victims," maintain their marginality to the dominant culture and, as Levy and Kramer put it, "take solutions, administer programs, and in so doing need never wonder if a complacent majority will one day rise to trample them, as happened to so many of the ethnics who fled their native lands for the 'gold sidewalks' of America."[41]

The Other Side of Racism

1. George Napper, *Blacker Than Thou: The Struggle for Campus Unity.* Napper's view of the integrationists is one that is usually attributed to the experience of blacks in general. As Lawrence W. Levine (*Black Culture and Black Consciousness*) and others have shown, the Negro experience in America was one of simultaneous acculturation and revitalization. See note 3, chapter 5.

2. Branden, *The Psychology of Self-Esteem*, pp. 177–78.

3. Hall, Freedle, and Cross, *Stages in the Development of a Black Identity.*

4. Rand, *The Virtue of Selfishness*, p. 130.

5. Dudley Randall, "The Melting Pot," in *The Black Poets*, ed. Dudley Randall, p. 141.

6. As pointed out in chapter 4, human beings need psychological and cultural visibility. The issue faced by race-conscious minorities is whether the visibility they seek will be collectivized or individualized. Most choose collectivized visibility and are torn between whether the locus of their search will be in the dominant culture or the Negro subculture.

7. Gwendolyn Brooks, with Ida Lewis, "Conversation," *Essence* 2 (June 1971): 72.

8. Gwendolyn Brooks, *The World of Gwendolyn Brooks*, p. 123.

9. Brooks, *Report From Part One*, p. 86.

10. Napper, op. cit.

11. E. Franklin Frazier, *Black Bourgeoisie*, p. 195. See also Nathan Hare, *The Black Anglo-Saxons.*

12. Talcott Parsons, "Some Theoretical Considerations on the Nature and Trends of Change of Ethnicity," in Glazer and Moynihan, eds., *Ethnicity.*

13. DuBois, *The Souls of Black Folk*, p. 3.

14. Quoted in Edgar A. Epps, *Black Students in White Schools*, from Frederick D. Harper, "Black Student Revolt on White Campuses," *Journal of College Student Personnel*, 10 (September 1969).

15. Charles Gordone, *No Place to Be Somebody: A Black Comedy.*

16. Parsons, "Some Theoretical Considerations on the Nature and Trends of Change of Ethnicity," in Glazer and Moynihan, eds., op. cit., p. 77.

17. Steven M. Lord, "Race Pride versus Self-Esteem."

18. Brewton Berry, "A Southerner Learns about Race," *Common Ground*, Spring 1942.

19. See Joyce Ladner, ed., *The Death of White Sociology.*

20. "Facing Up to the Holocaust," *Newsweek*, May 26, 1975.

21. "American Jews and Israel," *Time*, March 10, 1975.

22. Ibid.

23. *Newsweek*, May 26, 1975.

24. Ibid.

25. Ibid.

26. Anne Wortham, "Equal Opportunity versus Individual Opportunity."

27. Jeffrey Hart, "Victims in the Moral Melodrama."

28. For a discussion of the distinction between happiness as a moral goal and freedom as a political goal, see Machan, *Human Rights and Human Liberties*, p. 249.

For a related analysis of the *prima facie* rights theory that supports "welfare rights," see Tibor R. Machan, "Prima Facie versus Natural (Human) Rights."

29. Brooks, *Walls Come Tumbling Down*, p. 268.

30. In all fairness to lower-class and poor Negroes it must be said that even if they were inclined to reject many of the programs proposed or administered in their name, but from which they benefit little, they would find little support from the true beneficiaries: professionals, intellectuals, and bureaucrats among the Negro and white middle-class.

31. This study takes the position that institutional poverty is caused not by capitalism but by the *lack* of capitalism—most specifically the mixed economic system of freedom and controls that exists in the United States. For analyses supporting this position, see Tibor R. Machan, "Demythologizing the Poor"; Ludwig von Mises, *The Anti-Capitalistic Mentality*; Murray N. Rothbard, *America's Great Depression.*

For Harrington's indictment of free-market capitalism as the cause of poverty, see Michael Harrington, *The Other America: Poverty in the United States.* See also Fanon Frantz, *The Wretched of the Earth*; and Arthur I. Blaustein and Roger R. Woock, eds., *Man against Poverty: World War III.*

32. Elinor Graham, "The Politics of Poverty," in Gettleman and Mermelstein, eds., *The Great Society Reader*, pp. 226–27.

33. Ibid.

34. David Stoloff, "The Short Unhappy History of Community Action Programs," in Gettleman and Mermelstein, eds., op. cit., p. 236.

35. Daniel Patrick Moynihan, "The Professionalization of Reform," in Gettleman and Mermelstein, eds., op. cit., p. 471.

36. Ayn Rand, "The Age of Envy."

37. John Hospers, *Human Conduct: Problems of Ethics*, pp. 397 ff.

38. Stokely Carmichael, "What We Want," *New York Review of Books*, September 22, 1966, cited in Gettleman and Mermelstein, eds., op. cit.

39. Eugene D. Genovese, cited in Gettleman and Mermelstein, eds., op. cit.

40. Levy and Kramer, *The Ethnic Factor: How America's Minorities Decide Elections,* pp. 196–97.

41. Ibid., p. 221.

10

The Independent Militant

"If you can't lick them, destroy their world."

The only way to stop evil here is to have a revolution. Somebody have got to die.—Black Youth

As a sapling bent low stores energy for a violent backswing, blacks bent double by oppression have stored energy which will be released in the form of rage—black rage, apocalyptic and final.—William H. Grier and Price M. Cobbs, *Black Rage.*

On June 10, 1963, newly elected Governor George C. Wallace stood at the entrance of the University of Alabama auditorium to block a group of federal agents escorting two black students to register under an integration order from the federal district court. But when President John F. Kennedy federalized the Alabama National Guard and sent troops to enforce the admittance of the students, Wallace left the door and the students were registered on June 11. That evening Kennedy spoke to the nation on television saying that the civil rights demonstrations in Birmingham and elsewhere

> have so increased the cries for equality that no city or state or legislative body can prudently choose to ignore them. The fires of frustration and discord are burning in every city, north and south. Where legal remedies are not at hand, redress is sought in the streets in demonstrations, parades and protests, which create tensions and threaten violence—and threaten lives. We face, therefore, a moral crisis as a country and a people. It cannot be met by repressive police action. It cannot be left to

235

increased demonstrations in the streets. It cannot be quieted by token moves or talk. It is a time to act in the Congress, in your state and local legislative body, and, above all, in all our daily lives.

To his countrymen Kennedy posed the familiar, then 187-year-old question that could no longer be ignored and for which there was precious little time during which to arrive at an answer: "Are we to say to the world—and much more importantly to each other—that this is the land of the free, except for Negroes; that we have no second-class citizens, except Negroes; that we have no class system or caste system, no ghettoes, no master race, except with respect to Negroes?"

As the demonstrations continued in cities across the South, it became clear that there could be only one answer to Kennedy's question, and it could not be equivocal. The time had come when American values and political ideals had to be actualized, and whether or not the manner of actualization was agreed to by all Americans, it had to be pursued. In this much of their thinking, at least, the Kennedy administration and the civil rights activists were correct.[1] Thus, on June 19, Kennedy submitted a civil rights bill to Congress and on August 28, two hundred and ten thousand Americans marched on Washington petitioning for legislative and moral support of the bill, which was finally passed and signed into law by President Lyndon B. Johnson on July 2, 1964.

From Civil Disobedience to Anarchy

The March on Washington, writes Thomas Brooks, was "a part of a process, a cumulation of events that led to the passage of the 1964 Civil Rights Act," but it was also the beginning of the end of an era in the struggle of Negroes for civil equality. Social psychologist Kenneth Clark has characterized it as

> the end of innocence, the end of a period when we believed the rightness of the cause would be the chief weapon for attaining the ends of decency. We could approach civil rights from a moral perspective when we kept seeing it as a Southern problem. The morality left the issue when it came North.
>
> In the South, the purpose of the civil rights movement was pretty clear and specific and direct. There were segregated schools, segregated transportation, segregated waiting rooms, terror—things for which there were apparently rather direct, specific remedies.
>
> Now when that was changed, we all looked at it and said, "My God, progress has been made." And we celebrated the progress. But the black

236

in the Northern cities saw his kids were just as retarded in reading as they ever were, his home was just as deteriorated as it ever was. He was in the same fix he had been in before this great progress had ever occurred. So he started getting mad.

And his white allies in the North—who could deal with their guilt and a racial ambivalence by contributing to the N.A.A.C.P. and the Urban League—found the restless natives next door. And they were not prepared for this, and so they reacted by saying: "These ungrateful so-and-so's. I contributed to the N.A.A.C.P. and I contributed to the Urban League. I'm a white liberal. I'm without prejudice. What do they want from me?" Their response was backlash. You got this damned cycle of white backlash, white ambivalence, reacting to Northern urban black frustration. And this, then generated what I call the era of realism.[2]

The March on Washington was impressive, primarily because it was peaceful. And it was a success—"a living petition" had reached the hearts and minds of millions of Americans and its message heard around the world. But accompanying the elation and enlightenment of the months that followed was the smoldering frustration and discord in the Northern ghettos and increasingly strained relations among different factions in the civil rights organizations. Writes Brooks:

Although the march was a grand coming together of civil rights forces, it also marked a divergence between militants and moderates, a parting of ways. Lobbying for the civil rights bill became the provenance of the [Southern Christian] Leadership Conference, agitation increasingly that of the so-called "street Negro" and those who courted his favor. . . . There was a growing debate and division over strategy, tactics, and even goals. Black consciousness veering on black nationalism became a force within CORE and SNCC. It became difficult for whites, even in CORE, the most interracial of all the civil rights organizations, to achieve leadership posts. . . .

Before the march, on August 1, President Kennedy had expressed hope that "if there is a period of quiet . . . we should use it to redress grievances." The white liberal establishment tended to view the legislative struggle for the President's civil rights bill as such an attempt. Within the civil rights movement, however, there were other pressures boiling up behind the slogan "Freedom Now!"[3]

Civil disobedience was becoming less civil all the time, writes Brooks, "as the winds of change stirred the surface of black life in America, setting events into motion that were taking black Americans into increasing militant and uncharted courses of action." The growing militancy of some activists was evident at the March. In a speech that he was persuaded to tone down, John Lewis of SNCC

237

gave what Brooks calls "a mild foretaste of the ricocheting rhetoric of the later 1960s." "We will not wait," Lewis had planned to say, "for the President, the Justice Department, nor the Congress, but we will take matters into our own hands and create a source of power, outside of any national structure, that could and would assure us a victory. . . . We will march through the South, through the heart of Dixie, the way Sherman did. We shall pursue our own 'scorched earth' policy and burn Jim Crow to the ground—nonviolently."[4]

There was no Sherman-like march through the South, and Jim Crow was not burned to the ground; but just sixteen days after the passage of the 1964 Civil Rights Act (about which John Lewis had said, "We support this bill with great reservations, for it is too little and too late"), an "unplanned revolt" erupted in the streets of Harlem during a CORE-sponsored rally. Following the Harlem riot were riots in Brooklyn's Bedford-Stuyvesant community, in Rochester, New York, in three New Jersey cities, in the Chicago suburb of Dixmoore, and in Philadelphia. In all, the riots, which the FBI characterized as "a senseless attack on all constituted authority without purpose or objective," cost five lives and an estimated $6 million in property damages. Responsible black leaders condemned the riots, but, as Brooks points out, "many came to feel that the rioters had acted out the hostility toward 'whitey' felt by most, if not all black Americans. Overtly or covertly stated, this became a community stamp of approval for the wildest of excesses in the succeeding years."[5]

The violence of the 1960s engaged in by Negroes, peace demonstrators, students, and others has been attributed to psychological factors like frustration and alienation and environmental factors such as police brutality. This was partially true, but, as Rand points out in her discussion of the student rebellions, what made violence acceptable as a response to social and political disputes was the abandonment of reason and the "philosophical impotence" of the country's intellectual leaders.[6] Like the student rebellion, to the extent that the civil rights movement abandoned human rights in favor of arbitrary privileges, it also abandoned reason and opened the door to physical force and political coercion. One of the movement's contradictions was its effort to achieve justice for all at the expense of the rights of some. And proceeding as it did by the motive power of Martin Luther King, Jr.'s nonviolent resistance was its

238

second contradiction and final undoing as an exercise in civil disobedience; for inherent in the doctrine of nonviolence were the seeds of violence. In his critical analysis of the double standard entailed in King's philosophy, Lionel Lokos writes:

It is only a short step from the doctrine of civil disobedience to the criminal disobedience of the Negro riots. The more articulate rioters would probably say that they are simply invoking their right to disobey "unjust" policemen, exacting retribution from "unjust" storekeepers, and in general, declining to cooperate with "an unjust society." The liberal's protest that the rioters are being violent, while Martin Luther King was nonviolent, wholly misses the point. Once you permit a man to disobey laws he dislikes, you cannot later disapprove of the *form* that disobedience takes or the *motivation* behind it.

In compelling the abject surrender of law enforcement in community after community, in demonstration after demonstration, civil disobedience became the unwitting midwife of the urban riots. In both cases, it was mob action making impossible the orderly function of government. In both cases, it was taking a grievance into the streets instead of the voting booth.[7]

Taking a more sympathetic view of nonviolent civil disobedience, William Robert Miller writes:

Psychologically, defiance is a strong component of the capacity to endure hardship and suffering. The annals of nonviolence, from the early Christians martyrs to the *satyagrahis* of twentieth-century India, are filled with instances of nonviolent men under stress taunting their persecutors and flaunting their courage in what might be called a moral equivalent of violence, an irrepressible venting of righteous anger. Even a Gandhi, under acute stress and despite iron self-discipline, could unwittingly fall prey to this aggressive drive. . . . Rare is the man who could literally and actually love and forgive the enemy at the height of his agony and, *rare still the one who could do so when he feels he is gaining the upper hand after much suffering*" (emphasis mine).[8]

The civil rights demonstrations of the early 1960s were actually exercises of power, writes Miller, but, as he points out,

If power does not find avenues of persuasion, it does not evaporate and conveniently disappear. It becomes destructive. Whatever may be true of nonviolence as a spiritual force, it remains a transmutation of power which can take other, sublimated forms. The individual who develops the capacity to endure develops a courage that can, if sufficiently tempted, express itself in a terrible vengeance. And it can inspire in those who lack a certain degree of discipline enough boldness to do severe damage in their defense.[9]

239

Martin Luther King, Jr. never advocated violence, but he warned of its threat passionately and repeatedly. Though he remained committed to his formula that "mass civil disobedience can use rage as a constructive and creative force," he was in no way blind to the destructiveness to which rage could be put. Writes Miller: "He had few qualms about the use of armed restraint to enforce justice if it could not be secured directly by the moral appeal of nonviolence itself. . . . No one knew better than he the potential of the oppressed for violence, but he saw too that it had best be held back as a tragic last resort, for mob violence, black or white, spelled chaos."[10]

But by what standard was violence to be exercised as the "last resort?" Who was to determine when the last resort was to be brought into play? King did not answer these questions; though violence was an inherent component of his philosophy, he apparently did not care to extend his logic to include violence as an outcome of nonviolent resistance. Employing Hegelian epistemology, King saw nonviolent resistance as seeking "to reconcile the truths of two opposites—acquiescence and violence—while avoiding the extremes and immoralities of both." Defying the Law of Contradiction and embracing the "dialectical movement," he wrote: "The nonviolent resister agrees with the person who acquiesces that one should not be physically aggressive toward his opponent; but he balances the equation by agreeing with the person of violence that evil must be resisted. He avoids the nonresistance of the former and the violent resistance of the latter. With nonviolent resistance, no individual or group need submit to any wrong, nor need anyone resort to violence in order to right a wrong."[11]

Warning that "all who take the sword will perish by the sword," King put primary emphasis on the redemptive power of nonviolent suffering as "the ultimate form of persuasion." He continually exhorted Negroes to "rise to the noble height of opposing the unjust system while loving the perpetrators of the system." He set them on the road to achieving the most impossible goals: self-respect through self-sacrifice; growth through suffering; love through mercy; life through death. He wanted to stir the conscience of America even if it meant death. "If physical death is the price a man must pay to free his children and his white brethren from a permanent death of the spirit, then nothing could be more redemptive." Finally, from the philosophy of nonviolent resistance came not self-respect, but racial chauvinism; not growth, but violent destruction; not love, but

240

vengeance; not life, but death; not redemption, but retribution; not a "beloved community," but mob anarchy. As attorney Morris I. Leibman, who saw "an inherent contradiction in the concept of premeditated 'righteous' civil disobedience," said in an address before the American Bar Association just two weeks after the passage of the 1964 Civil Rights Act:

> While the idea of civil disobedience may evoke sympathy where the claim is made that the cause is just, once we accept such a doubtful doctrine, we legitimize it for other causes which we might reject. We must be even more careful in the sympathetic case because, in effect, that sets the standard of conduct which then becomes acceptable for cases not as appealing or for groups not as responsible. Thus, we substitute pressure for persuasion, and squander the carefully nurtured value of self-restraint and jeopardize the system of law.[12]

Ayn Rand also questions the validity of civil disobedience on the grounds that it is used not as a means of achieving justice, but as an assault on the law. The moral righteousness given to it by the civil rights movement has so obscured its meaning that few Americans are able to make the connection between the mass demonstrations of the early 1960s, the abrogation of rights that accompanied them, and the civil disorder that followed. Rand writes that civil disobedience is justifiable when an individual disobeys in order to test the legality of a particular law. But when mass civil disobedience involves the violation of the rights of others, it is a breach of legality as such.[13] One cannot be engaged in justifiable civil disobedience, for example, when he aims to test discrimination laws by occupying another man's property and thereby violating his property rights in the process. Civil disobedience is an act against the state, not individuals. In this review of Burton Zwiebach's *Civility and Disobedience*, journalist Richard Eder summarizes Zwiebach's theory of the role of civil disobedience in a constitutional democracy thusly: "The right and the usefulness of disobedience come in because in practice such a society will fall short of its ideal. Whenever an act of government or a law breaches one of the fundamental principles, whenever it abridges an individual's rights, there is at least a theoretical justification for disobedience. Even if such a law is democratically arrived at . . . there is still the right to disobey. Nor . . . should the citizen have to submit to a legal penalty for breaking a law if he does so for the sake of a basic right."[14]

It is very important to keep in mind that the civil rights movement of the early 1960s was basically a movement of reform; none of its leaders advocated a break with the country's political institutions. Indeed, every facet of the March on Washington, which stands as the symbol of mass protest, was planned and executed in consultation with President Kennedy and other political leaders and within the laws allowing such a demonstration to take place. The demonstrators came to Washington not to wage war on the government, but to petition for the nation's sanction of the use of political institutions as agents for solving social problems by legislative coercion.

"Our philosophy was simple," wrote CORE director James Farmer. "We put on pressure and create a crisis and then they react. I am absolutely convinced that the ICC order [banning the segregation of interstate terminal facilities] wouldn't have been issued were it not for the Freedom Rides."[15] Thomas Brooks tells how "they"— the Kennedy Administration—reacted:

> The upward spiral of arrests [of Freedom Riders] placed the Kennedy Administration, as it were, under the gun. It owed its presence in Washington to the black vote. . . . In this instance [of intervening on behalf of the civil rights protestors], the Attorney General worked out an imaginative solution that avoided costly court battles over the integration of interstate travel facilities. It was an extraordinary proceeding, one department of the government petitioning an autonomous agency, the Interstate Commerce Commission, to ban segregation by regulation. . . . By the time the ICC order took effect [November 1, 1961], there had been a dozen or more rides, involving over a thousand persons. . . . In 1962, CORE launched the Freedom Highways campaign, seeking to desegregate motels and highway restaurants across the country. . . . By the end of 1962, Farmer was able to report, "a Negro could drive along the national highways and know that when he was hungry or tired, there would be a place he would be welcome to stop and rest."[16]

By the occasion of the March on Washington, civil rights protestors and others in the black community had come to expect the agitation and pressure of nonviolence to result in government intervention on behalf of Negroes. As Lokos notes, Martin Luther King, Jr. saw agitation and intimidation as only a phase of the general four-step process by which civil rights activisits achieved their goals:

(1) Nonviolent demonstrators go into the streets to exercise their constitutional rights.

(2) Racists resist by unleashing violence against them.

(3) Americans of conscience in the name of decency demand Federal intervention and legislation.

(4) The administration, under mass pressure, initiates measures of immediate intervention and remedial legislation.[17]

"The mere threat of a boycott sometimes brought success," writes Brooks, "as in Philadelphia where the N.A.A.C.P. secured jobs for blacks as Trailways bus drivers or in Atlanta where 'Operation Breadbasket,' backed by the churches, secured white-collar employment in department stores."[18] In cases as these one has to wonder whether the acquiescence of Trailways and the department stores resulted from a change in the managements' conscience or from their fear of government coercion. From what has been said here and elsewhere, one thing is clear: although the civil rights leaders never openly advocated the initiation of violence, in order to achieve their goals through nonviolent resistance and mass civil disobedience, they required both the violence of racists and the reactionary coercion of the government. "Obviously, segregationist violence was the *sine qua non* of the success of King's nonviolence," writes Lokos. It should be remembered, however, that the "success" of the contradictions of nonviolent resistance and mass civil disobedience occurred *within* the political and economic framework of a semifree America—itself a contradiction—in which force is sanctioned as the means of settling political and social disputes.

Like the student rebels whom Rand says tried to establish a special distinction between *force* and *violence*, so too did the civil disobedient nonviolent resisters make the same claim. Force is what social scientists identify as power—the ability to command compliance against the person's will because he fears the threat of sanctions. Violence is literal physical force, the application of a threatened sanction so that the victim has no choice but to comply; it is destructive harm where injury results, and it can be illegitimate or legitimate. On the basis of such a distinction, demonstrators could occupy a college administration building and call that "force." If they were forcibly removed by policemen, that was called "violence." A thief who threatens his victim is said to be using force. If the victim retaliates and assaults the thief, that is violence. The right of self-defense becomes defined not as the resistance of force, but the initiation of force. By this reasoning, it is not the perpetrator of force who is condemned, but the victim.[19]

Having obtained sanction for the use of political force to implement their goals, through the 1964 Civil Rights Act, the civil rights leaders petitioned the courts to bar the prosecutions of "peaceful" sit-in demonstrators. Thus, on the same day that it upheld the constitutionality of the public accommodations section of the Civil Rights Act, the Supreme Court ruled simultaneously that this section barred state prosecutions of demonstrators who had tried by peaceful means to desegregate business places covered by the act. Wrote Justice Tom C. Clark: "The purpose of the civil rights legislation was to obliterate the effect of a distressing chapter of our history . . . now that Congress has exercised its constitutional power in enacting the Civil Rights Act of 1964 and declared that the public policy of our country is to prohibit discrimination in public accommodations . . . there is no public interest to be served in the further prosecution of the petitioners." The ruling overturned the trespass convictions by state courts of Negroes who had sought service at segregated lunch counters in South Carolina and Arkansas in 1960, and would affect some three thousand sit-in demonstration prosecutions awaiting action as far back as 1960 in southern states.

Of the four dissenting justices, Hugo L. Black opposed the idea of the law coming to the aid of those who "took the law into their own hands." However, the Supreme Court did more in its ruling than assault legality by legitimating pressure-group rule. In upholding the constitutionality of the public accommodations clause and in reversing the trespass convictions, it obliterated the very moral foundation of legality by violating human rights. It first declared that a restaurant owner's property was a public accommodation; then, on the basis of that contrived redefinition of private property, it declared that the owner had not the right to order from his property those with whom he chose not to do business.[20] Such was the absurdity of the legal and moral climate of the country at the end of 1964. It should be no mystery, then, that if the *trespass* of private property in the name of civil rights was made lawful, it would not take long for the actual *destruction* of property in the name of civil rights to follow.

Because it demanded the violation of human rights, mass civil disobedience had never been entirely civil to begin with. By the end of 1964 it had crossed the line and become criminal disobedience, mushrooming throughout the succeeding years to become tribal warfare, anarchy, and finally terrorism.

The Independent Militant

The most unjust and irrational of those who inherited the spoils of civil disobedience and heard in the rhetoric of nonviolence the rallying cry for violence was the race-conscious individual I call the Independent Militant. Adapted from Branden's Independent social metaphysician, this person is "the counterfeit individualist, the man who rebels against the status quo for the sake of being rebellious, the man whose pseudo self-esteem is tied to the picture of himself as a defiant nonconformist."[21] As Branden's profile of the Independent social metaphysician indicates, describing the Militant as "independent" does not refer to those positive qualities of self-esteem (i.e., self-confidence, self-respect, and self-assertiveness) that are normally included in the characterization of a person of psychological maturity and intellectual independence. "Independent," in this context, refers to the Militant's counterfeit individualism and his manner of expressing it in two areas: (1) his distortion of the *ethical-political* context of individualism (i.e., the requirement of rational self-interest and the supremacy of human rights for man's survival qua man) to mean "doing whatever one wishes regardless of the rights of others"; and (2) his perversion of the *ethical-psychological* context of individualism (i.e., the requirement of rational self-interest and intellectual independence for man's survival) to mean "It's right because *I* feel it," or "It's good because *I* want it," or "It's true because *I* believe it."[22]

During a television news program's analysis of the twenty-four hours of looting and arson that occurred in the slums of several New York City boroughs following that city's power blackout on the night of July 14, 1977, one of the newsmen asked a teenage looter why he had joined his neighbors in pillaging the small shops, supermarkets, and department stores. The young man's answer was simply: "Because I wanted to do it. I wanted to be like my friends." He did not deliver a flow of rhetoric on the exploitation of the poor by the rich or on the failure of society to end urban decay, punctuated by unemployment statistics, crime rates, and stories of racial discrimination. That was done by novelist James Baldwin, who shouted to the white newscaster: "*You* are the cause of this!" The young looter, who admitted that his action was wrong, simply said: "I wanted to do it." That is the only fundamental expression the Independent Militant can give of his "independence."

The Militant is in fact a parasitical subjectivist; and his rebellion is not against conformity as such, but against what he perceives as reality's "tyranny" over his whims and feelings. His defiance is against the requirement of reality that independent judgment should take priority over subjective whim; that feelings should not be substituted for independent thought. Says Branden of the counterfeit individualist: "existence is merely a clash between *his* whims and the whims of *others*; the concept of an *objective* reality has no reality to him."[23]

Unlike the weeklong series of racial riots that swept Harlem and Brooklyn's Bedford-Stuyvesant section in 1964, the billion-dollar rampage of looting and the wave of 1,037 fires during the 1977 blackout were not sparked by racial tensions. But as their interviews with the press indicated, many of the thousands of ghetto occupants who sacked their own communities, as well as sympathizers like Baldwin, and even some of their victims, were motivated by the same dilemma of race consciousness that characterizes the other prototypes of this study. These individuals are torn between the loyalty they have for their subcultural group and the approval and acceptance they seek from the dominant group. And all their activity is directed toward alleviating the dilemma between their natural need for self-identity and their attempt to acquire that identity through group affiliation. They would like to dispel their sense of inadequacy either by gaining the approval of the majority ("If you want to join them, be like them"); or, if that fails, gaining power over them in some area ("If you can't join them, lick them"); or, by declaring themselves beyond the majority's comprehension ("If you can't be like them, be like your own group"), or, as in the case of the Militant, by rebelling against the dominant culture of the majority ("If you can't lick them, destroy their world").

Branden makes the following observations about the Independent social metaphysician, in which category I include the race-conscious Militant:

> Overwhelmed by feelings of inadequacy in relation to the conventional standards of his culture, this type of person retaliates with the formula "Whatever is, is *wrong*." Overwhelmed by the belief that no one can

possibly like or accept him, he goes out of his way to insult people—lest they imagine that he desires their approval. Overwhelmed with humiliation at feeling himself an outcast, he struggles to conquer his sense of non-identity by maintaining that to be an outcast is proof of one's superiority. . . .

While he may profess devotion to some particular idea or goal, or even posture as a dedicated crusader, his primary motivation is negative rather than positive; he is *against* rather than *for*. He does not originate or struggle for positive values of his own, he merely rebels against the values and standards of others—as if the *absence* of passive conformity, rather than the *presence* of independent, rational judgment, were the hallmark of self-reliance and spiritual sovereignty. It is by means of this delusion that he seeks to escape the fact of his inner emptiness.[24]

Echoing Branden's description of the Independent as the person who rebels against the status quo for the sake of being rebellious, J. A. Parker writes of the militant Black Power organizations and their white New Left counterparts: "The new organizations preach revolution, racial consciousness, and hostility to all establishments, both good and bad. They are, in a sense, against things as they are, regardless of whether the things be beneficial or detrimental."[25] Although many leaders of the Negro militants disputed any attempts to link them with the predominantly white New Left counterculture movement, the fact is that their aims and tactics often converged and may be seen as variations on a larger cultural trend—not of rebellion, but of conformity. To be sure, the black and white radicals were not passive conformists, but their rebellious conformity made them no less members of the category of social metaphysician. As Rand notes of the relationship of the student rebels to the status quo they rebelled against: "theirs is a rebellion against the status quo by its archetypes."[26]

Professor of philosophy Leonard Peikoff, who shares Rand's perspective, identifies New Left radicalism as the political expression of the "spirit of the sixties" that could be seen in other forms: the "substraction art" of Pop Art; the reductive, antiplay theatrical principles of Absurdist drama; the "relevant" curricula and "open classrooms" of Open Education; the antiempirical "nihilistic repudiation," to quote Robert Nisbet, of the social sciences; the subversion of causality in the physical sciences; the blurring of the distinction between reportage and fiction in the "new journalism" and in docudrama television; the "primal" screaming-meditation-encounter-group-style of "new" therapy that promised inner harmony; the spectacle of Satanic cults, pornography, and filthy language in moves; the "atonal, athematic, arhythmic" music; the "black humor" of novels.[27]

As "heirs and successors of generations of liberal reformists," the New Left advocated "love" and defended "the people," while rejecting everything from conceptual awareness to the American system. "What kind of society was to replace the American system?" asks Peikoff. "What positive goal justified all the negative demands? What was the rebels' program? 'We haven't any,' declared youth leader Tom Hayden in 1968. 'First we will make the revolution, and *then* we will find out what for.' "[28] Spoken like a true independent social metaphysician.

It was, writes Peikoff, a field day of *nihilism*, a replay of the German youth movement of Weimar Germany, "stripped of any nineteenth-century vestiges and, therefore, incalculably more degraded in form, with nothing to conceal the brutish hatred at its root, or the lust for destruction." Although the nihilism of the New Left was shocking, it was not accidental. Writes Peikoff: "In every area, the rebels of the sixties accepted, and then carried out consistently, the philosophic fundamentals of the Establishment they cursed. The 'spirit of the sixties' was, at root, [as was the "Weimar culture"] the spirit of the eighties—the 1780's, the decade of the Kantian *Critiques*, and of everything which they unleashed on an unsuspecting world."[29]

The nihilistic spirit of the sixties was not "white." It was a phenomenon of the cultural bankruptcy of the society at large and Negro cultural nationalists (militants and pragmatists alike) were not the least among those who repudiated America's pro-reason, pro-freedom, pro-achievement sense of life. The cultural and political nationalists sought to enshrine black identification as a debunking mechanism that would transform the ethnic ideal into a crusade against capitalism, scientific objectivity, self-interest, and individual rights.

Like the student rebels, the Negro nationalists rebelled against the very cultural situation of which they were the products. These descendants of Pragmatism had been taught that the truth of a proposition is to be judged by its consequences. Hence, they took the consequences of America's betrayal of the classical liberal proposition of individual rights (one of which was the oppression of Negroes) to be proof that the proposition itself was invalid. They declared their own subordination as a consequence of the invalidity of individual rights and substituted that proposition for collective "rights." Since they and their parents had been taught that values are relative, the product of the cultural environment, they proceeded to proclaim "black" values superior to "white" values.[30] They took the consequences of racist-motivated social science research (the legitimation of racial inferiority) as "proof" of the invalidity of objective inquiry, and joined the New Left in its antiempirical bias.[31] As noted earlier, the nationalists held the growing Negro middle class in contempt—this, despite their own membership in the group—and joined white student radicals in their condemnation of the American system of competitive mobility. Both attacked the consequences of an open society—productivity, property, prosperity, and progress.

The radical conformity of the pragmatic and militant nationalists can be seen in their responses to several issues that have preoccupied Americans during the past two decades. Regarding the role they played in educational policies of the sixties, Christopher Lasch writes:

> In the late sixties, as the civil rights movement gave way to the movement for black power, radicals in the educational world began to identify themselves with a new theory of black culture, *an inverted version of the theory of cultural deprivation*, which upheld the ghetto subculture as a functional adaptation to ghetto life, indeed as an attractive alternative to the white middle-class culture of competitive achievement. Radicals now criticized the school for imposing white culture on the poor. Black-power spokesmen, eager to exploit white liberal guilt, joined the attack, demanding separate programs of black studies, an end to the tyranny of the written word, instruction in English as a second language. Ostensibly a radical advance over the middle-class movement for racial integration, *black power provided a new rationale for second-class segregated schools*, just as the radical critics of "traditional" schooling played into the hands of the educational establishment by condemning basic education as cultural imperialism. Instead of criticizing the expansion of educational bureaucracy, these critics turned their fire against the safer target of education itself, legitimizing a new erosion of standards in the name of pedagogical creativity. Instead of urging the school to moderate its claims and to return to basic education, they demanded a further expansion of the curriculum to include programs in black history, black English, black cultural awareness, and black pride.[32] (emphasis mine).

It is worthwhile to recall the point made in chapter 6 that the stated function of black identification was to to eliminate the ambivalence between (white) American ideals and the Negro world view, between Negro American identity and Negro racial identity, by establishing a set of ideals that would be commensurate with the reality of Negro life in America and to do so by excorcising the "white" American ideals from the minds of Negro Americans—to resocialize them to a "black ethos." The consequence of this rejection of "corrupt white ideals" would be the preservation of the world view of the Negro community that has developed within the context of its separate existence in America. But as Lasch points out, such "strategies of narcissistic survival" which propose "emancipation from the repressive conditions of the past" only "[give] rise to a 'cultural revolution' that reproduces the worst features of the collapsing civilization it claims to criticize."[33] Like other elements of "cultural radicalism," the antiwhite proposition of the ideology of cultural nationalism, which the militants translated into action, unwittingly provided support for the status quo, leaving it intact and reinforced.

As the militant student rebels were actually accommodating the status quo of the liberal Establishment they claimed as their enemy, the militant Black Power advocates accommodated their target of rebellion, the status quo of the racist Establishment. The dissimilarities in the kinds of status quo the students and race-conscious militants accommodated is less important, in this context, than the fact that in their defiance against things as they are, their rebellion often acted to extenuate the very things they said repelled them so. In the case of the Black Power militants, the Kerner Commission on Civil Disorders noted that although they were the most militant of the Negro protesters, "they have retreated from a direct confrontation with American society on the issue of integration and, by preaching separatism, unconsciously function as an accommodation to white racism."

The Militants accommodated more than the white racism that they claimed was inherent in "the System"; their theme of retaliatory violence was also an accommodation to the society's sanction of the assault on legality and human rights implicit in the egalitarianism advocated by the Conventional Integrationists. In other words, the Establishment against which the Militants rebelled was not just white, but black as well. Their contempt for Establishment blacks was aimed not only toward the coalition politics espoused by Integrationists, but also toward the pragmatic nationalism of the

Power-seekers, whom H. Rap Brown called "nothing but a bunch of potheads, bootleg preachers and coffeehouse intellectuals. They are caught up in that whole identity thing. They just discovered that they were Black, because they were working so hard all their lives to be white. They're further away from being revolutionaries than the poor people who are not militantly political. . . . [They] spend all their time trying to program white people into giving them some money. 'The man' has created a new type of Tom. They are willing to be anything, as long as they can be Black first. Black capitalists, Black imperialists, Black oppressors—anything, so long as it's Black first."[34]

In her call for revolution, Angela Davis also rejected the solutions advocated by the black Establishment. "The apologists for Black Capitalism are determined to render Black people oblivious to the reality that the most significant portion of this country's wealth rests with a small group of corporations and that, absent a revolution, there it will remain," said Davis. "As a Communist, I feel that it is incumbent upon us to reject Black Capitalism."[35]

Even Martin Luther King, Jr. met increasing disapproval and hostility from young militants who regarded him as representative of the status quo in the civil rights movement. Defending the Black Power movement as "a reaction to the failure of white power," but condemning its advocacy of violence as an imitation of "the worst, the most brutal, and the most uncivilized value of American life," King wrote of the militants' hostility toward him at a Chicago mass meeting:

For twelve years I, and others like me, had held out radiant promises of progress. I had preached to them about my dream. I had lectured to them about the not too distant day when they would have freedom "all, here and now." I had urged them to have faith in America and in white society. Their hopes had soared. They were now booing [me] because they felt that we were unable to deliver on our promises. They were booing because we had urged them to have faith in people who had too often proved to be unfaithful. They were now hostile because they were watching the dream they had so readily accepted turn into a frustrating nightmare.[36]

In all of their solutions to their dilemma of marginality, the actions taken by the other race-conscious types have been largely nonviolent, though sometimes with the aid of government coercion. Even when they advocate changes that require the abandonment of the principles on which the American political system was founded, they are, nevertheless, committed to the system. The Integrationist responds to his dilemma by giving priority to equality over freedom and imposing desegregation on those who discriminate against him and segregate him. The Power-seeker responds by employing his electoral power to secure policies and programs that give him preferential treatment on the basis of racial identity and collective victimization as defined and justified by the racial chauvinism of the Spiritualist. The other race-conscious types advocate solutions that are often unjust but not illegal. Indeed, their campaign is to transform their personal desires into law.

But the Militant differs from the others in that his behavior is often criminal, he has no respect for the legal system and no interest in preserving or reforming it. He has concluded that his survival depends on the destruction of the system, not its salvation. "America must be burned down in order for us to survive!" said Stokely Carmichael. Since he aims to gain control over men and their institutions, Branden calls the Militant the "brother-in-spirit" of the Power-seeker. The effective difference between the two is that the Power-seeker attempts to coerce men by the force of laws and the Militant does so by the force of physical violence and destruction.

The difference separating the Power-seeker from the Militant can be seen in the following reasons given by Branden for the Power-seeker's preference for nonviolent control over others:

> While his desire is to control the consciousness of others, he does not necessarily resort to physical force, even when opportunities exist. Manipulation, trickery and deceit are often chosen by him, not as *adjuncts* to coercion, but as preferred *alternatives*. There are several reasons for this. First, not all men of this type have the "stomach" for physical violence: they cannot bear the vision of themselves resorting to such means. Second, devices such as manipulation and deceit do not ordinarily entail the physical risks and dangers inherent in the use of violence. Third, to some Power-seekers, these nonviolent devices represent a *superior* form of efficacy, a more "intellectual" form, so to speak.[37]

Disappointed with the pace and achievements of the interracial campaign for integration, the Power-seekers and Militants embraced the Black Power movement, which began with an antiwhite philosophy broad enough to accommodate the violent and nonviolent tactics of both. As the report of the Kerner Commission on Civil Disorders describes it, the Black Power movement first articulated a mood rather than a program—"disillusionment, independence, race pride and self-respect, or 'black consciousness.' " As seen in chapter 8, the transformation of the Black Power doctrine into political and economic programs has been carried out by the nonviolent pragmatic nationalists among the Power-seekers. Functioning on the premise that only a well-organized and cohesive bloc of Negro voters can provide for the needs of the black masses, the pragmatic nationalists place emphasis on self-help, racial unity, and the implementation of ethnic exclusivity to achieve power and influence.

The pragmatic nationalists have responded to their disillusionment and alienation from the American mainstream by transforming the victimization of Negroes into a political advantage—a symbol of status used to manipulate the political system for their benefit. The militant reactionary nationalists responded by articulating the mood of Black Power in the form of rhetorical and retaliatory violence. When asked what program Black Power offered, Stokely Carmichael answered "None," conceding that "We have no infallible master plan and we make no claim to exclusive knowledge of how to end racism; different groups will work in their own different ways."[38] It was not electoral power the Black Power reactionaries sought but the power of the gun.

One faction of the reactionary nationalists, such as CORE, advocated "revolutionary" changes in the social structure. If there was to be any black-white cooperation it should be in the form of an alliance of Negroes and unorganized lower-class whites to overthrow the "power structure" of the white "ruling class," which allegedly exploits the poor of both races. The more militant of the reactionary nationalists, such as the Black Panthers, sought not to change the social structure but to destroy it and those who protect it. Both groups applauded the idea of guerrilla warfare and regarded riots as "the natural explosion of an oppressed people against intolerable conditions."[39] Whatever their justifications, the varying responses of the violent reactionaries and the nonviolent pragmatists were derived from the same root that fuels the impulse to violence. That impulse is, as Branden writes, "the desire to bypass and overcome the voluntary judgment of others, to affect others through the imposition of one's own will, against their desires, knowledge and interests—to gain a sense of triumph by cheating reason and reality. The desire to manipulate other men is the desire to manipulate reality and to make one's wishes omnipotent."[40]

253

The Other Side of Racism

Often the Militant will abandon the immediacy of violent destruction and become a conformist to the longer-range tactics of the Power-seeker. This was the case with the Black Panthers and their leaders. In the late 1960s Huey P. Newton, co-founder and chairman of the Black Panther party, wrote in the party's newspaper: "When the people move from liberation, they must have the basic tool of liberation: the gun. Only with the power of the gun can the Black Masses halt the terror and brutality perpetuated against them by the armed racist power structure; and in one sense only by the power of the gun can the whole world be transformed into the earthly paradise dreamed of by people from time immemorial. . . . The people must oppose everything the oppressor supports and support everything that he opposes. . . . The racist dog oppressors have no rights which oppressed black people are bound to respect."[41]

In 1974 Huey Newton fled to Cuba, jumping bail on charges of murder and assault. He returned voluntarily in 1977 to stand trial in San Francisco. In the time that he was in exile the Black Panther party put aside its guns ("armed in self-defense of our homes and communities against these fascist police forces") and concentrated on organizing "survival programs" for the poor and influencing politicians in the Negro community. Among its projects were a health clinic in Berkeley, a free food program, the Black Panther newspaper, and a private Oakland Community School purchased from a white Southern Baptist group. The school's director said: "We try not to teach anything in terms of philosophy. We don't want it to be too Panthery." During the spring of 1977, the party's voter registration drive in minority communities helped elect Oakland's first Negro mayor and the first Negro Alameda County supervisor. A fellow Panther was on the Alameda County School Board, and Elaine Brown, the party's leader from 1974 until Newton's return, was an advisor to the new mayor on transition goals his administration should undertake.

Newton, who once wrote, "We were forced to build America and, if forced to, we will tear it down," called on the mayor and the Panthers to join forces and "work for progressive change in our society." The party's aims, he said, would be directed toward "a national campaign for full employment and a reform of the political system as well as full participation in that political system. I think the position of a progressive revolution today is to make a reality out of what is possible rather than to talk about what could be."[42]

254

In 1977 the Black Panther party had become a respected community organization among the pragmatic nationalists. Bobby Seale, another co-founder of the Panthers, whose name had been expunged for undisclosed reasons from their official history, ran for mayor of Oakland in 1973. Even though he lost, the number of votes he received was substantial enough to indicate that the party had political influence.

No longer conducting campaigns of armed rebellion, spirited by violent rhetoric like "Off the Pigs," Newton claimed in 1977 that much of the rhetoric had been produced by Eldridge Cleaver, who had been the minister of information of the Black Panthers. He called Cleaver's rhetoric so detrimental "that if he wasn't a police agent he did more damage [to the party's image] than most." The Panthers branded him a "Judas" for allegedly informing on their activities.

In one of his outrages, as minister of information, Eldridge Cleaver told a group of San Francisco lawyers: "This whole apparatus, this capitalistic system and its institutions and police . . . all need to be assigned to the garbage can of history. . . . If we can't have it, nobody's gonna have it. We'd rather provoke a situation . . . that will disrupt cities and the economy so that the enemies of America can come in and pick the gold teeth of these Babylonian pigs."[43]

Like Huey Newton, Cleaver jumped bail on charges of attempted murder during his 1968 shoot-out with the Oakland police. Upon his voluntary return to the United States in 1976 after a seven-year exile in Havana, Algiers, and Paris, he disavowed the black nationalist aims of the Black Panther party manifesto. In 1969 Cleaver was an atheist who advocated the overthrow of "the American nightmare." But in 1976 his statements came from a new set of right-wing political views and fundamentalist religious doctrines. After spending nine months in jail, he was released on $100,000 bail arranged for by conservative Philadelphia millionaire Arthur DeMoss, who also contributed to his legal and family expenses. With the assistance of supporters like Reverend Robert Schuller of the "Hour of Power" religious television program, he spent the months following his release preaching the virtues of born-again Christianity and giving lectures denouncing his former third-world hosts and expressing his faith in "the limitless possibilities of the American dream." While former associates and black activists denounced his political and religious conversion as everything from "turncoat opportunism" to "schizophrenic," he was embraced by such Establishment figures as Daniel Patrick Moynihan, who contributed $500 to his legal defense; *Commentary* editor Norman Podhoretz, who held a fundraising party for him; and William H. Buckley, who praised Cleaver's "integrity" as "a matter for national celebration, toward which I light this candle."[44]

It is not necessary, for this discussion, to establish whether Cleaver's renunciation of his past and Newton's call for progressive social change were genuine. What is relevant is that as of 1977 their apparent transformation from revolutionaries to reformers was an accommodation to the system they once wanted to destroy. It is obviously more comforting to men like Buckley to hear Cleaver singing the praises of "America the bountiful" rather than denouncing "America the nightmare." But from the view of this study such accommodation represents only a variation in the means by which Militants-turned-Power-seekers attempt to defy "the tyranny of reality" by manipulating other men. Nonviolent though their campaign was, acting in alliance with Jesus Christ or the mayor of Oakland says significantly less about the change in tactical expression of their philosophy than it does about how entrenched is their desire to control the consciousness of others. The power-seeking means used by the Black Panthers and their former members to achieve their goals are now legal, but they are means that are often as unjust as their militant means of years ago. The difference is that they now compete with other special interest groups to impose their will on others by means of a legislative gun instead of a sawed-off shotgun.

The focus here on politically motivated Militants should not be construed to mean that all Militants seek political solutions to their dilemma of self-esteem and marginality. Most race-conscious Militants are not interested in any systematic defiance of the "white power structure" or the organized destruction of "the System." Most have no "plan," no thought of tomorrow, only their obsession with finding relief from frustrations of the immediate moment. They are the thousands of easily provoked rioters, arsonists, and looters who, in the words of Branden, "struggle to fill the void of the egos they do not possess, by means of the only form of 'self-assertiveness' they recognize: defiance for the sake of defiance, irrationality for the sake of irrationality, destruction for the sake of destruction, whims for the sake of whims."[45] Internal chaos wells up and, fired by political rhetoric, spills over and out into the external world to become a raging rampage of primitive pillage, as dramatized in the poem "Black People!" by Imamu Ameer Baraka (LeRoi Jones):

What about that bad short you saw last week
on Frelinghuysen, or those stoves and refrigerators,
        record players
in Sears, Bambergers, Klein's, Hahnes, Chase, and
        the small joosh
enterprises? What about that bad jewelry, on Washington
        Street, and
those couple of shops on Springfield? You know how to
        get it, you can
get it, no money down, no money never, money don't
        grow on trees no
way, only whitey's got it, makes it with a machine to
        control you
you can't steal nothin from a white man, he's already
        stole it he owes
you anything you want, even his life. All the stores will
        open if you
will say the magic words. The magic words are: Up
        against the wall mother
fucker this is a stick up! Or: Smash the window at night
        (these are magic
actions) smash the windows daytime, anytime, together,
        let's smash the
window drag the shit from in there. No money down.
        No time to pay. Just
take what you want. The magic dance in the street. Run
        up and down Broad
Street niggers, take the shit you want. Take their lives if
        need be, but
get what you want what you need. Dance up and down
        the streets, turn all
the music up, run through the streets with music, beautiful
        radios on
Market Street, they are brought here especially for you.
        Our brothers
are moving all over, smashing at jellywhite faces. We
        must make our own
World, man, our own world, and we can not do this
        unless the white man
is dead. Let's get together and kill him my man, let's
        get to gather the fruit
of the sun, Let's make a world we want black

257

children to grow and learn in
do not let your children when they grow look
in your face and curse you by
pitying your tomish ways.[46]

That such a poem could be written by any American—indeed, by any person of modern civilization—and that it could be published is evidence enough of the "intellectual vacuum" that, as Branden puts it, "flings the militants up from their cellars to the pinnacles of prestige." Its raving resentment of life and property does not spring from the times and places of arch-Militants like Attila the Hun, Adolf Hitler, and Idi Amin, but from the director of the Black Arts Repertory Theater, which was partially financed by government antipoverty funds. Its foulmouthed hatred was not presented to the world by way of some ink-stained, underground rag, but by one of the nation's leading publishers.

Though LeRoi Jones believed "the black artist's role in America is to aid in the destruction of America as he knows it," he did not refuse the assistance of the federal government and the publishing world in revealing the reeking spirit of the Independent Militant: since he cannot control men's minds, he destroys what their minds have produced; since he will not strive to achieve positive values, he will not allow others to benefit from their values; since he cannot escape the consequences of dealing with reality and the men in it, he attempts to destroy the men and thereby escape reality.

From Mass Anarchy to Political Terror

In a 1967 speech to his fellow liberals in Americans for Democratic Action, Daniel Patrick Moynihan warned that explaining away Negro violence was more likely to contribute to increased lawlessness than it would to racial harmony. He said: "All the signs declare that the violence is not ended. Worse still, a new set of signs tell us something that is painful, even hateful, to have to hear: We must prepare for the onset of terrorism. Indeed, it may already have begun. How widespread and how successful remains to be seen, but the probability is so great that ignoring it would be an act of irresponsibility or of cowardice."[47]

Writing in 1968, H. Rap Brown also predicted a future of more intense violence than had already occurred:

We stand on the eve of a black revolution, brothers. Masses of our people are in the streets. They're fighting tit for tat, tooth for tooth, an eye for an eye, and a life for a life. The rebellions that we see are merely dress rehearsals for the revolution that's to come. We'd better get ourselves some guns and prepare ourselves. . . . To desire freedom is not enough. We must move from resistance to aggression, from revolt to revolution. . . . May the deaths of '68 signal the beginning of the end of this country.[48]

The revolution did not come, but terrorism did. The battles with police, the looting, and the arson of street violence is quite a sufficient solution for some Militants. But for some, "the tyranny of reality" is more than they can bear. Their internal chaos cannot be assuaged by joining a rampaging mob in its attack on the property of others. They require bigger game—the lives of individuals and the fear of society. They are the terrorists—the most isolated and desperate of the Militants.

The annual predictions of "long, hot summers" of urban violence are no more. But in the spring of 1977, the Task Force on Disorders and Terrorism of the National Advisory Committee on Criminal Justice Standards and Goals warned: "The present tranquility is deceptive . . . and we must see in the current social situation an accumulation of trouble for the future."[49] Acknowledging the increase of international terrorism, the task force said it did not consider domestic terrorism currently alarming. But it warned that individuals should prepare for becoming hostages some day. It was a shocking prospect, but very real. In ten years Militants had gone from street violence and occupying college campus buildings to terrorist kidnappings, hijackings, and assassinations.

Civilians are not only vulnerable to domestic terrorism, but international terrorism as well. In August 1976 three employees of Rockwell International Corporation were murdered in Iran by enemies of the Shah. Between 1968 and 1974 terrorists in Latin America killed four U.S. diplomats and kidnapped eight others. Throughout the 1970s and since the headlines of the world have announced the latest acts by revolutionaries and killer bands, whose common objective is to focus attention on their political objectives. The groups spring from every part of the world and a list of them reads like a United Nations of Terrorists:

Armed Revolutionary Movement, Mexico
Arab Liberation Front, an arm of Iraq's Ba'ath party
Baader-Meinhof gang, West Germany
Basque Separatists, Spain

The Other Side of Racism

Croatian Separatists, Yugoslavia
Japanese Red Army
Marxist Popular Front for the Liberation of Palestine
People's Revolutionary Army, Argentina
Popular Liberation Front, Turkey
Popular Struggle Front, Lebanon and Jordan's West Bank
Provisional Irish Republican Army, Britain and Ulster
Quebec Liberation Front, Canada
South Moluccan Nationalists, The Netherlands

They are seemingly everywhere, in a world that hardly makes a distinction between villains and victims; where one man's (or one nation's) gain is seen as necessarily an achievement at the expense of another; where political grievances are accepted as the justification for murder and extortion; where national, tribal, racial, and ethnic affiliations are perceived as more valid sources of self-identity than an individual's character, personality, and values. In numbers, the impact of international terrorism has been fairly small, but in political terms, its impact has been far greater. As the Department of State's Coordinator for Combating Terrorism explained it: "When you have a situation where air travel can be endangered, where mail must be x-rayed for explosives, where international conferences can be disrupted by bomb threats, where embassies and diplomats can be hampered in their work, where justice is impaired as perpetrators of horrible acts of violence are given short sentences or let free, and where state authority is weakened as governments accede to terrorist demands—then you can see the consequences which uncontrolled terrorism could have."[50]

While international terrorism has grown and become increasingly dangerous as guerrillas acquire more accurate and destructive weapons, the United States has been plagued by its own domestic terrorist groups, the most notorious of which was the Symbionese Liberation Army, which abducted newspaper heiress Patricia Hearst. These groups consisted primarily of frustrated and desperate young people who were participants in the black and student riots of the 1960s. As psychiatrist David Abrahamsen explained it, they were the ones "who decided to call attention to themselves by deeds that would be more direct, more accurate and more threatening than anything this country had experienced—a more explicit and more directed version of what we saw in the 1960s."[51] Their threat to society is less visible than the militant anarchists, but far more deadly.

There was the Death Angels, a San Francisco group known by the code name "Zebra" and associated with the Black Muslim movement, whose members were charged with a series of indiscriminate shootings of whites in the Bay area.

Dissident Black Panthers known as the Black Liberation Army came into being in the late 1960s in Oakland, as a result of a dispute over strategy between Huey Newton and Eldridge Cleaver. The group's aim was to kill policemen in the hope that police departments would overreact and kill innocent black people, who would then rise in mass revolt with the Black Liberation Army as their leaders. Between 1970 and 1973, they added to bank robberies and bombings the ambush and murder of ten policemen in Georgia, Pennsylvania, New Jersey, and New York. More than two dozen officers were wounded.

The New World Liberation Front, a descendant of the Symbionese Liberation Army, was composed of white radicals who claimed responsibility for forty bombings and attempted bombings in California between 1975 and 1977. Their bomb threats so frightened public leaders in San Francisco that top officials were given twenty-four-hour police protection, and the entrances and corridors of City Hall were patrolled by teams of policemen.

The F.A.L.N., or Armed Forces of National Liberation for Puerto Rico, whose members are Hispanic-American, set fifty-eight bombs or incendiary devices between 1974 and 1977, exploding inside or near government buildings, large banks, or major corporations. An explosion at a New York tavern in 1975 left four people killed and fifty-five others injured. The F.A.L.N. demands, stated in notes left near the bomb sites, have included the independence of Puerto Rico from the United States. They also made threats if cancer-stricken Puerto Rican terrorist, Andres Figueroa Cordero, were not released from federal prison before his death. (In 1954 Cordero and three other Puerto Ricans fired into the House of Representatives chamber from the visitors' gallery, wounding five Congressmen. He was sentenced to 81 years in prison. In light of his advancing illness, President Carter pardoned him in 1977. He died in San Juan in 1979.)

Not all political terrorists act in groups. Some, like assassins Lee Harvey Oswald, Arthur Bremer, and James Earl Ray, are "loners"—typical of the American terrorist in the past—who tend to be psychotic and with short-term goals. Since the massacre of Israeli athletes at the 1972 Olympics in Munich and the S.L.A. kidnapping of Patricia Hearst, there has been an increase in the United States of lone desperadoes who use the taking of hostages, extortion, and blackmail as instruments of terror. In March, 1977, even as the government Task Force on Disorders and Terrorism warned Americans to prepare for becoming hostages, an outbreak of incidents involving hostages had occurred in Cincinnati, Indianapolis, New Rochelle, New York, and Syracuse, New York. By the end of March the fashion of taking hostages and making outrageous demands on society as the ransom for their lives had reached the point of contagion.

A week after the release of the task force report, in Cleveland a black former marine took a suburban police captain prisoner and freed him after two days only at the price of talking to President Jimmy Carter. Besides his demand to talk to the president, the twenty-five-year-old gunman demanded that all white people leave the planet with their "bombs, guns, bullets and ignorance." Less than an hour after his March 9 press conference, during which Carter agreed publicly to talk to him on the telephone, members of the Hanafi Muslim sect attacked three buildings in Washington, D.C. Apparently driven by his grief over the 1973 murders of his family by gunmen from the rival Black Muslim sect, Hamaas Abdul Khaalis, leader of the Hanafi group, and twelve followers held 134 hostages for thirty-nine hours at City Hall, the B'nai B'rith headquarters, and the Islamic Center. Brandishing rifles and machetes and vowing to "fight to the death," Khaalis demanded the removal of the film "Mohammad, Messenger of God" from movie theaters, the return of the $750 contempt of court fine levied against him during the trial of the murderers of his family, and the delivery to him of the six convicted killers of the Hanafi family, the three killers of Malcolm X, and two prominent Black Muslims, Muhammad Ali and Wallace Muhammad. After the motion picture was removed from the theaters and the contempt fine returned, the Hanafis released their captives and surrendered on felony charges with the promise from authorities that Khaalis would be free without bail pending his trial.

Before the month of March ended, there were six more incidents involving hostage-taking. The last one occurred on the night of March 26 when a gunman held four hostages for more than five hours in the office of New York City's Housing and Development

Administration. He surrendered to police without a struggle after issuing a rambling series of demands for $500,000 to convert a Harlem building into a mosque, "equal opportunities for Sunni Muslims," a suspension of alternate-side-of-the-street parking regulations on Muslim holidays, and elimination of the need for court orders to change Christian names to Muslim names.

Not all acts of terrorism are racially or religiously motivated. As psychiatrist Frederick Hacker, author of *Crusaders, Criminals, Crazies*, points out, besides the fanatical political or ideological terrorists, there are criminals who take hostages, such as in a bank robbery gone wrong; and psychotics, usually suffering from a severe lack of self-esteem, who seek publicity. The hostage-taking sieges cited above had none of the tactical sophistication of the Symbionese Liberation Army or the Black Liberation Army, and nothing approaching the long-term goals of political terrorists in Europe, the Middle East, and Latin America. But in the hostage-taking terrorist we can see in its crudest and most primitive form the fear that motivates all reactionary militants, whether they be the Ku Klux Klan, the Black Panthers, or the government of Iran. The terrorist is terrified—by the world without and the world within. As psychiatrist David Abrahamsen puts it, "Some terrorists may join a group out of their inner fears, which they hope, from the very beginning, will be eliminated by instilling fear in others."[52]

Forgetting or evading the active antithesis of violence in his synthesis of nonviolent resistance, Martin Luther King, Jr. wrote: "The ultimate weakness of violence is that it is a descending spiral, begetting the very thing it seeks to destroy. Instead of diminishing evil, it multiplies it."[53] Thus, it has been that since the early 1960s, mass civil disobedience, which relied on the initiation of violence, spiraled into mass anarchy that spiraled into guerrilla violence and eruptions of terrorism. Terrorists are of a wide range of politics, but what they all have in common, said a police psychologist, is their view of themselves "as victims of society—as losers. For them, taking hostages is a very creative act. It gives you real power." Since the terrorist cannot join society, he holds a gun and a group of hostages over the rest of society—a strength equal to "his own ruthlessness, recklessness, or the extent of his mental derangement," said the government task force report on terrorism.

For decades the Integrationists, Power-seekers, and Spiritualists have claimed that to be black was to be society's victim. And in the last decade they have transformed the victim status of Negroes into a source of political power. But while the other race-conscious types exact retribution from the majority society on the basis of the historical victimization of Negroes, the Militant, though inherently powerless, is desperate to give the *appearance* of strength, taking the course of least resistance. The others want to *acquire* power; the Militant wants to *exhibit* power. He exclaims desperately to the world that he is prepared to do or die. He will have what he wants—Now!—or he will take his own life or the lives of his hostages, trading on the fact that the preservation of life is among the highest of human values.

He declares his hate and exhausts his rage over radio and television to a world he perceives as indifferent and hostile. Newspapers carry glaring headlines with his name in 2 1/2-inch print—and all the community, or indeed a nation, waits at his bidding. The evening news lifts him up out of 220 million Americans, and for a brief time he is as important—and powerful—as the president. And once again, as they have so many times before, Americans ask each other incredulously: *Why?*

Why the Violence?

Standing near the B'nai B'rith building that was beseiged by Hanafi Muslims, a black psychology student told newspaper reporter Robert Lipsyte: "You know what Hanafi means? Upstanding."

"Then why are they doing all this?" asked Lipsyte.

"You shouldn't have to ask . . . ," he said. "But things are coming plain. Think about *Roots*, think about what Malcolm meant about chickens coming home to roost. . . . Think about how you have to hit the mule with a two-by-four just to get his attention."

The student confirmed what criminal experts and students of terrorism say is the principal ingredient in the "focused violence" of hostage-taking terrorism. "What really is going on in depth right now is a broad fringe group has learned that they can bring their social discontent to maximum public attention instantaneously," psychiatrist David Hubbard said of the groups active in the 1970s. "They wish to be the cynosure of all eyes. They're willing to die Beau Geste-like if at least for a moment in the bright flare they stand revealed."

264

Of course the student's statement implies that the Hanafi terrorism had more meaning to it than Hubbard's rather matter-of-fact explanation. For him the thirty-nine-hour siege carried the same meaning as the riots of 1967 had for the Kerner Commission on Civil Disorders: "the culmination of 300 years of racial prejudice." In other words, the cause of the Hanafi violence was to be found not in Khaalis and his armed gang, but in the effect that white racism had had on them. To understand their crime, said their apologists, one must see them not as perpetrators, but as victims.

Most explanations of the racial violence engaged in by the Militant are offered as *moral justifications* of the crimes committed; an attempt to absolve the individual of the responsibility for his action. The Militant is seen not as a self-defined individual capable of choosing his course of action, but as an explosive reactor to circumstances beyond his control. Deterministic social scientists bypass his value system and his cognitive state, preferring to depict him as yet another Negro stereotype: a mangled mass of madness whose " 'place' in America has been shaped by powerful forces"— whose identity is "a nearly bottomless well of self-depreciation . . . prepared by society and stands waiting, a prefabricated pit which [he has] had no hand in fashioning."[54] He is the product of the "powerful interlocking of family milieu and social attitudes [that] has presented a barrier to him and his black brethren which is felt by no other ethnic group in America."[55] He is a festering force of fury turned inward on himself and capable of destroying those without who created him.

Negroes have heard themselves described in this way so often that young criminals and troublemakers do not hesitate to defend their lawlessness in terms of the collective victimization of their race. And they expect to be taken seriously! During the 1970 "Panther 21" trial in New York City, which tried thirteen of the original twenty-one Black Panthers charged with conspiring to blow up five Manhattan department stores, defendant Michael Tabor told the questioning district attorney, "When I say that ultimately I was framed, I am saying that the conditions under which not only myself but black people per se in America are forced to live drive them to such desperation that they are forced to extend beyond what society defines as the bounds of law."[56]

There is no denying the fact that throughout their history Negroes have been "framed" by slavery, government-enforced segregation,

265

white prejudice, discrimination, and terrorism. Neither can there be any dispute over the fact that these factors have contributed to the poverty, unemployment, and illiteracy in Negro communities, and to the bitterness and resentment many feel toward society. But in reality that is where the causal chain ends; and even then the connection is relative, not absolute. Economic deprivation, ignorance, and social alienation brought on by racism do not in turn *cause* violence. White racism *is* a cause of black poverty, but poverty *is not* the cause of violence. Violence is one of several forms of behavior a person chooses in response to his own or his group's definition of his economic situation. Some Negroes eliminate poverty by going into business for themselves; others do so by working for someone else; some seek relief from public assistance; some seek private charity; others support social legislation that will provide for guaranteed wages; others support legislation that makes private racial discrimination illegal; and still others try to eliminate their poverty by robbery and theft. Whatever the response, it is not imposed on the individual by external forces, but *chosen* by him according to his own personal moral code and resources.

In attempting to understand why a person resorts to the violent alternative in solving his problems, it must first be acknowledged that the person engaging in violent behavior has, for whatever reasons, chosen to do so; that in committing violence he represents no one but himself—that he alone is the source and owner of his crime. This approach, which relates a person's behavior to his character as well as to environmental factors, has been employed by sociologist Edward C. Banfield in his book on the urban crisis, *The Unheavenly City*. A person's socioeconomic and political situation certainly influences his *propensity* for crime, writes Banfield, but the cause of his crime is determined by the choices he makes within that situation. "People decide whether or not to do illegal things in essentially the way that they decide whether or not to do other things," says Banfield. They choose to act according to the judgment they make regarding whether the action will be beneficial or inimical to their self-interest (which may or may not be rationally defined). And they weigh the "good" and "bad" effects of a choice against the moral and legal rules of right and wrong.

The Militant is among those whose morality is what Banfield calls "preconventional." That is, a person who "understands a 'right' action to be one that will serve his purpose and that can be gotten away with; a 'wrong' action is one that will bring ill success or punishment. An individual whose morality is preconventional cannot be influenced by [legal] authority (as opposed to power)."[57] The preconventional morality is very near to being no morality at all. The person influenced by it does not consider the universal right and wrong (*qua* man) of his action, only whether he can get away with it.

When Banfield speaks of a person's "propensity" toward or against a certain action, he means the "class-cultural and personality constraints" that influence the considerations the individual makes in choosing among various action possibilities. In addition to the person's morality, the other elements of propensity toward or against crime, or certain kinds of crime, are: (1) *Ego Strength*—"the individual's ability to control himself—especially his ability to adhere to and act on his intentions (and therefore to manage his impulses) and his ability to make efforts at self-reform"; (2) *Time Horizon*—"the time perspective an individual takes in estimating costs and benefits of alternative courses of action. The more present-oriented an individual, the less likely he is to take account of consequences that lie in the future"; (3) *Taste for Risk*; and (4) *Willingness to Inflict Injury.*[58]

Typically, the Independent Militant whose morality is preconventional is impulsive, with little ego strength and easily influenced by others; he is present-oriented, acting on range-of-the-moment whims, with no long-range goals; he has a fondness for risks and no qualms about doing bodily harm to individuals.

Banfield writes that these elements of propensity may be so great

> that situational factors would never be decisive. In fact, of course, situational factors are commonly decisive, even among persons of strong propensity in one direction or another. . . . It happens that individuals whose propensity toward crime is relatively high—especially those with high propensity for violent crime—tend to be those whose situation provides the strongest incentive to crimes of the common sorts. The low-income individual obviously has much more incentive to steal than does the high-income one. Similarly, a boy has much more incentive to "prove he is not chicken" than does a girl. In general, then, high propensity and high incentive go together.[59]

It must be emphasized, however, that while situational incentives and propensity go together, one is not the intrinsic cause of the other. Being rich does not make one any more morally conscious

267

than being poor; and being poor does not make one less moral. The poor person's situation may provide him with incentives to steal but the *reason* he steals or does not steal is located not in his empty wallet but in the content of his conscience. The Kerner Commission on Civil Disorders very emphatically named "white racism" and its effects as incentives to racial violence, but not all violence engaged in by Negroes is done for racial reasons. Writes Banfield:

> The assumption that if Negroes riot it must be *because* they are Negroes is naïve. If one rejects this as a starting place and looks at the facts instead, one sees that race (and, incidentally, poverty as well) was not *the* cause of any of the Negro riots and that it had very little to do with many of the lesser ones. Indeed, it is probably not too much to say that some of the riots would have occurred even if (other things being the same) the people in the riot areas had all been white and even if they had all had incomes above the poverty line. The implication of this view is, of course, that punishing police misconduct, providing decent housing, and so on will not significantly affect the amount of Negro rioting.[60]

As it was, a great many of the Negroes in the riot areas earned incomes considerably above the poverty line of $3,000. Quoting from a University of Michigan survey of those who had been arrested for rioting in Detroit in 1967, J. A. Parker challenged the validity of the Kerner Commission's conclusion that economic deprivation is the necessary root of social unrest. Writes Parker:

> In the main riot areas of Detroit, according to the University of Michigan survey, the median annual income of Negro households is $6,200. This is only slightly lower than the figure for all Negro households in Detroit—$6,400. And it is not far below the median white household income: $6,800.
>
> Educational attainment in Negro household heads (45 percent were high-school graduate or better) was higher in the riot area than throughout the city. Seventy percent of the Negro households in the riot area had automobiles available, and the Negroes living in the riot area were substantially better off in every respect than those who lived inside the deep core of the city. They were also somewhat better off than the whites who lived in the riot neighborhoods. Of those arrested, Detroit Police Department records show that only 10 percent of the Negroes were juveniles; 18 percent were between seventeen and nineteen years old, 24 percent between twenty and twenty-four years old, 17 percent between twenty-five and twenty-nine, and 31 percent over thirty. The Law Center survey of 1,200 nonjuvenile male arrestees shows that 83 percent were employed—40 percent of them by the three major automobile compan-

268

ies, and an equal percentage by other large employers. No income data was gathered, but annual wages of $6,000 and more can be assumed.[61]

Parker reports that Professor Irving Rueben, head of the University of Michigan Center for Urban Studies (which made the survey), concluded that solutions based primarily on improving schools, housing, and employment, as were those of the Kerner Commission, do not eliminate the causes of violence; instead, they sow the seeds of even greater trouble. And so it was that a decade later the *New York Times* carried a news story headlined, "*17 U.S. Urban Areas Troubled by Midsummer Racial Violence*"—this, after ten years of a steady stream of Great Society reforms, expanded public assistance, busing, affirmative action quotas, open admissions, public housing expansion, job training programs, and "black capitalism." The cities were still unheavenly and racial tensions still high. "We seem to be fast headed for a race war," said the Reverend Jesse L. Jackson of Operation PUSH. And still after a decade of evidence to the contrary, city officials continued to place the blame for race problems on high unemployment and cutbacks in funds for summer jobs and recreation.

Similar explanations were offered by community leaders, government officials, scholars, and journalists regarding the looting and arson during the 1977 blackout in New York City. But a national poll conducted by the *New York Times* and CBS News after the blackout found that 66 percent of Americans thought that those who took part in the looting did so "because they are the kind of people who always steal if they think they can get away with it." While 48 percent felt it was "because they are out of work and frustrated," 77 percent said it was *not* "because they are poor and needy." The Americans polled affirmed the view of historian Diane Ravitch, who points out that not every riot by poor people is connected to any lofty principle such as social justice. "History does not teach us that every civil disorder, every incident of mass violence, if committed by the poor, is a disguised plea for justice," writes Professor Ravitch. "History teaches us to make intelligent distinctions. . . . To confuse criminal behavior with civil disobedience unfairly demeans those who have struggled for justice and wrongly ennobles those who steal with no greater end than easy gain. This sort of moral confusion pretends to express sympathy for the poor but actually expresses contempt; it says that poor people should be absolved of responsibility for lawless behavior because not much more can be expected of them."[62]

Throughout this chapter the Independent Militant, in all his various forms, is presented as a person who attempts to solve his dilemma of self-esteem by imposing his will on the judgment of others. He is shown not as a victimized dissident hopelessly mired in the backwater of a race-conscious society, but as the hoodlum and criminal he is, whose violent behavior is an act of volition.

There is a more sympathetic view of the Militant that interprets violence as a response to frustrations caused by "the imposition of 'order' by a highly regulative political system." This view is put forth by Professor Butler D. Shaffer, of the University of Nebraska, who writes: "One can only wonder how much of the recent violence—some part of it directed by blacks against their own deteriorated neighborhoods, other parts of it directed against banks and businesses with large defense contracts—may be the product of displaced aggression against an amorphous but highly structured 'social order' that is created, maintained, and enforced by the political state for the purpose of restricting human activity and interfering with the processes of change, thereby frustrating the expectations of millions of people seeking greater fulfillment in their lives."[63]

Professor Shaffer's view of Negro violence as a consequence of "imposed order" is favored by some libertarians who see some similarity between the American Revolution for independence and the "Black Revolution." While they would condemn the crime and violence engaged in by the Militant, they often applaud his disrespect for political authority. Believing as they do that the authority of the state is inherently immoral and therefore should be abolished, some are empathetic to the Militant's challenge of officers of the law who enforce the state's authority.

But the Militant's rebellion is less often against the tyranny of the state (or its representatives) than it is against what he perceives as the tyranny of reality. For instance, while some of his accusations of police "brutality" are certainly justified, often what he calls police brutality (against him) is only the legitimate prevention and/or punishment of him for acts of abuse against the life, liberty, and property of law-abiding citizens. Such protection of all in the community may be experienced by the Militant as "brutality," but it is a proper function of the state, not an incident of statist tyranny.

While this study acknowledges the existence of statist tyranny, it holds that minorities seeking entrance into the American mainstream—indeed, even most mainstream Americans—perceive themselves as *beneficiaries* of the state, not its victims. In its interpretation of urban riots, looting, and certain acts of terrorism, this study agrees with journalist William Safire's view of racial violence as a response to failed expectations that government should do *more*, not less, to provide for the individual a guaranteed existence. The looters in New York felt justified in their "suspension of ordinary civility and morality," wrote Safire, for reasons embedded in the prevailing political philosophy that places increasing responsibility for solving personal and social problems on government:

> One reason for the I'm-entitled-to-what-I-want attitude is the philosophy that welfare is a right to be expanded and not a condition to be avoided by the able-bodied.
> Another reason is the claim that because minorities have suffered discrimination in the past, they are now entitled to reparations in the form of special treatment—and some carry that claim to extremes.
> Another reason is the notion that a job is something to be provided and not searched for, and that menial work is to be spurned as not a "decent" job.
> Another reason is the argument that crime is the result of poverty, and that poverty is nobody's fault but the System's; it follows that in this no-fault world, society is to blame for what a poor person does when the lights are out.[64]

If we take seriously the Militant's rhetoric, we must believe that the justification he offers for his lawlessness and destruction is not because he wants to throw off the yoke of the state's authority, but because of what he perceives as the state's insufficient response to his demands. It is not less state intervention and regulation he seeks, but more—decidedly more—particularly in the lives of those he disagrees with. The state is the Militant's enemy only in that it possesses a monopoly on power and force that he desires for himself. It is not that he is necessarily "framed" by society, but that *he* desires to frame society.

The grotesque absurdity of the present American culture is that its prevailing political philosophy provides the Militant with every reason to believe that he can indeed get away with it; that in a society where men accept the notion that man's mind is impotent, he can rise as the Prince of Anti-Mind, Anti-Morality, Anti-Life, while the intellectual, political, and economic guardians of the society stand helplessly by, asking: *Why?*

1. As I have indicated, so many of the civil rights goals amounted to the betrayal of American values and ideals, not their realization. See chapter 12 for my elaboration of this point and discussion of the pro and con views of the civil rights bill.
2. Ernest Holsendolph, " '63 March in Retrospect: Many Strata of Meaning."
3. Brooks, *Walls Come Tumbling Down*, pp. 229–31.
4. Ibid., p. 227.
5. Ibid., pp. 238–39.
6. Rand, *The New Left: The Anti-Industrial Revolution*, p. 34. There are many sociological, psychological, and political analyses of the rebellions of the sixties, but nowhere have I read a more accurate philosophical analysis than in this work. The lead essay concerns the student rebellions, but much of what Rand says can be applied to the civil rights activists, many of whom were also participants in the campus disruptions that plagued higher education for nearly a decade. Thus, the following discussion will be presented primarily against the points made by Rand in that essay.
7. Lokos, *House Divided: The Life and Legacy of Martin Luther King*, p. 462.
8. Miller, *Martin Luther King, Jr.*, p. 192.
9. Ibid., p. 159.
10. Ibid., p. 97.
11. King, *Stride toward Freedom*, p. 174.
12. Quoted in Lokos, *House Divided*, p. 80.
13. Rand, *The New Left*, p. 38.
14. Richard Eder, "The Struggle of Authority and Autonomy."
15. Brooks, op. cit., pp. 165–66.
16. Ibid.
17. Lokos, *House Divided*, p. 161. Quoted from *Saturday Review*, April 3, 1965, p. 16.
18. Brooks, op. cit., p. 233.
19. See Rand, *The New Left*, p. 40 for further discussion of this "moral inversion."
20. See chapter 12 for elaboration of this issue.
21. Branden, *The Psychology of Self-Esteem*, p. 178.
22. See Nathaniel Branden, "Counterfeit Individualism," in Rand, *The Virtue of Selfishness*, pp. 135 ff. See the discussion in chapter 5 regarding inner-direction and other-direction.
23. Ibid, p. 137.
24. Branden, *The Psychology of Self-Esteem*, pp. 178–79.
25. J. A. Parker, *Angela Davis: The Making of a Revolutionary*, p. 59.
26. Rand, *The New Left*, p. 29.

27. Leonard Peikoff, "The 'Spirit of the Sixties.' " In their analyses of recent cultural trends, Rand and Peikoff trace the intellectual roots of developments in the 1960s to Immanuel Kant, who "divorced reason from reality," and his intellectual descendants: Pragmatism, Logical Positivism, Linguistic Analysis, and Existentialism. The New Left declined with the defeat of George McGovern and was succeeded by debunking movements of the 1970s: the "peace" movement; the Women's Liberation movement; the antitechnology/ecology movement; and the new ethnicity movement.

28. Ibid.

29. Ibid.

30. See Imamu Ameer Baraka, "A Black Value System," John O. Killens, *Black Man's Burden* (New York: Trident Press, 1965); Lerone Bennett, Jr. *The Negro Mood*; Philip Mason, "The Revolt Against Western Values."

31. See Joyce A. Ladner, ed. *The Death of White Sociology*; Wilbur H. Watson, "The Idea of Black Sociology: Its Cultural and Political Significance," *The American Sociologist*, 11 (May 1976): 115–23; Richard F. Hamilton, *Class and Politics in the United States*, pp. 550–52.

32. Christopher Lasch, *The Culture of Narcissism: American Life in an Age of Diminishing Expectations*, p. 144. Much of what Lasch attributes to narcissism, Rand attributes to envy, the social-economic-political expression of which is egalitarianism. (See Rand, "The Age of Envy.") Many of Lasch's observations shed light on the cultural context of the Black Power movement and its ideology of cultural nationalism. But Lasch must be read with a caveat: like so many other cultural historians of our time, he blames all the things gone wrong on (1) capitalism's "welfare liberalism," not realizing (or acknowledging) that the erection of that political contradiction spelled the end of capitalism, not its continuation, and (2) on "the decadence of American individualism," without realizing that of the two contradictory ideals entailed in Puritanism—rational self-interest (or individualism) and self-sacrifice to the common good (or altruism/utilitarianism)—it is altruism (America's conscious philosophy) that is winning in its clash with individualism (America's sense of life). Remnants of capitalism and individualism exist, but the decadence and "cultural radicalism" Lasch denounces are *not* their manifestations.

33. Ibid., p. xv. Again, it should be noted that the collapsing civilization and status quo Lasch is referring to is "the culture of competitive individualism." Since the end of the nineteenth century the status quo in America has been altruistic utilitarianism; its institutional forms are liberal corporatism and the welfare state, neither of which were meant to serve the interest of the competitive individualism.

34. Brown, *Die Nigger Die!*, p. 104.

35. Parker, op. cit., p. 106.

36. Martin Luther King, Jr., *Where Do We Go From Here: Chaos or Community?*, pp. 32–66.

37. Branden, *The Psychology of Self-Esteem*, pp. 176–77.

38. Op. cit.

39. Kerner Commission Report on Civil Disorders, p. 234.

40. Branden, *The Psychology of Self-Esteem*, p. 177.

41. Parker, op. cit., p. 55.

42. *New York Times*, July 18, 1977.

43. Parker, op. cit., p. 59.

44. See T. D. Allman, "The 'Rebirth' of Eldridge Cleaver."

45. In Rand, *The Virtue of Selfishness*, p. 137.

46. Imamu Ameer Baraka, "Black People!", pp. 226–27, in *The Black Poets*, ed. Dudley Randall.

47. Quoted in Lokos, *The New Racism*, p. 497.

48. Brown, op. cit., pp. 114–15.

49. *U.S. News & World Report*, March 4, 1977.

50. Ibid., September 29, 1975.

51. Ibid., March 4, 1974.

52. Ibid.

53. Quoted in Blaustein and Woock, eds., *Man against Poverty*, p. 202.

54. William H. Grier and Price M. Cobbs, *Black Rage*, pp. 8, 13.

55. Ibid., p. 22.

56. Quoted in *Intellectual Digest*, August, 1973, from Murray Kempton, *The Briar Patch*.

57. Edward C. Banfield, *The Unheavenly City: The Nature and Future of Our Urban Crisis*, p. 161. I do not subscribe to the view, implied in Banfield's concept of "preconventional" morality, that morality is a matter of convention. Yet, since the social metaphysician equates morals with conventions, Banfield's concept is applicable in understanding the social metaphysician's sense of morality.

58. Ibid., pp. 161–62.

59. Ibid., pp. 162–63.

60. Ibid., p. 186.

61. Parker, op. cit., p. 66.

62. Diane Ravitch, "Not Always a Matter of Justice."

63. Butler Shaffer, *Violence as a Product of Imposed Order*.

64. William Safire, "Christmas in July."

11

The Ambivalent Appeaser

"If you can't join either group, don't let them know it."

If you choose to differ from others, or happen to be different from most, and still demand total acceptance by those you're different from, you just don't have the backbone to live with your choice of identity.—Tibor R. Machan, *Reason.*

As already pointed out, the marginal man's dilemma is not a political crux, but a psychointellectual dilemma that may or may not be given political expression. In none of the race-conscious types discussed here is that dilemma more poignant than in the Ambivalent Appeaser. Among race-conscious Negroes he is a silent minority whose self-esteem is eaten away by a quiet desperation that is seldom revealed. Like the other types his frame of reference is also dictated by significant others, but he differs from them in that his intellectual independence is significantly greater. It is this difference that makes him one of the most devastating casualties of the Black Power–black identity movement.

This type is adapted from Branden's *Ambivalent* social metaphysician and from a definition of appeasement by Ayn Rand. Branden writes of the Ambivalent type:

> His superiority to other social metaphysicians is evidenced, not only by his greater independence, but also by his desire to *earn*, through objective achievements, the esteem he longs for, by his relative inability to find real pleasure in an admiration not based on standards he can

275

respect—and by his tortured disgust at his own fear of the disapproval of others. Often, he tries to fight his fear, refusing to act on or surrender to it, exercising immense will power and discipline—but never winning his battle fully, never setting himself free, because he does not go to the roots of the problem, does not identify the psycho-epistemological base of his betrayal, does not accept full and ultimate responsibility for his own life and goals.

Among this type, one will find men of distinguished achievements and outstanding creative originality—whose treason and tragedy lie in the contrast between their private lives and their lives as creators. These are the men who have the courage to challenge the *cognitive* judgments of world figures, but lack the courage to challenge the *value*-judgments of the folks next door.[1]

The appeasement with which the Ambivalent Appeaser expresses his fear of disapproval, and his moral cowardice, is defined by Rand as "consideration for and compliance with the unjust, irrational and evil feelings of others. It is a policy of exempting the emotions of others from moral judgment, and of willingness to sacrifice innocent, virtuous victims to the evil malice of such emotions." The appeaser's usual rationalization for his fear of disapproval, writes Rand, is: " 'I don't want to be disliked.' By whom? By people he dislikes, despises and condemns."[2]

While the marginality of the other race-conscious types is evidenced by the conflict in their minds between their ethno-racial group and the dominant culture, the Ambivalent Appeaser experiences a conflict between his private convictions and his public denial of those convictions. Privately, he rejects aspects of both the dominant group and his own minority group. But publicly, he appeases them both, believing that to be the only "practical" solution to his problem.

In his mind there is not a question of whether he will subordinate his will to his subcultural group or the dominant group. He experiences no contest between the two for his soul. Rather, he perceives them as one and the same menace possessing two heads, one black and one white. His is not the ambivalence of divided loyalties to the two groups, but the ambivalence of divided loyalty to wanting to be right and not wanting to be disliked. If he is to be right he must reject the race consciousness of others; if he is not to be disliked he must embrace their race consciousness. Since he can neither publicly reject their race consciousness nor embrace it, he solves his dilemma by remaining silent and uninvolved. "*If you can't join either group*," he says, "*don't let them know it.*"

As stated earlier one of the assumptions that undercut the moral base of the integration movement was the belief by integrationists that people's respect for one's human rights should necessarily include their sanction of his individual character. The Conventional Integrationist wants to be liked—to be loved—and in his view the elimination of racial injustice is a symbol of society's confirmation of his self-esteem—his human dignity. He does not want to *earn* the esteem he seeks but makes it a condition of the civil rights guaranteed him by law (see chap. 7). However, seeing the difference between the protection of human rights and the regard individuals extend voluntarily to one another, the Ambivalent Appeaser *wants* to earn the respect of his fellows. While the Integrationist views such policies as affirmative action as public sanction of his worth, the Appeaser views them as an insult to his worth. But most of the society agrees with the Integrationist, and it's the fear he has of publicly opposing the society that grips the Appeaser.

So often he finds that without judging his character and personality, whites are willing to "love" him as a racial entity to atone for the sins of their ancestors against members of his race. On the other hand, blacks offer him the exclusive regard reserved for "brothers" simply because he shares their racial identification. In both cases, he is not seen as the individual he is and he is not asked to show evidence that he merits the esteem given him. Thus, he feels misperceived and experiences the lack of regard for his individuality as the height of disrespect for his personal worth. His problems begin when, like the Integrationist who equates the protection of human rights with the sanction of personal character, he equates his human individuality (a quality all men possess, whether they acknowledge it or not) with his personal worth (a quality of individuals that must be achieved). He is correct to feel misperceived, but his error lies in allowing the disrespect others have for human individuality (in general) to undercut his confidence in expressing his sense of worth.

He may appear removed and independent but that detachment is his exile; he remains trapped between his self-identity and "their" racial identification—between the truth of his convictions and the cowardice of his inaction—between contempt for racists and his desire for their approval—between his own standards and the standards of everybody else. Like the other race-conscious types, the Appeaser has one foot in his own subculture and one in the dominant culture but unlike the others he views neither group as objects of *cognitive* authority nor relies on them for a perception of reality. They arise, instead, as *evaluative* authorities to whom he is afraid to reveal his lack of ethno-racial allegiance. That is, while they do not dictate the *content* of his convictions, they do dictate whether he will *act* on those convictions. "Men have died in torture chambers, on the stake, in concentration camps, in front of firing squads, rather than renounce their convictions," writes Rand. "The appeaser renounces his under the pressure of a frown on any vacant face."[3]

Like the Conventional Integrationist, the Ambivalent Appeaser wants to join the dominant culture; but, unlike the Integrationist, he wants to join because he believes he has *earned* a place in the American mainstream. He desires the friendliness and acceptance of an integrated society, but he deplores the idea that such a society should be aimed for at the expense of the liberty and rights of the individuals of which it is composed. This preference of voluntary association over coercive integration is the right position to take, but the Appeaser does not dare defend it. He does not fear or resent economic and political competition with individuals of the larger culture as do the Power-seekers; rather he fears the disapproval of the Power-seekers should they learn that not only does he support free-market competition, but that he is also capable of such competition. Unlike the Spiritualists he does not seek black identification as a substitution for self-identity; neither does he claim victim status as the rationalization for the lack of self-responsibility. Rather, he feels guilty for being unable to assume the manifestations of "blackness," and he apologizes for his willingness and ability to surmount the disadvantages he may experience because of his race. His sense of self-reliance and his respect for the rights of others caused him to respond with disgust and contempt for the destructive and criminal acts of the Militants; but he makes no public statement of his indignation, for fear of becoming himself an object of some vicious renegade's epithet.

The Ambivalent Appeaser is an assimilated Negro, but he is not at peace with himself. He may enjoy integrated relationships, but his emotions and convictions are not integrated. He has not yet

278

achieved an attitude of indifference to the appeals of the other race-conscious types. "Redeem the white society at any cost!" say the Integrationists. "Damn whites!" say the reactionary Power-seekers. "Black solidarity is the answer." "Change the political and economic system to favor black interests," say the pragmatic Power-seekers. "Down with the system!" say the Militants. "Destroy the white menace." "Think black," say the Spiritualists. "Demand payment for our collective victimization." The Ambivalent Appeaser's rejection of these appeals would be interpreted as a rejection of his racial affiliation. His assertion of his lack of ethno-racial allegiance would be cast as neuroticism. Whites would call him a traitor to the civil rights cause; Negroes would call him an Uncle Tom; and everyone would be embarrassed by his presence. Such condemnation from all sides is simply more than he wishes to bear, but he cannot escape the disturbing fact that the daily price he pays for his agonizing silence is the continued loss of self-respect.

Moral Cowardice versus Cognitive Independence

It has been said that the marginal man's dilemma involves the conflict between his legitimate need for self-identity and his other-oriented attempt to acquire it through group affiliation. The search for group identification is a preoccupation of all the other race-conscious types, and they feel justified in their search. They believe that self-identity is bestowed by society. The Ambivalent Appeaser's dilemma differs in that it lies in the conflict between his need for self-identity and the guilt he feels for being unable and unwilling to seek it through group affiliation. He does not believe that self-identity is bestowed by society, but behaves as though he did.

Many Ambivalent Appeasers go through life continually compromising their intellectual independence to the race consciousness of others. But some do make sporadic attempts to exhibit the courage of their convictions. Such was the case with the character of Dr. John Wade Prentiss, the young Negro scientist who is brought home by his white fiancée to meet her liberal parents, in Stanley Kramer's award-winning film *Guess Who's Coming To Dinner?* In a heated argument with his father, who disapproves of the impending marriage, Dr. Prentiss, played by Sidney Poitier, says: "You and your whole lousy generation believes the way it was for you is the way it's got to be and not until your whole generation has lain down and died will the dead weight of you be off our backs.

You understand? You've *got to get off my back!* . . . You think of yourself as a 'colored' man—I think of myself as a *man!*"

Observing the performance of Sidney Poitier as Dr. Prentiss, one can see that it is not just blind acceptance the Ambivalent Appeaser desires, but the acceptance of his individuality by people who do not value individuality. This is not to imply that a commitment to individuality is a defining characteristic of the Ambivalent Appeaser. If it were, he would hardly want to compromise that quality and would thus not be ambivalent or appeasing. Cognitively, he is inner-directed, but evaluatively, he is other-directed. Even in his greater independence and momentary challenge of the values of others in his race, the Appeaser remains held in bondage by his fear that his rejection of the ideas of some in his racial group will be interpreted as a rejection of his racial (biological) attributes in preference to attributes of whites.

Besides the guilt they feel for their lack of ethno-racial allegiance, some Ambivalent Appeasers are burdened by a guilt of another sort. Like their white counterparts who assume unwarranted guilt for the sins of members of their race against Negroes, these Negroes assume unwarranted guilt for the sins of contemporary Negroes against whites. Because they are Negro they feel responsible for the actions of other Negroes. Thus, in their associations with Negroes and whites they go through a very complicated ritual of appeasing Negroes on the one hand in order to keep their approval and quietly apologizing to whites on the other hand to keep their approval.

They will not speak out publicly against the immorality of affirmative action statism, for instance, for fear of being denounced as siding with whites who are against it. But they will tell their white associates, "You know, I think quotas is taking things too far." Some are parents who are every bit as incensed by the insanity of busing as white parents, but they refuse to join whites in their protest for fear of being called traitors to the larger cause of integration.

Vermont Royster has observed that people refuse to speak out against such programs because they are seduced by their noble purposes. To criticize such programs "seems to criticize the intent," he has said. "As a nation we are so guilt-ridden over the past treatment of blacks and other minorities among us that it has become almost impossible to talk about such programs . . . as a means of correcting past inequities without becoming entangled in blinding emotions."[4] In a similar observation Nathan Glazer has pointed out that the enormous moral authority given to antidiscrimination policies makes it very difficult for people to oppose them and be taken serously. Even congressmen worry that they will be called racist for such opposition. "It is assumed that what is proposed is right and can only be opposed from an inferior moral position or an actually immoral one," writes Glazer. Advocates of affirmative action and school busing believe that these programs will result in a just and good society, says Glazer, "that they defend the best traditions of the United States."[5] What is seen as in the interest of Negroes and other minorities is perceived as in the interest of the society at large. Thus, a black person opposing these policies is seen not only as a neurotic who is ashamed of his "blackness" and a traitor to the special interests of blacks, but is also condemned as an enemy of freedom and justice.

The choices before the Ambivalent Appeaser are clear: he may challenge the purpose and implementation of such policies as immoral and unjust; or, he may remain silent, keeping his judgments to himself while pretending to others that he has no interest in the matter or feigning incompetence to make an "educated" judgment. Of course, he chooses the latter approach. Like all social metaphysicians, as Branden puts it, he "needs the approval of others in order to approve of himself." And since most people (especially members of his race) disapprove of the kinds of objections he has to antidiscrimination policies, he simply withholds them to spare himself what he perceives as their rejection of him personally (whether or not that is in fact the case). Of course, what is more detrimental to his self-esteem than the rejection by others of his values is *his own* rejection of those values under the pressure of disapproval. "Whether a person's motive is noble or ignoble, facts cannot be wiped out by self-made blindness," writes Branden, "the person who attempts it merely succeeds in sabotaging his own consciousness."[6]

Compensating for Alienation

As Nathan Glazer documents, "the history of American society in relationship to many of the groups that make it up *is not* a history of racism" (emphasis added), but is the history of a society expanding to reject ethnic exclusivity and to shape and maintain "this complex and distinctive pattern for the accommodation of group difference that has developed in American society."[7] Ethnicity, in the United

States, is voluntary, asserts Glazer. "It is voluntary not only in the sense that no one may be required to be part of a group and share its corporate concerns and activities; no one is impelled not to be part of a group, either. . . . In the United States, one is required neither to put on ethnicity nor to take it off."[8]

There have always been pressures within groups for members to retain their ethnicity and resist assimilation; but national policy has, for the most part, moved toward de-emphasizing the role of ethnic or racial affiliation, at least in the public sector of the American society. However, since 1964, when Negroes were guaranteed full political equality and it was decided that public policy in a multiracial and multiethnic society should be exercised without regard to race, color, national origin, or religion, the pressures to stress one's ethnic or racial affiliation have increased with every passing year. Indeed, the nation has entered what Glazer calls "a period of color- and group-consciousness with a vengeance." This atmosphere in which one's group category is given priority over individual merit and self-interest is particularly painful for the Ambivalent Appeaser who finds himself bogged in a sense of alienation from his own racial or ethnic group and lacking the counter-values to challenge their claim to special consideration and benefits.

Some Appeasers try to overcome their alienation by plunging deeper into their work; others cast their convictions to the winds and opt for approval. Public officials often find it especially difficult to function beyond the influence of their ethnic or racial groups and seek their approval at the same time. One example of how this dilemma is solved is in the case of Henry Kissinger, of whom *The New York Times* said, "Although in his public capacity he never alluded to his Jewishness, among Jews he would make a comment to demonstrate that indeed he was Jewish."[9]

Because of his "even-handed" Middle East diplomacy, Kissinger, the first Jewish secretary of state in American history, remained suspect in the minds of many American and Israeli Jews during all of his tenure as secretary. Moreover, many spiritualist-type Jews distrusted him because he is an assimilated Jew whom they view with as much disdain as the Negro Spiritualists view the assimilated Negroes they call "white Negroes." They required that Kissinger perform not as secretary of state for the United States but that he do so as a Jewish Secretary, just as many Negroes expected United

Nations Ambassador Andrew Young to represent not the interests of the United States but those of blacks and the "third world."

During his last days in office, in a speech before the Conference of Presidents of Major American Jewish Organizations, Kissinger answered his Jewish critics for the first time publicly:

> From my point of view, probably no criticism has hurt me more than if it came from this community. And probably from your point of view, it was especially painful if disagreements occurred between the Jewish community and the first Jewish secretary of state in American history.
>
> I thought it was important for the future of Israel and for the future of the Jewish people, that the actions that the United States government took were not seen to be the result of a special, personal relationship, but that the support we gave Israel reflected not my personal preferences alone, but the basic national interests of the United States.

He then asserted his personal connection with the Jewish heritage, and thereby appeased his critics: "I have never forgotten that thirteen members of my family died in concentration camps, nor could I ever fail to remember what it was like to live in Nazi Germany as a member of a persecuted minority."

The audience was pleased and following the speech the chairman said, "We have sought our brother and we have found him, and we are profoundly grateful for this experience."[10]

While Kissinger's statement reflects his awareness of the influence of the Jewish community on American policy in the Middle East, the focus in this discussion is on the fact that he felt it necessary to eliminate his personal estrangement from the Jewish community. He had to demonstrate to other Jews that he had not forsaken his Jewish heritage—that he was one of them. The scene of Kissinger ingratiating himself before his Jewish "brothers" is incongruous with the proud, self-possessing Kissinger who dominated American foreign relations for so many years. But it is not unlike Appeasers to behave in this way when they place such a high premium on the esteem of their subcultural group. To repeat Branden, "These are men who have the courage to challenge the *cognitive* judgments of world figures, but lack the courage to challenge the *value*-judgments of the folks next door."[11]

While Kissinger's public appeasement of his ethnic group is apparently unusual for him, similar behavior is not unusual for song-and-dance entertainer Sammy Davis, Jr., who has advertised for the approval of his people as well as that of whites throughout his career. Davis has said, "I don't want to look like I'm saying 'Please like me.' " But that is just what he does look like. He attempts to be all things to all people, as his inconsistent political activities suggest. Shortly after announcing his support for Richard Nixon's presidential campaign in 1972, he endorsed Black Panther leader Bobby Seale in his race for mayor of Oakland and then performed at a benefit for black militant Angela Davis. In that same year, during the Republican National Convention he hugged Nixon when the presidential nominee appeared in the middle of a rock concert in Miami's Memorial Stadium. Almost a year later, just two months after the Watergate break-in became front page news, Davis talked to a reporter about his support of Nixon and the public reaction to "the squeeze felt around the world."

"It hurts," he said. "This thing's left a scar on me that I will wear to my grave. They're really trying to infer that I don't care about my people. I'll match my caring with anybody: emotional, spiritual, financial. Say you don't agree, that you don't like me, but don't say I don't care. They say I'm a white folks' nigger. Nobody has got Sammy Davis."

The reporter wrote of Davis: "It's clear he has a deep need to be understood by blacks, partly because, perhaps, his widest appeal is among whites. He said the numbers of blacks in his audience increased, over the years, but slipped way down since he's been supporting the president."

"Things are easing up now," he told the reporter. "It was worse right afterward."[12]

Davis's support of Nixon was not the first of his actions to draw protest from the black community and others. Many vilified his marriage to Swedish actress May Britt; his conversion to Judaism in 1954 was upsetting to some; others sneered at his knocking around with Frank Sinatra's "rat pack"; and there are those who simply do not like his "white" music and his "Uncle Tom" motion picture roles. Despite the disparagement of him by blacks, he has continued to reach out to them through his many black self-help projects, benefits, and contributions. He has said, "You would like for the brothers and sisters in the community to know that somewhere along the way you did something."

In 1966 when Davis was named chairman of the N.A.A.C.P.'s Life Membership Committee, he said: "It's a matter of standing up and being counted. When my kids ask me 20 years from now what did I do in the civil rights movement, I want to tell them—I did my very best—if I didn't now, I wouldn't be able to look them in the face."

Davis has suffered insults and rejection not only from blacks but from whites as well. In 1960, he was booed at the Democratic National Convention in Los Angeles by a group of Southerners, and he was so hurt he cried. Still he continues his quest for the approval of blacks and whites, wishing his audiences "peace, love, and togetherness" accompanied by the Black Power clenched fist, and always joking away the contradiction of his appeasement. "Someone asked me to take a handicap on the golf course," he once said. "Handicap? I'm black, Jewish, and blind in one eye. What other handicaps are there?"

In trying to solve their dilemma of ethnic and racial alienation, both Kissinger and Davis attempted to appease their detractors by stressing the cultural ties that bind them to their groups. Kissinger cites his family's experiences in Nazi Germany and Davis enlists his support of various civil rights programs while each, in the meantime, continues to perform in professions that require transcending the demands of ethnicity. Some Appeasers find those demands so overwhelming that they engage in complete appeasement by adapting the solutions chosen by the other race-conscious types. In some cases, they become so disoriented that they resort to the violence and destruction of the militants. But more often they embrace the rhetoric of the integrationist with the belief that if the races are forced to integrate, the demands made on them from both groups would likely diminish and then they would be acceptable to both.

Another solution chosen by Appeasers is to become "blacker" than the nationalists and spiritualists to whom they want to prove their blackness. George Napper found this solution widely employed by Negro students on white campuses. The following excerpts of statements by some of these students in interviews with Napper demonstrate the tragic sense of guilt the Appeaser has for being who he is, and his ultimate betrayal of his identity in order to gain the approval of those he does not respect.

From a female graduate student whose parents' combined income exceeded $20,000:

> You know, because I haven't had to confront the kinds of problems that most blacks have faced, like problems of economics and housing and all

285

that, I often felt very guilty; and people try to make me feel less black because my experiences have been different from those blacks in the ghetto. When I first became aware of the blackness thing I was kinda shaky and I was afraid to mingle with the black community around here because of the emphasis on being black and blacker-than-thou and all that stuff, but often having been around the blacker-than-thou's—who do not impress me—I'm not overly concerned about being black enough. . . . But before I got to this point in my thinking I tried to be as black as I thought the others were.[13]

Another student described the pressures he experienced as follows: "If your statements aren't a certain way you are stereotyped as not being black. Plus, if you don't have a certain background, like coming from a poor neighborhood or having certain experiences or being able to relate to certain things, you are made to feel different, like you did something wrong. I guess because my hair was straight and I was light skinned didn't help much either."[14]

A third student described her "overcompensation" for her lack of blackness as follows:

Because I don't come from the ghetto or a black neighborhood, I've felt for a long time that I've been missing something. I haven't felt as black as people coming from this background, so I've had to overcompensate. When I first came here I had to readjust to a totally new thing: middle-class blacks cloaking themselves in a different class; everybody acting like they're lower class. I found myself trying to take on those values. I tried to act like them; imitate them rather than be myself whether they accepted me or not.[15]

Many of these students are the children of Negroes who have worked hard to assimilate into the larger culture. Having concluded that their middle-class home environment and the values they have grown up with are "wrong" because they reflect "whiteness," many of these young people reject the values of their families and take on those of the nationalists and spiritualists. Others seek to relieve their alienation from the "blacker-than-thou" attitudes of their peers by withdrawing from the social scene and plunging deeper into their academic studies. Whether they maintain their values in secrecy or openly reject them for other standards, Appeasers such as these students find that the one thing they cannot escape is the nagging sense of guilt they experience over the fact that their life circumstances do not put them in the category of the disadvantaged.

Implicit in the pressure on Appeasers to relate to the black experience and "act" lower class is the expectation that they will also assume the role of victim. As pointed out in chapter 9, the new victim status asserted by Nationalists and Spiritualists has as part of its definition the idea that victimization is an inherent quality of one's blackness. To be black, they say, is to be, by definition, white society's victim, whether one suffers that victimization personally or not. And to deny that one is victimized is to deny one's blackness.

The black identification movement contains also an element of envy toward middle-class Negroes who have surmounted the adversities of racial discrimination and assimilated into the American mainstream. These Negroes are resented by others as having been "socialized into accepting white standards." Advocates of black identification say that middle-class blacks could not have achieved their economic and social status in racist America without rejecting identification with the Negro and his traditional culture. Thus, the symbol "black" means not just the assertion of pride in the black component of one's ancestry; it is also a symbol of disdain for the differences in achievement among Negro individuals.

It happens to be true that, until recently, in order to advance *meritoriously* most Americans of all races have had to transcend (but not necessarily reject) the narrow context of their ethnicity. In fact, the civil rights movement was for many decades devoted to making it possible that one's individual merit. rather than one's race, would determine one's success. Booker T. Washington, who is still maligned as an "Uncle Tom," embraced this American ideal when, recalling his 1884 address before the National Education Association in Madison, Wisconsin, he wrote:

> I said that the whole future of the Negro rested largely upon the question as to whether or not he should make himself, through his skill, intelligence, and character, of such undeniable value to the community in which he lived that the community could not dispense with his presence. I said that any individual who learned to do something better than anybody else—learned to do a common thing in an uncommon manner—had solved his problem, regardless of the colour of his skin.[16]

At another point he wrote: "Say what we will, there is something in human nature which we cannot blot out, which makes one man, in the end, recognize and reward merit in another, regardless of colour or race."[17] Washington's emphasis on the achievement of nonracial (human) values was and still is interpreted by many Negroes as a nonblack and, therefore, prowhite sentiment. In truth, what Washington urged for was neither a black nor white outlook, but a human, individualistic approach to race relations consistent with the ideals on which the nation was founded.

Today, the emphasis has shifted from self-reliance, meritorious achievement, and equal justice to the elimination of the effects of collective victimization and adversity by granting political and economic privileges to individuals on the basis of race, religion, sex, creed, and national origin. Politicized ethnicity has become a significant force in the formation of American public policy and victimization is the fodder used to keep it active.

Thomas Sowell, a Negro professor of economics, has complained of this trend as it forms the basis for practices and policies of programs for black students at leading colleges and universities. Why, asks Sowell, is it that thousands of the black students who score in the top half on standard tests attend the lowest level of Southern Negro colleges—nondescript and often unaccredited institutions—while many other black students without necessary academic skills are being maneuvered through top-level colleges at a cost to the integrity of the educational process that is exceeded only by the psychic costs borne by the students themselves?

He answers that

> social conscience requires that help be concentrated on those who need help most—that academically able students "will make it anyway" (this assertion carries with it a definition of intellectually oriented students as being middle-class in outlook, whatever their social origins, and therefore not qualified for help offered "authentic" ghetto types). This basic goal of helping those who need help most, rather than those who can use it best is not confined to the campus but pervades many programs sponsored by Government agencies and private foundations as well. The aim is not to cultivate the most fertile soil but to make the desert bloom.[18]

Sowell cites several illustrations of this attitude at work, one of them involving "a young black woman with an IQ of 142, and grades and recommendations to match. She was told by a national organization which finances black law students that she would be eligible for financial aid in law school if her scores were *low* enough! Her scores were, of course, not low enough, so she is now going $2,000 into debt to finance her first year of law school."

To go against the trend of providing special benefits for the so-called needy at the expense of the capable, and to realize one's version of the American dream on the basis of one's merits is to be envied and resented. And many Negroes who have managed this feat find that not "belonging" with their favored brothers of victim status is more than they wish to be penalized for. So they attempt to gain acceptance by going through the ritual of appeasement—by being sufficiently "black," even if their education, income, and social standing show that they are anything but victims.

This solution is not one chosen just by Negroes. Nelson W. Aldrich has written of similar acts of appeasement by Harvard students who feel guilty because of their "greater advantage."

"Certainly I feel guilty," one student told Aldrich, "guilty for being privileged. I'm embarrassed in the outside world to say that I come from Harvard. You can feel that people resent it."[19]

Students like this one, whom Aldrich calls "the party of fairness," find the privileges of wealth and the privileges of intellect offensive and try to assuage their guilt by donning construction boots, jeans, and plaid flannel shirts to ward off the envy of the less privileged in the Cambridge community. But, for assimilated blacks, changing one's clothes is not an effective defense against the envy and resentment of black-identity nationalists and spiritualists. And the pressure to identify with the less privileged is far more complicated.

Alienation—The Price of Assimilation

Some Appeasers try to escape the pressure to be "ethnic" by moving to all-white or ethnically mixed neighborhoods. Although some, particularly mulattoes, are known to think that behaving and living as whites do will spare them the burdens of being "black," their object is not necessarily to be "white" but to escape the pressures of black race consciousness. Some have tried to escape the issue of race entirely by living as expatriates in Europe. But whether in Europe or white suburbia, they often find that the pressure to stress one's racial and subcultural attributes comes as strongly from whites as it does from blacks. Thus, assimilated Appeasers find that not only must they cope with estrangement from their ethnic group but that their lack of certain ethnic attributes is often suspect by whites who have a stereotyped idea of what someone from their group should be like.

A black reporter from Mississippi who lacks a Southern or "black" accent and who uses "words of more than one syllable and breathing" related his experiences with white friends who could not

see beyond his skin color to the person he is. A blond girl he had
known for more than a year complained during one of their dates
that she could not "relate" to him. "My problem, she said, is that I
am not 'black enough' for her. . . . She complained about never
knowing where my head is on the important issues affecting black
people." Dating him, she concluded, was just like dating a white
boy.

At their first meeting, a woman he had spoken to over the
telephone said: "You didn't sound black over the phone." Then
there are all the questions asked at suburban parties and business
luncheons. "Frequently I feel like a harassed welfare applicant," he
wrote, "answering questions about family size, number of brothers
and sisters who slept in the same bed, family income and diet.

"The situation is so ridiculous I was afraid to watch Alex Haley's
"Roots" on television. I feared my friends would want to repent or
relate how it put them in tears. Yet I knew I couldn't escape the
inevitable. One man asked me if [my name] was an African name
like Kunta Kinte. Another asked if I would do a search similar to
Haley's."[20]

The scourge of the assimilated Appeaser is that he is not a "social
product" and is therefore not easily understood by people who insist
on viewing themselves and others as packaged and labeled
constructs rather than as the individuals they are. While many
Negroes may feel alienated from the larger culture they are all, to
some degree, involved in the process of cultural give and take. Most
blacks are assimilated and all of the prototypes discussed here are
assimilated. Even as he exhorts Negroes to take pride in their
blackness, the Spiritualist, who advocates resistance to assimilation,
does so in ways that are peculiarly "American," employing literature
and music, theater and motion pictures, fashion and lectures to
make his appeal. Perhaps the best example of how assimilated
Negroes are is seen in the use of the nationalist term "black
capitalism" to describe business activity in the Negro community,
whether it be wholly private or government subsidized. The concept
is, of course, a contradiction, as capitalism, properly defined, entails
no reference to the biological or cultural categories of the
individuals who produce, buy, and sell in a free market. Black
capitalism is derived instead from the present political economy that
functions under the heels of a mixture of freedom and controls.
Existing in a society that rejects laissez-faire capitalism but still

290

places some value on private enterprise, black capitalism represents the contradictions that permeate so much of the assimilation engaged in by Negroes.

So much of the Negro subculture mirrors the dominant culture that the only way one can know the difference is by the skin color of the participants and, in some instances, the geographical separation of Negro and white communities. But even when imposed segregation and discrimination prevented the association of the races on an equal basis, Negroes have, since slavery, shared the values and attitudes of most other Americans. Thus, while they have desired desegregation, integrated association, and equal justice, they have sought these ends within the context of the general American cultural framework. And each succeeding generation has experienced an increasing awareness of its American nature. The territorial Separatists have had no success in reversing this trend and even the Spiritualists who interpret assimilation as a one-way process of giving up one's cultural heritage to become "white," have not succeeded in halting the actual give-and-take that goes on between Negroes and whites.

To be sure, there are individuals among Negroes who resist assimilation, but, as a group, Negroes have eagerly engaged in the process and encouraged their children to do so. For all practical purposes, with the exception of recent immigrants, the assimilated Negro—the *American* Negro—is no longer just a theoretical possibility residing in sociology texts. His characteristics are a reality and so embedded in the psyche of Negroes that it takes a visit to Africa or a conversation with a recent black immigrant for them to realize just how assimilated they are—how utterly "American" they are.

However, as pointed out in chapter 4, there are many factors that influence the nature and rate of a person's assimilation. Generally, the process may be self-assertive and self-interested or self-immolating and altruistic. It is the nature of his assimilation that distinguishes the Ambivalent Appeaser from the other race-conscious types discussed here. He perceives himself as self-created (even when he is not entirely), while the others perceive themselves as culture-created. Functioning on the premise that they are products of their environment, the latter rely on significant others to create their ethno-racial identity while the Appeaser desires the visibility one experiences in relationships with individuals.

Although they never totally resist assimilating themselves, the Nationalist, Spiritualist, and Militant think of it as a dis-value. To both Negroes and whites in these groups the Appeaser is a sociological freak—a neurotic phony trying to be white. His insistence on achieving personal happiness, professional fulfillment, and interracial associations without reference to race is seen as a desire to deny his racial affiliation. His ability to appreciate the achievements of individuals in other cultures is viewed as a preference for another cultural heritage over that of the Negro subculture. His lack of personality traits that reflect the stereotyped view that both blacks and whites have of Negroes is considered an affectation. Though he rarely expresses them so they may be judged, his ideas that conflict with the popular rhetoric of civil rights activists would be called racist if expressed by whites. He is maligned by Negroes and whites who refuse to believe that a person like him is possible. He simply does not belong. That he cannot accept the virtue and responsibility of not belonging is his cowardice. That he wants to belong with people who despise him is his shame. Indeed, he is the most tragic of all race-conscious men, for he carries inside him a truth of human relations that he dares not let see the light of day.

1. Branden, *The Psychology of Self-Esteem*, pp. 180–81.
2. Rand, "The Age of Envy."
3. Ibid.
4. Vermont Royster, "The Emperor's Clothes."
5. Glazer, *Affirmative Discrimination*, p. 219.
6. Branden, *The Psychology of Self-Esteem*, p. 87.
7. Glazer, *Affirmative Discrimination*, p. 7. In this statement, Glazer is not denying the fact of racism in American society. He is asserting, instead, that the trend in group relations has been toward the deinstitutionalization of racism, even during the height of slavery. Of course this does not absolve racist institutions of their role in the continuation of racism.
8. Ibid., p. 29.
9. *New York Times*, January 19, 1977.
10. Ibid.
11. Branden, *The Psychology of Self-Esteem,* p. 180.
12. Dorothy Gilliam, "Sammy Davis—Political Enigma."
13. Napper, *Blacker Than Thou.*
14. Ibid.
15. Ibid.
16. Washington, *Up From Slavery*, p. 142.

17. Ibid., pp. 165–66.

18. Thomas Sowell, "Black Professor Says: Colleges Are Skipping over Competent Blacks to Admit Authentic Ghetto Types." See also Thomas Sowell, *Black Education: Myths and Tragedies.*

19. Nelson W. Aldrich, Jr., "Harvard on the Way Down."

20. Burnis R. Morris, "I Am Curious (Black)."

PART IV. COMMENTARY ON RACE RELATIONS AND PUBLIC POLICY

12

Antiracism versus Human Rights

In the cause of freedom, we have to battle for the rights of people with whom we do not agree; and whom, in many cases, we may not like. These people test the strength of the freedoms which protect all of us. If we do not defend their rights, we endanger our own. —Harry S. Truman, quoted in *The New Dictionary of Thoughts.*

The preceding profiles of race-conscious Negroes show that race consciousness is a human problem, one that afflicts blacks as well as whites, and that minorities are every bit as capable of transforming their race consciousness into public policy as are members of the majority. The issue of race consciousness is not political as such, but a question of psychology and morality; it is, by definition, a personal problem of self-esteem. It is a social problem only because it is the orientation of so many people and because they act on it in their relations with others. When it is transformed into public forms of racism that are established and enforced by the government, it becomes a political issue that cannot be ignored. Racism in the United States is generally thought to be of one kind—white racism—and it has been roundly condemned by most Americans as evil and detrimental to individual freedom and harmonious and peaceful community relations. But there continues to be disagreement as to what should be done to eliminate it.

297

The Other Side of Racism

Coping with Racism

"What kind of program can be advanced to cope with the sheer humanness of racism?" asked journalist Tom Wicker in his introduction to the *Report of the National Advisory Commission on Civil Disorders*. The commission answered Wicker's question with: "Only a commitment to national action on an unprecedented scale can shape a future compatible with the historic ideals of American society. . . . The major need is to generate new will—the will to tax ourselves to the extent necessary to meet the vital needs of the nation."

Any American who can cite the Preamble of the Declaration of Independence knows what the historic ideals of American society are. But there is hardly any agreement on how those ideals should be implemented in the realm of race relations. The question of what can be done to cope with the problems of prejudice and discrimination in America has been argued since the beginning days of the republic. Thomas Jefferson died without having reached an answer in his own mind. Sometimes the social and political solutions put forth have been consistent with American ideals, but more often they have been advanced and implemented in betrayal of those ideals. The disagreement has been over means and ends and is generally argued from two perspectives represented by Supreme Court decisions separated by eighty-one years of change in the American government's approach to civil rights. In 1875 Congress passed a Civil Rights Act that forbade operators of hotels, theaters, and transportation facilities to discriminate against Negroes in the rendering of service. But in 1883 the Supreme Court declared this "places of public accommodation" law unconstitutional on the ground that it was a police power measure regulating private conduct and as such beyond the scope of the powers granted Congress in the Constitution. In 1964, the Supreme Court upheld the constitutionality of the public accommodations section of the 1964 Civil Rights Act. The Court unanimously ruled that the Constitution's commerce clause, which gave Congress the power to regulate interstate commerce, gave Congress broad enough authority to ban racial discrimination that might affect interstate commerce.

The differing interpretations of the Constitution by the Supreme Courts of 1883 and 1964 reflect not only the extent to which the

American government is willing to go to eliminate racism, but it also shows the degree to which the concept of human rights has been redefined during the twentieth century. The 1883 Supreme Court ruling against the unconstitutionality of the 1875 Civil Rights Act was consistent with the definition of human rights as natural, absolute, and objective, the exercise of which should be protected from the interference of others. It also sanctioned private conduct as a realm that must not be interfered with by the government. But the 1964 Supreme Court decision expresses the theory of human rights as arbitrary, absent of any universal standard of right and wrong, and defined according to what the law prefers at any given time. "The original notion of the natural right to freedom," writes Tibor Machan, "was that people in a human community are free to do wrong within their own spheres, *with what is their own*—print wrong ideas, buy dirty literature, and even select to trade only with those who belong to one (favored) race. That is the liberty which human rights guarantee, even in the face of public condemnation. [Now, according to] U.S. Law, one has no rights to do what the 'public' considers wrong. (That is, what those in power identify as wrong, sometimes with and other times without public or the majority's explicit or tacit support.)"[1]

It is their concept of human rights that has determined the direction Americans and their government have taken in deciding how to solve the problem of racism. The question before them always is whether the humanness of racism is to be dealt with according to the standards of human rights, or whether it is to be eliminated by whatever legislative and judicial decree those in power happen to think best at a given time. Two speeches by Lyndon B. Johnson, separated by sixteen years of change (in the man and in the nation), further illustrate the division among Americans in answering this question. While running for the Senate in 1948, Johnson denounced the civil rights portions of Harry Truman's Fair Deal Policy as

> a farce and a sham—an effort to set up a police state in the guise of liberty. I am opposed to that program. I have fought it in Congress. . . . I am against the FEPC [Federal Employment Practices Commission] because if a man can tell you whom you must hire, he can tell you whom you cannot employ. I have met this head-on.[2]

But in 1964, sixteen years later, Johnson was president, representing a broader constituency than the state of Texas he sought to represent in 1948, and as president he signed the Civil Rights Act, saying:

> We must not approach the observance and enforcement of this law in a vengeful spirit. Its purpose is not to punish. Its purpose is not to divide, but to end divisions—divisions which have lasted too long. . . . [The act] relies first on voluntary compliance, then on the efforts of states and local communities to secure the rights of citizens. It provides for the national authority to step in only when others cannot or will not do the job. . . . We have come to a time of testing. We must not fail. Let us close the springs of racial poison.[3]

So it was that Johnson, like so many Americans, had come to believe that closing "the springs of racial poison" justified the restriction of human rights as called for in the Civil Rights Act, yet all the while referring to the act, in the words of Whitney M. Young, Jr., as "the greatest single triumph for human rights in our country since the Emancipation Proclamation."

There were those who were not so enthusiastic, however. "You can't legislate goodwill, and therefore the only thing that will eliminate discrimination and segregation is education, not legislation," said Black Muslim leader Malcolm X.

Governor George C. Wallace of Alabama warned, "It will take a police state to enforce it."

In his announcement on June 18, 1964, that he would vote against the bill, Senator Barry Goldwater had said that while he was opposed to all discrimination, he believed it to be a problem that "is fundamentally one of the heart." Some law can help, he said, "but no law . . . [with] provisions which fly in the face of the Constitution and which require for their effective execution the creation of a police state." Goldwater, who was campaigning for the presidency at the time, was denounced by many as a racist demagogue and Governor Nelson Rockefeller said Goldwater had "effectively abandoned the Republican party on the most fundamental issue of our time."

It is now seventeen years since the 1964 Civil Rights Act and while a great deal of discrimination and segregation has been eliminated, Americans are still divided on the morality of using legislation to eliminate private racism. One position, the laissez-faire approach, taken partially in Johnson's 1948 speech, is that the problems of race relations are best left to private, voluntary action for solution; that (antiracism) legislation cannot be enforced in the private sector without violating the rights of individuals; that such laws are unenforceable because they represent an attempt to overcome prejudice and discrimination by law, a venture that is doomed to failure; that they only stir up new antagonisms, thereby interfering with private, voluntary efforts to improve race relations.

The second position, the statist approach, taken in Johnson's 1964 speech, favors antiracism legislation on the basis that racial discrimination, in private as well as public affairs, is antisocial and un-American and it is proper for the state to outlaw it; that no right is ever absolute; that all rights are subject to restriction where the greater social good overrides the individual interest; that while outlawing racial discrimination does not produce an overnight utopia, the presence of such laws on the statute books, coupled with an enforcement program, speeds up the absorption of minority groups into the mainstream of American life; that the choice of methods to eliminate racial discrimination is not an "either/or" one between compulsory regulation under statutes and voluntary action through education and similar methods, but that law and education both have roles to play in safeguarding the civil rights of minorities.

"It is evil that the nonviolent resister seeks to defeat, not the persons victimized by evil," wrote Martin Luther King, Jr. "If he is opposing racial injustice, the nonviolent resister has the vision to see that the basic tension is not between races. . . . The problem is not a purely racial one, with Negroes set against whites. In the end, [the struggle for equality] is not a struggle between people at all, but a tension between justice and injustice. Nonviolent resistance is not aimed against oppressor but against oppression. Under its banner consciences, not racial groups, are enlisted."[4]

By so divorcing men from their actions, civil rights activists advocated an integrated society without reference to the individuals living in the society. Their goal was not just to challenge unjust laws and statutes against the rights of Negroes, but also to "seek a social order of justice permeated by love"—to change the hearts and minds of white America and, as Miller put it, "rescue the wrongdoing oppressor from his misdeeds" by enlisting the law as a regulator of morality and conduct. But while legal action was taken to correct injustices incurred by the subjection of Negroes to the will of white racists, the enforcement of those laws had the effect of subjecting

301

those whites to the will of Negroes. Thus, the rights of racists are now restricted in order to achieve the greater good of a nonracist society.

In choosing to eliminate racism without consideration for the human source of racism—i.e., individuals and their natural right to free thought—antiracism legislation has necessarily broken the historical pattern of the American sanction and protection of individual rights. Indeed, the implementation of such legislation by enforcement programs as affirmative action has resulted in the unprecedented politicization of ethnic and racial categories. American public policy has coped with the humanness of racism not by making it insignificant in social relations but by making it more important than ever before.[5] Glazer draws the picture of the assault by antiracism legislation on human rights thusly:

> Larger and larger areas of employment came under increasingly stringent controls so that each offer of a job, each promotion, each dismissal had to be considered in the light of its effects on group ratios in employment. Inevitably, this meant the ethnic group of each individual began to affect and, in many cases, dominate consideration of whether that individual would be hired, promoted, or dismissed. In the public school systems, questions of student and teacher assignment became increasingly dominated by considerations of each individual's ethnic group: Children and teachers of certain races and ethnic groups could be assigned to this school but not to that one. The courts and government agencies were called upon to act with ever greater vigor to assure that, in each housing development and in each community, certain proportions of residents by race would be achieved, and a new body of law and practice began to build up which would, in this field, too, require public action on the basis of an individual's race and ethnic group. In each case, it was argued, positive public action on the basis of race and ethnicity was required to overcome a previous harmful public action on the basis of race and ethnicity.[6]

For the first time the federal government gives legal status to ethnic and racial categories and the wrong of racism is "corrected" by the wrong of still more racism. What has made it possible for antidiscrimination laws to become the tools by which reverse discrimination is implemented? What has enabled the quest for equal opportunity and equal justice to degenerate into legal sanction of preferential treatment? Very generally the cause lies in the changing American consensus, which subscribes to the priority of equality over freedom and individual rights, the redefinition of equality of opportunity to mean equality of condition or result, the

302

practice of sacrificing principles to pragmatic expediency, and the reliance on government to force into existence solutions to social problems. Specifically, however, the instrument of such programs as busing, "open admissions" in colleges and universities, preferential hiring, and affirmative action marketing plans for even statistical distribution in housing is the 1964 Civil Rights Act.

Five of the act's eleven titles variously prohibit segregation or discrimination "on the ground of race, color, religion or national origin." The act could be read, writes Glazer, "as instituting into law Judge Harlan's famous dissent in *Plessey v. Ferguson*: 'Our Constitution is color-blind.' " In his analysis of the act's legislative history and passages from the act itself, Glazer demonstrates that the context of the law and the "clear and unambiguous intent" of Congress was "granting not *group* rights but *individual* rights." This was indeed the *stated* intent of the act, but, in giving government a role in banning private discrimination, it contradicts that intent and its provisions extend the administrative context to allow for subsequent affirmative action rulings and enforcement plans.[7]

It does not matter that during the debate on the bill several congressmen expressed abhorrence to the idea of quotas, preferential hiring, busing, and the like, and so specified this sentiment in the provisions of the act. What cancels out their lofty intentions and nullifies the language of the provisions is the breach of property rights in the public accommodations and employment titles. It is in the antidiscrimination clauses of these titles that the act grants administrative agencies the power to discriminate in favor of some citizens at the expense of others, and thus does not grant *rights* but political *privileges* instead. It is here that it violates an individual's right to discriminate on the basis of race, color, or national origin. Granted, such nonviolent discrimination is immoral, but its immorality does not justify legislative prohibition of it, no more than does the desire to reduce discrimination justify the use of coercion to bring it about. Yet, the use of coercive legislation against persons engaging in private racial discrimination is just how the American people have chosen to cope with the humanness of racism.

Rights of the Discriminator

For ninety-five years, since the Declaration of Independence until the ratification of the Thirteenth, Fourteenth, and Fifteenth Amendments to the Constitution, the United States developed

303

under the black cloud of being a nation in search of freedom for white men while denying it to Negroes. However, eliminating slavery did not eradicate the contradiction of racial oppression existing in the land of the free. For another eighty-four years until 1954 the contradiction persisted with legal discrimination and segregation succeeding slavery as the breach of the human rights of Negro Americans. Then within a year after the March on Washington in 1963, Congress passed more legislation to protect the rights of Negroes than it had during the whole period since 1875 when the first civil rights bill was passed. With the 1966 Civil Rights Act, "the legal foundations of [white] racism in America had been destroyed," as Brooks puts it.

"*Southern Segregation Falls Silently, Without Violence*," reported the Columbia, South Carolina *State* on July 4, 1964.[8] But the contradiction of the nation's guarantee of civil rights for some at the expense of the human rights of all continued. (For instance, while the 1966 Civil Rights Act assured the selection of state and federal juries without regard to race, it banned racial and religious discrimination in the sale, rental, and financing of about 80 percent of all housing in the United States.) The walls of segregation and discrimination came tumbling down, but what of the segregationist and discriminator? What of *their* rights?

On July 2, 1964, the day Congress passed the Civil Rights Bill and two days before the 187th anniversary of the signing of the Declaration of Independence, Lester G. Maddox, owner of the Pickrick Restaurant in Atlanta, Georgia, declared his rights to a group of Negro civil rights activists who had come to test the new law: "You're not going to eat at the Pickrick today or any other time! This is my property, my business, and the Constitution guarantees me the right to operate it my way!"[9]

When one of the men continued to leave the car to approach the restaurant, Maddox, armed with pistol and pick handle, ordered him off his property. "Get out of here now," he said. "I have the right to protect my property and myself, and that's what I'll do."

Most twentieth-century Americans have no sympathy for Maddox's position and every Supreme Court since 1964 would surely rule against his assertion of his right to property. But at that moment Lester Maddox, the dissenter, was championing a fundamental principle of human survival and human liberty and in so doing joined the ranks of the men who signed the Declaration of Independence and the Constitution of the United States. The drama of the moment—Maddox wielding gun and pick handle as the blacks approached him—was unpleasant and ugly, to be sure, and its star, a contemptible fellow to many; but none of these elements have any bearing on the fact that Maddox was justified in his disobedience. The three Negroes disagreed and sued Maddox, contending that the public accommodations clause of the Civil Rights Act required him to serve them. On July 22 a three-judge federal panel in Atlanta ordered the Pickrick Restaurant to admit Negroes within twenty days. Ruling that the restaurant was subject to the powers of Congress to regulate interstate commerce and thus bound to obey the public accommodations clause, the panel issued a temporary injunction for its integration pending a possible ruling by the United States Supreme Court on whether the public accommodations clause was constitutional on all grounds.[10]

On August 10 Supreme Court Justice Hugo L. Black denied Lester Maddox's motion to delay the integration of his restaurant past the August 11 deadline set by the panel in Atlanta. On December 14 the Supreme Court upheld the constitutionality of the public accommodations section and ruled simultaneously that the section barred state prosecutions of demonstrators who had tried by peaceful means to desegregate business places covered by the act. President Johnson hailed the court's decision and declared: "There already has been encouraging and widespread compliance with the act during the five months it has been law. Now I think we all join in the hope and the resolution that this kind of reasonable and responsible acceptance of law will continue and increase."[11]

Not everyone felt that such acceptance of the law was reasonable or responsible. Indeed, there were responsible people who questioned the very existence of the law. In a 1963 article on racism Ayn Rand had written: "If that 'civil rights' bill is passed, it will be the worst breach of property rights in the sorry record of American history in respect to that subject."[12] On August 13, before the Supreme Court ruled on the constitutionality of the public accommodations section, Lester Maddox announced that he was closing his restaurant. Why did he not comply with the law—allow Negroes to eat there—and keep his business open? Maddox writes: "It was simply that I was not going to knuckle under to a law that I believed went against the basic precepts of freedom as set forth in the Constitution, and so I shut down my business rather than violate a law I felt was unjust, as many were doing in the so-called civil rights movement."[13]

To many Americans, especially the liberal press, the Pickrick became a symbol for the South's holdout segregationists; its closing was a symbol of the triumph of Negro demands for equal rights, equal opportunity, and an integrated society. But for Lester Maddox, the Pickrick represented the business "I had painstakingly built over a period of two decades." For him the "closed" sign he hung on the door in September 1964 was not a symbol of the triumph of civil rights but "symbolic of the door that had been closed to individual opportunity and private property rights all over this land."[14]

After his 1974 defeat in a bid to return to the Georgia governorship, ten years after the passage of the Civil Rights Act, Maddox reopened his Pickrick Restaurant and Negroes went through the cafeteria line just like everybody else. "If it's something you can't do anything about," Maddox told a reporter, "you go along with it. The battle is all over." He did not say whether he meant his personal battle against integration or the battle to preserve individual rights. It is likely that to Maddox they were one and the same battle: his right to discriminate had been sacrificed to imposed integration. And in losing his battle to determine who he would allow to patronize his restaurant, he had lost a measure of his right to property, as well as a measure of his right to freedom of expression. As journalist Edith Efron puts it: "A free mind and a free market are supportive of each other and one cannot be violated without violating the other. Men who cannot think freely cannot produce freely. And men who are prohibited from free production are not free to think."[15] Maddox's freedom of expression had been constrained but he had not lost his *right* to think. "By its nature, internal thought, reason, is free, it is *literally* an inalienable right," writes Efron. "It does not need a First Amendment to protect it. It cannot be regulated by the State. It is totally autonomous, totally self-regulated, totally private. Indeed, *there is no form of private property more absolute than the ownership of his own thoughts.*"

The law was imposed to regulate Lester Maddox's behavior, but his thoughts were the same in 1974 as they had been in 1964. His restaurant was now integrated but he remained a segregationist. "I believed then, as I do now, that it was my right under the Constitution to serve whomever I chose to serve in my place of business," he writes in his autobiography. "I am a segregationist and I chose to operate my business on a segregated basis. Because of this I was called a racist, although the words are far from synonymous. A segregationist is an individual—black, white, or any other color—who has enough racial pride and racial integrity and love for his fellow human beings to want to see all races protected and preserved."[16]

Maddox's observation that segregationists exist in all races is correct. His concept of segregation comes very close to the separatism once advocated by the Black Muslims. The similarity is there even though Malcolm X saw in them a distinct difference:

> Every time I mentioned "separation," some of them would cry that we Muslims were standing for the same thing that white racists and demagogues stood for. I would explain the difference. "No! We reject *segregation* even more militantly than you say you do! We want separation, which is not the same! . . . *Segregation* is when your life and liberty are controlled, regulated, *by someone else*. To *segregate* means to control. Segregation is that which is forced upon inferiors by superiors. But *separation* is that which is done voluntarily, by two equals—for the good of both!"[17]

What is interesting about the Black Muslims' concept of separatism is that apparently it does not require the force of government for implementation, as does the territorial separatism advocated by Roy Innis and the economic nationalism implemented by government-subsidized "black capitalism" schemes. This is not to say that Black Muslim separatism is at once antistatist, only that its voluntary implementation is not a statist position. This is, of course, not true for most forms of segregation practiced in the United States. The "Black Codes" of Reconstruction, Jim Crow laws, as well as the separate-but-equal doctrine sanctioned by the Supreme Court were all forms of institutionalized, coercive segregation.

Maddox claims not to advocate coercive segregation but the protection of his right to discriminate, and in this his position is like that of the Muslims who, until 1976, did not allow whites to participate in their schools and businesses. The law has regarded the activities of the Muslims in a different light from those of Maddox, however. Black Muslims could demand to be served in Maddox's restaurant and be assured of legal sanction. But Maddox would not likely receive such legal insurance were he to have demanded to patronize Muslim schools and shops. A similar double standard has operated in the area of higher education. Since 1954, one after another of the all-white universities and colleges have opened their doors to black students under the threat of punishment by federal agencies. But no law has been imposed on black students who demand that the universities provide them with all-black living quarters and cultural centers. The difference between private segregation and voluntary separation is that while the former is outlawed, the latter is allowed as the quid pro quo for law and order. Malcolm X's description of racial segregation as a means of control is correct, but so are coercive integration and voluntary racial separatism.

Both the white segregationists and the hard-line black separatists advocate the protection and preservation of their races and both deny being racists. But it is hard to imagine a nonracist advocating *any* scheme to protect and preserve the races, let alone that of segregation. One might ask: protect and preserve them from what?—the answer to which is: from each other. Why? To prevent their mixing, say the segregationists. To escape their control, say the separatists. But why is this necessary? To ensure the "purity" of that race which is superior, say the segregationists. To ensure a means of gaining power, say the separatists.

If the desire of the segregationist or the separatist to see all races protected and preserved is interpreted as the desire to prevent the biological mixing of the races, and if they are against such amalgamation and miscegenation because each believes another race mixed with his own will somehow taint his with "inferior" traits, then one would have to call them racists. Even if they are not against miscegenation where it exists but merely want to associate with people of their own race, one would still have to describe their attitude as race consciousness or racially prejudiced.

The ideas of Maddox and those of Malcolm X are clearly racist, and racism is most assuredly immoral. But was Maddox's dissension on July 2, 1964, a matter involving his prejudiced ideology or his property rights? Should his closing of the Pickrick Restaurant be seen as the act of a die-hard segregationist, or the act of a man who would rather close his place of business than have the government or other citizens tell him how to run it? Only Maddox knows what his motives were. But whether his was an act of courage or villany, no one had the right to force him into such action.

Before the passing of the 1964 Civil Rights Act, the law protected the right of men like Maddox and Malcolm X to practice voluntary racial segregation; the same law protected the right of men like Martin Luther King, Jr. to practice voluntary racial integration. It also sanctioned their right to persuade others to follow their ideas and actions, but it did not recognize a right to force others to think and act as they did. Yet to force Maddox's thinking and action is precisely what the Civil Rights Act provided for. At the price of his property rights, blacks were granted the privilege (not the right) to force their ideas of integration on Maddox. As already noted, political privilege cannot exist without the violation of human rights in the process. The standard used to determine whether Maddox should keep his business was not that of property rights, but the standard of political force. The question decided was not whether he could compete (successfully) with other restaurants on the segregationist terms he chose, but whether he would obey a law forcing him to integrate against his will. Of course, we will never know whether Maddox could have remained in business as a "holdout segregationist."

Human rights do not entertain the question of whether men *should* possess certain attitudes and values, but whether they are free to express those attitudes and values in a manner that does not interfere with the rights of others. A man may hate others merely because they look and act differently from him. He is wrong in his judgment but he has *the right to be wrong*, and that right ought to be protected by law. Objective law should not take a position one way or another on the morality of a person's ideas; it ought to exist solely to protect his *right* to those ideas. Those persons hated by the discriminator may feel a lack of dignity because they are so hated; they may wish to change his attitudes, but they may neither seek legislative coercion to do so nor destroy his property in protest against his ideas. To quote Rand: "Racism is an evil, irrational and morally contemptible doctrine—but doctrines cannot be forbidden or prescribed by law. . . . Private racism is not a legal, but a moral issue."[18] One man's private expression of his race consciousness may conflict with the desires and preferences of others, but it does not interfere with their rights. But institutional racism necessarily entails the violation of individual rights, whether it be in the form of oppression as with public segregation ordinances or in the form of redress, as in the case of preferential hiring policies "to correct past discrimination."

We simply cannot begin to justly cope with the humanness of racism without first accepting the fact that every human being has the right to be wrong and that no one has the right to force an individual to be good. Adolph Hitler had the right to dislike Jews and others who were not of his illusionary "Aryan race"; and the German people had a right to blame their economic and political troubles on the Jews and other minorities. But they had not the right to force these immoral and prejudiced beliefs into practical expression because the only way such ideas could be so expressed was by punishing those whom they wrongly judged, and thereby violating their rights. Hitler did not think the Jews had the right to exist, but he did not have the right to remove them from existence. So long as Hitler's ideas remained just his own thoughts and he did not attempt to transform them into concrete reality, no one had the right to harm a hair on his head. But when he began to put his ideas into action by initiating force against the lives of those whom he hated and feared, he forfeited thereby all rights to his own life and deserved the retaliation that should have been immediately directed against him.

It may seem preposterous to suggest that so vile a man as Hitler could have the right to hate Jews. But the objectivity of human rights requires that private racism be regarded as the breach of morality that it is (and therefore not subject to legal punishment) until such time that it becomes the motivation for criminal behavior. And even then, it is the *crime* that should be punished, not the motive. Unfortunately, in its attempt to eliminate prejudice and discrimination, civil rights legislation has intruded on the morality of men and made a crime of their hatred and fears. How, then, should the government respond to the ideas and noncriminal behavior of discriminators in our society? In an essay critical of the introduction into our legal code of the category of "political crimes," Ayn Rand offers what seems to be the best approach to coping with the humanness of racism. She writes that under the American system of law the state may neither penalize nor reward an individual for his ideas. "It may not take any judicial cognizance whatever of his ideology." It may neither punish the noncriminal who holds and propagates the most reprehensible ideas nor allow to go unpunished the criminal whose ideas are considered most edifying. Since ideas do not violate the rights of others, they cannot be called a crime and cannot serve as the justification of a crime.[19] It is not a crime to believe that whites are biologically, intellectually, and morally superior to Negroes. However, one's belief that all men are created equal is no justification for initiating force against a white supremist. In a free society, the egalitarian and the racist have the same status under the law: it is between the criminal and noncriminal that the difference in status exists.

In this instance, what should be the proper relationship between citizens and the government is equally valid for private relations among citizens. For example, the regents of a private university may deplore the Marxism and racist rhetoric of Angela Davis and for that reason refuse to give her a teaching position. Miss Davis has the right to hold any views she pleases but she does not have the right to force the university to hire her. The issue here is not which doctrines are right, those of Davis or the regents, but whether each will be allowed to hold his ideas without sacrificing his judgment to that of someone else. A free society simply must allow for men to disagree, and its system of justice must extend even to those whose ideas are thought to be the most irrational and immoral.

Rights of the Discriminated Against

When Rosa Parks decided to sit in the front of a city bus in Montgomery, Alabama, she challenged a mode of transportation financed by her taxes as a citizen of that city. The city could not morally operate a segregated transportation system so long as it was run for the benefit of all the citizens and paid for by them. Mrs. Parks disobeyed the law in order to challenge its injustice. She said her feet were tired and she wanted to sit down, a purely personal desire, but resting her feet in the white section of a city-owned bus, as she did, turned the incident into a matter of public concern.

However, Lester Maddox's desire to run a segregated restaurant was never a matter that should have involved the society at large. He owned the restaurant and for twenty years had poured his labor into it without public assistance. Thus, it was an extension of his person. Its purpose was to offer a service to the public, but it was owned neither by the public nor a political agent of the public—i.e., the government. Thus, according to natural law and the Constitution, all members of the public and the government were prohibited from interfering with Maddox's ownership of the service he offered or the manner in which he offered it. But even though the Fifth and Fourteenth Amendments respectively prohibit the federal and state governments from depriving him of his right to property, that right has long since come to be treated as less than absolute by both government and citizens alike. It is generally thought that liberty and property are not absolute when the welfare of society is involved. And as civil rights leaders, legislators, and the Supreme Court saw it, how Lester Maddox ran his restaurant was a matter involving the welfare of society as they defined it at the time. Thus, while their definition of society's welfare required that legal protection be given to Mrs. Parks's right to sit where she wished on a public bus, that same definition required that protection be *denied* to Lester Maddox's right to serve whomever he chose in his privately owned restaurant.

The Parks and Maddox cases show that, having rendered human rights as arbitrary, legislators and the courts have progressively evaded the differences between public and private property. In addition they have become even bolder in applying the double standard of denying the rights of discriminators in favor of the rights of the discriminated against. But there is no way in a free society that the law can be used to the advantage of one citizen at the expense of another without infringing on the rights of both. Thus, once the government was given the power to violate the rights of men like Lester Maddox in behalf of the discriminated against, the way was also opened for men worse than Lester Maddox to use political force to violate the rights of the latter. As Maddox himself put it: "I was trying to protect not only the rights of Lester Maddox, but of every citizen, including the three men I chased off my property, for if they could violate my right of private property, then there would be nothing to prevent me from violating theirs."[20]

In 1964 not many people were in sympathy with Maddox's concern for a single standard of justice for discriminators and the discriminated against. But five years ago, his position was explicitly supported by the events surrounding a civil rights case in Mississippi that threatened to bankrupt the N.A.A.C.P., one of the defendants.[21] The circumstances that led to the court case began in 1966 when, in order to pressure officials of Port Gibson, Mississippi, for job programs and voting rights, the N.A.A.C.P. joined other civil rights groups in a boycott of white merchants, which lasted from April 1966 to February 1967 and continued on and off during the decade that followed. In a 1976 ruling, which awarded twelve white merchants a $1.2 million settlement against the N.A.A.C.P. because of the boycott, Judge George Haynes of the Chancellery Court in Hinds County, Mississippi, called the boycott *illegal* because the merchants had no say in the granting or withholding of the civil rights sought and therefore the boycott was "secondary"—a distinction between "public issue activity" (primary) and "private issue activity" (secondary).

The lawsuit was filed after a law was passed by the Mississippi legislature that sought to outlaw "conspiracies" to boycott businesses. The law had been introduced by a Port Gibson legislator who was one of the twelve complaining white merchants. Judge Haynes ruled that the N.A.A.C.P., the Mississippi Action for Progress, a federally funded antipoverty organization, and 132 persons had "wrongfully combined and colluded a civil conspiracy." He said the defendants had "illegally created a monopoly" for black businesses and "unlawfully interfered with business relations between the merchants and their customers."

The ruling said that the black objectives were "highly laudable and praiseworthy for the most part" but that the dispute had been between blacks and public officials in Clairborne County, not between blacks and white merchants. Citing Mayor Charles Evers of nearby Fayette, who was then the N.A.A.C.P. field secretary for the state, as the "unquestionable leader of this endeavor," Judge Haynes wrote, "The white merchants were conscripted into the controversy because the defendants believed them to be in a position of control or having the power to exert pressure to compel the public officials to grant their demands."

In a plea to Judge Haynes to overturn his ruling the attorney for the N.A.A.C.P. argued that the boycott had concerned "public issue activity" rather than "private issue activity" and thus had been "primary," and therefore legal, rather than "secondary." To hold that the boycott was illegal would be tantamount to abridging the right to free speech, he said. "The defendants were attempting to persuade the merchants of the town to abide by the laws of the United States."

The attorney for the merchants countered that "the fact that the boycott was designed as a means to an end and that the end might have been lawful does not make the boycott lawful." He added that

313

because he frequently represented labor organizations in court, authorization of secondary boycotts would "give me and my clients a great weapon. But that is not the law, and I don't think it ever will be."

Having no legal expertise nor a working knowledge of the laws of the state of Mississippi, I cannot comment on the legality of the Haynes ruling, but I can question the moral implications of his statement and, therefore, whether the suit against the N.A.A.C.P. was just. (What is legal or illegal does not always square with what is just.)

The right to liberty entails the right to act, without the use of force or fraud, according to dictates of one's conscience. It also entails the requirement that one bear the consequences of his actions, which includes the judgment held of him by his fellowmen. They may be mistaken in their judgment of him but their right to liberty entails their right to think as they please (in this case, about him) and to act accordingly, without violence unless in retaliation of violence. The N.A.A.C.P. and civil rights activists in Port Gibson apparently felt that they would need the support of the white merchants in the town in order to secure jobs and voting rights. (News reports did not say whether blacks had sought employment from the twelve merchants.) When the merchants refused to use their influence, the civil rights groups called on blacks to boycott their stores. The issue is not whether the boycott was justified or even legal, but whether those who felt discriminated against had the *right* to boycott the businesses of those merchants they believed were supporters of the discrimination against them.

Judge Haynes was correct in characterizing the boycott as an interference with business relations between merchants and customers, but he and the Mississippi legislature were unjust in making such activity "unlawful." For a private economic boycott (for whatever reasons) can be deemed illegal only by abrogating the economic relationship between merchant and customer and violating the rights of both.

The relationship between merchant and customer ought to be based on the fact that each has something the other wants. Each ought to be free to produce and trade what he produces. However, in a free society the businessman may not force the customer to purchase his product and the customer may not force the businessman to sell his product. The buying and selling that results between them should be determined by each man's choice to solicit what he needs from one who has it in exchange for a value equal to that of the goods, service, or money sought. The extent of the buyer-seller arrangement between merchant and customer is determined by the nature of their reliance on each other and the availability of the commodity or service each has to offer. Many buying and selling arrangements are secured by contracts that hold each party to an agreement that is binding over an extended period of time. But most transactions between buyer and seller are immediate, involving products that are in abundance and for small amounts of cash.

The primary interest that the merchant and customer have in each other is economic. The freedom to exercise his right to property entitles the merchant to create and otherwise acquire goods and sell them to willing buyers. The customers exercise their right to property by offering their monetary earnings or some other form of payment in exchange for the goods. Each person has the right to create, own, and dispose of his *own* property, not that of someone else. Accordingly, each may *withhold* his property from the market in general or from individual buyers or sellers and for whatever reason he may choose, whether wisely or foolishly. Provided that neither party is bound by contractual relationships with the government that dictate the nature of his participation in the market, the action taken is entirely personal and private. Thus, Judge Haynes was correct to call the black boycott a private issue activity and the N.A.A.C.P. attorney committed a disservice to his clients by insisting that theirs was a public issue activity (implying that public action should meet with greater favor from the law than private action). But the Mississippi law and Judge Haynes were unjust in outlawing the boycott on the basis of its private nature. They would have been more justified had it been indeed "public"— i.e., action against private merchants by government agents or representatives.

I have said that the primary interest that merchant and customer have in each other is economic, but their action in the market may be *motivated* by anything *but* economic concerns. When a merchant opens his business each day he places himself in the position to be judged by customers not only on the basis of the goods and services he sells but also on the basis of his attitudes and behavior in the community. Some customers may refuse to give him their patronage simply because he does not offer the goods or services they would

315

like to purchase. Others may withhold their business because the merchant is known to hold certain views they disapprove of. Customers have passed up certain merchants because they are members of certain racial or ethnic groups. In some cases even the sex of the merchant makes a difference to customers. The reasons for doing business or not doing business with a merchant are as varied as there are customers. But however motivated, the customer's purchasing power, which is entailed in his right to property, is inalienable, sanctioned by the Constitution, and ought to be preserved and protected by the law. The Mississippi court chose to do precisely the opposite: it called the purchasing power of the black boycotters an "interference" and punished them for it.

No law or statute is just that purports to protect civil rights at the expense of the basic human rights from which they are derived. Yet it was in the name of justice that the federal government violated the property rights of Lester Maddox, the discriminator, and the Mississippi state government violated the right of free speech of the N.A.A.C.P., the discriminated against. In providing that a person exercising his "right to demand service" at any business in a "named category" cannot be "lawfully" ejected from it or arrested for trespass, the public accommodations title of the 1964 Civil Rights Act violated the rights of merchants who chose to withhold their goods and services from customers of a given race, color, religion, or national origin. The Mississippi law prohibiting economic boycotts violated the rights of customers who chose to withhold their patronage from merchants whom they believed were supporters of racial discrimination. As blacks had claimed the right to demand *service* from men like Lester Maddox, the Mississippi merchants claimed, in effect, the right to demand *patronage* from blacks. The judicial system that had made trespassing legal in 1964 was now making boycotting illegal in 1976. The system that punished white men for refusing to sell was now punishing black men for refusing to buy! When such injustices are suffered by both discriminators and the discriminated against in the name of equal justice for all, one has to wonder whether such solutions will contribute to the elimination of racism in America or to the reinforcement of it.

The Steady State of Justice

When the Constitution abolished slavery and involuntary servitude it also made illegal the use of force to obtain service from another. A businessman who cannot serve whom he pleases is not a businessman but a slave. The only right customers have is to *request* a man's services; but they have no right to force him to *provide* that service. In its sanction of a man's choice to request the services of another and in its simultaneous sanction of that person's right to refuse the service wanted, the Constitution reflects the principle that there are no conflicts of interest between rational men, that one man's gain is not necessarily another's loss. The only way such an imbalance can be created in the affairs of men is when they resort to the rule of force instead of the rule of reason. In throwing its weight behind enforcing the alleged "right" to demand service the government necessarily violates the actual rights of the individual who owns that means of service. And, thus, it attempts to get around reality by claiming that the existence of property has no cause, no effect—no reason for being.

In a free society one is free to hold contradictory premises—that is, an individual may be prejudiced *against* others or prejudiced *in favor* of them and participate in an open market that makes no distinction among men except in the realm of their economic role in the community. He may express his prejudice through various acts of discrimination for or against certain individuals or groups. He is free to express his biased judgment of others; but he is *not free* to escape the consequences of that choice, and he is not free to force others to implement his judgment or to comply with it. As he owns his business, so too does he own his bigotry and is responsible for the consequences of holding such an attitude.

If he is a restaurateur who discriminates against Negroes, the consequence of his bigotry is that I am forbidden to eat in his restaurant. What means do I have to change this consequence? I may attempt to change the attitudes that make the consequence possible by persuading him of the irrationality, immorality, and injustice of his bigotry. If I fail to persuade him I may act to punish the consequences by affecting the economic expression of his bigotry: either by persuading his patrons to boycott the restaurant and thus cause him to lose profits, or by setting up my own restaurant (or encouraging others to do so) and force him out of the market by competition. These are the only *just* and *voluntary* actions I may take without violating his rights. As Tibor Machan puts it, "Knowing what is right does not entitle one to force others to do what is right."

But I may take another route—the *criminal* action. I may act to change the consequence of his bigotry by forcing him to serve me (acting against his judgment) at the point of a gun. I may affect the economic execution of his bigotry by blackmail, by destroying the restaurant itself, or by killing him.

Or, I may seek *legislative* action against him that would declare his discrimination against Negroes illegal. Thus by making his ideas and behavior illegal I have used the law to force into existence the consequence I preferred (integrated restaurants) and prevented the consequence he preferred (segregated restaurants). But have I been just? Race consciousness is immoral; the expression of it in acts of prejudice and discrimination is unjust. But should we, on the basis of its immorality and injustice, make prejudice and discrimination illegal?

An answer to this question lies in Machan's observation that the implementation of moral values by edict with equality and efficiency would be impossible because "those doing the implementing would necessarily enjoy unequal status."[22] Men must be free to discover the right and the wrong, the good and the bad; but their being free is no guarantee that they will choose to be good or bad. Political freedom is necessary for the expression of man's good, and it is just as necessary to identify the bad. Morality legislation interferes with the individual's ability to judge what or who is good or bad, beneficial or inimical to his interests.

The issue of political freedom is not to judge the moral rightness or wrongness of sociopolitical decisions by individuals (and to assign consequential rewards or punishments to these decisions), but to determine the best means of assuring that such decisions may be made without coercive constraints from other individuals or institutional entities. Just laws do not sit in moral judgment on those decisions, but judge whether they are freely made, whether the person executing them is engaged in voluntary or compulsory activity, and whether that activity threatens the freedom of others. In other words, the concern of political liberty is not to decide what decisions men should (or should not) make within the boundaries of their own lives, but to determine that they are able to make such decisions (rightly or wrongly) in the absence of coercion and that they have the freedom to experience the consequence of those right or wrong decisions.

When morality legislation makes it illegal for a prejudiced restaurateur to follow the dictates of his conscience, it not only punishes him for his ideas and his consequential behavior at the expense of his right to private property, but by preventing the actualization of his bigotry, the law removes from reality the factual evidence men need by which to judge his character. Once he is forced to act against his biased judgment, those deploring immorality such as his and committed to fairness are no longer in a position to know whether he is a racist or not and are therefore without means to oppose him. The flow of justice is further interrupted when, finding that there is now no rational way to perceive the "intent" to discriminate, civil rights administrative agencies such as the Equal Employment Opportunity Commission (EEOC) now equate the "underrepresentation" of minorities in jobs with "exclusion" and "discrimination." Statistics and percentages—i.e., quotas—have become the means by which discrimination is proved or disproved.[23] Contrary to the very backbone of the American judicial system, employers are considered guilty (by ommission or commission) until *they* prove *themselves* innocent of discriminatory practices.

It would be well to remember that a restaurateur or merchant owns his place of business not as a means for intimidating Negroes as such, but for the purpose of providing a livelihood for himself. And this is the ground on which he must be objectively rewarded or justly punished. That a restaurant owner is prejudiced and that this is his motive for refusing service is irrelevant in judging whether he has violated a potential customer's rights. What is relevant is that he is the owner and may determine how his establishment should be used, who should use it, whom he should hire and fire, etc.

That he may not purchase goods and services from someone who wishes not to sell (for whatever reasons) is the only fact the customer can consider in judging whether he has been treated fairly. That he believes integrated restaurants make the best kind of restaurants and contribute to racial harmony is irrelevant. What *is* relevant is that *he does not own the restaurant* and may not impose his morality on the person who does. In a free society, the rules of ownership of an enterprise and the terms by which the enterprise is conducted are set by the owner. Patrons and other entrepreneurs who disagree with how an establishment is run are, as Rand puts it, "free to go elsewhere and seek different terms."[24]

319

There are those who argue that while this prescription may be suitable in dealing with just one discriminator, surely the application of justice must be altered when there are a thousand such merchants discriminating against all Negroes as a group. But such a proposal negates the objectivity of the standards of justice. The whole point of justice is that its principles are universal and absolute, that they must be applied to the same degree whether in relations between two people on a desert island or among the nine million inhabitants of New York City. The nature of justice and the extent to which it is applied are not determined by the number of people involved but by the laws of reality and the natural rights that all men possess.

Justice does not ask whether an action is "fair" according to conventional standards. It is, rather, the rule of conduct that repels or retaliates action inimical to the requirements of human nature (rights) and encourages action beneficial to human survival. The legal minded Romans of antiquity, whose mission it was to give laws to the world, defined justice as "the steady and abiding purpose to give every man that which is his own"—what Rand defines as "neither seeking nor granting the unearned and undeserved, neither in matter nor in spirit." The purpose of justice, then, is to establish and maintain a steady state between the rights inherent in human nature and the implementation of those rights. As Rand points out, justice forbids "the material implementation of [rights] by other men; it includes only the freedom to earn that implementation by one's own effort."[25]

Justice is the maintenance of a steady state between the facts of reality and one's moral appraisal of his fellows, what Rand further defines as "the act of judging a man's character and/or actions exclusively on the basis of all the factual evidence available, and of evaluating it by means of an objective moral criterion."[26] That objective moral criterion must be based on man's nature as a rational being who requires certain rights of existence and whose survival depends on his capacity to think and choose among alternative ideas and actions he judges to be in his self-interest.

Every human being owns his person, his thoughts, his actions, and their consequences. When we force consequences into existence other than those that would naturally occur as the result of a person's thought and action, we upset the balance between his identity and the laws of reality. Some consequences must be prohibited—such as those of the criminal—in order that the consequences from the implementation of rights may be manifest. We must prohibit or punish stealing, for example, as the just consequence for men who take from others what they have not earned or produced, and as a protection of men who produce and earn their means of livelihood. This is why men in a rational society establish the law—to curtail action and to punish action taken in violation of it. But not all laws are just. Laws like the public accommodations title of the 1964 Civil Rights Act, Affirmative Action regulations, and the Mississippi antiboycott ruling are offensive—offensive because they strike at justice and because the enforcement of them requires exempting men from the laws of reality and exempting reason from their nature, nullifying it as the requirement of their survival.

The purpose of moral (just) law is not to regulate morality, but to prevent or punish the violation of human rights. "The law may not make a man love me," said Martin Luther King, Jr., "but it can keep him from lynching me." The law may punish the violation of an individual's rights, but it has no inherent power to reform the attitudes of the violator. Yet, the expectation of the civil rights movement was and is that under the condition of being forceably brought together, men will come to love one another. No consideration is given to the rights of the individuals involved and every effort is directed toward imposing on some men the ideal of a "good society" held by others.

The desire for a "beloved community" has no value outside the context of the rights of those who are to compose such a community. The desire for a "social order of justice" has no value outside the context of justice. The goal to change the hearts and minds of men has no value outside the context of man's right to his ideas and actions. The struggle for equal opportunity has no value outside the context of man's independence. The achievement of racial integration has no value outside the context of voluntary association. The desire to cure the "disease of racism" is of no value outside the context of the lives of the men so "infected."

The end does not justify the means.

On August 28, 1963, amid what one writer called "a mood of quiet anger and a mood of buoyant exuberance," before a sea of over two hundred and ten thousand Americans that stretched from the

Washington Monument to the Lincoln Memorial, Martin Luther King, Jr. told the world about his "dream" for his country, his fellow Negroes and his children:

> I have a dream that one day this nation will rise up and live out the true meaning of its creed: "We hold these truths to be self-evident; that all men are created equal."
> I have a dream that one day on the red hills of Georgia the sons of former slaves and the sons of former slaveowners will be able to sit down together at the table of brotherhood. . . .
> I have a dream that my four little children will one day live in a nation where they will not be judged by the color of their skin but by the content of their character.

And he dreamed of the day when all men could join hands and sing: "Free at last! Free at last! Thank God Almighty, we are free at last!"

It was a noble dream and the millions who heard it felt ennobled by it. Said one writer: "It was no private vision, nothing esoteric, but a personalized translation of the American heritage taught to every schoolboy, forged anew in a context of the Negro experience and detailed in terms of his, Martin King's, identity as part of that experience, its legacy and destiny. . . . Right out of elementary civics, the lesson, in this context, formed an ironic exegesis of our democratic platitudes."[27] But however noble and however deeply embedded it lies in the American expectation, the dream of brotherhood cannot be forced on men as the solution to the "humanness of racism."

Two wrongs never make a right.

1. Machan, *Human Rights and Human Liberties*, p. 43.
2. Gettleman and Mermelstein, eds., *The Great Society Reader*.
3. *Facts On File*, July 2–July 8, 1964, p. 220.
4. King, *Stride toward Freedom*, pp. 82, 175.
5. See Levy and Kramer, *The Ethnic Factor*.
6. Glazer, *Affirmative Discrimination*, pp. 31–32. It should be noted that Glazer does not question the morality of affirmative action, only its effectiveness, its necessity, and the justice of its implementation. His criticism of preferential hiring, for instance, is not on principle but because it generally does not do anything to benefit those who need it. He writes: "For me, no consideration of principle— such as that merit should be rewarded, or that governmental programs should not discriminate on grounds of race or ethnic group—would stand in the way of a program of preferential hiring if it made some substantial progress in reducing the severe problems of the low-income black population and of the inner cities."

7. For my discussion of Titles 1 and 8 as the basis for extending the statistical-distribution approach to education and employment, see Anne Wortham, "An Open Letter to Nathan Glazer."

8. Quoted in Brooks, *Walls Come Tumbling Down*, p. 260.

9. I have purposely chosen Lester Maddox's situation as an instance where the discriminator's rights are violated because he is so despised by so many people for his segregationist views. But segregationist or not, Lester Maddox is human too; and as such, he has human rights as do all the rest of us.

10. The panel's injunction applied also to the Heart of Atlanta Motel, the owner of which sued to stop the government from enforcing the act at his motel, maintaining that travelers ceased to be involved in interstate commerce once they entered his establishment.

11. Quoted in *Facts On File*, December 10–16, 1964, p. 434.

12. Rand, *The Virtue of Selfishness*, p. 134.

13. Lester G. Maddox, *Speaking Out: The Autobiography of Lester Garfield Maddox*, p. 69.

14. Ibid.

15. Edith Efron, "The Free Market and the Free Mind."

16. Maddox, op. cit., p. 54.

17. Malcolm X, *The Autobiography of Malcolm X*, p. 2;6.

18. Rand, *The Virtue of Selfishness*, p. 134.

19. Rand, *The New Left: The Anti-Industrial Revolution*, p. 99.

20. Maddox, op. cit., p. 57.

21. The facts of the case are cited here from reports in the *New York Times*, (August 12, October 1, 9, 21, 1976).

22. Machan, *Human Rights and Human Liberties*, p. 49.

23. Thomas Sowell, *Affirmative Action Reconsidered: Was It Necessary in Academia?*

24. Rand, *The New Left: The Anti-Industrial Revolution*, pp. 41–42.

25. Rand, *The Virtue of Selfishness*, p. 97.

26. Rand, *Introduction to Objectivist Epistemology*, p. 49. See also *Atlas Shrugged*, pp. 1019–20.

27. Miller, *Martin Luther King, Jr.,* p. 166.

13

Statement of Challenge

We do not "solve" race problems—we move in directions. And there are only two alternatives. One leads to persecution, hatred, and bestiality. The other is the one I believe Americans have slowly but hesitantly trod—the path of acceptance, cooperation, and democracy.—Brewton Berry, *Common Ground.*

The very nature of man's survival and well-being requires that his social freedom and his individual freedom complement each other. At best, a man must take the responsibility for his intellectual freedom, even if the social system in which he lives is such that his social freedom is restricted. But at no time and under no circumstances does man's nature as a reasoning, self-regulatory being allow for the situation in which his sociopolitical liberty is *greater than* his internal, individual freedom. Such an imbalance goes *against* man's nature. Yet, this is the contradictory situation in which the race-conscious Negro found himself during the latter half of the 1960s.[1] His dilemma, then and now, stems from the fact that his increased social freedom is made incomplete by his lack of individual sovereignty. It is a dilemma of self-alienation compounded by the pressures and risks of external socioeconomic opportunities he had not been confronted with before and by political privileges he had not been granted before.

There are those who say that the transformation of the civil rights protest movement into the Black Power movement was a good thing. The shifts from tactics of civil disobedience to urban violence, to cultural nationalism combined with political action within the system are viewed as legitimate stages within a people's quest for freedom. Civil disobedience, violent and nonviolent protest were great movers of the American Revolution. Violence, H. Rap Brown, has told us, is as American as apple pie; the search for cultural determination or ethno-racial identification has been the goal of immigrant minorities since the founding of the republic; and political action within the system to change the system is seen as the very expression of democracy in our country.

Of course, the legitimate retaliatory violence necessary to protect lives and property or to maintain sovereignty against hostile nations is not the same as the criminal violence initiated against individuals and their property just because they disagree with us. The fact that so many thousands of immigrants have sought cultural determination and ethno-racial identification at the expense of their self-identity does not make the action any less prohibitive of the achievement of authentic self-esteem. When we identify political action as a means of changing the social system we must determine whether the action engaged in will change the system to the benefit of human liberty or to its detriment.

The Flight from Freedom and Self-Identity

The civil rights movement is most often portrayed as a campaign for justice and human dignity—a moral revolution for freedom as opposed to a movement for power and coercion—a search for interracial harmony rather than unfair vengeance and retribution. Indeed, a great many activists of the integration era and their supporters were truly committed to the achievement of goals appropriate for a free and open society. Their diligence has had beneficial effects on the American social system and the lives of individuals—in their achievement of the right to vote, the elimination of government-enforced discrimination, and the desegregation of publicly financed institutions and services.

But the civil rights movement has not always embraced purposes and goals consonant with justice, freedom, human dignity, and social harmony. While some in the movement sought freedom, others were engaged in a flight from freedom. While some desired equal justice, others sought political privileges. While the cry of many of the movement's leaders for sociopolitical and economic integration was genuine, the cry of others was merely an exercise in rhetoric to divert attention from their personal schemes to rise to prominence on the wave of the hopes, fears, and uncertainties of their followers.

If the political and cultural nationalism that succeeded the integration movement aimed for the achievement of freedom, as its leaders claimed, then there is a great deal of explaining that they have yet to do. If freedom was the end they sought, why did they use means that can only deny freedom?

In 1954 the Negro said he should have equal educational opportunity in order to achieve integration and he was granted that opportunity. What did he mean, then, in 1967 when he demanded "relaxed" admissions standards so that he could attend the "best" schools? After being admitted under lowered standards to top universities, why did he then demand his own black-taught Black Studies program in 1970? Having been given his own branch of studies in 1971, what did he mean in 1972 when he demanded separate Afro-American living quarters and "ethnic cultural" centers? What meaning could his 1954 demand for social and academic integration have now that in 1973 he was given separate living quarters?

What did he mean in 1971 by "equal educational opportunity" when he pressured the City University of New York to adopt an "open admissions" policy that allowed him to be admitted regardless of secondary school grades or entrance examination scores?

What had he meant by equal opportunity when, after being openly admitted, he insisted that remedial makeup classes be given as credit courses?

What was the meaning of his burning down black-owned businesses in his own community in 1964, if in 1963 he had demanded equal economic opportunity? What did he mean in 1968 when he opted for government-subsidized "black capitalism?" If in 1970 he advocated a separate black economy, what had he meant in 1963 when he demanded economic integration?

If for several decades he demanded political integration and it was guaranteed him in 1964, what did he mean in 1968 when he embraced separatist power politics? Why does he tolerate the Congressional Black Caucus in Congress if he is interested in the representation of all the people?

327

If in 1971 he demanded "preferential hiring," what had he meant in 1963 when he demanded equal employment opportunity?

Did he want to put an end to the injustice directed toward him, or did he want to establish a social system that would favor his desires at the expense of the rights of others? Did he want justice and opportunities, or favoritism and privileges?

If we are to answer these questions and come to any understanding of the contradictions implied in them, we must begin to examine race relations and the civil rights movement not just from the perspective of the discriminator but from that of the discriminated against as well. We shall have to determine whether the suffering of those who are discriminated against is self-caused or externally caused, or both, and we shall have to determine whether *any* suffering can be offered as the moral justification for violating the rights of others.

We need to go behind the politics of the civil rights movement and examine its content—its constituents, their rhetoric, and manner of logic—its motive power and inner dynamics—its conscious philosophy, as well as its sense of life. We need to identify which aspects of the civil rights movement constitute a legitimate, moral quest for freedom in response to external discrimination and racism and which are but a revolt against freedom as a response to the internal dilemma of self-esteem.

For the past four decades our response to civil rights activism has been to ask beleagured minorities: "What do you want?" and to provide what is demanded whether or not it is necessary, just, or even feasible. But in our eagerness to satisfy—to content the discontented—to ease our own conscience—we have absolved them of the responsibility for their demands and sacrificed our own self-interest in the process. We have failed to ask "What do you mean?" and find ourselves overwhelmed by what Daniel P. Moynihan calls the "maximum feasible misunderstanding"—i.e., the belief held by pragmatists and utilitarians that social problems can be solved by means of government intervention. And what distortions of human dignity are left in the wake of the forty-year-old attempt to order into existence a Great Society of equality and ethno-racial harmony?

We have seen the concept "equal rights" transformed into yet another surrogate concept for social parasitism and is now a euphemism for equality of results and equal conditions. We have seen "civil rights"—a valid concept deriving its objective meaning from the principle of human rights—stripped of all rational meaning and used as a legal weapon against the very principles of natural rights of which it is a subcategory. There is nothing figurative about "civil rights," but it has become a euphemism for political privileges forced into existence at the expense of the rights of others. It is employed by everyone, from storefront social workers to federal justices, in order to legitimate the transformation of personal desires into public policy.

It is time to end the unprincipled, unjust compliance with the demands of the liberationist whose means of seeking liberation can only result in enslavement. The time has come to ask questions and to hold him accountable for his ideas and actions. The assumption that he who uses the language of freedom is necessarily an advocate of freedom does not stand up against the evidence to the contrary. We must know whereof he speaks when he addresses us.

We have seen anticoncepts like "black mind," "blackness," "black awareness," "black pride," and "black identity" become a part of the conventional language as symbols of disdain for individual identity and achievement, kept afloat by intellectuals and politicians who ardently seek to destroy the validity of man's individuality, to obliterate the objective definitions of the human mind and awareness, to divorce the content of consciousness from the fact of consciousness. We have seen such concepts rise from the philosophical swamp of subjectivism and determinism for the purpose of turning valid concepts inside out, rendering man's cognition nonexistent and his judgment impotent, with the ultimate goal of forcing irrational whims into existence as the embodiment of the Public Purpose with little or no opposition.

We should ask ourselves: Is there some essential characteristic about the minds of Negro individuals that justifies the phrase "black mind"? Is there some essential distinction about the awareness of Negro individuals that justifies the term "black awareness"? What is the cognitive necessity of "blackness"? Is it a quality that all Negroes have by virtue of their racial characteristics and the reactions of others to it? Does the lack of "black identity" imply a lack of self-identity? What is "black pride"? What should determine pride in a person—*any* person—his biocultural ancestry or his achievements? What should determine his identity—his genetic endowment or the character and personality he creates? Are these concepts indigenous

329

to the rational liberation of a group of individuals—or, are they symbols used to promulgate moral altruism, political collectivism, and social psychological determinism?

For too long the fate of the Negro race has been analyzed and portrayed without any reference to Negroes as the causal agents of their existence. Their life in America has been oversimplified by rhetoric, statistics, and sentimental sociohistorical examinations to the point that there is hardly a trace left of the fundamental element of that existence—the individual Negro himself. For too long the socioeconomic and political limitations that face them have been identified as the only agents acting to frustrate their existence. So, too, have white prejudice, discrimination, and racism been too quickly designated as the evils that undermine the self-esteem of Negroes, with no thought given to the fact that an undermined self-esteem is the consequence of *inappropriate* responses to an irrational social environment. A man without self-esteem cannot overcome socioeconomic and political limitations; he cannot respond rationally to prejudice, discrimination, and racism. If such injustice and hardships assume such great importance in his view of himself and reality, it is because he has no countervalues to offset them. And they become the psychointellectual content of the void that is his pseudo self-esteem.

Being the object of government-enforced segregation, racial discrimination, and general race consciousness is undoubtedly humiliating, but neither government policy nor one's prejudiced neighbors are the *causes* of the alienation a person might experience. Some Negroes have assimilated some of the worst aspects of the culture around them, but neither the dominant culture nor one's own subculture are *causes* of self-immolation. While there is nothing wrong, per se, with having an interest in the history of one's biological ancestors or fashioning one's hair and dress after their cultural customs—or favoring only the achievements of individuals whose race is the same as one's own—these preferences do not *cause* self-acceptance. They are not the agents of pride and they certainly do not constitute the "essence" of one's identity. To quote Branden:

> A man's social environment can provide incentives to think or it can make the task harder—according to the degree of human rationality or irrationality that a man encounters. But the social environment cannot *determine* a man's thinking or non-thinking. . . . The social environ-

ment can provide him with the incentives for good or evil, but . . . an incentive is not a necessitating cause. The environment consists only of facts; the meaning of those facts—the conclusions and convictions to be drawn from them—can be identified only by a man's mind. A man's character, the degree of his rationality, independence, honesty, is determined, not by the things he perceives, but by the thinking he does or fails to do about them.[2]

The point is that as human beings, Negroes are just as subject to the requirements of human nature as any other group of men. Being discriminated against, humiliated, and oppressed by laws abusive of their rights does not relegate them to the outer fringes of what defines the nature of the human being; such treatment does not render them *less* human. Neither does their "victimization" elevate them beyond the laws of reality entitling them to a special set of rules by which to function; they are not *more* human. A man's self-identity may be evaded by others, but they cannot shape it; only he has the power to create the personality and character from which self-identity is derived. Others may abuse his humanity, but they cannot ignore it. Every man is his own creator—responsible for his own existence, the content of his consciousness, and the nature of his actions. He may surround himself by hundreds of thousands and march the streets of the Seat of Liberty, proclaiming his "dream" of an open community without prejudice, discrimination, and racism, but in the final analysis only he can create the personal sovereignty on which the establishment and maintenance of such a community must rest.

This is not to absolve discriminators from the responsibility they have for creating conditions that aggravate the striving of those discriminated against. Rather, the intention here is to challenge the tendency to exempt the discriminated from *their* ownership of the suffering *they* experience. What we need to recognize is that whether it is rational or not, the *behavior* of Negroes in response to an irrational social environment is not created by those engaged in discrimination but by Negroes themselves. The fact that ours is a race-conscious society does not explain the manner in which some individuals respond to that state of affairs. When a Negro responds in acts of civil disobedience, it is *he* who is acting. When he responds in acts of violence, it is *he* who is responsible for the violence—not white racism. When he responds by advocating special legislation to curtail the private actions of others, it is *he* who is doing the advocating. When he responds by judging himself inferior, inadequate, and unimportant, it is *he* who is so judging.

Acknowledgment of the self-responsibility of Negroes is not to lay moral blame but to assert the fact that even when many Negroes complain that they have been robbed of a self-identity, we cannot exempt them from the self-ownership and self-responsibility that self-identity entails. As Branden puts it, man cannot escape his nature.

If the plight of Negroes as a group continues to be a hardship, it is, to a large degree, because so many individuals in that group either do not know or refuse to accept the fact that self-determination and self-identity can be neither achieved nor destroyed by political means. If the civil rights movement has failed to create the black and white "togetherness" advocated during years past, it is because a large part of the movement was a product of an attitude of race consciousness and the politics of collectivism that would accept nothing less than the self-sacrifice of both Negroes and whites. And no benevolent or beneficial relations can ever result from self-sacrifice.

As I have pointed out, even in its moralistic attack on white racism, the civil rights movement was itself an expression of ethno-race consciousness and racism on the part of Negroes. Even as the nonviolent demonstrators, the protest marchers, the "liberators," and the "revolutionaries" declared their "self-determination," they had already sacrificed their self-identity and self-awareness to ethno-racial identification and collective awareness; theirs was a view of themselves and others as racially determined beings; their policy of social interaction was to judge individuals by the ethno-racial attributes of their group; prejudice and antipathy laced their attitudes toward those in other groups. Even as the dream of integration was piped through the airwaves of America via the calculated cadences of Martin Luther King, Jr., many Negroes desired to institutionalize their race consciousness by political means—to institute a sociopolitical system that discriminates *in favor* of individuals and groups of individuals on ethnic and racial grounds. Even as racial harmony was put forth as a goal to be achieved, many of its advocates longed to escape from self-responsibility through mindless conformity to the values of others; and their idea of cultural give and take amounted to cognitive parasitism, psychointellectual blackmail, deceit, manipulation, role playing, and appeasement. They complain of the oppressive white racism that pervades our semifree society but do so in the manner of men consumed by their own race consciousness and craving for retributive minority racism. These have been the major underlying motives of the regression of the civil rights movement from the quest for political equality and justice via nonviolent civil disobedience and petitions for the legitimate redress of grievances to destructive vengeance via criminal violence and anarchy, to the demand for privilege by fiat via power politics. And uniting these stages of social and political action has been the desire to relinquish to "society" the responsibility for the achievement and maintenance of personal freedom.

Their flight from freedom has been a flight from their own consciousness. Their revolt is not just a strike against what constitutes a free society but against the necessity of man's intellectual freedom to his survival. It is not only external, social freedom they want to strangle, but their own free will as well.

The Preservation of Freedom and Individual Sovereignty

How do we improve race relations in the United States? We begin with a hands-off policy from the government in matters of private morality and interpersonal relations between Negroes and whites, and the repeal of much of the civil rights legislation regulating these affairs and equalization policies such as busing and affirmative action. As to the relations between Negroes and whites, and other ethnic and racial groups, they should simply coexist as traders, exchanging material and intellectual values for their mutual benefit. Nothing more should be required or expected of them and nothing less should be acceptable to them.

In no sphere of their daily lives should Americans allow their ethno-racial identification to assume primacy over their self-identity. And this conception of ourselves should not be taught and learned merely as an abstract ideal, never to be realized in practical life. One's character and personality need not be shaped by one's biological and social categories; and there need not be a tug-of-war between one's self-identity and one's categorical attributes. The individual of authentic self-esteem *is* possible!

As Everett Stonequist said so well: "to confront the issues [of race relations] with courage will not necessarily solve the whole conflict,

333

for the action of one person cannot eliminate, although it may significantly modify, the objective social situation. . . . But those who maintain their personal integrity—the 'I am myself' attitude—do reaffirm the rights of personality in the face of external pressures, and so become pioneers and creative agents in that new social order which seems to evolve as narrower group loyalties gradually give way to larger human values."

While I disagree with those sociologists who debunk "assimilation," "acculturation," or "cultural pluralism," I do agree with the Glazer-Moynihan view of ethnic groups as interest groups and with the Levy-Kramer one that with their increasing political participation and visibility ethnic Americans hold the key to the political future of the United States. But I oppose the Levy-Kramer notion that minorities are justified in using their ethnicity as an electoral trump card with which to extract statist benefits and solutions from the government. They could indeed change the direction of American politics but *for the better*, by breaking their alliance with the government. Minorities could work to lose their dependency on the Great Benefactor, the modern-day Master of the Big House—the enslaver who picks the pocket of one citizen to ensnare the self-sufficiency and self-responsibility of another. For once they could say "No" to politicians who wish to buy their votes with legislation that cripples the economy and interferes with the rights of us all. They could say "No" to coercive integration, affirmative-action quotas and preferential hiring, busing, open admissions, ethnic diplomacy, food stamps, welfare, etc.

Many Americans would denounce these suggestions as inhumane. Sure, people should try to be more independent, they say, but you cannot expect this until they are educated. Minorities need more and better education if they are to successfully coexist and compete with the majority, they say, and the government must do something to guarantee this. "You leave too much for people to decide among themselves, which just can't be done," they say. "Everyone's not like you—or me. Most people can't make it alone."

I do not believe this. I believe that most people—black or white, rich or poor—do make it alone and would do so more efficiently and effectively were it not for the unjust and patronizing interference of others. The idea that most people need to be kept by their brother, neighbor, or a bureaucrat is not only untrue but immoral and an insult to what most men can achieve if given only half the chance—

i.e., being left alone by their brothers, neighbors, and bureaucrats. As Rand has pointed out, those who advocate such policies either want to be taken care of by someone else or they want to command the dependence on them as dispensers of material and spiritual values.

If it is freedom, human dignity, and self-respect that we Americans want, then we must reject much of what has been offered to us in the name of freedom, human dignity, and self-respect. We must reclaim the objective meanings of those values and actualize them in our private and public lives. To those Negro and white egalitarians who would enslave us with ethnic mysticism and welfare statism, we must say: *No! The equality you urge on us is not a requirement of our existence as beings of volitional consciousness and we reject all your efforts to make it so. We reject your attempts to make us exceptions to the rules of human existence simply because of our skin color. We do not want the results of our action to be "equal" to everyone else's. We do not want any private doors opened for us by the force of government intervention. We do not want a guaranteed livelihood paid for by the expropriated resources of others. We do not want to be spared the responsibility and risks of surviving by our own means. We do not want "assistance" given as blackmail paid to silence a militant's gun to prevent a looter's rampage. We do not want an education at universities we are not qualified to attend. We do not want positions of employment we are unqualified to hold. We do not want "preferential treatment" in order to be spared the risks of competition by achievement. We want no honors we do not deserve. We want no rewards we have not earned. We want only to be free! What you seek in our behalf and in the name of justice is unjust, immoral, and antihuman; it requires that some men exist at the expense of others; it requires the law of the jungle. But we will no longer participate in our own destruction. We will no longer help you pretend that what you do is right and just. We will not help you use freedom to destroy freedom.*

The faults in race relations in America lie in most of us and the solutions can be found in each of us, not HEW, EEOC, FCC, or HUD. We do not need "ethnic power" to move us closer to the American dream; we need no charismatic saviour to redeem us from the sins of our intolerance and discord. We need only to break from the tradition of imposing our will on others and to rid ourselves of the fear and resentment of another man's freedom.

335

Some will complain that these proposals and expectations are too high for mankind in general and Americans and Negroes in particular. Look about you, they will say, it's man's nature that justifies our Leviathan—forgetting man's nature in the process. Anyone who does not evade man's nature cannot exempt any of us from the possibility of being better than we are—and being so freely. We must not accept the notion that we cannot be all that we are capable of. And we cannot pretend for one moment that we have done our best.

There is yet a great distance to travel in our social development before we reach the reality of the free society that protects and preserves human rights and promotes individual sovereignty and harmonious, beneficial relations among men. Most of the world does not want to approach this social order, but the fact that it is shunned by most men is no reason to conclude that they are therefore incapable of it *because* they are men. Let them turn their backs on their nature and the requirements of successful human existence, but let it not be said that they could not help it, or did not know better.

When we address the concerns of Negroes and their response to the contact and conflict between the races, we should do so within their contemporary context as *legally free Americans* possessing all the rights to which their citizenship entitles them. While we must acknowledge the dark history from which this context is derived, there is no reason to be bound by it as the reference point from which Negroes should fashion their present and future participation in American life. There is no more cause to base the free relations between contemporary blacks and whites on slavery and the Civil War than there is for basing relations between Great Britain and the United States on colonialism and the Revolutionary War. The voice of the past speaks to us, but it emits echoes of the deeds of men before us from whose tragedies and triumphs we can learn but can neither change nor claim as our own. There comes a time in the lives of individuals and in the history of groups of people when it is wise to take Shakespeare's advice: "Things without remedy, should be without regard; what is done, is done."

With the exception of the American Indians, no ethnic group has suffered more injustices at the hands of government and its fellow citizens than the Negro race. But the debt has been paid. The protection and preservation of the human rights and liberty of

336

Negroes is no longer a dream deferred; there is no cause for predictions of a "fire next time." Were Thomas Jefferson alive to see this day, he would smile in relief that, though the "fire-bell in the night" was sounded and the Union split, the slaves were indeed emancipated as he had hoped and that the "sacrifice of themselves by the generation of 1776, to acquire self-government and happiness for their country" had not been entirely "thrown away by the unwise and unworthy passions" of future generations. He would be pleased to see that Negroes have at last "the opportunities for the development of their genius" and that they have achieved "their reestablishment on an equal footing with the other colors of the human family." But I believe he would be as disturbed, as we all should be, that having secured the blessings of liberty, many among them now join that coalition of the unwise and unworthy who are committed to liberty's abuse. Hearing so well the voices of their distant and recent history, Negroes should be more vigorous than most in leaving the past and turning the country in the direction of freedom.

"Other people" is never a good reason for free men to give as the sole reason for their failures or successes. For the extent to which "others" are responsible for our fate—whether voluntarily or under duress—is the extent to which we cannot claim to be free. If it is freedom we desire for Negroes, then we cannot rob them of their self-responsibility by relieving them of it. We cannot make Negroes an exception to the rules of a free existence. There are too many examples of individual Negroes who, by their psychointellectual independence, have and do transcend the stifling atmosphere of "significant others" for anyone to accept that excuse for a whole race. It just will not do.

Negroes have certainly been treated as outsiders, but in *actual*, *historical* fact they were not and could not be outsiders. They have been segregated and discriminated against, to be sure, but they have not been total outcasts. They are too much an elaboration of the American culture to be outcasts within it. That so many Negroes have chosen to remain psychological and intellectual outcasts has to be seen, in part, as a matter of their own choice. Unfortunately, it is a choice of error that all Americans, black and white, pay for. No other group, except the Indians, has faced as many barriers to structural and cultural assimilation as Negroes, and for this reason the group should have stressed the individuality of its members more than most. For if the group is to benefit justly from its freedom is must rely on the individuals who compose it. This, they must not lose sight of. The Negro race will not be free until individuals commit themselves to the achievement and maintenance of freedom.

But there are those who continue to evade their potential to liberate and to be liberated, foremost among whom is the social metaphysician. He hangs onto the misdeeds against his ancestors like a leech, drawing from them the blood of a nation. He does so even in the face of drowning himself and his countrymen in the tidal wave of statism of which that blood is composed. In hiding behind the parasitic skirts of victimization and demanding unrealistic reparations for the enslavement and segregation of his ancestors, he becomes an agent for enslaving us all. He is a hard taskmaster, brutal and unrelenting in his demands that men sacrifice their own self-interest for his collective whim. The price he asks us to pay for his survival is too great.

In alliance with other ethnic and pressure groups, statist intellectuals and appeasing businessmen, he has conned Americans into believing that in order to be moral they must sacrifice morality; that in order to achieve values, they must sacrifice virtues. In order for institutions of higher learning to be the mainstay of intellectual excellence, they must give up excellence. In order for employers to remain in business, they must give up standards of achievement, production, and free-market competition. In order for employees to enjoy the fruits of their labor, they must give up their wages to someone else's need. In order for government to protect equal opportunity, legislators, bureaucrats, and the courts must impose policies of "preferential treatment." And on it goes.

For too long the other-directed among us has made his personal problems a matter of public policy. He makes his conflict of self-esteem a national conflict; he persuades legislators, social institutions, educators, clergymen, social workers, and intellectuals of all descriptions, as well as his neighbor, that *his* crisis is their crisis. He even goes so far as to accuse them of being the *cause* of his crisis, whether they are or not. That a nation as advanced as the United States should allow his problems to exist is unforgivable, he tells us. That he should suffer so in a country that is dedicated to the pursuit of happiness is a sin, he admonishes. That he should own so much less than the president of the company he works for in a country that values "equal rights" is a shameful disgrace, he complains. That his self-esteem is so undermined by his environment that he is compelled to splatter the walls of a modern metropolis with graffiti is damnable in a nation that values beauty, he says. That he should have to kidnap the wealthy in order to draw attention to his poverty is not his fault, he says, but the fault of the injustice of capitalism.

The nation is diseased, he says, and he is the symptom of the disease. We must do something to relieve him of his situation—Now! We must commission researchers to study what is wrong with him and determine how his problems should be solved. We should pass legislation to permit government-enforced policies to be implemented in his behalf. We must remove the blindfold from justice, he says, and extend the context of the American legal system beyond what he calls its "narrow confines" of "lifeless abstractions." The law must be "humanized," he says, so that the courts cannot evade the real issues of the "imperiled aspirations of thousands of black Americans."

We must *free* him, he says. But the freedom *he* wants is not something any man can give him. The only way he can obtain it is by force and destruction, because the freedom he seeks is *freedom from the judgment of others.* He has not yet faced the fact of freedom—that he is not and cannot be a slave to anyone except by his consent, which is impossible. He will have to accept the fact of individual pride and reject the rhetoric of ethnic and racial pride. He will have to accept the fact of individual separateness and reject the politicization of ethnic exclusion. He will have to assert the fact of his own mind and reject the notion of a racial ideology. He will have to accept the responsibility of standing alone—not behind the mask of ethnicity, but naked before the sunlight of truth and liberty.

For three hundred years Negroes and whites in America have talked of no single subject more than freedom—personal and political liberty. Its promise has run like an unending thread through the fibers of this land—even when those fibers were weakened by slavery, segregation, and discrimination. The obsession of freedom has gripped other people in other lands at other times, but in no nation has it been the obsession of so many people for so long a time as it has been for the American people. They have written about it, preached about it, sung songs about it, marched for it, fought and died for it, and suffered from the lack of it.

Thomas Jefferson died believing that the presence of that peculiar institution of slavery was an abomination that would have to be removed by the future generation. And so it was. Abraham Lincoln died believing that the wounds of a divided nation would have to be healed by the future generation. And so they were. And Booker T. Washington died believing that the separation of the races would have to be ended by the future generation. And so it was.

Always there has been the hope that there would be peace between the races; that one group would not begrudge the other its freedom; that every individual would work toward harmonious relations with his neighbors, respect the rights of others, walk with dignity, and carry pride in his heart. The hope still lives but amid the intense argument between those who desire freedom and political equality of opportunity and those who advocate controls and metaphysical equality of result.

Do we dare allow our desire to cope with the humanness of racism lead us to institute equality as the priority over freedom? I think not. Can we afford to leave the issue to be settled by future generations? I think not. We can no longer afford the obsession of freedom as a hope and a promise. We must, each of us, commit our very existence, on an hourly basis, to the actualization of freedom—both psychointellectually and politically. Human liberty and the rights it entails must cease to be merely a dream; *it must be lived*. There simply is no longer the time for anything less.

1. In the commentary that follows, my use of the term "the Negro" refers to the particular kind of individuals focused on in this study. It does not refer to all Negroes as a group.

2. Branden, *The Psychology of Self-Esteem*, p. 45.

Bibliography

Aldrich, Nelson W., Jr. "Harvard on the Way Down." *Harper's*, 252 (March 1976): 39–42.

Allen, Robert L. *Reluctant Reformers: Racism and Social Reform Movements in the United States*. New York: Doubleday, Anchor Press, 1975.

Allman, T. D. "The 'Rebirth' of Eldridge Cleaver." *New York Times Magazine*, January 16, 1977.

Allport, Gordon W. *The Nature of Prejudice*. 2d ed. Garden City, N.Y.: Doubleday & Co., 1958.

Anderson, Charles H. "The Intellectual Sub-Society Hypothesis: An Empirical Test." *Sociological Quarterly*, 9 (Spring 1968): 210–27.

———. "Marginality and the Academics." *Sociological Inquiry*, 9 (1969): 77–84.

Atonovsky, Aaron. "Toward a Refinement of the 'Marginal Man' Concept." *Social Forces*, 35 (October 1956): 56–62.

Bailey, M. Thomas. "The Attitudes of Thomas Jefferson toward Slavery during the Revolutionary and Early National Period." *Journal of Social and Behavioral Sciences*, 19 (Summer, Fall 1972).

Baldwin, James. *The Fire Next Time*. New York: Dial Press, 1963.

———. *Notes of a Native Son*. New York: Bantam Books, 1964.

Baldwin, James, and Margaret Mead. *A Rap on Race*. Philadelphia: J. B. Lippincott Co., 1971.

Banfield, Edward C. *The Unheavenly City: The Nature and Future of Our Urban Crisis*. Boston: Little, Brown & Co., 1968.

Banks, James A., and Jean D. Grambs. *Black Self-Concept: Implications for Education and Social Science*. New York: McGraw-Hill Book Co., 1972.

Baraka, Imamu Ameer (LeRoi Jones). "A Black Value System." *The Black Scholar* (November 1969): 54–60.

Bartlett, John. *Familiar Quotations*. Boston: Little, Brown & Co., 1938.

Bell, Daniel. "On Meritocracy and Equality." *Public Interest*, Fall 1972.

Bennett, Lerone, Jr. *The Negro Mood*. Chicago: Johnson Publishing Co., 1964.

Bensman, Joseph and Arthur J. Vidich. *The New American Society: Revolution of the Middle Class*. Chicago: Quadrangle Books, 1971.

Berry, Brewton. "A Southerner Learns about Race." *Common Ground*, Spring 1942.

———. *Race and Ethnic Relations*. Boston: Houghton Mifflin Co., 1958.

Blaustein Arthur I., and Roger R. Woock, eds. *Man against Poverty: World War III*. New York: Random House, 1968.

Bonacich, Edna. "A Theory of Middleman Minorities." *American Sociological Review*, 38 (October 1973): 583–94.

Boorstin, Daniel J. *Democracy and Its Discontents*. New York: Vintage Books, 1975.

Branden, Nathaniel. *The Psychology of Self-Esteem*. Los Angeles: Nash Publishing Co., 1969.

———. *Breaking Free*. Los Angeles: Nash Publishing Co., 1970.

———. *The Disowned Self*. Los Angeles: Nash Publishing Co., 1971.

Brooks, Gwendolyn. *The World of Gwendolyn Brooks*. New York: Harper & Row, Publishers, 1949.

———. *Report From Part One*. Detroit: Broadside Press, 1972.

Brooks, Thomas. *Walls Come Tumbling Down: A History of the Civil Rights Movement 1940–1970*. Englewood Cliffs, N.J.: Prentice-Hall, Inc., 1974.

Brown, H. Rap. *Die Nigger Die!* New York: Dial Press, 1969.

Brown, Susan Love. "The Rape of the Black Mind." *Reason*, January 1975.

Brudnoy, David, ed. *The Conservative Alternative*. Minneapolis: Winston Press, 1973.

Carmichael, Stokely, and Charles V. Hamilton. *Black Power: The Politics of Liberation in America*. New York: Vintage Books, 1967.

Catrevas, C. N., et al., eds. *The New Dictionary of Thoughts*. Standard Book Co., 1960.

Cummings, Scott, and Robert Carrere. "Black Culture, Negroes and Colored People: Racial Image and Self-Esteem among Black Adolescents." *Phylon*, 36 (September 1975): 238–48.

Delaney, Paul. "Civil Rights Unity Gone, In Redirected Movement." *New York Times*, August 29, 1973.

———. "Blacks Gaining Politically But Still Feel Frustrated." *New York Times*, June 1, 1976.

DuBois, W.E.B. *The Souls of Black Folk*. New York: Washington Square Press, 1970.

Duchêne, François, ed. *The Endless Crisis: America in the Seventies*. New York: Simon and Schuster, 1970.

Eder, Richard. "The Struggle of Authority and Autonomy." *New York Times Book Review*, December 14, 1975.

Efron, Edith. "The Free Market and the Free Mind." *Reason*, August 1975.

Epps, Edgar A. *Black Students in White Schools*. Worthington, Ohio: Charles A. Jones Publishing Company, 1972.

Fanon, Frantz. *The Wretched of the Earth*. New York: Grove Press, 1965.

Franklin, John Hope. *From Slavery to Freedom: A History of American Negroes*. New York: Alfred A. Knopf, 1956.

Frazier, E. Franklin. *Black Bourgeoisie*. London: Collier-Macmillan, 1962.

Friedman, Neil. "Has Black Come Back to Dixie?" *Society*, May 1972, 48–53.

Friedman, Norman L. "Problems of the Runaway Jewish Intellectuals: Social Definition and Sociological Perspective." *Jewish Social Studies*, 31 (January 1969): 3–19.

Gettleman, Marvin E. and David Mermelstein, eds. *The Great Society Reader: The Failure of American Liberalism*. New York: Vintage Books, 1967.

Gilliam, Dorothy. "Sammy Davis—Political Enigma." *New York Post*, June 9, 1973.

342

Gilman, Richard. *The Confusion of Realms.* New York: Random House, 1969.

Glazer, Nathan. "America's Race Paradox." *Encounter,* October 1968.

_____. *Affirmative Discrimination: Ethnic Inequality and Public Policy.* New York: Basic Books, 1976.

Glazer, Nathan, and Daniel P. Moynihan, eds. *Ethnicity: Theory and Experience.* Cambridge: Harvard University Press, 1975.

Goble, Frank. *The Third Force: The Psychology of Abraham Maslow.* New York: Grossman Publishers, 1970.

Goldman, Peter. *Report From Black America.* New York: Simon and Schuster, 1970.

Golovensky, David I. "The Marginal Man Concept: An Analysis and Critique." *Social Forces,* 30 (March 1952): 333–39.

Gordon, Milton M. *Assimilation in American Life.* New York: Oxford University Press, 1964.

_____. *Human Nature, Class, and Ethnicity.* New York: Oxford University Press, 1978.

Gordone, Charles. *No Place to Be Somebody: A Black Comedy.* New York: The Bobbs-Merrill Company, 1969.

Grier, William H., and Price M. Cobbs. *Black Rage.* New York: Basic Books, 1968.

Hall, William S., Roy Feedle, and William E. Cross, Jr. *Stages in the Development of a Black Identity.* ACT Research Report No. 50. Iowa: American College Testing Program, April 1972.

Hamilton, Charles V. "The Nationalist Versus the Integrationist." *New York Times Magazine,* October 1, 1972.

Hamilton, Richard F. *Class and Politics in the United States.* New York: John Wiley and Sons, 1972.

Hare, Nathan. *The Black Anglo-Saxons.* New York: Marzani & Munsell, 1965.

Harrington, Michael. *The Other America: Poverty in the United States.* New York: Macmillan Co., 1962.

Hart, Jeffrey. "Victims in the Moral Melodrama." King Features Syndicate, February 27, 1975.

Hofstadter, Richard. *The American Political Tradition.* New York: Vintage Books, 1974.

Holsendolph, Ernest. "Black Colleges Are Worth Saving." *Fortune,* October 1971.

_____. " '63 March in Retrospect: Many Strata of Meaning." *New York Times,* August 30, 1973.

Hospers, John. *Human Conduct: Problems of Ethics.* New York: Harcourt Brace Jovanovich, 1972.

Howe, Harold. "Integration: The Lost Momentum." *New York Times,* December 10, 1972.

Hraba, Joseph, and Jack Siegman. "Black Consciousness." *Youth & Society,* 6 (September 1974): 63–90.

Hunter, Charlayne. "A Black Professor Urges Softening of Racial Issues." *New York Times.* April 1, 1976.

Jones, W. T. *A History of Western Philosophy.* New York: Harcourt, Brace & World, 1952.

343

Kempton, Murray. *The Briar Patch.* New York: E. P. Dutton and Company, 1973.

Kerckhoff, Alan C., and Thomas C. McCormick. "Marginal Status and Marginal Personality." *Social Forces,* 34 (October 1955): 48–55.

King, Martin Luther, Jr. *Stride Toward Freedom.* New York: Ballantine Books, 1960.

_____. *Where Do We Go From Here: Chaos or Community?* New York: Harper & Row, Publishers, 1967.

Ladner, Joyce A., ed. *The Death of White Sociology.* New York: Random House, 1973.

Lasch, Christopher. *The Culture of Narcissism: American Life in an Age of Diminishing Expectations.* New York: W. W. Norton & Co., 1978.

Levine, Donald M. and Mary Jo Bane, eds. *The "Inequality" Controversy.* New York: Basic Books, 1975.

Levine, Lawrence W. *Black Culture and Black Consciousness: Afro-American Folk Thought from Slavery to Freedom.* New York: Oxford University Press, 1977.

Levy, Mark R., and Michael S. Kramer. *The Ethnic Factor: How America's Ethnic Minorities Decide Elections.* New York: Simon and Schuster, 1973.

Lincoln, Eric C. "Color and Group Identity in the United States." *Daedalus,* 96 (Spring 1967): 527–41.

Lippman, Walter. *The Public Philosophy.* New York: New American Library, 1962.

Lokos, Lionel. *House Divided: The Life and Legacy of Martin Luther King.* New Rochelle, N.Y.: Arlington House, 1969.

_____. *The New Racism: Reverse Discrimination in America.* New Rochelle, N.Y.: Arlington House, 1971.

Lord, Steven M. "Race Pride versus Self-Esteem." Boston: Individuals for a Rational Society, 1973.

Machan, Tibor R. *The Pseudo-Science of B. F. Skinner.* New Rochelle, N.Y.: Arlington House, 1974.

_____. *Human Rights and Human Liberties.* Chicago: Nelson-Hall, 1975.

_____. "Demythologizing the Poor." *Alternative,* May 1975.

_____. "Law, Justice, and Natural Rights." *Western Ontario Law Review,* 14 (Fall 1975): 119.

_____. "Libertarianism: Has Its Time Really Arrived?" *Reason,* 7 (December 1975).

_____. "Prima Facie versus Natural (Human) Rights." *Journal of Value Inquiry,* 10 (Summer 1976).

MacIver, Robert M., ed. *Discrimination and National Welfare.* Reprint, Port Washington, N.Y.: Kennikat Press, 1962.

Maddox, Lester G. *Speaking Out: The Autobiography of Lester Garfield Maddox.* Garden City, N.Y.: Doubleday & Company, 1975.

Malcolm X. *The Autobiography of Malcolm X.* New York: Grove Press, 1969.

Marx, Gary T. *Protest and Prejudice: A Study of Belief in the Black Community.* New York: Harper & Row, Publishers, 1967.

Maslow, Abraham H. *Motivation and Personality.* New York: Harper & Row, Publishers, 1954.

————. *Toward a Psychology of Being.* Princeton: D. Van Nostrand Co., 1962.

————. *The Psychology of Science.* New York: Harper & Row, Publishers, 1966.

————. *The Further Reaches of Human Nature.* New York: Viking Press, 1971.

Mason, Philip. "The Revolt Against Western Values." *Daedalus,* 96 (Spring 1967): 328–52.

Meier, August, Elliott Rudwick, and Francis L. Broderick, eds. *Black Protest Thought in the Twentieth Century.* Indianapolis: Bobbs-Merrill Co., 1965.

Meier, August, and Elliott Rudwick. *From Plantation to Ghetto.* 3rd ed. New York: Hill and Wang, 1976.

Merton, Robert K. *Social Theory and Social Structure.* New York: Free Press, 1968.

————. "Outsiders and Insiders: A Chapter in the Sociology of Knowledge." *American Journal of Sociology,* 77 (July 1972): 9–47.

————. *The Sociology of Science.* Chicago: University of Chicago Press, 1973.

Miller, William Robert. *Martin Luther King, Jr.: His Life, Martyrdom and Meaning for the World.* New York: Weybright and Talley, 1968.

Mises, Ludwig von. *The Anti-Capitalistic Mentality.* Princeton: D. Van Nostrand Co., 1962.

————. *Human Action: A Treatise on Economics.* Rev. ed. New Haven, Conn.: Yale University Press, 1963.

Morris, Burnis R. "I am Curious (Black)." *New York Times,* March 7, 1977.

Napper, George. *Blacker Than Thou: The Struggle for Campus Unity.* Grand Rapids, Mich.: William B. Eerdmans Publishing Co., 1973.

National Advisory Commission on Civil Disorders. *Report of the National Advisory Commission on Civil Disorders.* New York: Bantam Books, 1968.

Nisbet, Robert A. *The Quest for Community.* New York: Oxford University Press, 1969.

Okun, Arthur M. *Equality and Efficiency: The Big Tradeoff.* Washington, D.C.: Brookings Institution, 1975.

Ozick, Cynthia. "All the World Wants the Jews Dead." *Esquire,* 82 (November 1974): 103–7.

Park, Robert E. *Race and Culture.* Glencoe, Ill.: Free Press, 1950.

Parker, J. A. *Angela Davis: The Making of a Revolutionary.* New Rochelle, N.Y.: Arlington House, 1973.

Peikoff, Leonard. "The 'Spirit of the Sixties.' " *The Objectivist Form,* 1 (April 1980).

Peterson, Merrill D., ed. *The Portable Thomas Jefferson.* New York: Viking Press, 1975.

Pettigrew, Thomas F. "Segregation." *World Book Encyclopedia.* Chicago: Field Enterprises Educational Corp., 1974.

Rand, Ayn. *The Fountainhead.* Indianapolis: Bobbs-Merrill Co., 1943.

————. *Atlas Shrugged.* New York: Random House, 1957.

————. "America's Persecuted Minority: Big Business." New York: Nathaniel Branden Institute, 1962.

————. *The Virtue of Selfishness.* New York: New American Library, 1964.

————. *Introduction to Objectivist Epistemology.* New York: Objectivist, Inc., 1970.

———. "The Age of Envy." *Objectivist*, July 1971.

———. "Don't Let It Go." *Ayn Rand Letter*, Vol. 1, No. 4, November 22, 1971.

———. *The New Left: The Anti-Industrial Revolution*. New York: New American Library, 1971.

———. *The Romantic Manifesto*. New York: New American Library, 1971.

———. "Moral Inflation—Part III." *Ayn Rand Letter*, Vol. 3, No. 14, April 8, 1974.

Randall, Dudley, ed. *The Black Poets*. New York: Bantam Books, 1971.

Ravitch, Diane. "Not Always a Matter of Justice." *New York Times*, July 27, 1977.

Rawls, John. *A Theory of Justice*. Cambridge: Harvard University Press, 1971.

Reich, Charles. *The Greening of America*. New York: Bantam Books, 1971.

Riesman, David. *Individualism Reconsidered*. New York: Free Press, 1954.

Riesman, David, with Nathan Glazer and Reuel Denney. *The Lonely Crowd: A Study of Changing American Character*. New Haven, Conn.: Yale University Press, 1950.

Rinder, Irwin D. "Strangers in the Land: Social Relations in the Status Gap." *Social Problems*, 6 (Winter 1958–59): 253–60.

Roche, George. *The Balancing Act*. La Salle, Ill.: Open Court Publishing Co., 1974.

Rothbard, Murray N. *America's Great Depression*. Princeton: D. Van Nostrand Co., 1963.

Royster, Vermont. "The Emperor's Clothes." *Wall Street Journal*, February 23, 1977.

Rustin, Bayard. "The Failure of Black Separatism." *Harper's*, January 1970.

Safire, William. "Christmas in July." *New York Times*, July 18, 1977.

Shaffer, Butler. *Violence as a Product of Imposed Order*. Studies in Law, No. 4. Menlo Park, Calif.: Institute for Humane Studies, 1976.

Shenfield, Arthur A. "Equality Before the Law." *Modern Age*, 17 (Spring 1973): 114.

Sherif, M., and C. Sherif. "Black Unrest as a Social Movement Toward an Emerging Self-Identity." *Journal of Social and Behavioral Sciences*, 15 (Spring 1970): 41–52.

Shibutani, Tamotsu, and Kian M. Kwam. *Ethnic Stratification: A Comparative Approach*. New York: Macmillan Co., 1963.

Sowell, Thomas. "Black Professor Says: Colleges are Skipping over Competent Blacks to Admit Authentic Ghetto Types." *New York Times Magazine*, December 13, 1970.

———. *Black Education: Myths and Tragedies*. New York: David McKay, 1972.

———. *Affirmative Action Reconsidered: Was It Necessary in Academia?* Washington, D.C.: American Enterprise Institute for Public Policy Research, 1975.

Stonequist, Everett V. *The Marginal Man: A Study in Personality and Culture Conflict*. New York: Charles Scribner's Sons, 1937.

Thomas, C. W. *Boys No More*. Los Angeles: Glencoe Press, 1971.

Truman, Harry S. *See* Catrevas, C. N., et al., eds., *The New Dictionary of Thoughts*.

Tuccille, Jerome. *Radical Libertarianism: A Right Wing Alternative*. Indianapolis: Bobbs-Merrill Co., 1970.

Washington, Booker T. *Up From Slavery*. New York: Bantam Books, 1970.

Wilson, William Julius. *The Declining Significance of Race: Blacks and Changing American Institutions*. Chicago: University of Chicago Press, 1978.

Woolman, Myron. *Cultural Asynchrony and Contingency in Learning Disorders*. Bethesda, Md.: National Institute of Mental Health, 1965.

Wortham, Anne. "Equal Opportunity versus Individual Opportunity." *Freeman*, July 1975.

———. "An Open Letter to Nathan Glazer." *Reason*, October, 1977.

Yinger, J. Milton. *A Minority Group in American Society*. New York: McGraw-Hill Book Co., 1965.

Young, Whitney M. Jr. *Beyond Racism: Building an Open Society*. New York: McGraw-Hill Book Co., 1971.

Index

Index

Index